Marine Rifleman

21 Feb 08

to: Pvt Hitchcock.

Semper Fi

Wesley Fox

Related Titles by Potomac Books

The Outpost War: U.S. Marines in Korea, 1952, vol. I,
  by Lee Ballenger

The Final Crucible: U.S. Marines in Korea, 1953, vol. II,
  by Lee Ballenger

Medal of Honor: One Man's Journey from Poverty and Prejudice,
  by M. Sgt. Roy P. Benevidez, USA SF (Ret.), with John R. Craig

Wonju: The Gettysburg of the Korean War,
  by J. D. Coleman

This Kind of War: The Classic Korean War History,
  by T. R. Fehrenbach

The Korean War: The Story and Photographs,
  by Donald M. Goldstein and Harry J. Maihafer

*Brave Decisions: Fifteen Profiles in Courage and Character
  from American Military History,*
  by Harry J. Maihafer

Command Legacy: A Tactical Primer for Junior Leaders of Infantry Units,
  by Lt. Col. Raymond A. Millen, USA

Marine Rifleman

Forty-Three Years in the Corps

Col. Wesley L. Fox, USMC (Ret.)

Potomac Books, Inc.

Washington, D.C.

First paperback edition 2003

Copyright © 2002 by Wesley L. Fox.

Library of Congress Cataloging-in-Publication Data

Fox, Wesley L.
  Marine rifleman : forty-three years in the Corps / Wesley L. Fox.—
1st ed.
      p. cm.
Includes bibliographical references.
  ISBN 978-1-57488-425-8 —ISBN 978-1-57488-529-3 (pbk.)
1. Fox, Wesley L. 2. United States Marine
Corps—Officers—Biography. 3. Marines—United States—Biography. I.
Title.
  VE25.F69 A3 2002
  359.9′6′092—dc21   2002002649

Printed in the United States of America on acid-free paper that meets the American National Standards Institute Z39–48 Standard.

Potomac Books, Inc.
22841 Quicksilver Drive
Dulles, Virginia 20166

First Edition

10 9 8 7

To my wife and to my mother

They stayed home and worried for my life every single day while I was off doing my Marine thing, though most of those days were an enjoyable walk in the sun.

And to all the Marines who have lost their lives while serving their country.

Contents

List of Maps   *ix*

Acknowledgments   *xi*

Prologue   *xiii*

1. Private, USMC   1
Family background and adolescent days—Recruit experiences at
Parris Island—Alligators, DIs, heat, and sand fleas—Maltreatment,
physical and verbal abuse—Rifle qualification

2. Private First Class   21
2nd Marine Division at Camp Lejeune—En route to the Korean
War—Combat with a rifle company—Squad personalities—
Corporal Davis, Squad Leader—Accidental discharge—Whisky
raid on the Army

3. Corporal   46
Difficulties due to promotion—Rear guard action following
Chinese breakthrough on flank—Hilarious meeting with
Chinese patrol—Listening post assignment—Chinese night attack
and breakthrough—Hall killed, enemy behind us—Grenade mal-
function—Closing the breakthrough—Assignment in No-Man's
Land—Bodies of 38th Regiment's soldiers recovered—Wounded
in assault on enemy machine gun—Squad Leader

4. Sergeant   81
Armed Services Policeman, Washington, DC—Guard duty in
postwar Japan—Rifle Company Platoon Sergeant in Korea—
1st Marine Division returns stateside—Drill Instructor duty

5. Staff Sergeant   105

Recruit hazing and maltreatment—Shakeup of Marine Corps following death of recruits at Parris Island—New way of making Marines—Flirt with Hollywood—Recruiting duty

6. Technical Sergeant   122

Recruiting quotas and quality recruits—Daily life and work of a recruiter—Pathfinder 1st Force Reconnaissance Company—POW, Escape, Evasion, and Survival training—Marriage—Parachute and SCUBA training—Deployment to Okinawa—Riptide sweep seaward—Brush with death in parachute landing

7. Gunnery Sergeant   172

Sport parachuting and parachute malfunctions—Parachute Demonstration Team—Brain concussion from parachute landing —Competitive rifle and pistol shooting—First child—Seeking assignment to Vietnam lands duty in Paris, France—Supreme Headquarters Allied Powers Europe—Promotion to 1st Sergeant— Selection for temporary commission

8. 2nd Lieutenant   184

2nd Force Reconnaissance Company—Personality conflict with company 1st Sergeant—Submarine escape trunk training—Locking out of and entering a submerged, underway submarine—Loss of friend in parachuting accident—Vietnamese advisor training at Fort Bragg

9. 1st Lieutenant, Section 1   202

Advisor duty with Vietnamese Marine Corps—Overcoming Vietnamese counterpart's objection to working with an American lieutenant—Vietnamese leaders use war as means of making money —Personality conflict with only other American assigned—Enemy Tet offensive—Three Marines take on an enemy battalion—R&R with wife in Honolulu—Extension of combat tour

10. 1st Lieutenant, Section 2   231

Assignment as Company Commander, Company A, 1st Bn, 9th Marine Rgt—Opportunity to hone the fighting skills of Marines— Company A locks on with an NVA battalion—Miraculous performance of Marines despite loss of all platoon commanders— Recommended for the Medal of Honor

11. Captain   267

Leaving Vietnam—Student and Instructor—Nixon presents the
Medal of Honor—Marine Security Guard duty in Eastern and
Western Europe—Embassy Marines and Physical Fitness Test—
Operations Officer, 3rd Reconnaissance Bn on Okinawa—
Student, Western State College

12. Major   296

Colorado outdoor sports—Graduated cum laude—Reconnaissance Officer, Development Center—Testing and evaluating new
equipment—Multiple parachute malfunctions—Parachute offset
delivery techniques—Hang gliders

13. Lieutenant Colonel   316

Battalion Command—Preparation for deployment—Combined
Arms Exercise—Training challenges—Proactive leadership
options—Long foot marches and zero disciplinary problems—
Battalion to the top of Mount Fuji—Army War College—
Director of Staff, NCO Academy

14. Colonel of Marines   348

Sea duty—Joint Plans Officer—Oslo, Norway—Officer
Candidate School—Keep only those who will make good leaders
—Determining who can think and react properly under extreme
stress—A question on one's integrity is a ticket home

Glossary

Notes

Maps
Korea: 1st Marine Division Tactical Area of Operation, 1951
Korea: 1st Marine Division Tactical Area of Operation,
    April–May 1951
Vietnam: US Marine Tactical Area of Operation, 1968 and 1969

Acknowledgments

A man's memory is influenced by many things: impressions, experiences, mental and physical capabilities, desires, and aging. I find that I remember my earlier experiences with events, people, and names more readily and clearly than my later ones. Nevertheless, I have written my life story as a Marine the way I remember it. What you read is what Marines and I experienced at the time. Most were good events but some, if I had them to do over, would be done differently. Several names have been changed to avoid embarrassing anyone.

I have many people to thank for making this book possible. In 1964 a sergeant in Public Information commented that I should tell my Force Reconnaissance story. Since then many Marines have stated an interest in hearing more about my experiences, asking, "When will you write your book?" Finally, here it is.

I thank Col John Greenwood, editor of the *Marine Corps Gazette,* for publishing my early articles, one of which received the Marine Corps Association's Wilcox Award. Col Tom Taylor's insistence that I had a story to tell was a motivating factor, and Col Edward Schwabe, USA (Ret.), at Virginia Tech helped me get focused with his first edit of my collection of words. Mrs. Rebecca Bier Stevens of Christiansburg, Virginia, was my English editor and proved most helpful in producing the final manuscript. Two young cadets, Robert A. Hannum and Tyson M. Murphy, prepared my maps. Col John Glasgow of the Marine Corps Association, Col John Ripley and Chuck Melson of the US Marine Corps History and Museums Division authorized the use of their maps. My thanks also go to Danny Crawford and his staff in the Historical Archives for providing me with Historical Diaries and Personnel Rosters.

This book would never have happened without the support and encouragement of my wife, Dotti Lu. My brother James, an author in his own right, was helpful throughout with ideas and grammar corrections. My story would have been in print ten years earlier if he had written it, as I requested. My daughters helped with the grammar, but they tended to get wrapped up in the story and read on to see what happened next, usually with teary eyes.

I wish to recognize Col Joe Alexander, the author of several good books about Marines, who had a major play in the publishing of this book when he convinced Richard A. Russell, the Acquisitions Editor of Brassey's, to ask for my manuscript. Rick has made this first-time author feel as though he were part of the publishing team, and he has been most helpful in bringing me through the publishing business, by-the-numbers (the way Marine recruits learn Close Order Drill).

Finally, my thanks are offered to the thousands of Marines who trained me, led me, set the example for me, served beside me, motivated me, followed me, and saw enough in me to promote me and keep me in the ranks for forty-three years. They made my story. It has been a great life, and it was all possible because of God's blessings.

Prologue

Searching the blackness forward in the early morning hours, I concentrated on trying to see any movement or threat. There was no illumination; everything was lost in the black. The words "The Chinese are coming up the hill" were still ringing in my ears. Where were the Chinese if we were under attack? Sounds that could be troop movement came through the darkness, but I was not sure of what I heard. Unable to place a direction on the sound, I considered it my imagination.

PFC John Hall's BAR opened up close on my left. Hall mashed the trigger with no letup. I knew that he was pressured because Hall was a good BAR man and normally fired in three-round bursts. Immediately other weapons and grenade blasts joined Hall's BAR. Although his position was about fifty meters to my left, I could not see anything. Over the scrubby pines around Hall's position I could see flashes of light from grenade explosions. As close as I was to Hall and with no enemy threat against me, I considered the firing to be coming only from our line.

I had learned that Marines fire only when they have a target. In spite of all the firing in the draw to my immediate left, there was no target; there were no muzzle flashes amid the blackness of the scrub pines forward of our positions. If enemy soldiers were not on our hill, my buddies were shooting at ghosts. Reality suddenly struck hard.

Hall's BAR and most weapons ceased firing. Intently searching the blackness forward, I was shocked by a voice close behind me. From my left rear and almost on top of me came loud, crisp orders in a foreign tongue. Every sense and nerve was instantly alerted as I realized that the enemy was behind our line of defense. They were behind me; I was next.

I would explode a grenade on the ground by my hole; that might give me a chance to get out. Removing a grenade from my belt suspenders, I placed my middle finger in the ring, and pulled. Nothing moved! To avoid accidental explosions, which had cost the division several Marines, we were directed to mash the cotter pin flat against the fuse handle. Now, in the haste of the moment and the black of the night, I did not attempt to straighten the pin; I applied more force. The ring came away without the pin.

I did not have to see it to know that the cotter pin had separated, releasing the pull ring but leaving the two halves of the pin in the fuse. Working by feel, I attempted to remove the two halves, but gave up because it was time consuming. I had to move. Foreign commands were shouted all around me while burp guns fired on the ridge by my shelterhalf.

Taking my second and last grenade, I straightened the pin and pulled the ring. Everything worked. Releasing the spoon that activated the fuse, I placed the grenade just outside my hole. Then I compressed myself as well as I could in that little hole and waited for the explosion. I failed to count off the four to six seconds between releasing the spoon and the explosion. To emphasize the eternity of seconds in a firefight, I thought that the grenade was a dud. It should have exploded!

Enemy soldiers were talking around me. Dud or not, I was going out anyway. An instant before I sprang, the grenade exploded. The timing could not have been better. Full advantage of the shock effect of that explosive force was mine. I came out of my hole so closely behind the blast that I was a part of it. No enemy soldiers were in my way or took me under fire in the blackness.

Baker was not in his hole; light from exploding ordnance helped determine that fact. Franzone and Foran were also gone; I continued toward the higher knoll on the right portion of our squad position. Weapons' fire and grenade explosions increased behind me around my position.

"Halt! Who's there?" Came a challenge out of the darkness.

"Fox," I responded while moving forward. At that moment a Chinese concussion grenade hit me in the chest, bounced off, and exploded while airborne. It exploded within arm's length, and except for temporary hearing and night vision loss, I was not scratched! I felt invincible, like I was ten feet tall.

All squad members were now on the knoll; we set up across the ridge, making an L-shaped position. Riflemen farthest from the breakthrough manned their original positions, making the long part of the L. My fire team refused the line across the ridge, making the base of the L. Weapons fire and grenade explosions continued in and around my vacated position and John Hall's. The battalion's 81 mortars joined the fight; their tubes were popping in the valley close behind us with fire-for-effect missions.

With no pressure against us, our weapons remained silent. What was the enemy's objective? As we lay quietly in the dark, I had time for thought. I mentally moved to the events that had placed me in this precarious situation; thoughts of my family and home filled my mind. I had wanted to fight my country's battles since a child, and I remembered my dad's concern for me when he learned of the uniform I had chosen.

1
Private, USMC
1128290/9900

4 August 1950

I was born to John Wesley and Desola Lee (Crouch) Fox near Herndon, Virginia, on 30 September 1931, their first of ten children. My dad was tall and slender with a quiet, sincere personality. He was a rock in my young world, and I was surprised later to see him cry at the funeral of a distant family member. Mom was a Christian, loving, and dedicated. She gave her all to her husband and her children. She probably had more influence on my adult outlook, as dad and I conversed very little. There were times that we worked together all day with neither of us saying much to the other. There was never a question of love; our nature was simply not to waste time talking but get on with the work at hand. My personal values came from both of them and the hard life they shared.

My parents had their hands full with the start of their family: I had scarlet fever at eighteen months, when my brother Ray was five months old. As if a sick child were not enough in the early thirties, work was scarce due to the Great Depression. Coal oil lamps, a water bucket in the kitchen, and an outdoor privy supported our home life.

I liked to speak of my parents having two families. The first six of us, two boys and four girls, were born about a year apart. Molly, the youngest, was five when Jim came along in 1942. David and Linda followed closely, and then in 1949 Elmer arrived to wrap up the younger family. My two oldest sisters, Betty and Dorothy, received early experience in raising children as they helped mom with the second family. Ruby was too small to help much, but she was a tomboy anyway and was always considered aligned with Ray and me against the other three sisters in our play—soldiers, cowboys, and baseball. We were very close.

Dad sold our forty-acre farm in Fairfax County when I was seven and bought an old house with fourteen acres near Front Royal. The privy was farther from the house, but we did have electricity, with a wire running across the ceiling from one bare light bulb to another.

1

My dad worked for eight years as a bricklayer at the American Viscose Corporation, a rayon manufacturing plant that we could smell from miles away. Concerned about the chemical environment of the plant, he quit and followed with building construction work. Believing that idle hands get into trouble, he kept his sons busy with farm chores—milking, feeding, and gardening—and construction work. He built a nice brick home for us and later subdivided and built two more homes before we sold.

I grew up along the south fork of the Shenandoah River in Warren County; that river and the mountain trails captured my heart. I often left home as if going to school but instead enjoyed the day doing my thing in nature's playground. Although I was not learning reading, 'riting, or 'rithmetic, I did learn the forest and outdoor life. These outdoor skills—tracking, reading movement signs, etc.—would be helpful later, especially as a scout or point man in a Movement to Contact. The rifleman's life on the ground in the Korean War reminded me of my early outdoor experiences.

My great grandfathers served in the War between the States. My maternal Great Granddad John Washington Lackey volunteered at the age of eighteen and served under General A.P. Hill in southern Virginia and North Carolina. Great Granddad Stephen Fox enlisted on 3 May 1862 in Bland County, Virginia, to fight against Yankee aggression. Young Steve served with Company G of the 36th Virginia Infantry in the Shenandoah Valley and was with General Jubal Early at the battle of Waynesboro. Captured, he spent the remainder of the war as a POW and was released from Fort Delaware on 20 June 1865. My later family tree shows a limited military exposure until World War II was under way. In the '30s, an older cousin, Nelson Brambier Fox, had joined the Army but did not stay.

The Japanese bombing of Pearl Harbor introduced me to military things and thoughts. On 7 December 1941, we returned from a family visit near Charlottesville, sharing US Route 29 with a long northbound military convoy. Stopping at a gas station, Dad learned that our nation was at war: Tojo had bombed Pearl Harbor. I was impressed with the soldiers seated in the truck beds, and my dad's comment, "They are going to fight the Japs." The thought that my dad would have to fight bothered me. We would learn later that his age and six kids would keep him home. The next day, an Army truck broke down in front of our school playground. I handled my first bayonet as the soldiers enjoyed the rapt attention of a crowd of young Virginians caught up in the anxiety of going to war.

Although I was too young for service, I lived the part. The Warren County School daily regimen started with the Lord's Prayer, the Pledge of Allegiance, and singing one of the armed force's hymns. I would become very emotional while singing the hymns, and I greatly enjoyed participating in the morning recess calisthenics led by a teacher. This gave me a comfortable regimented feeling.

Most of my cousins were involved in the war. Nelson had earlier found the Army not to his liking. During his long, unauthorized absence, World War II started. Nelson wrote to President Roosevelt, telling him that fighting was the reason he had joined, and now that the Army had some fighting to do, he wanted back in the ranks.

Roosevelt responded favorably, and Nelson was assigned to an US/Canadian outfit, the 1st Special Service Force (not to be confused with today's Special Services). He fought at Anzio and Normandy and was shot up badly in France. We welcomed him home to his family farm on a Sunday; he was pale and frail from his near-death experience but he returned to us as a decorated hero. Medically retired on full disability, Nelson was a big influence on my young, someday to be military, mind. I dreamed of being another Sergeant Fox.

I was not motivated to do well in schoolwork. Eventually, my dad caught me playing hooky and said, "If you aren't going to school and making something of yourself, you won't just lie around in the mountains." I quit the ninth grade, my dad bought a larger farm near Round Hill, and we moved.

Money was tight after buying the farm, livestock, and equipment. Our money crops were cattle, hogs, wheat, and corn, but the market was low in 1948. The farm did not pay for itself; my dad continued with bricklaying, and I did the farming. I plowed with a three-horse team pulling a 16-inch bottom-turning plow, cut corn by hand, and shucked it out ear by ear over the long winter. Wheat was cut with a horse-drawn binder, shocked in the field, and threshed when the threshing machine came through our neighborhood.

A young sow was my sole money source, and her first litter went to market in the winter of 1949. That sum ($250) purchased my first car, a 1938 Buick sedan. We had a family car, an old, brush-painted, faded blue '36 Chevy with broken fenders, but I needed my own car.

My chance to wear a uniform came when the North Koreans attacked across the 38th parallel on 25 June 1950. I loved the farm, the work and everything connected with the land, but I had to leave it. My cousins who had fought in WW II were home, starting families and getting on with their new lives; Korea was my war, my chance to fulfill my dreams of serving my country. There was no active selective service induction in 1950, but the recruiting offices were doing a heavy business.

My parents knew of my desire to join the armed forces, but they always had reasons why it was not a good idea. Therefore, I did not discuss my latest intentions, even though they were very much involved because of my part in working the farm. Ray had another year before he graduated from high school, and I knew that if I stayed home, he was gone. We both shared the same ideas of service in uniform; it was now or never, him or me.

My first problem was deciding which uniform I wanted to wear. An older friend and Army war veteran advised me against joining his branch of the service; he felt that I would be unhappy as "just another soldier." When I asked for clarification, he responded with, "You are the Marine type," and closed the subject. Between that and Nelson's influence, I narrowed my options to the Army Airborne and the Marines.

Nelson and friends had told me about the Army. The role of a paratrooper suited my taste, but a paratrooper was, after all, just a soldier. My knowledge of the Marines was limited to "Sands of Iwo Jima," "The Raiders," and other Hollywood versions of the Corps, but I liked what I saw. Further, the Army recruiting posters in 1950 did not impress me: JOIN THE ARMY AND BE TREATED LIKE A GENTLEMAN was not the experience I sought. The Marine Corps's posters stated simply, BE A MARINE. The challenge was there along with something else— a certain mystique.

I solved my problem with a simple scenario approach. Mentally placing myself in each uniform, one at a time, I visualized my reaction upon meeting a member of each of the other services. Being a Marine was the only position that did not give me an overshadowed feeling when meeting another service member. Equally, when I imagined myself in any of the other uniforms and meeting a Marine, I would wonder where he had been and what he had done. I wanted firsthand experience on the cutting edge.

Summers were busy on the farm, and it was several weeks after the war started before I could get a day off. On a rainy day in July, a neighborhood friend and I headed for Washington, DC, in my Buick to find a Marine Recruiter. I had never been downtown in that city, much less driven in it, but we found the recruiting station located in the temporary wartime buildings on the Mall. Excitement and a feeling of adventure added to my day, but my undertaking, not what this great city presented, caused it.

My recruiter learned that I was interested in both the paratroopers and the Marines and solved my problem by asking, "Why not be a Para-Marine?" Great! The Para-Marines were tailor-made for me, sign me up. (I would later learn that the Para-Marines had been disbanded during WW II.)

We were in the middle of the wheat harvest and I asked to leave after the threshing machine had completed the neighborhood circuit; I would be ready in two weeks. That was acceptable to the recruiter, who agreed to ship Delbert and me together. I left the recruiter thinking that I had been enlisted, which turned out not to be the case. Passing the medical officer's door, I learned that Delbert had failed his physical.

We stopped by Lawson's country store on our way home for a bottle of pop and to tell of our latest experience. My dad later stopped by Lawson's coming from work. When he pulled the old Chevy into the front yard, I met him on the front porch. Before I could tell him what I had done, he asked, "Of all the services, why did you pick the Marines?" He sat his tired body on the front porch steps and said, "Don't you know that the Marines are the spearhead, the first to fight?" I answered affirmatively while thinking to myself that this was the very reason I chose the Marines. Though aware of his concern for his children, I was still disappointed that he did not know me better and want me to be with the best.

The weather remained dry and two weeks' work completed the neighborhood wheat-threshing season, with me taking much kidding about what lay ahead. Four August was my report date, a Friday and a workday; Dad went off to his brickwork. Mom and my sisters bid me a tearful goodbye and Ray drove me to Round Hill in my Buick, which was now his. There was no reason to drive me to Washington; I could catch the milk truck as it came through Round Hill on its run down Route 7 to the city dairy. Ray returned home to cut a field of hay.

Neighbors had suggested that the milk truck was a sure ride, but I began to wonder after an hour's wait. Finally, a milk truck appeared from the Hillsboro direction, and the driver was sympathetic to my cause. The dairy turned out to be in Clarendon, and somehow this hayseed caught the right trolley car and found his way to 1400 Pennsylvania Avenue. The office was full of young men taking on the same task as I. There was not much talking; we were about to assume an unknown role, in another world.

Captain W. F. Lloyd talked to his group of recruits before he gave us the oath. I remember him saying that most of our future paychecks would not be deserved based on work and effort put forth. "But," he said, "there will come a time when our countrymen can not pay you enough for what you will do for them and our country." He swore us in, issued travel orders, a one-way Pullman ticket, and $2.50 for three meals. That was a lot of money in 1950, but it did not buy much food on that train. We departed Washington at 1825[1] and would arrive in Yemassee, South Carolina, at 1320 the following day.

This way my first time out of Northern Virginia, and I was on my way to Parris Island, South Carolina. My new companions could not believe I had never heard of Marine Corps boot camp. I looked forward to basic training, running obstacle courses, and the physical challenge of getting in better shape, but this boot camp thing was getting my attention. I had much to learn, and it was not long in coming.

A new friend identified my service number on my orders, stressed its importance and suggested that I memorize it before we arrived on the island. I'd had trouble with memory retention throughout school, but 1128290 quickly became a part of me.

The world was sunny when we pulled into Yemassee, but the corporal boarding our railroad car cast a dark shadow over it. He informed us of his desires with loud, profane threats, finishing with, "Get off and get on the buses." My day grew darker, spinning madly as we were herded from place to place. The spin slowed enough for me to assess my situation as I lay on my rack at 0200 that night. I reasoned that my Lord would allow me to say my nightly prayer in this position rather than on my knees as I was in a top bunk, and the corporal had clearly yelled, "Get in 'em!" It was foolish to do anything that would cause him to scream any more. My mom, dad, brothers, and sisters were lovingly blessed, and I had time to wonder what I had gotten myself into.

Although I was exhausted and the hour late, sleep did not come quickly. Sleeping with the lights on was a new experience, and there was a big light directly over me. We were in Casual Company; training had not started, and we had not yet met our DIs. Who or what are DIs? What do you mean that this form-up week in Casual Company does not count?

I lucked out with only two days in Casual Company; Platoon 88 formed fast. General MacArthur had asked for Marines in Korea, and the Commandant of the Marine Corps (CMC) had obliged. There was a need to train us quickly and provide a personnel pipeline to feed the 1st Marine Division (MarDiv) in Korea.

Our Drill Instructors (DIs) introduced themselves to us, their new herd. "I am Corporal Reiser, and I am your Senior Drill Instructor.

(Slender, of average height, Reiser presented a hard, tough personality. We would learn to fear him because of his full control of our lives. We could breathe only when he so allowed.) Reiser continued with, "You will know me as Sir and you will address me as SIR. This is PFC Daves, he is your Junior Drill Instructor, and you will address him as SIR. In fact, the first and the last word out of your slimy mouths will be SIR. Is that understood?"

"Yes Sir!"

"I said the first and the last word out of your slimy mouths would be SIR! IS THAT UNDERSTOOD?"

"SIR, YES SIR!"

"I can't hear you pussies!"

"SIR, YES SIR!"

"Together, we will make Marines out of you shitheads from Yemassee or kill you trying. Do you understand?"

"SIR, YES SIR."

"DO YOU UNDERSTAND?"

"SIR, YES SIR!"

"There are only two ways off this f—ing island: as a Marine or in a box. And, I'll tell you pussies right now that some of you don't have what it takes to be a Marine. Some of you shitheads might think that you can just up and leave this nice, little summer camp when you get enough and want to quit. Now hear this, because I am only going to say it once.

"Some shitheads have tried it. They have never been seen or heard of since. Their mammies still cry for them, wondering what happened to their babies. I'll tell you what happened to their shit-for-brains babies. My gators ate them. My f—ing gators need to eat, and they are not fussy. They will eat your stinking ass the minute your foot hits the water.

"So, there are MPs on the only gate and water all around us. You don't have to take my word about the gators, just decide that you don't want to be a Marine. Your leaving just makes my job easier, as I don't have to put up with your stupid shit."

Corporal D. W. Reiser took us first to the Hygienic Unit and Clothing Issue. When it came my turn, I stepped through the Hygienic Unit door to face a big, overweight, ugly individual with many stripes on his arms. His khaki shirt had huge dark areas under his arms from heavy sweating. Sergeant Ugly looked at me, pointed to my chest, and grunted, "Take 'em off."

I had my polo shirt over my head when he hit me with a sack of clothes, screaming, "I said TAKE 'EM OFF."

Thoroughly confused about what he wanted and finding his manner of expressing himself distasteful, I must have given him a "Fox look." He hit me again, saying, "Don't look at me like that, you son-of-a-bitch!" My shoes, trousers, and shirt came quickly off in that order while I quietly decided that I would not hold this animal responsible for his mistake concerning my mother.

Hair was next off as the Corps's routine quickly reduced us to the lowest mental common denominator. Man's spirit weakens when he stands bare, for all to see. Our individuality was stripped and shorn, making us one in appearance, purpose, and fear. The nakedness of our bodies reflected the nakedness of our souls. Can these skinny boyish figures, this frail collection of tomorrow's manhood, be from the stock of those who crossed the beaches on Iwo? I wondered.

Next was body cleansing with a special foot solution, hot water showers, plenty of soap, and a heavy coat of delousing powder. The processing trail seemed endless as we moved through the dimly lighted bowels of the huge, old building. My concern for what I had gotten into increased as I moved through the shower unit.

A salty DI in starched, bleached khaki with a leather riding quirt was squaring away a black recruit. This was the first Negro that I had seen at Parris Island, and I assumed that the Marines did not take colored people. I did not have a problem with colored folks. During wheat-threshing days, the colored men ate in the kitchen while the white folks ate in the dining room. The farmers had separate washpans and towels for the crew based upon race. I grew into that way of life and accepted it as the way things were. However, this was going too far.

The recruit was nude, standing at attention while the DI repeatedly struck him with his quirt. His verbal abuse included reminding the recruit that he was a nigger, and that he was attempting to get out of his element in life. After each assertion, the recruit agreed with a loud, "SIR, YES SIR." The DI continued with his rationale that niggers could not fight and therefore could not be Marines. I felt sorry for the recruit and became truly concerned for what lay ahead as I moved quickly through the area. I saw that corporal frequently; his platoon was in our training cycle. We had no colored recruits in Platoon 88, and I saw only two or three during my time in boot camp.

Reiser formed us up in three lines (we learned that was a formation) according to height on the first day. This made the tall guys immediate squad leaders. They were always under Reiser's eye in Close Order Drill (COD), and they were the first to react to commands such as column movements. Some could not handle it and, after much abuse, were replaced by the recruits next in line. For once in my life, I was grateful that I was not taller.

(Our seventy-five-man platoon was halved into sections.) Two tall recruits were our section guides and they endured. Besides marching as right guides, they were next in command below the DIs. The guides caught much flak but took it well. The rest of us recognized a special DI allowance for D. W. King, a six-foot, five-inch, 240-pound football player from Tennessee who went on to play for Parris Island, and J. S. Thompson, older, also tall and strong, with prior Navy time. Reiser probably weighed 130 pounds. Our Junior DI, Daves, treated King and Thompson as equals; we later learned that he had graduated from boot camp himself shortly before our arrival.

Dressed in heavy, herringbone dungarees (later called utilities) and light brown, rough-side-out, crepe-rubber-soled, ankle-high boondockers, we began learning to move from point to point in an orderly manner. This meant COD to Reiser; it meant sweat to us. We struggled to learn and to get it right, but Reiser would become so disgusted at times that he would throw his hands in the air, issue a torrent of vulgarity, and walk away. Daves would take over and the drill would continue.

I never considered myself very religious, but the first time that Reiser exploded with "Jesus F——ing Christ," I truly expected a bolt of lighting from heaven. It did not happen, and ironically, getting away with this blasphemy increased his stature.

That August, the Parris Island heat and humidity were tough even for a hard-working farm boy. We were constantly drenched in sweat, day and night. My clothes were never dry; my socks were always soaked, causing major blisters with new shoes and marching. The nights provided no relief as the barracks trapped the heat of the day, and we added to that the body heat from seventy-five recruits. I lay on my rack in wet skivvies and wet sheets.

As bad as the heat and the DIs were, we had a bigger enemy, the sand flea. There was no getting away from the little bloodsuckers; they were on the drill field, in the chow hall, and in the barracks. The worst place was the drill field or any place where we were in formation because they ate at their pleasure. Unless standing at ease in formation, we were not allowed to remove the hungry little devils. Marines at attention do not move their eyeballs unless commanded to do so. We marched, stood at Attention or Parade Rest and the sand fleas ate. We learned the hard way as Reiser charged through the ranks toward his target.

"Shithead, did I see you move?"

"Sir, yes sir." The response was followed by Reiser's expected punch in the recruit's stomach.

"You don't move an eyeball unless I tell you, Shit-for-Brains."

"Sir, something was biting my neck, Sir."

"Oh, you poor little pussy. Something was biting her little neck so she just decides on her own to remove it. YOU MOVED WHILE YOU WERE AT ATTENTION, ASSHOLE. YOU DO NOT DO THAT. DO YOU UNDERSTAND ME?" To emphasize his point, Reiser grabbed the recruit's dungaree cap visor and pulled it down over his face. He followed with, "That was my pet, and it is his chow time. All sand fleas are my pets, and they will eat on you when they feel like it."

Reiser gut-punched the recruit again and addressed the rest of us. "You do not move while at attention. You do not wipe your runny little nose, scratch your ass, or bother my sand fleas while you are at the position of attention. Is that clear?"

"Sir, yes sir."

"IS THAT CLEAR?"

"SIR, YES SIR."

Washing clothes became the one enjoyable social occasion on the Island. Wash racks were built between the barracks where we washed everything from skivvies to khaki uniforms with scrub brushes and bars of strong laundry soap. Our wash was hung on a clothesline with our tie-ties, small braided rope provided for that purpose in our PX bag. After the first Sunday's wash rack experience, I looked forward to the next; the DIs left us alone, and we could talk and get acquainted. I learned to take my dungarees off the line before they were completely dry and smooth them out on my footlocker, giving them a somewhat pressed appearance.

Receiving mail in our second week was sweet and sour; we all wanted to hear from home and friends, but the price was high. Reiser walked into the squadbay and sounded off with "Mail call. Gather around." He proceeded to call off names while throwing the letters in the direction of the "SIR, HERE SIR." Reiser checked both sides of each envelope; those with anything other than the correct address in the proper format received his attention.

"HOLCOMB."

"SIR, HERE SIR."

"Come here Holcomb. What is this shit S. W. A. K?"

"Sir, that is a letter from Private Holcomb's girlfriend, Sir."

"Is her name Swak or is that her mental makeup, Holcomb?"

"Sir, that is sealed with a kiss, Sir."

"No shit, asshole. Do you think I or anyone else cares about the bullshit you and your pussy play in? You keep that shit inside the envelope. I don't want to see it. Is that clear?"

"Sir, yes Sir."

"Give me fifty push-ups, Holcomb."

"PANGRACE."

"SIR, HERE SIR."

"Get over here, lover boy. This damn platoon is full of lover boys and there is not the making of a Marine among you. I don't know what the Marine Corps is coming to. What is this shit on this envelope, Pangrace?"

"Sir, those are the lip prints of Private Pangrace's fiancee, Sir."

"Well Private Pangrace, seeing as you are so hungry for those lips, let's not waste them. Eat them." He threw the letter; Pangrace caught it, tore the back of the envelope out with his teeth, and began chewing.

I reflected on my good fortune to have no girlfriend and no buddy who knew about Marine boot camp. Several fellow recruits received letters addressed to them as lieutenant or sergeant from friends that did it for the laugh. The laughs might come later, but there were none in Platoon 88. My weekly letter from Mom never caused me any stress.

My first great concern for my future as a Marine came during our day at Classification. We were tested on intelligence and capability so that the Corps could put us in the right jobs. We were to inform the Corps of the Military Occupational Specialty (MOS) we wanted. Clearly told to write in our first three choices, I only had one. Not one of my buddies wanted infantry; all wanted some technical job. There should be plenty of infantry openings, and I saw no need to chance putting down other choices. I only wanted to be a rifleman; getting any other MOS was unacceptable. From my perspective, being a Marine was being a rifleman.

The smart clerk-type PFC who received my form thought otherwise. After some loud screaming about me already qualifying for the infantry because I was not intelligent enough to follow orders, he returned the form for two more choices. Tanks and artillery were entered, and I worried about it until we finally received our MOSs just before graduation.

Reveille included all lights on, DIs yelling, and recruits running in place while shaking both sheets. I awoke on my way to the deck from my top bunk. Dragging my sheets with me, I shook them, one in each hand while trying to get my knees to shoulder level as demanded. Three minutes of this routine from a sleeping start is exhausting, but it does get one awake.

Platoon 88 was in the 2nd Recruit Training Battalion, and we appreciated living in wooden barracks. We learned later at the rifle range, where we lived in Quonset Huts, that we did not have the best deal. Recruits lived in the huts and tents by squads, which meant that a platoon was located in six areas, and the DIs could only be in one place at a time. So, while they were raising hell in one hut, the rest of us were not involved. In the barracks, with all of us in one big squadbay, we were right under their thumb. When one recruit screwed up, we all got the treatment.

Reiser's pet remedy for our screw-ups (anything from a recruit sounding off incorrectly to a dirty rifle) was the lockerbox drill. This drill had many variations, standing or moving, depending upon his mood. We stood by our bunks and performed what he called, "Up and on shoulders." Our full lockerboxes were held straight out in front of us, over our head, followed by extending them to each side. We did this exercise to his commands by the numbers. Then we marched around the inside of the barracks with the full boxes extended out at arm's length. Fingers softened the impact of lockerboxes crashing into each other.

When Reiser thought we really needed motivating, he had us put on our wool overcoats and ponchos. With the footlocker held forward at arm's length, we would double-time out one hatch of our squadbay, up the outside ladder, through an upper squadbay, and back down and around. This was in August, and a dozen such trips made the juice flow.

One of the DIs' favorite remedies for dropping a rifle was to have the recruit extend his arms straight out forward. A rifle was placed on the extended fingertips and bayonets were used to discouraged the lowering of exhausted arms. One bayonet handle was placed in each side of the recruit's cartridge belt with the blade points propping up the underarm.

Reiser also had a remedy for recruits who put their hands in their pockets; they filled their pockets with sand and sewed them shut. The sweat-soaked material chafed their skin, but they learned: Marines do not put their hands in their pockets.

Only once did Reiser touch me, and then with his boondocker. Two hours on the hot drill field had made me extremely thirsty, and I planned to catch an unauthorized drink on the way into our barracks from formation. (Canteens were not used in the mainside area.) Fellow recruits had grabbed a drink on occasions in the past, though we were warned otherwise.

We halted in front of the barracks and Reiser stated, "On the double, I want you inside standing by your racks." With the command "DISMISSED," I raced for the barrack's door. First inside, I stopped at the scuttlebutt and let the cold water enter my parched mouth.

Reiser normally followed the platoon; this time he must have run with the lead. He sounded off behind me, "Shithead, did I tell you to drink water?" I was already moving when his boondocker contacted my rear, and I remained in full flight until standing by my rack. To my surprise, he did not pursue the matter.

Nothing we did was right or good enough. Our racks were ripped up repeatedly because we did not stretch our blankets tightly enough. Initially, we all had to rip up our inspection-ready racks and remake them; we advanced to finding individual racks ripped apart. Returning to barracks and finding my rack made up was one of the first signals that maybe, just maybe, I could get through this place. We cleaned the barracks and heads with toothbrushes, and began to understand why only our mothers could love us. Throughout it all, we marched and marched. Getting better at drill was not good enough for our DI who wanted to hear our eyeballs click on the command of Eyes Right.

During the second week of training, Reiser decided to light the smoking lamp with the platoon formed up in front of our barracks. Reiser sounded off with, "Smoking Lamp Is Lit." He followed with a class on fieldstripping cigarette butts and emphasized that Marines never throw trash on the deck. Trash and discards provide our enemy with good intelligence; even a cigarette butt tells him more than we want him to know.

Then Reiser did his part in support of the tobacco industry by ordering all nonsmokers to fall out and form up on him. Seventeen of us complied. Reiser then directed us to get on line and police the area, picking up everything that did not grow or was not painted. We did so with much under-the-breath grumbling because we were working while the smokers enjoyed a rest.

Days passed and there was another lighting of the smoking lamp. This time, there was only one nonsmoker in Platoon 88; everyone but me now had the habit, and I policed up alone. After one more round of the one-man police detail, I was allowed to stand in ranks and breathe secondhand smoke.

We moved to the Rifle Range for our fifth week of training and the pressure eased. Reiser took leave to get married. (I learned later that most DIs enjoy a wedding with each of their platoons.) The bucket was passed, and we each donated a wedding gift. We were big income guys at $78.00 per month. Income tax came out of this, but living expenses were low: haircuts were 25 cents; shoes resoled and heeled, $1.50; and trousers cleaned and pressed were 30 cents.

We were like children without their parents during Reiser's absence. Our Junior DI was more like an older brother; his short time in the Corps did not provide him with the backbone to cause us to take him seriously. Daves was just too much of a nice guy. He made most of his demands upon us through the two section guides. PFC K. R. Murphy joined us when Daves received orders for Korea. Murphy had to put his foot down at the range, and we lost some movie nights.

DI-induced stress was purposely reduced at the range so that we would fire better scores. Recruits reasoned that the change was because the rifles we drew at the range had firing pins in them, while our drill rifles at mainside did not. That sounded good; the DIs might be afraid of us if we had rifles that would fire. Better shooting was probably the real reason.

Safety is paramount on Rifle Ranges, and DIs had their manner of emphasis. The M-1 Rifle cannot fire with the bolt locked in the rearward position. Therefore, the standing order was that all bolts be open, and anyone found with a closed bolt anywhere other than on the firing line was in trouble. Recruits found with closed bolts were made to open the bolts with their noses. A smart hit is required to open the bolt with the left thumb, and the soft nose is a poor substitute. It will, however, move and lock the bolt to the rear with accompanying DI threats and in-the-face yelling. No recruit ever had to open his bolt more than once with his nose. Platoon 88 had several broken noses and much lost skin, but no one died from an accidental discharge.

Shooting an expert score on qualification day became an obsession with me. While shooting all other weapons and "snapping in" with the service rifle, I dreamed of wearing the crossed rifles of the Expert Badge. I knew that I would shoot an expert score, as I had been pleased with my shooting ability in the past.

Firing week provided a different slant on my abilities and hopes. Nothing went well, which included hitting the bull's-eye. Each day, including pre-qualification, I was lucky to qualify. The monkey was on my back; the little rascal would grab my rifle barrel and with me hanging on, swing me around in huge circles. That expert rifleman badge appeared to be beyond my capability.

In spite of praying for good weather on record day, 27 September arrived badly with a hurricane coming ashore. The day meant so much to me that something had to change; I changed. I walked off the 200-yard line down six points from the hundred possible. Those were dropped in the Off-Hand position while I fired a possible score of 50 during the rapid-fire, sitting string. My average drop here for the week of firing was twenty points with fifteen of those being in the Off Hand. This was as it should be; I could shoot this big-bore rifle.

On the 300-yard Sitting and Kneeling, Slow Fire, I dropped four points where my average drop was fifteen. With two strings of fire left, and the most difficult ones behind me, I was on my way for a high score if not a recruit range record.

As I moved up for my 300-yard prone, rapid-fire string, Murphy, standing beside my scoreboard said, "Hang in there, Hawkeye, we are counting on you." That did it. The little monkey returned, and I dropped fourteen points on that string.

I blew the easiest string of all to fire, the one most shooters expect to drop only one or two points, if any at all. Here my average point drop was two. My ten rounds were in a tight group but few were in the black. There was little consolation in noting that the wind affected all shooters on that relay by putting all out of the black in the same area. Thinking that I had blown my Expert chance, my spirit sank.

Adding up my score, I realized that I could still qualify as Expert if I fired 44 or better on the 500-yard line. With this strong, squirrelly wind over that distance, that score would be a feat in itself. Worse, I had not broken into the 40s on the 500-yard line all week.

We moved back and I lost hope as I watched the relays ahead of me firing with poor results due to the rain and tricky wind. My turn came; following two bull's-eyes, my confidence returned. With the shifting, gusting wind, however, I could not hold in the black and some spotters started to appear out of the bull. After nine rounds down range, my last round had to be in the black if I were to shoot 220 and qualify Expert. It was!

While I did not shoot any great score, I did make my desired qualification. The platoon's high score that day was 220. Three of us fired 220 for Expert, six fired Sharpshooter, and nineteen failed to qualify, with the remainder shooting Marksman. Our 500-yard-line score was used to determine the platoon high shooter, and my 44 points on the 500 gave me the honor. Eugene G. Gunderson, who fired Expert all week, was retained as a coach. He went on to be a competitive shooter, spent most of his career as a top gun on the Marine Corps Rifle and Pistol Team at Quantico, and retired as a Master Gunnery Sergeant.

Recruits who fail to qualify are referred to as "drops." While the goal was zero drops, most platoons averaged three or four on qualification day. Platoon 88's nineteen drops indicate how badly the weather affected our scores.

We returned to our billeting area to find our personal effects dumped and scattered over the deck, and our lockerboxes missing. A platoon just arriving at the range was short lockerboxes, and in the tradition of the times, went out and got some. Mine was one of the missing, but my wallet and money were present. Murphy located the guilty platoon, and our lockerboxes were recovered.

The DI pressure was almost bearable after our return to mainside, but Reiser looked for new and different things to entertain us. Our barracks were built on posts that kept the deck above ground level, with two feet of space between the sand and the bottom of the joists. Plumbing and heating pipes reduced this space, making it difficult in some places to crawl from one side of the building to the other. Reiser did not miss the opportunity. He released us in a line on one side, warning us not to be last getting into ranks on the other side. This exercise did not produce the camaraderie for which the Marine Corps is known. Instead, it was dog–eat–dog, get through anyway and anywhere you could, do not be last.

The barracks crawl was later combined with a pet peeve of the DIs. We understood from comments that reservists were the lowest form of humanity on earth. We were constantly reminded that we were lower than whale shit, and that was on the bottom of the ocean. These "weekend warriors" were even lower, and they were treated so by all DIs, including their own.

DIs got together and put a regular platoon on one side of the barracks and a reserve platoon on the other. The regulars were told what was happening and given instructions that no reservist should make it under the barracks. The reservists were only told that it would be tough on the last one to form up on the other side.

The results were not those expected by the DIs. Recruits met under the barracks, and it was shameful to realize that one Marine hopeful could do such a thing to another wanting to wear the same uniform. Several reservists were hauled to sickbay and the hospital. Their platoon was readily identified by their many bandaged recruits in casts and on crutches straggling along behind the formation. That reserve platoon DI was relieved of duties.

Another memorable experience was the Gas Chamber. The justification for this bad moment was to give us confidence in our gas masks.

Platoon 88 marched to that ugly little shack in the pines where twenty recruits went inside at a time. We moved into the building with our masks on and stood while doors were shut and tear gas activated. As briefed, we marched twice around the inner walls with our masks on proving that they worked. Then, told to remove our masks, we marched counterclockwise while singing the Marine Hymn.

We were instructed to file out of the building in an orderly manner when the hatch opened. Recruits just passing the hatch should continue to march and sing until they arrived again at the hatch. There would be no stampede for the outside. The gas was not heavy where I unmasked, causing me to think that this would not be a problem. Halfway around the building, the gas hit my eyes and lungs solidly.

My eyes burned so badly that I could not open them, and I stopped breathing while coughing up a storm. Just as I passed the hatch after completing the one required tour, it opened. I saw the light through my eyelids while realizing that I had one more circle in that building before getting out. Coughing, with burning eyes and no air in my lungs, I continued with a hand on Murphy to my front.

By the time we reached clean air, I thought I would never recover. Saliva and mucus covered my face; I was not alone with that makeup, but I was not doing as well as the others. My eyes were extremely painful, and my lungs felt as if they were burnt. Few of the recruits, including Murphy who received the same dosage as I, seemed to be hurting as badly. I respect tear gas, and yes, the mask is a necessity in chemical warfare.

We received instruction on the components of the five Marine Corps packs. From smallest to largest, they were the light marching, marching, field marching, transport, and field transport packs. Components of the pack system were the haversack, knapsack, blanket roll, and belt suspenders. The long or short blanket roll was added to make the two field packs while the knapsack was added to make the two transport packs.

The blanket was rolled inside the camouflage shelterhalf and carried in a horseshoe shape around the pack. Greenside or brownside out (showing) was always a problem with the shelterhalf. Falling out with the wrong color outboard was a problem because it took two men and time to stretch and do the blanket roll neatly. Wrong side out was not a problem in Platoon 88 because we all worked together. Several months later in the 2nd MarDiv, color was a problem. There were always a few greensides out in winter when brownside was the uniform. The outboard-color problem also included the camouflage helmet cover. Someone always failed to get the word on the uniform, and one could not go by the season of the year. The piney woods of the Carolinas are green the year around.

Platoon 88, with field transport pack, marched to Elliott's Beach for tactics and infantry training. We pitched shelter halves, ate C-rations, received some instruction, and chased rabbits. We spent most of the time on a platoon line, moving through the boondocks, and chasing down rabbits. Reiser must have liked rabbit stew because he took home a good supply.

In 1950, there was no Infantry Training School; Marines were combat ready after boot camp and were Korea bound. Most of the instruction and especially the tactical training in the field came from the DIs. Therefore, what recruits gained from a field exercise was limited to the knowledge and abilities of the two young Marines assigned. As luck would have it, I did not learn much in tactics and fieldwork that was helpful to me later in Korea. The Korean War itself was the reason for this shortcoming.

On 25 June 1950, the Marine Corps's strength was 68,000 Marines scattered over the world. After sending a hastily collected division and air wing with supporting forces to MacArthur in Korea, General Clifton B. Cates, CMC, did not have many Devil Dogs left to perform other Marine duties. MajGen Robert Pepper, the CG of the Recruit Depot, had to get his training mission accomplished as best he could with whatever and whoever was available. Therefore, in the fall of 1950 some mature recruits, such as Daves and Murphy, were retained at Parris Island to serve as drill instructors.

The members of Platoon 88 were getting salty. We looked it in our faded dungarees, (caused by hard scrubbing at the wash racks), and our attitudes reflected it when we were among the "boots" on the Island. Reiser, however, kept us honest to the cause; our heads never became so big that we forgot who we were. A sand flea incident makes my point.

Platoon 88 stood at Parade Rest in the street waiting for our time to go in the mess hall. Evenings were the worst time for sand flea feeding, and my eyes focused on one crawling up the neck of the recruit standing forty inches to my front. The recruit tried to discourage the flea by twitching his muscles and shoulder without catching the DI's attention. The flea moved unhampered up his neck, on to his ear, and disappeared inside. The recruit was having a smothered volcanic reaction: his body was a mass of motion and action yet no real movement was seen.

In spite of the tension, heat, frustration, and concern for the recruit, I had to suppress real laughter for the first in a long while. Knowing what the recruit was going through was part of it, as was the lack of visual body movement to remove the flea. The flea ate, and the recruit lived the role of a Marine; he did not move.

Our time for feeding the sand fleas was nearing the end. The last event was the final personnel inspection by an officer. This was my first contact with one of those lofty, seldom-seen officers. What could I expect? Would he scream and yell meaner and louder than our DIs? Our corporal enjoyed a position somewhere equal to God, so I expected the worst. Detailed preparation ensured that my rifle and uniform were spotless. All I had to worry about were his questions and my performance of a perfect Inspection Arms movement.

Watching the captain move down the front ranks did not help; I dreaded his approach while wondering if he would ever make it this far. He was very detailed and missed nothing while spending time with each recruit. He was not loud, and I could hear very little of what he said. I knew better than to look at him, but I did not miss much of what was happening. Stress and apprehension began to take its toll while the inspector moved through the first two ranks. There was a disadvantage to being in the 3rd Squad: the dread of the Inspector's approach lasted longer. My body felt so stiff that I wondered if I could move; I felt as if I were a permanent fixture on the drill field.

The worst part was while he inspected the recruit beside me. Knowing I was next, I doubted that I could get my arms to move the rifle through the inspection manual properly and hit the operating-rod handle smartly to the rear. Worse, I had to respond to his questions, and I did not trust the functioning of my brain-housing group.

My arms did move and I mechanically went through the action. He slapped my rifle from my grip, and I dropped my arms as though the rifle were hot. Action was relief; I was functioning.

"Recruit, what is the zero of your range rifle at five-hundred yards?"

"Sir, the zero of this recruit's range rifle at five-hundred yards is eighteen elevation and four left windage, Sir."

"Who is the Commandant of the Marine Corps?"

"Sir, the Commandant of the Marine Corps is General Clifton B. Cates, Sir."

My rifle was returned; I closed the bolt, pulled the trigger, and went to Order Arms while enjoying a new feeling of weightlessness.

We passed the inspection. The end came; 17 October finally arrived. That distant bright spot that we had dreamed of for so long, which never seemed to get closer, was upon us. We paraded with a Pass in Review, and with one exception, were all promoted to PFC. It had been a hard, demanding eleven weeks, an experience that I would not want to go through again. I had my share of weak moments, but I never lost sight of my objective: I was going to be a Marine. Now that it was over, the end justified the means. I have never been so pleased and proud of my accomplishments as becoming a US Marine; the Eagle, Globe, and Anchor is in my heart forever.

We boarded a Trailways bus and headed home on a ten-day boot leave.

Lessons Learned

1. Well-thought-out commitments, regardless of difficulty, are easily kept.
2. Eleven weeks of boot camp make a Marine for a lifetime.
3. Discipline and heritage are the makings of a Marine.
4. Every person ought to experience a feeling similar to that of a Marine graduating from boot camp.

2
Private First Class
1128290/0300
17 October 1950

Leaving Parris Island was the high point of my nineteen years. (My nineteenth birthday came during bootcamp; I kept that fact to myself.) I was proud of what I had accomplished and proud of my uniform. Our bus was filled with recruits; we removed our "Vandegrift" jackets and laid our seats back for the long ride to Washington, D.C. There was a strong awareness of freedom in the areas of expression, choice, and action outside that depot gate.

The reclined positions did not last, however; we were too keyed up with thoughts and expectations of our new roles as Leathernecks. We were also not used to resting with the sun up; our departure was early afternoon. The radio was on, and we caught up on the latest: "Mona Lisa" and "Good Night, Irene" played repeatedly, while on the country side, "Movin On" by Hank Snow was the top hit.

Arriving in D.C. at midnight, I learned that the next bus for Winchester would leave at 0930. I placed my seabag in a locker and experienced my first night in a bus terminal. The early hours went fast, as many of my buddies were there as well. Their individual departures were the final breakup of Platoon 88.

"Good Night, Irene" and "Mona Lisa" continued to play on the coffee shop jukebox and sleep did not come easily on the terminal benches. Departure time came, and I was on the next to last leg of my journey home. As I moved down the aisle on the bus, a gentle older lady offered me the seat beside her. As we talked, I realized that she probably did so out of curiosity.

I had not been in my seat long before she asked, "What country are you from, Sonny?" At first I could not believe this woman's question, then remembered I had not seen a US Marine before my visit to the recruiter. Upon hearing my response, she apologized with embarrassment. Then I was glad that I had not responded with the smart "Russian Para-

21

trooper" answer that had entered my mind with her question. We spent the rest of the ride talking about a subject we had in common, farming.

I got off the bus in Round Hill, left my seabag at the barbershop, and started the five-mile walk. There was no taxi service, which would not have been a consideration anyway. My folks had no telephone; they did not know that I was inbound. Rides were easy to get as few people passed up a uniform. The friendly barber probably helped as the Deputy Sheriff came along shortly offering a ride. We never saw the law enforcement out our way, and here I had a ride to my front door.

My leave was great; one might have gotten the impression that I had returned from the war rather than just boot camp. Mom fed me as if I needed to put on weight, and Dad got my attention by introducing me as "My boy in the Army." I knew that, to him, anyone in the military service was in the Army. Country people used the word in a general sense to cover all boys in uniform. That introduction, however, did not stand; I immediately made the correction. My dad repeated the act for the next several years before I got through to him that the difference mattered to me. Moreover, I felt that he took a certain pride in having a Marine in the family.

There was no need to correct Dad verbally: I wore the uniform. As with the lady on the bus, if they did not recognize the uniform, the difference probably did not matter. My uniform was a part of me. Everywhere I went away from the farm I wore Greens; while aboard the farm I wore Marine dungarees. I had given Ray my civvies upon enlisting; I was a Marine, and I intended to look like one. During my first enlistment, I wore only uniforms, and did not own one civilian shirt. Marines wore the Vandegrift jacket for casual occasions and the coat (known as a blouse) for dressier times. Our summer uniform was all khaki, and the tie was always required.

Boot leave ended and, on 29 October, I reported to the 2nd MarDiv at Camp Lejeune. The division and camp were in turmoil because of the Korean War. The regular Marines had shipped out, leaving the base for the follow-on Marines. Reserves were now aboard and trying to get organized while training everyone up for combat. All Marines, regular or reserve, old or new, were bound for Korea. The leaders in Baker Company, 1st Bn, 2nd Marines, including the corporals, were reservists. The majority of them had been in during WW II and knew Marine business. The problem was that events had happened so fast. No one expected America to be involved in a shooting war so soon, and disruptions of private lives and plans were taking adjustment time. So, with reservists shaking off their civilian suits, and recruits fresh out of boot camp adjusting to thinking for themselves, we organized and started training.

Assigned to a rifle squad, I asked for and received a Browning Automatic Rifleman (BAR-man) billet. I liked the way that weapon had fired in boot camp, and I liked all that I had heard about it. The Browning Automatic Rifle, Caliber .30, Model 1918-A2 with bipod was an air-cooled, gas-operated, magazine-fed, shoulder weapon. Each of the three fire teams in a rifle squad had a BAR, for a total of nine in each platoon. That was a lot of firepower; at that time, an Army platoon had only three BARs, one per squad.

The short life expectancy of a BAR man in combat did not bother me. (The rumor was two minutes on the Pacific beaches in the Big Two.) Combat was a long way off. In addition to the BAR's firepower, I liked the fact that the fire team was built around that rifle. It was the most important weapon in the team, and the Marine carrying it was next senior to the team leader.

Military subjects were presented on outside bleachers; reservists relearned while they taught. Our tactics training was basic and on the platoon level. We went into the wooded area within walking distance and rotated through attack and defense problems while aggressing each other. Blank ammo was not even a thought; we made a "Bang! Bang!" by mouth, not unlike my soldier games as a kid. Blank ammo and training dollars were unheard of in the 1950 2nd MarDiv.

A night tactical march in the nearby woods created some excitement. We were moving on a dark night while maintaining contact by holding onto the entrenching tool on the back of the Marine ahead. There was a pause following a commotion toward the front. The word came down the line, "Fix bayonets! There is a bear forward!" Metallic clicks were audible as riflemen fixed bayonets. BAR men and those armed with pistols were issued K-Bar knives in place of bayonets; the bear would have to get closer to us. Although the march was completed without further incident, I was disturbed by the thought that over 200 of my great Marines should be concerned with one bear.

PFC C.J. Holland, who had been in Platoon 88 with me, was also in Baker. He brought his 1937 Buick back from boot leave, and on the Saturday of our second weekend at Lejeune, he sponsored a liberty run. Four of us from Platoon 88 exercised our liberty rights and hit the towns.

J-ville (Jacksonville), the nearest town, was first, and then we moved up to New Bern. These guys' ideas of fun was drinking beer in a dimly lit bar with thick cigarette smoke. No one wanted to go to a movie; we could see those on base. I found the night dragging after several sodas, and thereafter spent my free time aboard the base. With Christmas coming, I needed money to go home on leave. My PFC pay was $86.00 a month, but I was helping with the farm payment. A $50 monthly allotment went home, and after deductions, I received $13 a payday (Marines are paid twice a month).

The 2nd Marines were in Area Two. Our brick barracks were almost new, built ten years earlier during WW II. Barracks life was comfortable, and our daily schedule was easy after boot camp. As in boot camp, rifle racks lined the center of each squadbay while bunks and wall lockers were positioned along both bulkheads. All rifles, including BARs, were kept in the racks. The need to lock our weapons was unthinkable. There was no guard in the barracks other than firewatch at night, but no one thought that a weapon might disappear. (Five years later, Marines would use bicycle locks to secure weapons to rifle racks or bunk rails. Some commands later required weapons to be locked in personal wall lockers.)

Weapon loss was not a problem because there were few automobiles aboard the base, probably six cars in Baker Company. We all lived in the barracks, including the staff NCOs, so there was not much movement through the main gate. In addition, we still believed in law enforcement in general and the FBI in particular. The word was that if a weapon came up missing, the FBI would come up with the weapon and the culprit.

Platoon 88 missed mess duty, but the reservists saw to it that my training was complete. Two weeks in the mess hall had me putting on weight. It was no wonder that cooks and mess sergeants tended to be big in the waistline. I was relieved of mess duty to go on Christmas leave. Half the command could go for Christmas; the other half could go over the New Year's holiday. Most preferred New Year's leave. I would get my leave, the others would not.

Because I had been home two months earlier, it was not hard to get back into the swing of things on the farm. Christmas went by, another ten-day leave passed, and I was again reporting in at Lejeune. I arrived at 2300 and the Duty NCO told me to report to the gym and draw cold-weather gear. We were shipping out. At midnight, the base was busy, and the gym was full of Marines receiving cold-weather clothing. Receiving mine, I returned to the barracks at 0300, too keyed up to sleep.

To put my mom's fear to rest, I had assured her that I needed more training before being sent to Korea. Now, with good-bye hardly out of my mouth, I was going. There was no phone on the farm; all I could do was write a letter, which gave Mom a few more peaceful nights.

A pay call cleared our record of pay due plus $4.50 a day for meals during the four-day train ride to the West Coast. From that amount it sounded as if we would eat well. As I would not need money in the war zone, I sent my pay home and kept only my food money.

On 6 January 1951, the 4th Replacement Draft boarded seven trains for the first leg of our journey to Korea. My company boarded a troop train in Morehead City at 0300. What made this qualify as a troop train was that no one would pay to ride it. The cars were old, dirty, and in need of paint, with torn upholstery covering the seats. The Pullmans were no better with lumpy mattresses and worn out pillows.

The chow was tasty enough, but the portions were so small that a bird would feel hunger pangs. One of my buddies asked about seconds only to find out that there was no such thing. We could order another meal or any part of a meal. Our waiter stated, "You want food, and I want money. You won't need money where you're going, and I have kids in school. That takes a lot of money. You give me money, and I will give you food."

That "won't need money where you are going" part did not strike me well, and the more I thought of it, the madder I became. My family needed my money, if I did not. Some Marines put money on the table and received more food; I did not have that option.

The train experience became old, fast. We lived out of field transport packs, which compounded the problem. The blanket roll was not needed, and the haversack and knapsack held so little gear that we lived like bums. We did not look any better wearing the wrinkled dungarees from our overstuffed packs.

Our time was spent sleeping and writing letters that were handed to strangers in one of the many stations where we stopped. We were not allowed off the train, though some gutsy individuals did seek out handy neighborhood bars on several stops. We were seeing our nation as we passed through the states. My first sight of our country truly impressed me, especially the difference in the terrain. The treeless hills of California made me feel I was entering a foreign country.

Our train sided on a San Francisco Port pier; we dismounted at 0230 on 11 January and walked aboard the USNS *General William O. Darby* (T-AP-127). I did not know it at the time, but 1,000 members of the draft flew to Korea while 799 of us went by ship.[2] Ships do not roll while tied up at piers, however, I felt a fluid movement while going up the gangplank, which was my first signal of coming seasickness.

Amid that confusion, we were assigned compartments and racks. Then came the problem: how to get two seabags, rifle, pack, cartridge belt, helmet, and myself on a canvas six feet long and thirty-one inches wide. It was twenty-two inches to the rack above and with a body on it; one did not get twenty-two inches of space. Racks were stacked from the deck to the overhead, five to six high depending on what utility ducts and piping were attached to the overhead. Two sets of racks were attached side by side, and there was an aisle of about two feet before the next tier.

A voice came over the 1-MC: "This is the Captain speaking. Welcome aboard, Marines. My men and I are here to make your ocean journey as pleasant as possible, and I will talk to you more about that later. Bad weather and high seas are forecast to hit this area today, so we will sail when all are aboard. I hope to get ahead of the storm."

We sailed and the storm hit. I stayed in my rack and it was not long before I was rolling from side to side. I was propped in solidly with my gear, but my insides rolled. Sick Marines grew tired of hassling with their seabags and kicked them onto the deck. Some took the ship's rolls better than others; I did not try to get up for two days. There is nothing to indicate the passing of days in the bowels of a troop ship except messages over the 1-MC.

About the third day, I realized that I should drink and eat something. Halfway up the ladder to the galley, I felt sickness coming, gave up, and moved quickly back to my rack. Sometime later, I attempted to get a drink of water. Moving to a scuttlebutt in our compartment, I found it full of vomit. I almost did not make it back to my rack without adding to what others had unselfishly given of themselves. Later, I found a clean scuttlebutt and was able to eat some food. The ship did not roll so violently, and I began to feel better.

Merchant seamen were no more receptive to us than the train waiters; they hassled us from place to place, leaving us unsure of what to do with ourselves. Troop compartments were secured for cleaning; Marines not doing the cleaning were moved topside to the weather decks. The compartments remained secured until after the Troop Commander's inspection which sometimes took several hours. Meanwhile, deck crews roped off deck areas for swabbing. We could not stay on deck, and we could not go below. We survived by standing on the ladderways, by moving from place to place, by trying to find somewhere to get away, get lost, and be hassle-free. Some poker games took place under the tarps of the "out of bounds" lifeboats, but few Marines were caught.

Marines formed up in the chow line, as we spent most of our time in one anyway. You either waited on the ladderways for the mess deck to open or you waited in the long, slow moving line once it did open. The mess deck was small for the number it served.

The *Darby* pulled into Yokohama, Japan, after a thirteen-day crossing. We stored our seabags containing issued uniforms, and seventeen-year-old Marines and reservists who were not graduates of boot camp were screened out and left in Japan. We were trimming down to fighting weight, and that action was noted. Noise, chatter, and laughter were greatly reduced; we were maturing. Very soon, we would take on tasks feared by most men, and the price would be high. Many among us would never see this ocean or a ship again; they would not return home. We were issued ammo and assigned to units while aboard ship. I was pleased to be assigned to the 5th Marines.

Our ship dropped anchor in Pohang Harbor, South Korea, on 27 January. (Map, page 30) It was freezing on the weatherdeck, but I wanted to see this country, this Korea that had triggered my enlistment. There before me, looking innocent in the distance, was the country with the war. It looked peaceful enough with the white caps dancing on the water lapping its shore and mountains framing the background.

In late afternoon, we were called to our debarkation station in order of our unit assignment. My 3/5 unit was among the last called. For a change, the ladderways were clear of Marines as I made my way to the weatherdeck; the ship was almost empty. The wind had increased and it was colder; the white caps were twice the size of those I saw earlier. We went over the side wearing cold-weather clothing topped off with fighting equipment and the field transport pack. Naval safety policy dictated that gloves not be worn on the cargo net—freezing weather and no gloves!

I became concerned before I was halfway down the net. The frozen Manila hemp tore into my hands, but the hurt became less as my hands grew numb. Without feeling in my hands, I could not be sure of a positive grip on the rope. In addition, our numb hands had to do double duty with the loads on our backs. The forty-pound weight of clothing and equipment was enough under normal conditions with functional hands. Gloves, pier side, or an easier way of unloading were not available; unload the Marines.

A fall into the water from the cargo net was certain death, a man would be crushed between the ship's hull and the pounding landing craft. As we labored down the net, I expected one or more Marines to fall. Several did lock arms through the cargo net while trying to get feeling back in their hands, but no one fell.

With an extra measure of determination, I made it down into the pitching, bucking DUKW (Army's amphibious truck). One instant it was there, ready for me to step into it, and the next it was ten feet below me. A sergeant yelled for us not to jump, but on the next rise of the DUKW, I did the next thing to a jump. Descending Marines who held on to the net were again high over the landing craft. Finally, we had a load, and headed for the beach. The flying bow spray soaked us, but the soaking did not last, as our clothing quickly froze.

Several machine guns began firing in the distance when we were halfway to shore. The MGs and the freezing spray made a major negative impact on my spirit. That was one of the low points of my entire war experience; I was not then mentally ready to meet the enemy. I hoped that the guns were friendly and used in training or test firing. Our DUKW kept its place in the line of amphibian vehicles, rolled up on the beach, and entered a dirt road.

We passed a small mud-walled, straw-roofed house with wood smoke coming from under the floor on one side. In the gray of the winter day the house looked isolated and primitive. The extreme cold and lateness of the day probably kept the few Koreans indoors. I saw no one but thought of the barren life these poor people must live. My home and loved ones came to mind, and I realized how fortunate we Americans were.

We dismounted at the Division CP and boarded trucks. Next stop was a Marine camp in Yongchon where we joined the 3rd Bn, 5th Marines. (Map, page 30) Sergeant Charles W. Eckert met those of us assigned to Item Company. Platoon assignments were made, and with a few hours left until dawn of the 28th, we bedded down in an empty freezing squad tent.

Assigned to 3rd Fire Team, 3rd Squad, 3rd Platoon the following day, I got my weapon of choice. Others did not want the extra weight, the responsibilities, or the additional risk associated with the BAR. Unit-unique equipment was issued that amounted to trading M-1s for BARs or carbines and getting grenades and more ammo. We had brought everything else with us. For the next two days, we new guys were introduced to the way Marines did their thing in Korea.

Launching up and forward after hitting the deck in a fire and movement exercise received my immediate and full attention. That BAR belt loaded with twelve magazines weighed twenty pounds and practically nailed the center of my body to the deck. Though I had been a BAR man in the 2nd Marines, I had never carried a load of ammunition.

I was shocked at how the weight all but stopped me from rising from a prone position. Was it possible that I could repeatedly move swiftly up, forward, and down as required to stay alive during an assault under fire?

Now I understood why BAR men had such a short life expectancy in a firefight. At a minimum, the training at Lejeune should have included a twenty-pound weight in the ammo belt. I worked on it, however, and lived every minute of the day with that weight on me. Within two weeks I was handling my BAR load as well as some riflemen handled their lighter load.

Each Marine carried two fragmentation grenades; the rest of his load was based on his weapon. BAR men had the greatest load: the weapon with full magazine and bipod weighed twenty-one pounds; total weight with ammo belt and grenades was forty-five pounds. Machine-gun ammo carriers also packed a load, as each carried two cans of gun ammo at 40 pounds plus a carbine with its ammo.

Our sleeping bag served as a pack, and our personal gear, such as toilet and writing material, went inside. Most Marines used comm wire to make shoulder loops on the rolled bag. With all the pockets in our clothing, a pack was not necessary. The different ways that the sleeping bag was carried caused us to look like the proverbial Cox's Army. Occasionally, a bag would work out of a loop and unroll with one end falling to the ground and the Marine dragging it along.

It did not rain in the winter, so the shelterhalf and poncho were excess gear, left behind or discarded. Similarly, most Marines discarded their entrenching tool (E-tool) with the hard-frozen ground providing the justification. Those who kept them stuck the E-tool into the roll of the bag. At one time, my E-tool was the only one in my fire team.

We wore up to five layers of clothing, wool-lined mittens, and a pile-lined cap with pulldown ear covers. The only clothing items carried were leather gloves with wool liners for working and fighting, and two pairs of heavy wool ski socks with felt insoles for daily rotation. We carried the socks and insoles under our armpits, between the woolen underwear and the middle layer of clothing, to dry them for wear the following day. Two pairs of socks and insoles were worn with the fourteen-inch shoepac that was made of rubber around the foot and leather uppers. Not insulated, it was a wet-climate boot rather than cold-weather.

Second Lieutenant Donald R. Brimmer was our platoon leader. A mustang (an officer with prior enlisted time), he would later express that fact by wearing his old dungaree jackets with patches sewn over the chevrons stenciled on the sleeves. Fair-haired, with smooth facial features,

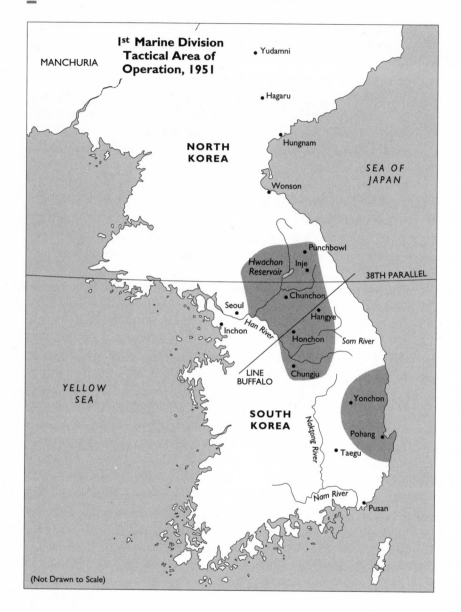

1st Marine Division Tactical Area of Operation, 1951

MANCHURIA

• Yudamni

• Hagaru

NORTH KOREA

• Hungnam

SEA OF JAPAN

• Wonson

Punchbowl

Hwachon Reservoir

Inje

38TH PARALLEL

• Chunchon

Seoul •

Hangye

Han River

• Inchon

Honchon

Som River

LINE BUFFALO

• Chungju

YELLOW SEA

SOUTH KOREA

• Yonchon

Naktong River

Pohang

• Taegu

Nam River

• Pusan

(Not Drawn to Scale)

he was older than the average 2nd Lieutenant. The Marine Corps does not have the "ninety-day wonders" that I heard about through my Army friends. By Marine standards, Brimmer had been around awhile.

Eckert was the platoon sergeant, and Corporal Myron J. Davis was my squad leader. I was pleased with each of my leaders; I had lucked out with the very best. Davis impressed me from start, and he grew in stature with each passing day. John Wayne, for his role as Sergeant Stryker in *Sands of Iwo Jima*, could have learned much from my corporal. A soft-spoken Marine from Pocatello, Idaho, Davis was my first mentor in the demanding field of leading Marines. His first name was Corporal until it later changed to Sergeant, and he was my first experience with a truly gungy Marine.

Gungy is the Marine nickname for the Chinese term *gung ho* that means to work together. A Marine's definition of the term includes those who are all for the Corps and the Corps's way of doing things, those who live, look, and perform the positive role of the ideal US Marine. To outsiders, all Marines probably appear gung ho; within our ranks, however, only a few measure up to the title. Gungy types see two ways to do things, the wrong way and the Marine Corps way. The title is attached to those who comply with regulation when the opposite is the norm. For example, I was called gungy because I wore my leggings and helmet cover. My view was that these two items made me stand out as a US Marine from among the other uniforms in that war. The practical viewpoint was that the leggings were too much of a bother to lace up daily. Anyway, no one seemed to care whether we wore them or not. Few Marines of any rank wore their leggings, but Davis wore his.

That rationale also applied to the camouflage helmet cover, which was strictly a Marine item of uniform during WW II and up to the latter part of the Korean War. Helmets were used almost daily as wash basins and to heat shaving water. Removing and replacing the cover was too much of a hassle. Therefore, the commonsense guys wore a black-smoked steel pot on their heads as did their Army brothers.

Corporal Davis had a long, blond, handlebar mustache that was an immediate clue to how long he had been in combat. Marines did not wear hair on their faces otherwise. He had a caliber .38 revolver holstered low on his right hip. The pistol had belonged to a 3rd Squad buddy killed crossing the Han River. Not trusting the rear echelon to return the pistol to the father, Davis intended to do that himself. He did not just wear it for looks.

During an attack, Davis was usually the first to enter a bunker following the clearing grenade, and this practice began to bother me. Aware of just how important he was to us, I talked with him about a change of bunker-clearing duties; a BAR man should be first in a bunker following the grenade. He countered my statement by showing how much quicker he could cover a threat from an unexpected corner. He could turn the muzzle of his pistol in a third of the time that it took me to swing the long-barreled BAR. Before I thought of a counterargument he said, "No other hand will touch this pistol."

The best example of Davis's performance in leading Marine infantry in combat happened after the rains started. In the attack for days through rough terrain, we had received little sleep with a 50 percent watch each night and poor rations. (We were provided with C-rations; the problem was thawing them so they could be eaten. The tactical situation did not allow a fire after dark, and we were on the move during daylight.) Then came the rain.

Item Company moved off the line with sleeping bags and clothing thoroughly soaked. Besides the misery of being hungry, wet, and cold, the rain-soaked gear added weight to our backs. An Army unit relieved us, but instead of going to the rear where we could rest, we moved to the flank. We suspected that we were committed to take an objective that some other unit could not handle. We plodded along knowing that the situation was only going to get worse. The squad morale was dangerously low; my spirit was down in the mud with my feet. Because of my weakened physical condition, I was mentally lower than when I came ashore in the landing craft at Pohang.

A voice seeped into my consciousness; someone was singing. After my initial disbelief, I tuned in Davis singing, "Never saw the sun shining so bright, never saw things going so right." The words did not fit our situation, and I resented the sentiment. Then I realized that I really had to listen closely to hear the words; the corporal was not making a show of his singing.

My thoughts shifted to, "I know his game; this is all part of leadership. He is just trying to make us feel better, raise our spirit." I refused to be influenced. We trudged on, and the words and tune continued, not forced or obnoxious, but audible if I listened closely enough. Our gloom gradually faded, someone made a remark, and soon we were talking, even if it was bitching. The squad spirit returned and we moved into night bivouac ready to do what had to be done.

My corporal had come to Korea with the 1st Provisional Marine Brigade in August 1950. A Refrigeration Repairman by MOS, he was later assigned to Item as a rifleman replacement for the casualties taken during the Pusan Perimeter fighting. Davis was an example of the Commandant's desire: every Marine a rifleman. He was with Item for the amphibious assault at Inchon, the attack on Seoul, the Wonsan landing, and the fight out of the Chosin. There were other Brigade Marines with us, but they had rejoined the squad from the hospitals where they had a break from the everyday life of the infantry Marine. When I arrived, Davis was the only 3rd Squad member to go through it all. My focus on Davis is getting ahead in my story; I will return to the bean patch near Yongchon and my first week in Korea.

While the Chosin veterans rested up, we replacements received a few days of training in our new roles. The 1st MarDiv received the mission to eliminate the 8,000 enemy troops caught behind our line. Broken into small thirty- to fifty-man bands, they operated as guerrilla forces. This operation turned out to be an excellent opportunity for the new Marines to become a part of the great 1st MarDiv team while not under fire. We patrolled and attacked, but our objectives were never defended. Most of us were not shot at in anger.

Our basic operation was trucking to a certain point, dismounting, and walking the ridges and valleys. Item covered miles in areas that were seldom, if ever, seen by humans, but we made no contact with those for whom we searched. Sometimes the trucks would drop us off at one point, pick us up at another, and move on for a second drop. Signs and evidence that the enemy had been in the area were plentiful, but they did not wait for us.

The enemy had no organization or plan, and that made determining their next move and action difficult. They were just banging around inside the pot, and any encounter with them was purely by chance. The village people did not support the enemy; therefore, the guerrilla idea did not work. The only success the enemy had in the villages was when they assaulted and killed all the people; then they could eat without having to rush into hiding. Otherwise, the people kept us informed of the enemy's movement and location.

Poor roads and a primitive communication system favored the enemy bands. By the time we learned of an enemy sighting and reacted, the band had departed. Troop-carrying helicopters would have been a great help, but that asset was still in the future.

The enemy left dead behind them, not only the farmers and woodsmen of the countryside but also their own. They were starving to death, dying of wounds and diseases. In the later stages, they did not bury their dead; they lay where they fell. While we did not catch them, we hurt them. Fresh signs became fewer, and we found more skeletons on the ridgelines.

The weather was cold and dry with snow falling now and then, but no rain. The only roads were dirt, and heavy truck traffic ground the frozen surface into inches of fine dust. While I did not care for long hikes, I despised the truck rides more, and wondered if the dust would kill us. It coated our parkas, ruined an unprotected weapon, and went right down into our lungs. We spit mud long after dismounting and walking the ridgelines.

We tried to keep our faces covered in spite of warnings to stay alert for convoy ambushes. We were covered quickly one way or the other, by cloth or by dust, and we could not see any better either way. Breathing was a chore without adding another almost impossible task. Because a Marine's first concern is his rifle, we gave special concern to our weapons.

Once, on the way to a drop-off, I was seated by the truck tailgate with observation responsibility to our rear. As we came out of a sharp hairpin turn on a mountain road, my eyes were drawn to an object over which we had passed. The perfectly flat item, looking like a cutout paper doll, was the remains of a man. So many heavy trucks had passed over him on the frozen road that he was literally mashed paper thin. War has a way of dulling one's humanity, but I was bothered by the lack of concern for that man, even if he was the enemy. Why was the body not moved from the road?

With the high speed of the convoy on that narrow, winding road, I realized that the drivers had no choice. Stopping suddenly (the body could not be seen until we were on top of it) would cause a pileup of trucks with untold Marine casualties in the open truck beds. An additional consideration was that the enemy might have placed the body there to stop us within his ambush kill zone. There was no time for any thought process on that mountain road. The order had been issued, "No stops—Roll 'em."

Several times, we arrived at a village just hours behind the departure of the enemy band, or at a campsite with coals from his cook fires still warm. To shorten the time-distance factor in our reaction, we moved out of our camp and set up patrol bases. Item Company made no contact.

We were benefiting from the patrolling. Humping the hills whipped us into shape, and we were beginning to work together as expected of a Marine rifle squad. While our bodies were getting hard, we were also learning to live with hunger pangs. Because of the extreme cold weather, we needed extra calories for body heat. We did not get the extra food; worse, we had to get by on less. During our days in camp, we received only two hot meals and a soup call for lunch. The soup amounted to colored hot water with crackers, and neither of the two meals left a young man feeling satisfied. (C-rations were issued while on patrol, and if they were warm, I at least felt as if I had eaten.) The word on the need of a soup call was that rations were in short supply and we were making do. Marines by their very nature also make do, and we assumed the task of supplementing our meager rations.

We butchered a calf and had a real feast that included roasting the meat over a bed of coals. Life in the squad was really looking up while we enjoyed full stomachs and the camaraderie around the fire. The next day a Korean farmer approached our CO with the complaint that Marines had eaten his calf. I never learned what the CO's action was with the farmer. I suppose the legal officer paid him more than the calf was worth. As for the 3rd Squad, we made do with government issue thereafter. We received a loud and clear signal that if something like this happened again, some people were going to the stockade.

In the middle of February the 1st MarDiv turned the guerrilla problem over to the Army, and the 5th Marines relieved the 187th Airborne for Operation Killer, a major UN offensive planned to drive the communists from Korea. We moved by truck through Chungju, located in the center of the Korean peninsula. There was no problem with dust this time; the rain had started. In open trucks, we soaked up the rain, and after dismounting south of Wonju, we walked and soaked up more.

A convoy moved to the rear as we hiked forward in file on both sides of the road. Each truck appeared to be loaded with uniformed bodies stacked higher than the truck cabs. Looking back, I saw that they were loaded with soldiers, truckloads of corpses with arms and legs extended in all directions. They were stacked like cordwood, side to side, front to rear, to a height over the truck-bed sides.

I did not need to see that sight, especially on this miserable, dreary day. War is costly in lives, but to see bodies stacked in such a manner, without a tarp over them, was gruesome. Similar situations have since taught me that this was a practical way to do the job. That first picture, however, implanted in this young Marine's mind, will be there forever.

We continued by foot to our Attack Position north of Wonju where we would jump off in our attack toward Hoengsong the following morning. Our battalion was the right flank of the division attack, and Item was on the battalion's right flank. We halted after dark on a rocky ridge with scattered waist-high pines.

Told to dig in, I found the rocky, frozen earth impossible to dent with my entrenching tool. That little shovel bounced off the ground with a sound of steel clanging against steel. The few of us with E-tools gave in to broken shovels, exhaustion, darkness, and the rain; I made do on the hillside. (Marines set in their defense on the military crest of the hill, rather than the top of the ridge or true crest. The military crest is down from the ridge and at a rise or swell in the grade that allows observation farther down the slope and better fields of grazing fire.) To stay on the hillside, we positioned our sleeping bags against rocks or bushes.

We could not build fires to thaw our rations. I needed food for body heat, strength, and endurance, but my sleeping bag interested me more than sucking on frozen hamburgers-with-gravy chipped out of the can by bayonet. My bag had been dry in a waterproof container. Outside and in use, only a water-repellent cover protected the sleeping bag. I made a bed of my soaked outer clothing, crawled into the comfortable environment, and immediately went to sleep.

A 50-percent watch was set, and my assistant BAR man took the first hour. He was also exhausted and probably did not last any longer than I. When I awoke, I knew that I had been sleeping longer than an hour, confirmed by the luminous hands on my watch. I had slid twenty yards down from my earlier position, and my bag was wet.

Rain was still falling, and I could not see anything in the totally black night. The sky could not be differentiated from the ground. I considered getting out of my still-warm bag and crawling up the hill, however, my personal-tactical situation seemed secure to my sleepy brain. I reasoned that if the enemy should find his way to our hill in this darkness, he would never find me down here on this slippery slope. My buddy had not turned over the watch, so I slept.

Dawn found us scattered all over that hillside with the job of collecting and packing up our wet gear. Fires were okay during daylight, but starting one with the rain-soaked wood was impossible before we jumped off in the attack. The small pine bushes around us were of no help, as they were too green to burn. Davis stated that he would get a gas Coleman stove for the squad even if he had to hump it. He did so at the first opportunity, and he did hump it, but that morning we moved in the attack, cold, wet, and hungry.

Our attack north found most of the hilltop objectives vacated by the enemy. Initially, they did not fire a shot but faded before us. We knew they had been there recently because we could smell the odor of cook-fire smoke and kimchi.

Our biggest problem was getting up the hill, knowing that there was always a steeper one ahead. Our loads made the climb tough and physically exhausting, but I learned to hate the descents more so. Our shoepacs were two sizes larger than our feet to allow the warmth of two pairs of socks. That combination was all right in a static situation, but it was murder on our feet while moving down mountains. Going up was not a problem as the heel normally rides against the back of the boot, but downhill with the extra toe room was another story. The foot slid forward causing the toes to rest against the boot front. One or two movements downhill were not bad, but all day with the weight we carried caused the toes to become painfully sore.

Climbing in the attack on the flank and in rough country with no roads, we carried our worldly possessions and needs. Our CO usually called several pauses for breathers on steep climbs. The problem was that the Marine having difficulties never knew how long to the next pause. We all had problems, especially the BAR men and the crew-served weapons teams. Initially I grew concerned because that BAR and its load of ammo literally mashed me into the deck. Approaching my physical limit on our first long, steep climb, I wondered about the fact that everyone else was making it. I could not be the first to fall out. I would never fall out consciously, but what if I reached my limit (up to now an unknown experience) and passed out?

About the time I became concerned, others slowed their climb or stopped for a breather. Individuals stood to the side of the trail as we passed in the climb or started dropping so far behind their unit that the column passed them on the move. The realization that I still had some energy gave me a fresh charge of strength and motivation. My BAR became lighter and there was no doubt of my making the climb.

The MG ammo carriers probably hauled the toughest load. Two metal boxes of gun ammo at twenty pounds each connected by a pack strap worked against the carrier in two ways. Not only did the forty pounds mash him to the ground, but with one box on his chest tied to the other on his back, it also put a forty-pound squeeze on his lungs.

PFC Thomas Stubblebine, a reservist from Pennsylvania, was an ammo carrier in the 3rd MG Squad. A small man of light build, he did not weigh much over a hundred pounds. He could never make it up the long, steep ridges with his load that was well over 50 percent of his body weight without his own rest stops. I knew that falling out bothered Stubblebine, as more than once his eyes filled with tears of self-disgust for falling short of what others were doing.

My charge of strength upon realizing that I was making it was enough to allow me to help others. I always took a load off someone who had fallen out or was moving at a slower pace. After a while I began to look for Stubblebine to relieve him of his gun ammo. In our first encounter, I had to take the cans away from him; he insisted that he needed no one to carry his load. He had the gungy spirit and would insist on at least carrying my BAR, with which I would not part company. Instead of that extra forty pounds beating me down, it gave me a lift, a renewal of energy. Stub let me help, but he never let me carry his ammo for long. We panted up many mountains one behind the other—a Yankee and a rebel together in the attack.

Assigned a reserve mission, our battalion moved into a valley for rest. Hot chow was served, but I never ate it hot. Temperatures well below freezing, an outside kitchen, cold metal mess kits, and a truck fender or tailgate all combined to ensure that the food was not even warm. Many times, before I could find a spot to place my mess kit, my coffee and food would be forming a skin of ice.

Marines took advantage of the fast freeze in that extreme cold and made ice cream. Condensed milk and sugar were mixed in a mess kit and placed outside our small shelters. In a few hours, we had ice cream, chocolate if we added C-ration cocoa. While we did not need the extra body chill, the sugar and the novelty of doing something different was welcome.

C-rations came three meals to a box. For a day's issue, it was not bad, except that there was only one can of fruit. The problem came when one meal was issued (which was usually the case because we did not need the extra weight in the attack) and three buddies would have to divide the contents of the box. Who gets the fruit? Who gets the beans with pork? And, who is stuck with the corned beef hash? Cpl Davis issued the meals to his fire team leaders, and rotated himself from one team to another, saying, "Give me the meal that's left." He never took advantage of his rank, and he never argued for a favorite meal. Fighting for an edible meal was a pastime for the rest of us.

The Korean Civil Transport Corps carried supplies for us in rough areas without roads. Older Koreans considered too old for the rigors of combat served in something like the National Guard. These men carried heavy loads on their back-mounted wooden carriers known as A-frames. Two five-gallon cans of water strapped on the A-frame was a typical load for a man who weighed not much more than they did. Cases of C-rations bulked out before they weighed too much for the man with the A-frame. We left our sleeping bags to be carried up by the labor trains, known to us as Gook Trains, when we assaulted tough objectives. These men carried our wounded and dead from the ridges on their return trips, and we all appreciated and respected their contribution to the war effort.

Several days of rain impressed on us that ponchos were essential gear; they were brought forward and issued. PFC Estel Tuggle was now my assistant BAR man and we made a warm hooch with our new ponchos. We carried corn fodder from a nearby field for our deck, sides, and beds. With the ponchos for the roof, we were ready for bad weather. The following is part of a letter written to my parents on 26 February 1951:

> . . . We are dug in on a hill just across from one that the gooks are on, only they are a little higher up. Our aircraft are bombing and strafing along the ridge top like they really have located a good target. The flyboys are using a new rocket that is located and fired on the wing. It sure packs a wallop, or at least it makes a big noise. I like to watch the planes peel off and come in on their runs to the target. A dogfight up there would be more interesting, but there is no opposition.
>
> You ought to see our foxhole (Tug is still with me as the assistant BARman). It is about two-foot square at the top, we went down three feet and dug back under the hill. We have a sleeping cave, all under ground, and it sure is cozy.
>
> Like I wrote before, we don't do much. We bump into the enemy or our planes spot them, we then pull back and let the air work the enemy over. The planes hammer the gooks until there is nothing left; then we walk up and take the hill. I don't know what the gooks are thinking about as they have no planes, no big guns or mortars and no tanks while we have all of these weapons. Still, they want to keep the fight going.
>
> I did see plenty of those Russian T-34 tanks that were supposed to be so tough and hard to kill. Remember we read about them last July and August and the fact that they couldn't be stopped by US forces. They were all along the road between here and where we started, and they surely had been stopped by something.
>
> I'm having a nice camping trip and having fun. . . .

Tug and I did not get much return on our efforts with our sleeping hooch, however. Item was back in the attack. Third Platoon was the assault force, and our 3rd Squad had the point when we jumped off for our mountaintop objective. If it had been defended, we would not have fared well because of the obstacles placed as barriers. Trees had been cut within small-arms range, a 200-meter band around the hilltop. The hill was thickly covered with trees, all dropped with their tops downhill, against us. We literally had to crawl and weave ourselves through those trees.

Every branch resisted my movement as I worked against the lay of the limbs that were also more compact on the ground. Footing was poor on the slick tree trunks, but the fallen trees were so thick that I could only move by walking uphill on the trunks. From the top of a tree to the bottom, one tree after another, I worked uphill around the many limbs slanted in my direction. My BAR was never ready for instant fire: I needed both hands for movement under, around, or over the limbs. My equipment constantly snagged and caught fast. The assault squad was dead if the enemy opened fire.

Before I cleared the barrier, a strong odor of garlic and wood smoke hit me, indicating the enemy's presence. My alerted senses went into survival mode, and I expected the eruption of their killing fire. Not wanting to be caught in the tree barrier, I used every second allowed to get through it. First out of the barrier, I felt ineffective in a one-man assault on the ridge. However, I had a better chance moving alone than waiting for others to get through.

The feeling of being in an enemy machine gunner's sights pushed me. No enemy was on the hill, but they had just left: their rice was in warm pots, cooked and ready to eat. Our airstrike on the objective before our jump off no doubt persuaded them to move hastily. With that barrier, I had to wonder why. One sniper would have cost us dearly. Luck was with us; the enemy was falling back with little resistance to any of our assaults. The 5th Marines continued forward with only light casualties.

Item Company came out of the hills in the first part of March, and set up on a small plain containing the road through Hoengsong and Hongchon. Our regiment was in division reserve, which normally means a rest. It was a rest in that we did not move with a load on our backs, but the temperature was so low and the wind so strong that we were miserable outside our sleeping bags.

Third Platoon's mission was manning a roadblock on that open, flat ground. We lived for two days in our sleeping bags when not actually standing duty on that road; one-hour shifts were all that we could handle. We were so miserable doing anything outside that we lost ourselves in our bags.

During the night of the second day, the wind ceased, the temperature climbed somewhat, and I awakened to a heavy snowfall. Waking up in a sleeping bag under freshly fallen snow is an other-worldly experience, with the blanket of snow trapping my breath inside my bag and insulating me from the cold wind. I was warmer than I had been for some time, the deathly quiet making me wonder if I was alive.

That day we were resupplied with food, ammo, clothing, and PX rations by airdrop. With goodies to eat, plus nylon parachutes to make living more like home, Leathernecks might get soft and start to expect the good life. Item Company moved out the following day.

Before jumping off in our attack, Davis approached me, saying, "Give your BAR to Tug; you are now the 3rd Fire Team Leader." The position promotion was all right, but I felt that I could also handle the BAR. I had developed a personal attachment to my rifle so it was mine for a few more days. Besides, Tuggle was not enthused with the idea, saying that he had carried his share of BARs. Davis, however, had a different opinion on which weapon his team leaders carried. He listened to my reasoning, but I swapped Tug for his M-1. That rifle trade was soon to be directly responsible for a big embarrassment.

UN forces jumped off 7 March on Operation Ripper, immediately following Op Killer, with the 5th Marines in reserve. That bit of luck lasted two days when 3rd Bn was attached to the 1st Marines with another flanking mission. Item started winding up the ridges in the attack. No fires and no talking was the word and actively enforced by all leaders. We were on the flank, and our commander did not want to take on the entire Korean and Chinese armies. I thought it odd that we could not talk, because the enemy would have to be on the ridge with us to hear. If he were, we would not be able to avoid him or a fight. Davis merely reminded me: "It is not mine to reason when or why, but mine to do or die."

About midday, the company took a break while scouts checked out the next hill. Seated on my helmet, I chose this time to get to know my new rifle. I took my trigger-housing group out to get familiar with the trigger squeeze. The safety must be off to do this. Tiring of the play, I put the trigger housing group back into my rifle. (The hammer is cocked automatically while the trigger-housing group is inserted.)

Five minutes later and still seated on the ridge, my eyes registered on a large tree knot fifty meters away. That knot made a natural bull's-eye that caused my rifle to move to my shoulder. Lining up my sights, I took up the trigger slack. I had done this often knowing that the safety had the hammer locked. When that rifle exploded, I had to be the most surprised and embarrassed human on earth. What? Me? Accidental Discharge?

Conversation was not allowed, and I had fired off a round! I knew I was dead! Feeling foolish and dumb, I was on a level with the ants at my feet. I just wanted to go into a one-man attack against the next ridge, to go down fighting. Not putting the safety on after playing with the trigger-housing group was the problem. The fact that the knot changed its appearance was small consolation.

Our platoon sergeant came down the line asking the obvious question. One look at me and he asked no further. A second surprise occurred when he heard my story and did not chew me out. He even appeared to be trying to suppress a grin. Brimmer never brought up the subject but my squad buddies did not let the incident die.

Combat support units played an important role in our everyday life. While all enemy positions were not defended, a small force fighting a delaying action was left behind in some positions. This resistance increased as we moved north. The stay-behinds would fire a few rounds upon our approach, causing us to hold up to place air and/or artillery on the position.

Air was our first choice if we were at the limits of gun range, which was Item's case 50 percent of the time. Marines could no longer depend on our air support to arrive upon call. The word was that the Air Force now handled all air requests. Marine infantry units now waited hours for an air strike that sometimes never arrived. Later we would go in the attack without a softening of the position.

Almost as bad as no air support were the slick-lined jets that responded to our request and did their bombing and strafing from such an altitude that we could not see the cockpit canopy. From those heights the ordnance usually went anywhere but where we needed it, including hitting our hill. This kind of air support was like firing artillery beyond maximum safe range. Marine flyers in their Corsairs came down to their target and us. Not only could we see the canopies but also the pilots' heads and now and then a wave of a hand. One group knew the business and had trained for it while the other had interests elsewhere, and it showed.

The US Army provided moonlight when the real stuff was not available. Dark nights are those when there is no illumination from the moon and stars because of cloud cover. Rainy nights were the darkest. On those nights, big searchlights were set up behind the line and aimed forward and up to bounce off the clouds with the same illuminating effect as a full moon. Those lights and the men who serviced them really made my nights easier. When I could see into my field of fire, I felt that I had a chance. While off on the flank of the attack, we enjoyed our man-made light.

Sometime in early March, our battalion was on the move again to the flank. This move was behind our line and therefore administrative, meaning there was no concern for security. The hurt of the hump was there and we were not told that we were going in reserve. Again, we were moving parallel with our lines; there would be no break, no rest. Some commander had called for help and a higher authority was moving the force to do the job. These actions were always hard on our morale, but we did get satisfaction from the knowledge that if no one else could do it, "Call in the Marines."

Two hours into the night we stopped; completely exhausted, we grounded our packs. Lt Brimmer called us into a bunch and passed the word: "We are in an Army regiment's camp, and we will jump off to-morrow morning. I will issue the attack order when I get it. We will sleep on the ground where we stand, and warm Cs will be passed out. Get some rest."

Marines! Brimmer had barely gotten his guidance out when we were gone, faded into the night. Secure area! Army CP! A Marine understood both of those statements to mean take advantage of the situation. The have-nots were now in an area of the haves. We forgot how footsore and tired we were. We forgot the "Cs," they would wait for us. Marines were interested in something better to eat, and we knew that the Army had the gear.

I teamed up with guys looking for whiskey. I did not drink alcohol, but I knew all other Marines rated booze highly. Other members of the booze team were PFCs Robert L. Minyard and Francis J. Ryan. Minyard suggested that we find the CO's tent; he would have whisky. Our objective was easily identified by its flags. A reconnaissance from the shadows revealed a jeep guarded by an armed soldier near the tent. Our plan was that Ryan, who could talk the trunk off an elephant, would approach and distract the guard while Minyard and I hit the jeep.

The guard was accommodating as he approached Ryan halfway to the CO's tent. He even kept his back to the jeep while Ryan laid the words on him. Our quick walk to the jeep revealed a full case of Canadian Seagrams Seven in the back seat. That was enough; we disappeared into the shadows with the case of whisky.

Back in our platoon bed-down area, we split the case three ways. I kept one for later barter material, gave one to Davis, and the other two to my fellow squad members. Other Marines had not been so successful. Because of the lateness of the night, no food other than C-rations was found. Several did replace their M-1s with Army BARs; these would be useful in the attack tomorrow. That was the routine for some Marines: heavier weapons needed, take them; need goes away, replace them with something lighter.

Sunup the next morning found us on the road and hurting. More than half the squad had worse than a sore head; they were drunk. There was at least one open bottle still making the rounds as we moved down the road. We were lucky that Item drew the reserve mission; we moved in trace of George and How. Both companies had hilltop objectives that were mutually supporting. If Item was committed, I hoped that the 1st and 2nd Platoons received the mission.

During the past night, we learned from soldiers that they had been trying for days to take these objectives. The enemy's defense was built with mutual support around and between the two hills; that made the task difficult and costly in casualties. Soldiers attacked until they took casualties then withdrew, throwing more artillery rounds at the objectives. George and How jumped off and took both objectives by mid-afternoon.

Army battalions relieved George and How on the newly gained objectives that day, and we moved to the rear for the night. I never knew if it was on purpose that we did not go back into the Army regimental area or if it was out of our way. That CO probably did not want us in his area again. We bedded down with a 10 percent watch, and the Seagrams continued to flow.

We moved on a wide dirt road the next day with the word that we were going in regimental reserve. As we plodded along, I realized that I needed to replace my boondockers. They were newly issued upon turning in my shoepacs but they were too small. Major blisters were heating up on both feet. My pain and misery must have been obvious because an Army chaplain stopped his jeep and offered me a ride. That was a good gesture, but if he could not haul the entire squad, he was no help. Another mile, however, and I wished for a second chance at that ride. Help in another form came along.

A convoy moved through us going in our direction. One truck went by with a Marine from the platoon behind us in the covered bed throwing out pairs of Army wrap-around combat boots. The pair I caught was not my size, but I did not allow the occasion to pass. I ran, caught the truck, climbed aboard, and searched for my size.

Preparing to jump to the ground with my new boots around my neck, I noticed an Army colonel in the jeep following the truck. There was a moment of hesitation as I realized I was caught in the act. In the same moment, however, I realized that he did not seem to care one way or the other, and I needed those boots.

Later a rumor circulated that the Army lost both hills the second night. We expected to have to do it over, but it did not happen. Instead, the 3rd Bn enjoyed a few days of rest in the rear with the gear.

Around the middle of March the 5th Marines attacked through the 7th Marines for Line Buffalo with the 1st Marines on our right. (Map, page 30) We were back into business, and the enemy was beginning to resist our moves with more determination. Smoke from green–wood fires was heavy in the air. It did not reduce our observation forward as planned, but it did burn our eyes and throats.

Lessons Learned

1. The spirit of a unit outweighs training in mission accomplishment two to one.

2. Helping others gives us additional strength.

3. Strength and endurance are factors of motivation.

4. Marines should train with the weight loads they will later carry in battle.

3
Corporal
1128290/0311

21 March 1951

Our platoon runner brought the word for Davis and me to report to the platoon leader. At the CP, Lt Brimmer promoted Davis to sergeant and me to corporal. His handshake was the extent of our ceremony; he told us that the paperwork would catch up later. My squad buddies' reception, however, was something else. The Old Salts did not wish the Boot Corporal well, and they freely expressed their contempt for this latest addition to the NCO ranks. Several jealous individuals responded with, "Well, you might be a corporal now, Fox, but just wait until you get back in the States and have to pass a written test[3] for the rank." The point of the test was that I would have to do well on paper to keep my stripes; we all missed the fact that performance in combat was the real test.

Marines stenciled rank on their sleeves in the early 1950s; since ink and stencils were not available, I could not wear my new rank. We could not go by what we saw on sleeves anyway, as we received recycled clothes—anything from a private's to a master sergeant's jacket—at the showerhead. Rank was the position of leadership, not something worn on the arm.

April saw the 1st MarDiv crossing the 38th Parallel on its way north. The terrain changed from the scrubby pine of the south to heavily timbered forests. On 2 April, my battalion, supported by an army DUKW unit, crossed the Soyang-gang (River) in the attack. Enemy resistance disappeared, and the ridgelines were ours for the climb.

Though there were no defenders, we could feel the enemy's presence in our bones as we moved into their backyard. It did not take a Von Clausewitz to figure that the Chinese were falling back to regroup. Our commanders were also on the chessboard, as the 7th Infantry Division relieved our regiment and the Korean Marines on 5 April.

The first call came out for Brigade Marines to go home. Sgt Davis showed that he could be like the rest of us by questioning the wisdom

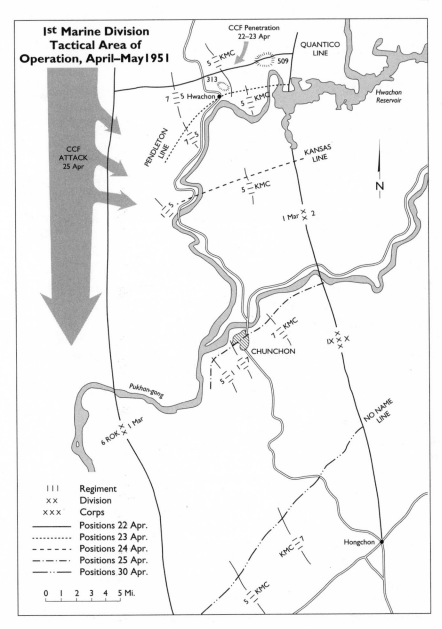

1st Marine Division Tactical Area of Operation, April–May 1951

CCF Penetration 22–23 Apr

QUANTICO LINE

CCF ATTACK 25 Apr

5 — KMC

509

313

7 — 5 Hwachon

5 — KMC

Hwachon Reservoir

PENDLETON LINE

7 — 5

KANSAS LINE

5 — KMC

N

I — 5

1 Mar ×× 2

7 — KMC

IX ×××

CHUNCHON

5 — I — 7

Pukhan-gong

6 ROK ×× 1 Mar

NO NAME LINE

| | | Regiment
×× Division
××× Corps
———— Positions 22 Apr.
----------- Positions 23 Apr.
– – – – – Positions 24 Apr.
–·–·–· Positions 25 Apr.
——··—— Positions 30 Apr.

0 1 2 3 4 5 Mi.

KMC — 7

Hongchon

5 — KMC

Courtesy of the Historical Branch, Headquarters Marine Corps, modified from *US Marine Operations in Korea*, Vol IV. CCF Offensive Starting 22 April and Subsequent Marine Withdrawals.

of higher leadership. Only those Brigade Marines with Purple Hearts or hospitalized for frostbite were leaving. Davis had been through it all, and the only reason he did not have a "Heart" was that the enemy could not shoot fast enough. He had been through more than most: long nights of wondering if he would see the light of another day, never-ending foot marches, poor rations, and good-byes to all of his old squad buddies, many of whom were dead. He was the only Brigade Marine left in the squad, and yet his combat time was not over in this Marine line company. Not yet! For the first time, I heard Davis express something resembling a complaint: he bitched like the rest of us about the higher brass not being attuned to the happenings. This Marine was human after all.

The 1st MarDiv continued the attack toward Line Quantico on 21 April, with the 5th Marines in the line. (Map, page 47) The 7th Marines were on our left and the Korean Marine Corps (KMC) was on our right. We held the Korean soldier in contempt, but his brother in the KMC was worthy of our respect. Korean Marines did everything we did, and did it well, whether taking hills or holding ground. I learned firsthand how they handled discipline.

A few squad buddies and I spent time socializing, trading, and learning words of Korean with the KMC company on our flank. There was a stir of excitement during one of these visits when the company formed up quickly on the hillside. The Korean CO appeared and stood on a tree stump while the First Sergeant brought forward a Marine with tied hands and hobbled feet.

From a distance of two feet, the Captain uttered a few words, raised his pistol, and shot the Marine in the forehead. This was a court martial; the Marine had left the hill without permission, was caught, found guilty, and sentence served. That incident shows why the KMCs had a low desertion rate. They were effective against the enemy for the same reason: better to die by an enemy bullet than the commander's.

Our regiment arrived on Line Quantico and the Hwachon Reservoir having met only light resistance. The terrain flowed into long slopes leading up to higher elevations and narrow ridgelines, not the worn down ridges found in eastern America. These higher ridges put us farther away from our water supply. Many were the times that I watched with a dry, parched mouth and an empty canteen as the water flowed in a stream far down in a valley. There was no relief while moving on the ridgelines unless we crossed a stream or spring. A water detail would be assigned after defensive positions were established. Unlucky Marines with a collection of canteens would go down for water then make the long climb with their loads. We carried one canteen inside our parka in winter to keep the water from freezing. We were looking for a second one as the temperature rose; however, two canteens were not issued in 1951.

The good time was not to last. On 22 April the 7th Marines on our left were heavily engaged throughout the night. Heavy small arms and MG fire along with the thump and crunch of grenades, mortars, and artillery filled the night air. We could hear and see a major battle taking place to our left; we went to 100 percent alert. Third Squad was ready for the enemy after two days' rest on the ridge, but no threat appeared. That day we learned that the 6th Republic of Korea (ROK) Division broke to the left of the 7th Marines, and Chinese were pouring through the gap. In a short time, a major enemy force would be behind us. The Chosin Reservoir encirclement was foremost in our minds as we prepared mentally for a fight in the opposite direction. We spent another sleepless night on the ridge before receiving the word to withdraw.

Item was rear guard for the battalion with 3rd Platoon bringing up the company rear. Third Squad covered the platoon movement, and it was well into the afternoon before our platoon moved out. Earlier, Davis had positioned our fire teams to cover the entries into the company frontage. Watching Marines move out, leaving my team to face the enemy, did not set well.

This was a different feeling from being in the assault force, where the dead and wounded are left in friendly hands. In this action the dead and wounded had to be carried by the fighters. Four men were needed to carry one man any distance in those hills, and the carriers could not do much fighting on the ends of a poncho litter. Our under-strength (nine men) squad was very likely to have some tough times.

Finally, we received the word to move out and none too soon. Individuals attempting to conceal themselves in the undergrowth appeared on the ridge to our front. They were probably enemy scouts from the attacking units searching us out. We placed artillery fire on their position and moved to the rear. Several ridges lay between us and the Pukhan River, our link-up point with the main force.

We moved with urgency, not slowing our pace on the steep climbs. If we made the river, we would be beyond the enemy's threat. Though Chinese soldiers could have gotten around us, we moved rapidly up and over the hills with little regard for potential danger areas. We moved in a tactical column on the ridgelines with our weapons at the ready. We expected to fight, but no enemy challenged us by fire or otherwise. The more distance we put behind us, the better I felt about our chances.

After what seemed an eternity, we walked down our last ridge; the forest opened and showed the river below. There was the pontoon bridge loaded with southbound Marines. Our rear guard mission was complete as we closed the trails behind us with artillery concentrations.

It was late evening when we started over the bridge. Halfway across, tanks on the south side of the Pukhan opened fire with their cannons and 50-caliber MGs against enemy soldiers appearing on the ridge behind us. That action put wings on our feet, and we flew over that long bridge. Cannon fire from the gun tanks cut the bridge loose from the north bank while we were still on it. The north side pontoons floated down stream in a pivoting action from the south bank as we approached the south side.

Time lost its relevancy after we crossed the river. There was no concern now for enemy activity; we had passed through friendly forces on the south bank of the Pukhan. Item continued to move at a forced march speed with a file on each side of a wide dirt road that allowed vehicle movement in the center. Trucks and artillery passed through us going south. While Hank Snow was singing it back in the States, we were doing it south of the Pukhan, "Movin' On." Following are several Marine verses to Hank's song:

> Ten thousand Chinks coming through the pass
> This old daddy is shagging ass
> I'm movin on . . . . I'm movin on
>
> The lieutenant says we're digging in
> Says see you Louie, but I don't know when
> I'm movin on . . . . I'm movin on.
>
> Old Joe Chink coming down the pass
> Playing the burp-gun boogie on the doggie's ass
> I'm movin on . . . . I'm movin on.

Exhausted from the excitement and non-sleep activity of the past two days, I walked in a semi-sleep mode, somewhat conscious of the Marine to my front. My mind was foggy, and numbness overcame my physical awareness. Others, to allow more unconsciousness, held on to the pack of the man to their front. Finally, it was our turn for a ride, and we boarded trucks for the remainder of the movement.

On 26 April most of the 5th Marines were positioned on No Name Line northwest of Hongchon. (Map, page 47) Item received the battalion reserve mission that allowed mail, rest, hot chow, all the water we wanted including a shower unit, and clean clothes. This was the first real body-cleaning opportunity I'd had since entering Korea, three months earlier. Extreme cold, no hot water, little time, or some other reason had limited the few earlier attempts. This experience had all the right elements, and I relaxed in plenty of hot running water and soap. I was pleasantly surprised to note how my body had changed since I last saw it. My muscles were more developed, solid, and hard and my chest boasted more hair than I could count.

Sergeant Davis's day came, and on 4 May, he left us for the States. His leaving was hard on the squad; it was difficult to think that we could get by without him. But like all good leaders, he had ensured that our squad life would go on as usual. My bottle of Seagrams had been humped long enough. Instead of getting the fifty bucks for which I had been carrying it, I opened it for our farewell to Davis. Leaving was not easy on him; he choked up as he tried to make his carefree good-bye to each of us. Corporal Orville L. Miller moved up to squad leader.

The following is an excerpt from a letter to my folks dated 4 May 1951:

> The rest of the guys are still sleeping; I had the last watch this morning. It is about 0700 and the day promises to be too pretty to go to sleep. We are still at the same place where I wrote my last letter, about the fourth day on this hill.
>
> There are some big white cranes fishing in the river below us and flying around. The cock pheasants are crowing in the pine brush on the hillside around us. Artillery is quiet and there are no planes overhead this morning. There is no sound but Mother Nature; the birds are singing all around. So you see, Korea can't be as bad as they say.
>
> Sgt Davis is leaving this morning at ten, going home. He is on pins and needles. He is my squad leader and sure is a nice guy. Davis is about the last of the old guys that were up north. He's seen it, having been here a little more than eight months. While I am happy for him, I hate to see him go (if that makes any sense). . . .

The Chinese Spring Offensive wore down as its forces outran their supply lines, and the enemy commander was unable to maintain pressure along the front. With no enemy activity forward, we started heavy patrolling in an attempt to regain contact. All commands up through regiment moved forward and set up patrol bases.

Item moved up a broad valley while dropping 3rd Platoon to move up a smaller valley on the company's flank. The platoon operated in the same fashion by sending squads up the feeders from the platoon valley. Third Squad, minus my fire team, set up at another junction of smaller valleys and deployed across the valley floor. My team moved up on a ridge overlooking the squad, to see and hear all.

From the ridge I watched Marines on the open, grass–covered valley below do their thing, lie in the sun, sleep, and eat chow. After an hour in position and while checking the area around the sunbathing Marines, I spotted movement in a creek bed.

Ten soldiers were coming toward me down the creek, five hundred meters from my squad's forward position. I first thought that they were friendly because they were so near and moving in such a nonchalant manner. Then I recognized their mustard-colored uniforms.

I had to alert my squad leader. My team and I were on a wooded ridge, so I could not get his attention by waving something, which the enemy would also see. I decided that the squad needed to be warned even if the enemy did hear, and I started yelling, but there was no response. The Chinese continued their slow movement in the sunken creek bed, and Marines were aware only of the sunrays. I added the voices of my entire team; we were not heard.

I ran down the wooded slope to pass the word, hopefully in time. As I neared the meadow after a reckless downward plunge, I saw that the enemy squad had left the creek bed and was moving up a washed-out gully in 3rd Squad's direction. Waving my arms for attention, I raced across the open field toward my squad and the enemy force. I could no longer see the soldiers, as they were in the gully. Out of breath at the center of my scattered squad, I tried to get up some interest in the approaching enemy force from my fellow Marines. Every one looked at me like, What are you drinking? What enemy, where? I was impressed with their stubborn response; nothing, even combat, was going to interrupt the pure joy of the peaceful, warm sun.

To help me make my point, the enemy squad walked out of the gully in single file, coming from left to right across our forward right flank at three hundred meters. They had to see us in the open field, but they moved closer as though we were members of their force. They were in no hurry as they did the infantry thing while moving one behind the other: their eyes focused on the ground cleared by the boots ahead.

Several Marines voiced the thought that this must be an ROK unit. Most squad members had left their rifles at their sunbathing spot and stood with bare backs and bare hands. Nobody was doing anything. What would Davis have done? Meanwhile the squad that was clearly wearing the enemy's uniform was approaching a tree line at the start of the hill on our rearward right flank.

Still breathing heavily, I assumed a kneeling position to take the enemy under fire. If they were UN forces, they had chosen the wrong color of uniform. A trail led away from us through the grass valley, a hundred meters from and parallel with the edge of the woods on our right. The enemy leader had almost reached the trail as my M-1 fired. Now running, he turned left on the trail moving away from me rather than running for the cover of the woods.

On this course, he would be in the open for another four hundred meters. Each soldier, still in single file, followed in the tracks of their leader. They did not move immediately away from my fire but continued to expose their flank until they reached the trail. They each turned at the trail, following their leader.

My score was not good with flanking fire; I did not drop anyone. At that distance, I could not even tell if I hit anyone. Going away from me one behind another, they presented a group target. I must have gotten close to the last soldier if I did not hit him. When my rifle cracked, he jumped high on the back of the soldier to his front. Both fell to the ground but rose immediately and continued running, passing two of their buddies in a comic manner. My M-1 ammo clip ejected with a metallic ring, locking my bolt to the rear. I had fired eight rounds and must reload. No enemy soldier lay on the ground, and no other squad member opened fire.

This might have been a different story if I had known my rifle's zero and had placed the correct elevation and windage on my rifle sight. This lack of military preparedness was the offspring of a nation that one year earlier believed that it would never again need ground-fighting forces. Our rapidly built force was of the come-as-you-are-with-what-you-have type. If any of my leaders knew the importance of zeroing rifles and test firing, they never expressed it. We fired our weapons only when we had the enemy in sight.

Plumps sounded in the rice paddy around us within a few minutes of the enemy's disappearance. We realized that the sounds were rifle bullets impacting the soft ground. The sound of rifle fire on the high ground overlooking the little valley followed the impact by several seconds. Our enemy was too far away to be effective, but they might have kept it up had they known how close their bullets were hitting.

After the patrol base operation, we spent a couple of days resting with a reserve mission. The easy life never lasted long, however, and on 19 May, our battalion rolled out on trucks. Where to this time? Marines were the fire brigade, sent in to make a difference.

Trucking forward, I observed a lone soldier without a weapon moving to the rear. There were more singles, then couples, then groups; we met hundreds of men in the US Army uniform moving to the rear on that narrow dirt road. These soldiers were all black, all were without weapons, and all moved with a slow, withdrawn attitude, their eyes to the ground. Even as we barked and yelled at them, not one looked up or gave any sign that they knew we were on the road. We knew soldiers as doggies; barking and howling was typical Marine conduct anytime we moved near Army units.

The convoy stopped with my truck beside an Army jeep parked in the ditch. Marines in my truck began to bark and make other dog sounds. Being closer to the jeep occupant, I noticed that he was a gray-haired US Army colonel, the first officer, and the first white man, we had seen. In tears, he looked at me and said, "I wish to God that I had you Marines with me last night." His words came through, but it was twelve hours later that I understood what he was saying. I never learned the identification of the unit we were relieving because there was no one in position.[4]

Our platoon moved up on a nearby low hill with a reserve mission, and George and How moved forward to the MLR (Main Line of Resistance). (Unknown to any of us in 3rd Squad, George and How, upon arriving on the MLR to relieve the two forward Army battalions, found the positions abandoned. Not knowing the enemy situation, Major Holiday, our Bn CO, pulled the two companies back on line with Item.)

Meanwhile, we set up with positions along the ridge oriented forward, as was our routine in reserve missions. We did not expect to defend, so my team immediately set up housekeeping. We pitched shelter-halves and elected to use the existing small one-man fighting holes, obviously dug by Orientals. The chance of receiving incoming was slim; otherwise, the holes would not be needed.

We had mail call during which I received an Easter package of candy and cookies. The contents were a welcome relief from the C-ration sweets. Sodas and beer were issued, our first in a long time. I traded my two cans of beer for sodas with PFC John B. Hall of the 2nd Squad. John and his assistant manned the next hole to my left.

It was a warm spring day, and we lazed around on the hill. My fire team consisted of PFC Girdley Baker as rifleman, PFC Amedeo U. Franzone as BAR man, and PFC Robert L. Foran as assistant BAR man. As darkness fell, we learned that we were on the front line when How moved to the right on our ridge, saying they were tying in on our flank.[5]

Brimmer confirmed this assumption by sending word for me to man a listening post two hundred meters forward from dark to daylight. Baker and I took the first half of the night with our LP tour ending at 0200. Leaving Baker on watch, I moved up the finger to awaken our relief. Baker did not wait long but arrived on the ridge as the two prepared to move out. To my question, he responded that he was not staying out there by himself. I reminded him that I had given him his choice, and he had not wanted to wake our relief either. Now, with no one on the finger, we could not know if the enemy had moved up and was covering the position.

Aware of this uncertainty, I nevertheless was furious when Franzone said that he was not going out without knowing the situation. Foran naturally agreed with his partner. Baker stated that he could not find the position when I told him to take the BAR team to the LP.

The only thing for me to do was to take the team out, which I did with a strong display of disgust. With the contempt of an inexperienced leader trying to make a point, I aggressively and noisily led the team down the finger, tearing through the bushes that blocked my path. Arriving at the LP, and in a condescending tone, I reminded the two Marines of their mission. We would not have had a chance if the enemy force had arrived two hours earlier.

My predicament was caused by my promotion over those with more time in the service. Except for Baker and Ryan, who also were directly out of boot camp, the others were activated reservists. Franzone and Foran were making me earn my extra stripe. The LP situation was an example of the hurdles constantly placed in my path.

Returning to the ridge, I crawled into my shelterhalf. Almost immediately it seemed, Franzone called to me from outside. Mixed in my sleep-deprived brain with dreams of home were his words, "The Chinese are coming up the hill." He only said it once.

My thoughts were that he had followed me back up the ridge, and this was another attempt to avoid the LP assignment. I stated words to that effect but received no response. Franzone had moved on without determining if he had awakened me. Grabbing my M-1 and cartridge belt, I felt my way forward to my fighting hole, twenty meters away.

Rifle fire and grenade explosions broke the night silence while I oriented myself in the small fighting hole. I assumed that my team members were manning their holes to my right. Franzone surely would have awakened Baker. The blackness of the night, as a multiplier, greatly increased the thirty meters' distance between our positions.

★ ★ ★

The close explosion of a mortar round brought my mind back to the present. Our mortarmen were walking rounds close to us on our ridge. What was the Chinese objective? There was still no pressure against 3rd Squad although there was an occasional string of automatic fire and grenade explosions around the breakthrough. Perhaps the Chinese were going down the hill for easier targets; our mortars and the battalion CP were both set up at the foot of our low hill and close. Did they know the enemy had penetrated our line?

I voiced my concern to the nearest Marines, suggesting that maybe we should move down and protect the mortarmen. Franzone was in full agreement, so I approached Miller, who seemed unsure about the plan and removed himself from the decision making. Six of us headed for the rice paddy at the foot of our hill, moving toward the muzzle flashes of the mortar tubes. Arriving at the mortar platoon, we were led to an officer who listened to our story. The lieutenant needed no help, and he took us back to our position on the ridge. My earlier thought of defending the mortar platoon and H&S was not the proper action.

Gaining the ridge, I led the detail left in the direction of the fight that now included several MGs firing straight down the ridgeline. Tracer bullets lit up the ground around us as they moved en masse several feet above us. It was an odd feeling to walk under that heavy fire, even at a low crouch, and feel nothing of the sudden and certain death a few feet above.

Miller had moved farther up the ridgeline from our night position, away from the breakthrough. I found him with PFCs H. G. Lyke and W. J. Chambers (both had recently returned from hospitals in Japan after recovering from wounds received in earlier actions). Solid infantry Marines with several years in the Corps, they understood Marine business in holding ground, a point that I realized I was just learning. BAR men PFCs Estel Tuggle and John W. Thurston also remained on the hill with Miller. While Tuggle and Thurston had arrived in Korea in the 4th Replacement Draft, both had seen combat in WW II and were now unhappily activated reservists.

Morning light dawned on the ridge, and things began to take shape as we moved forward against no opposition. Still to the right of our squad's right-flank position, I realized that we should have contacted How Marines. They were to tie in with us; I had not thought of them earlier.

Looking around as the world began to take shape, my eyes came to rest upon two mummy figures on the forward slope about 100 meters down from the ridge. My first thought was that the Chinese had burp-gunned these Marines in their sleeping bags. With a feeling of guilt for leaving the ridge, I moved alone down the hill to check on them. Why had someone not warned them of the attack? Better yet, why did they not know from their own sources? Who was on watch?

My conscience eased when I could see that a burp gun had not chewed up the sleeping bags. The comforting sounds of heavy snoring relieved my concern. It was strangely ironic to hear peaceful everyday sounds amid all that MG fire. I woke four more sleepers before I arrived at How's left flank position.

How had not tied in physically with us because its position was forward on the military crest. No one in How was hurt, and all were surprised to learn that they were in the middle of a battle. These Marines were exhausted from their action the day before when, along with George, they went forward over several ridges, dug in, and prepared positions. Then told to pack up, they moved back the same distance, dug in after dark, and prepared positions. They simply passed out from exhaustion; once inside a sleeping bag, even a war could not arouse them.

Item Marines assumed that their 3rd Squad, 3rd Platoon no longer existed, as Chinese were all over our positions. Four company guns were employing grazing fire along the ridge; their fire reduced in volume with the improved morning light. The enemy's last hold was on the small knoll where 3rd Squad had collected after the breakthrough.

Pushing against the breakthrough, I paused behind a pine tree on the ridge crest. Tuggle crouched in an old fighting hole slightly forward and to my right about five meters. Standing in this hole, he raked the ridge forward of us with his BAR. He emptied his magazine and dropped to one knee in the hole to insert another.

An enemy soldier sprang up fifty meters to our front and ran toward us. I lined my sights on his center mass and squeezed the trigger. There was a snap as my hammer hit the firing pin but no explosion of a round. He dropped in some brush twenty meters away. Immediately I saw a black smoke trail leave his position, arch through the gray-morning air, and unbelievably go into Tuggle's hole. Pulling my rifle's operating-rod handle to the rear, I yelled, "Tuggle, was that a grenade?" He never heard me over the battle noise. Discovering that my rifle was failing to feed automatically, I chambered a round by hand. In that instant the grenade exploded.

The Chinese soldier sprang into a hard return run for the top of the knoll. I found him in my sight and squeezed; he fell and lay on the ridge. Manually feeding another round into my chamber, I fired into his prone body to keep him down.

The concussion grenade went off under Tuggle's shin, and that small enclosure directed all the blast upward to his leg, blowing away part of it. He was blown from his hole and rolled to a position behind me. In excruciating pain, Tuggle rolled on the ground and repeatedly begged me and others to please shoot him; he could not stand the pain. Medical help was not available since we were cut off from our platoon, and I did not think of How Company corpsmen.

I held my position while Tuggle's Team Leader, Cpl James B. Roop, tended to him. Tuggle needed immediate help, and my one thought was to close the gap and unite with our company. As I moved forward (getting away from Tuggle's pain and pleading was an active motivator), camouflaged helmets appeared over the bushes to my front. The gap was closed; the ridge again belonged to us, but we had paid a price.

Thurston was hit hard in our assault on the knoll, and we thought he was dead when we carried him from the hill. HQMC records show that PFC John W. Thurston USMCR died of wounds in the Yokosuka Naval Hospital, Japan, on 16 June. Private John B. Hall USMCR was killed in his position during the initial enemy assault. Counting Tuggle, 3rd Platoon lost three gungy Marines, one-third of the platoon's BAR men.

While my Squad suffered no other wounds, we had lost two-thirds of our BAR men. This was in keeping with the life expectancy of that position as understood by all Marines. A few good men carried the M-1918A2 Browning Automatic Rifles, but not for long.

A lone bugle sounded from the ridge to our front with a thin high-pitched wail. I assumed that it was recall of the attacking force, but I had to fault the commander for being so late. His force was stopped, and many of his soldiers would never answer his call.

We moved back into our squad position to find the ground covered with bodies. John Hall's position and my fighting hole had the heaviest concentration; the soldiers lay as they fell, shoulder to shoulder.[6] Company guns probably accounted for many of the dead on my side of the ravine. Hall's position was defilade to the gunfire; those bodies went down under his withering BAR fire. They killed Hall, but he took his Marine's share with him. His assistant BAR man managed to get out of their position without a scratch. My grenade had taken its toll, and the bodies around my fighting hole supported my earlier decision to move. Mom's Easter package lay inside my burp-gun-riddled shelterhalf; the contents were gone.

The enemy force may have been an element of the 44th CCF Division.[7] All the soldiers had weapons, but while most had burp guns and rifles, some had only grenades and a stick with a bayonet tied crudely on one end. Those with stick-knives, I suppose, were to pick up the rifles of fallen comrades. The cost to the Chinese (not counting their wounded) was 152 dead and 15 prisoners.[8] Third Platoon losses were one killed in action (KIA), one died of wounds (DOW), and one wounded in action (WIA).

A Chinese mortar and two MGs lay near my fighting hole. These heavy weapons made it to the ridge, but thanks to the plundering soldiers, were never set up for action. The signs read that the enemy was too busy looking for food, including C-rations, to exploit their success or set up a defense. Concerned with plundering and eating, they died an hour later under the withering fire of Item's guns. These soldiers were not starving; most bodies had rolls of rice attached or looped over a shoulder. Like Marines, they were looking for something tasty and different.

Their assault force, part of a regimental attack[9], came up the draw in a column directly into the front of John Hall's position. Their commander thought that the old defenders were the force, if any, on the hill. He expected no opposition. Their routine was to move to the objective, throw a few grenades, and then take possession as the defenders fled the hill.

Our prisoners were shocked to learn that Marines, whom they called "Cloth Tops and Canvas Legs," owned the hill. "Cloth top" came from our helmet cover and "canvas legs" came from our leggings. There would have been no attack if scouts had identified the defenders of their objective as Marines. Those were comforting words at a time when I needed a morale boost.

Physically and mentally exhausted by the events of the past twelve hours, I needed sleep and I hoped for a reserve mission. Besides the need for sleep and food, I did not feel well with all the carnage around me. Then word came for 3rd Squad to pack up, which suited my need. We did so hurriedly and moved out to the platoon CP. Others would bury these Chinese. After much sitting around waiting for the word on where to locate, we were put back in the front line.

Instead of being on the line, we extended forward from the line and down a finger running into No-Man's Land. This finger was like the one on which I had manned the LP but several feeder ridges over. More prominent, the left side was a steep grade, almost a cliff. The MLR was broken here, as there were no positions manned on the steep grade. There were about 400 meters of steep, brush-covered space between the manned position on the ridge and the next manned position in the valley. Third Squad's new position extended forward to protect this gap. I did not want to believe what was happening. Not only had we lost an opportunity for rest, but this position was worse than our previous position. My spirit was low but it had not bottomed out. Shortly, two more negative events would complete my day.

Individual fighting positions were yet to be assigned, and late morning found us sitting in a group on our new position. Forward of the MLR, we bitched about our run of luck while the Squad and Platoon Leader walked the ground and decided where they wanted each fighting hole.

A soldier appeared forward of the MLR about 300 meters from us on the next finger as though he came out of the draw between us. He was walking uphill away from us and in no hurry. Because of his casual manner, I first thought that he was a Marine but then recognized his uniform as Chinese. I pointed him out to my fellow squad members who showed no interest in him or any action.

Alone, I took the enemy soldier under fire. Again, I did not feel quite right in doing so because of the others' lack of action. It was not right to allow that soldier to walk away; what if he had done a reconnaissance on our position? I had replaced my malfunctioning rifle with a casualty's M-1 at the platoon CP earlier. Having had no chance to sight the rifle in, I was not a threat. I made him move faster, but I saw no sign that my rounds were close before he disappeared.

Miller returned and began placing us in positions. Who was to get the fighting hole farthest from the security of the line, the last position down the finger, but me? I could not believe my luck and would have cried if I'd had the energy. There was no hope of surviving an assault in that forward position. This deployment might be good tactics on the company level, but it was suicide for the two forward Marines.

Should the enemy come up our finger, they would have the pleasure of taking us on, one by one, and me first. Forward fire (considering the MLR) from all 3rd Squad positions was masked by each position. Our squad's principle direction of fire was to my right and parallel with the MLR, ideal if the enemy was to repeat his past performance on one of the fingers to our right. A gun team arrived and set up to fire parallel with the MLR, but no help to me.

Our platoon and squad shifted personnel to adjust for the casualties taken that morning. The best and most senior PFCs took over the three BARs. PFC Vinyard[10], who had earlier been a platoon runner, became my rifleman and hole buddy. He was tireless in spite of his slight frame, weighing about 100 pounds. I accepted him well enough, and we dug in. The work finished, Vinyard disappeared on one of his social runs.

In Vinyard's absence, I concentrated on what I might do to give me a better chance of surviving this bad situation. Twenty meters down the finger was an old hole; I freshened up the dirt, rigged a dummy wearing a helmet, and placed a stick across the dummy's front. I hoped this makeup would appear to the enemy at night as a Marine with his rifle. This dummy would give me warning of attack, and maybe a chance. Fragmentation grenades were plentiful; I tied several to trees. Straightening the pins, I ran communication wire from the rings across paths to trees or bushes.

Just when I figured that things could not get worse, they did. My sleep deficit increased and my overall situation dropped below zero that night in the dark when Vinyard offered me morphine. I did not know about drugs, but he began to tell me. Shoot up with morphine and I would not need sleep, would never get tired, and "You just don't worry about things." That did not sound like a combination to get me out of this mess alive, and I refused. From that moment on, I was in that hole alone because I could neither depend on nor trust my buddy. I slept in fitful catnaps during the one-hour watches he stood. Morphine was the source of his staying power, as well as his buddy relationships with several corpsmen who carried morphine in their Unit-Ones (corpsman's medical bag).

Our spirit returned, and in two days, 3rd Squad was its old self. While several earlier incidents suggested a lack of motivation in my squad members to kill the enemy, there were exceptions. We could see forward for several miles into a broad farm valley running from the base of our ridge. A well-graded dirt road serviced the valley and the surrounding hills. Far out, a bicyclist was coming up the road toward us, and someone talked the machine gunner into taking the rider under fire. The range was well over 2,000 meters, which was the issue. Could the gunner hit someone that far away?

My thought was that this was not an enemy because he wore the Korean white dress and because he was coming toward our lines. If we did nothing, he would run into our roadblock on the low ground to our left. We routinely had line crossers who brought back information on the enemy force. No one listened to my reasoning, however, and the gunner opened fire.

Tracers in gun ammo show where the rounds are hitting. Like directing the force of water from a garden hose, the gunner merely raised his gun barrel until the tracers were hitting the bicycle. Man and bicycle went over the far bank of the road, and we never saw him again. I could not shake the thought that the man (it could have been a woman or child) was probably a line crosser on his way back to us with information. The gun was cleaned and the incident forgotten.

All of my concern for that exposed position was for nothing, and my dummy never had a chance to fool anyone. While I received little sleep during the night, it was not because of enemy activity; all was quiet forward. I made up for my sleep loss during the day, as we had no patrol activity. We lazed around our positions, and tried new ideas on how to better prepare a meal of C-rations.

On the 23rd, the 1st and 5th Marines jumped off in the attack. We were not told anything about our objective and assumed that it would be a routine movement forward. Isolated within our combat-infantry-squad environment, we had no knowledge of what was going on within the total force. The *Stars and Stripes* newspaper was not available to us so we had no way of knowing that the day would be a tough one.

My fire team was the point for the company attack; we moved right on our ridge and then left down a finger of Hill 719 into the valley. Crossing the valley, I held up the column and checked out a farmhouse nestled against the rise of Hill 710.

Three fresh mounds of dirt that looked like graves were piled near the house. My rifleman and I checked them out while my BAR team checked the outbuildings. The earth mounds did not reveal anything, as there were no headboards or markings. I assumed that the farm family had been killed and buried near their house.

Next, I checked out the house where I was surprised to find the entire family, including the adult males in their sleeping loft, under bed covers in spite of the heat of the day. They did not acknowledge our presence in their small home but ignored us. I could see that they were not well. Besides looking weak and undernourished, they had huge sores on their faces and arms. The house was a mess and filled with an unpleasant odor. Deciding that they were not a threat to the passing company, we went outside.

The BAR team found a dead US soldier in a shed and carried him to the front of the house. His hands and feet were tied with comm wire. A wooden pole lay between his arms and legs so that two men could carry him with the pole resting on their shoulders. He had been carried in the manner that hunters carry a deer, with the animal swinging between them.

A bullet had gone through the center of his left upper arm, entering the left side of his chest, and probably hit his heart, causing death. He had not bled much, but the condition of the arm where the bullet had gone through indicated that he had been carried after the shooting. The bone was shattered, and the body weight tore and twisted the flesh at the wound. Finding the body created many questions: Should we dig up the graves? What was the farm family's involvement? I sent word for the Lieutenant and the interpreter.

At that moment, members of 3rd Squad (waiting on the trail with the company strung out behind them) opened fire on movement in the tree line. We hit the deck, but there was no return fire and it was over quickly.

A man wearing a US Army uniform with neither weapon nor boots walked out of the tree line with his hands held high. This soldier[11] said he was a replacement from the States; he had joined his company, and the enemy hit them during his first night. In the confusion of the attack, he had found himself alone in his squad's sector. Everyone had bugged out without him.

Captured along with others, he was herded barefoot down a ridge after daylight. Their captors forced them over a steep decline and opened fire as they tumbled downward. Firing continued as the bodies came to rest in the bottom of the draw. This soldier was one of the first to go over and was at the bottom of the heap with bodies over him stopping the bullets. He not only survived; he was unhurt. Not daring to move, he lay there under that blood and mess most of the day. Since then, he had lived on berries and stream water while hiding from anything that moved.

Wearing the dead soldier's boots was not a problem; he removed them quickly and pulled them on his raw feet. Full of talk, his words centered on his squad members bugging out on him. He would fight with the Marines and do anything that we wanted. However, he would never go into combat with the Army again.

My point action was taking time; the CO wanted to move. His radio call to Brimmer, who had joined me, received actions. I left everything with the lieutenant and led my team up the trail.

At this point, we had received only a light introduction to what lay ahead. I later learned from the 3rd Bn Historical Diary that we had spent the last three days on No Name Line, jumped off in the attack by crossing the Line of Departure, Hill 719, at 1215 for Battalion Objective 3, Hill 710. Regimental Objective 1, Hill 975, followed and was secured by nightfall. Hill 1051, known as Kari-san and Division Objective Peter, was secured on the 24th.

Two hundred meters from the farmhouse, we entered the tree line and total carnage. The 38th Regiment's lines started there, and soldiers were still there in death. Some were in their holes and bunkers while others were scattered on the ground.

Holding up our advance, we checked out the bodies, looking for survivors. There was no odor, but these men had probably been dead for the time that our soldier friend had been living off berries. I had not expected to find this situation, and I was trying to read the signs, to make some sense of what had taken place. After a time, Brimmer sent word for me to move out.

Bodies of US soldiers were scattered along the trail to the main ridge. The story was the same on the ridge, which had been the MLR, only there were more corpses.[12,13] Sturdy earthen bunkers spaced fifty meters apart were on the forward slope with few bodies inside; most were scattered across the open ridgetop.

The enemy had gotten on the ridge and moved against the bunkers' blind side. We referred to that technique as Rolling-the-Ridge-Line; it is an easy tactic once a force is on the ridge and attacks against the flank of a forward-oriented defense. We moved through so much death that only the exceptional caught my attention. Fight and flight were evident everywhere.

A blond soldier with a long, hawk-bill nose lay across the footpath in the center of the tree-bare ridge. My attention was captured by a military entrenching pick deeply embedded in his chest. His pale-blue eyes were open to the heavens, causing me to wonder about his last moments. He had a bandage on his left upper arm from an earlier wound, but nothing more of his story could be told. We passed a Command Post situated on the back side of the ridge from the bunkers. Soldiers wounded earlier were lined up on stretchers; all were dead from gunshots to the head. Many of those killed around the CP had received earlier wounds; they had probably gone to the aid station thinking they were excused from the war.

The CP had stockpiles of rifle and mortar ammo, grenades, and weapons. The enemy no doubt helped themselves but they did not make a dent in the supply. I loaded up on grenades. My WW II Marine utility jackets, with two map and grenade pockets covering the entire front, came into use. I filled my pockets. Those jackets will hold thirteen Mark II fragmentation grenades, I learned, and I had a feeling that I would use all of them that night.

We did not care for a night on that ridge, and our leaders must have felt likewise as we moved off and continued forward toward Kari-san. We set in on high ground just before dark and dug deep fighting holes. That long night finally passed with no enemy activity other than huge fires in the distance beyond Kari-san. The fires would flare up and go out immediately. We took them to be enemy signal fires, but they may well have been the enemy burning gunpowder. They were enough to keep a little excitement stirring in the squad.

Awakened for my third turn on watch in the early morning hours, I was pulled from a deep sleep and a dream of being home. This was another of my "at home dreams" that seemed touchably real with Mom and Dad going about their daily routine and me involved with my brothers and sisters. Those dreams were so true to the life I had known that it was depressing, harsh, and cruel to move instantly from a loving farm family in Virginia to a dark fighting hole on a Korean hillside. From love and security to instant threats to my life, I sat there in the dark trying mentally to move back into the warmth of that other world.

I experienced this dream situation more than once that winter, and it became worse after the Chinese night attack. Nights are rough on an infantryman when rest comes in one-hour sleep periods, mixed with one-hour watches spent trying to determine if what you saw or heard in the darkness was real or imaginary. Little rest at night is compounded many times over while in the attack. A ten-minute break on the trail usually ends in sleep.

Just before daylight, I exploded my extra grenades far down the hill. After daylight, those of us who carried some chow ate our first meal in twenty-four hours. No one had had an appetite for food the previous day. Kari-san and the ridges around Hill 1051 were ours for the climb. The next few days helped us to clear our minds of the fate of the 38th; we were again in a hard, driving attack.

There were no more climbs in the sun; the enemy was fighting to hold its hills. Chinese leaders detailed the North Korean Peoples Army (NKPA) troops to hold in place, meaning to die in their positions.[14] This action was to allow the Chinese time to regroup and rebuild their shattered force. Also, the NKPA guys were now fighting for their home-land; we were again nearing the 38th parallel.

The rifleman's job became harder; to take a hill meant that Marines would die. We could not call in air or shoot artillery on every hill that we had to walk up or near. Therefore, as we moved forward, we were paying with lives while finding out which objectives were manned by the enemy and needed softening before our ground assault.

Marines were also learning that it was not smart to attack ahead of the forces on our flanks. We would be cut off forward by enemy forces when one or more major units on our flank could not keep the pace or do their job. Marines had found themselves alone in this war too often. The farther north we walked and fought, the farther to the rear we had to fight when the flanks gave away.

Shock troops do not make good line troops. They can handle the job; the problem comes with the commander matching flank units. All units must be able to keep up with the attack pace or the elite unit is wasted. Reining in the elite unit to a slower pace is also a waste of valu-able assets.

May ended with our division taking Yanggu. Third Battalion went into regimental reserve on 1 June, and we received rest, hot chow, and money. The paymaster's visit to our battalion was his first in a long time. Because of my allotment home, my monthly pay was not much, but it had accumulated to the sum of $150.00. I drew it to send home, but a post office was needed to get a money order. Our location was only one ridge to the rear of the front line, and rear area facilities were not avail-able. Pay call served only the poker players. Money in the form of mili-tary scrip was useless to the rest of us. Scrip could not be mailed home, and of course, there was no place to spend it. Now was not a good time to carry that amount of money.

The 5th Marines were in the attack for Line Kansas on the southern rim of the Punchbowl and our final objective on 5 June. Hill 729 and four higher ridges lay in our way with these ridges forming cross-compart-ments to our direction of attack. These ridges made forward movement difficult, especially with supplies and combat support units such as ar-tillery.[15] Within the next few days, our regiment would see some of its hardest fighting since the Chosin Reservoir. We were on the enemy's home turf, and they were not giving it up without a fight.

Item received the attack mission for 8 June. Our platoon was com-pany reserve; if the attack went well for the 1st and 2nd Platoons, we had the day off. That was not to be. We moved out behind the two attacking platoons and held up on the finger leading up to the main ridge and our company objective, Hill 821. Hill 1038 and the commanding peak of Taeam-san, Hill 1316, were just ahead with a promise of difficult times.

Seated on my helmet, I ate all the good portions of the three meals issued that morning. Since the when and where of our next resupply was unknown, we carried a day's ration. I did not have a positive feeling about the day so I ate the good portions of my rations. Without thinking much about it, I felt that I would not need three meals, and I did not save any goodies for later. I sensed that I would not be with my squad by day's end.

Unable to get direct air support to prep the objective for their assault, 2nd Platoon called for artillery fire. Terrain cross-compartments did not allow our artillery to move; they were firing at maximum range and the rounds fell short. Instead of hitting the enemy, rounds fell on the platoon, immediately taking them out of the fight. The cry for "Corpsman Up" pulled our corpsmen forward to help with the 2nd Platoon wounded. Dead and wounded were carried down the hill as we moved up to take over the assault role.

We held up just forward of the 2nd Platoon's position and waited for an inbound air strike. We would now have air support; maybe so many friendly fire casualties influenced the decision of some big guy. I sincerely hoped the arriving planes would be gull-winged, F4U Corsairs; we needed help from flyers who knew how to get down with us. They were!

We stood one behind the other on the feeder ridge and watched the Corsairs circle out to our left for their run on the target. As I watched, I realized that the lead plane coming in low was lining up directly on us. He had the wrong hill! He thought we were the enemy!

With shouts of "Get down!" Marines scampered for cover in the rocks and wherever they could find it. Taking my air panel (used to identify friendly ground positions to aircraft) from inside my helmet, I raced to a nearby clearing on the plane's approach side of our ridge. I mounted a huge boulder and stood fully exposed to the aircraft, desperately waving the panel. If the pilot did not see me, we would join the 2nd Platoon in field hospitals and Graves Registration.

The plane continued with an attack angle that had me boresighted. Flame leaped from the wings of the cannons fired, causing me to brace for the impact. I had failed. With the speed of a bullet, I realized that I was not the target. The pilot passed low over me with his cannons rattling and his empty shell casings dropping around me. That pilot knew our objective; I did not.

We were moving up a ridge that capped out in elevation about 300 meters above us. The enemy was close to our right front on an adjoining knoll that was connected to ours by a smaller ridge. We assaulted and secured the first hilltop; however, the nearby enemy force had the hill covered with machine-gun fire.

PFC James E. Quinn of our 3rd MG Squad positioned his gun on the hilltop and traded rounds with the enemy gun that had the advantage of elevation. To make things worse, our ridge was open with little underbrush, while the enemy position was difficult to locate due to thick foliage. Quinn located the gun by following the tracers to their source.

I crawled forward of Jim for a position behind a tree and began firing at what I thought was the gun position. The small tree trunk did not cover much of me, but I tried to keep my chest behind it.

I had fired several clips of ammo when something exploded behind me causing a sharp pain in my buttocks. There was no blood, at least none coming through my clothing. The explosive sound confused me, as there were no enemy soldiers within grenade range, and Marines were behind me. I felt as if I had been spanked, but there was no one close to me. Quinn's gun continued to rattle.

Brimmer passed the word to move on the reverse side of the hill for another air strike. We ceased fire and moved back. Baker asked me what happened to my pack so I removed it. That pain in my buttocks also needed checking; how could I hurt so badly and not be bleeding?

To my shocked surprise, four MG-bullet holes were in the side of my blanket roll. The rounds had entered on my left, went through my pack and out the right side of my roll. For lack of carrying space inside the haversack, I had placed two cans of C-ration meals in the blanket role straps. A can of corn beef hash had a bullet hole through it, and my entrenching-tool handle caught the sixth bullet. At least six bullets had raked over me at a distance of from one-half to two inches. In that position, my E-tool handle lay on my buttocks, and the bullet that splintered the handle caused the exploding sound and my spanking. I was shocked to realize that gunfire was so close without my knowledge, other than the round through the handle. Of course, the other rounds hit at the same instant. Dropping my trousers revealed splinters in my buttocks, a skinned, bluish area, and light bleeding.

My buddies advised, "Report to the corpsman. Go to the rear for a couple of days. You've earned it." A wound in that part of my body was not one that I would want to talk about, so I let the opportunity pass. Within the hour, I would meet that gun again.

Miller reorganized the squad due to the casualties just taken. We were down to six Marines plus the Squad Leader, half of a squad. Counting Miller, four of us were corporals. Miller established one fire team under Roop, leaving Robert (Bob) H. Levangie and myself as extras or "Corporals at Large." When Brimmer issued his attack order, we learned that not having a team worked against us.

We would jump off in the attack with 3rd Squad in the assault. Brimmer stepped into his squad leader's business by stating that Levangie and Fox would be the point in our squad's assault on the gun position. The air strike would end with three dummy runs to keep the enemy buttoned up while we moved.

The enemy guns were silent while the Corsairs worked over the ridge. Third Squad moved to the base of the higher hill held by the enemy while the Corsairs made their runs on the target. The word would be passed when the planes started their dummy runs.

Squad leaders did not have radio communications, which made our mission connection clumsy. We received the word by runner to move out after the last plane had pulled up from the dummy run. Because the order to start was late, I did not expect the dummy run to be much help. Again, our assault formation was a column of files, a one-man front: the tactics of the 1951 come-as-you-are Marine Corps. Bob and I moved up the ridge, not aggressively, but more like we expected to be called back, as if this action was a mistake.

A surrender leaflet signed by LtGen James A. Van Fleet caught my eye. As I moved around the bush upon which the leaflet was caught, I wondered what the general was doing at this very moment. He was not moving toward certain death but enjoying the comforts and safety of that huge rear area. He was the reason I was doing this mad thing; I hated him. With feet that weighed a ton, I forced myself forward.

We moved in a stretch file up the slope, one behind the other. No tactics were involved, just guts, and mine were measuring extremely low, if any at all. I knew that we ought to move rapidly up the hill to take advantage of the airstrike. Now, however, the Marine thing was not working.

Bob and I supported each other as we moved cautiously toward the enemy position, one forward, then the other. Finally, approaching the crest of the hill, I realized that we would be under fire if the enemy were on the hill. Just when I convinced myself that the enemy had withdrawn, I spotted a gun.

Ten meters uphill and partially hidden with bushes was the ribbed barrel of a Chinese heavy MG pointed directly at us. We had almost walked into it without seeing it. Brush covered most of the gun, and fire from the napalm delivered by the Corsairs burned just to my right of it. Pointing the gun out to Bob, I suggested that we throw a grenade, although the gun appeared to be abandoned.

Bob readied and threw a grenade that sailed high over the gun; I knew he had missed. I pulled the pin on a grenade as Bob's exploded well behind the gun position. Instantly that gun began firing straight down the hill into 3rd Squad.

Fortunately, the gun was locked in position on its traversing and elevating mechanism, causing it to fire between Bob and me. Bob ran to the left, and I ran to my right front into and through the napalm fire. Throwing my grenade at the gun as I ran, I also missed. There was no letup in the gun's heavy rattle of fire.

I paused behind a tree on the gun's left rear to get my bearing and prepare for the next action. The enemy had probably moved off the hill during the airstrike. Because of the aircraft dummy runs, the gun crew had just returned to their position as we approached. That gun was chewing up my squad; it had to be taken out. Where were the riflemen supporting the gun, and how many were there? I felt that my movement through the fire and smoke was not observed. Feeling alone against the entire North Korean Army, I also knew I was in a good position to assault his flank and make a difference. These thoughts went through my mind in a flash; my decision was to assault, and I tensed for the task.

I regained consciousness tumbling like a ball down the steep slope. When I stopped rolling, I did not have my rifle, and my pack had come off my shoulders. My left hand, arm, and foot felt as though red-hot needles were sticking in them. An enemy soldier must have seen my movement and hit me with a concussion grenade. The explosion knocked me out and blew me down the hill while showering my left side with light metal and wood shrapnel. The MG was still firing above me, and I was down the hill to the right of our earlier attack route. Needing a rifle and feeling very naked without one, I moved up to intersect with the rear of 3rd Squad.

First Squad had moved into position behind the 3rd, preparing to go forward and do what we had not done. Third Squad casualties were being carried down the hill, and Baker came staggering along with a head wound as I reached the path. He seemed to think that he was now out of the game, and the gunfire no longer concerned him. Adding to his pain by pulling him faster and keeping him low, I at least kept him alive.

We arrived at Brimmer's position, which was forward from where he had issued his attack order. In response to his question, I filled him in on what had taken place and the enemy position. I then asked for a rifle, thinking that I would continue the attack, but he told me to take Baker to the company aid station, a couple of hundred meters behind us. He then sent his runner forward to have the squads pull back for another airstrike.

That fight ended for me at the aid station with the corpsman filling out my medical evacuation tag. He did not have to twist my arm to convince me that I needed medical attention beyond what he could provide in the field.

My first aircraft ride came in an HO3S-1 that lifted out with two wounded. Any other day, the ride might have been a highlight, but it was no big thing with what had been compressed into this day.

Company E, 1st Medical Battalion was busy because of heavy fighting at the front. Doctors took care of the seriously wounded, and it was well into the night when they got around to me. A young doctor probed each of my wounds, removing the shrapnel without anything to ease the pain. My wounds were dressed and my butt punctured with needles to ward off infection.

The security of being in the rear was a great comfort. I claimed a cot, a real off-the-ground-sleeping cot, and almost immediately went into a deep, restful sleep. My few worldly possessions were lost along with my pack, but they would be full of bullet holes anyway. My wallet was with me; the next day I bought a money order and mailed the money I had been carrying to my dad.

The following form message was received by my parents from CMC:

14 June 1951

Regret to inform you that your son, Corporal Wesley Lee Fox USMC has been wounded in action 8 June 1951 in the Korean area in the performance of his duty and service to his country. I realize your great anxiety but nature of wounds not reported and delay of receipt of details must be expected. You will be promptly furnished any additional information received.

The message continued with a mailing address for the Marine Directory and was signed: "for the Commandant, J. T. Walker."

Life in the Med Bn included hot chow, movies, and a secure, dry, soft place to sleep. There were no threats lurking in the darkness, no sharing the night with your buddy or you awake. I could not, however, enjoy what was available to me. What was happening with my Squad?

Fighting in the Punchbowl area was heavy, and I learned that the 5th Marines were in the middle of it. How badly had that gun chewed up my squad on the 8th of June? Two squad members were at Easy Med with me. Were the rest at the morgue? What had happened to Levangie? I wanted to be with my buddies to get answers to my questions regarding that enemy gun. Higher authority also wanted able bodies returned to the line, and 18 June saw many of us trucking back to our units.

We dismounted at the Battalion Command Post (CP) in the valley south of the Punchbowl. Placed with Korean resupply trains to the different companies, we started up the trails to the southern lip of the bowl that was Line Kansas, the new MLR. We met a train coming down, and both groups took a break together. The Koreans were carrying down dead Marines in poncho-covered stretchers, and they grounded their loads beside the trail.

The boondockers extending from one poncho looked familiar. They had a personality of their own, and I knew that the feet in them would be those of Sgt Porter. Walking over, I removed the poncho from the face, knowing I would see Sgt Porter. I did; it was.

Sergeant Horace H. Porter Jr. USMCR had recently been promoted. Although his MOS was 0143, Administration, he was our Gun Section Leader. I had a problem visualizing the scenario that would involve him in rifle squad action or something that would get him killed. He normally moved with a command group and never with anything smaller than a platoon. As guns were always attached, he had spent much of his time with his 3rd Gun Squad and our platoon. We liked him; he was one of the few older NCOs who had time for us junior Marines.

My problems began upon arriving at the company CP. Because the 2nd Platoon was the lowest in personnel, that is where I was assigned, not back with my buddies. I had seen a little of the 2nd Platoon while in rear areas, but most of the time, they were another unit on our flank.

The platoon had caught my attention because their PltLdr, being an older lieutenant, looked more like a staff NCO. Obviously another mustang, he also carried an odd rifle, an M-1941 Johnson semi-automatic. Another difference was that the platoon had the only black Marine in Item. Neither was a reason for not wanting to join 2nd Platoon. I wanted to be with my Marine family.

I was not happy with my assignment, and I did not feel any better after meeting the members of my new squad. Yes, they were Marines, but they were not my buddies. Maybe because of my attitude or because I was the new guy, no attachment developed with the members of this squad. Truthfully, I did not give it time to work, but in combat these things have to move fast.

Receiving a negative response to my transfer request from the platoon sergeant, I started thinking that, when wounded again, I would have a chance of returning to 3rd Platoon. Time that I spent on that thought only kept me more to myself. Standing my watch alone and desperate in my fighting hole the second night, I took the matter in hand.

About 0400 in the morning I pulled the pin on a grenade and tossed it just out of my hole. Standing upright, exposed from the lower ribs upward, I placed and held my helmet over my face, with my arms in front of my chest. I felt that all my vitals were covered, and I should receive only flesh wounds. After a very long four seconds, the grenade exploded far down the hill. I had forgotten how grenades roll on the hillside. What else had I forgotten? The explosion shocked me out of the depths into which I had dropped, and I had no interest in trying it again. I would wait for the enemy.

Daylight found me feeling no better; time passed and then it was nature's call. With my E-tool, I went down the hill for a bowel movement. When I saw the white, squirming mass that came out of my body, I realized that I had my ticket off the hill. Other squad members at different times had left us for periods of up to a week for the same problem; almost everyone had worms at one time or another. Carrying the proof on my shovel, I went directly to the corpsman. He allowed that I needed treatment and directed me to collect my stuff; worms meant a trip to the Battalion Aid Station (BAS).

I'd had the worms for a month, but there had been no good time to leave 3rd Squad. We had been in the attack since I learned of my situation, and we were always shorthanded. I had planned to take care of the problem when we were in reserve. While at Easy Med, I had forgotten the worms, helped by the fact that we used wooden heads with seats over ground pits. There was no visual reminder, and I felt fine. Having worms was common enough that I never thought much about it. Now, the 2nd Platoon assignment gave me the incentive to do something about my personal health.

I went off the hill with the supply train. Three days at BAS and it was back up the hill to Item. A replacement draft had come in the day before, and I could go to any platoon I wanted. I chose the 3rd Platoon and Brimmer returned me to the 3rd Squad. However, no one was around from our attack on the gun. All faces were new; the three members of my fire team were boots. I never did learn how the final action with the MG on 8 June played out other than that 3rd Squad was not involved. Levangie's story also ends with his run to the left when that gun fired. I never learned more about him other than he is not listed in the historical record as a casualty that day.

Our days were filled with patrols with one platoon going into the Punchbowl each day. The other two platoons would send squad patrols down the mountain and back by different routes, morning and afternoon. The squad patrols could be done in three to four hours, but the platoon patrol was an all day affair. Also, with a platoon forward in the bowl, we did not sweat enemy contact on the near patrols.

Our platoon was assigned a deep patrol to the north side of the bowl. Because of the heat and distance, we left before daylight with one meal and one canteen of water. Though Marines were issued one canteen, some of us were getting smart and taking the canteens of casualties, who no longer needed them. The mentality in 1951 was that you could condition yourself to get by on little water. We crossed some creeks on patrol that day, so we would condition ourselves later. Other than mortar rounds thrown in our direction on the far side of the bowl, we returned after dark with no action.

Now that we were no longer advancing, our days on the ridge were relaxing. Other than the platoon patrol, we had at least half a day to rest, sometimes a full day. The daylight hours were easy, but late afternoons and evenings were rough on me. I dreaded the coming of night when the shadows grew longer and darker. Once darkness had fallen, I was all right. The enemy and I were equals after darkness arrived, and I could see well. If there were natural or man-made illumination, my concern went away until the next evening.

We were in fixed positions that allowed the enemy to locate and study us in spite of our aggressive patrolling. They could and would pick their time and place to hit us. My nature suits the Marine Corps' philosophy: keep moving, stay in the attack, never stay two nights in the same place. The attacker keeps the defender off balance. The defender never knows for sure about the what, where, when, and how. His reconnaissance teams have a problem collecting information on a moving force.

One of our restful days on the ridge cost me a Marine. We were seated around a fire when PFC Channing J. Potter, carrying a new 38 pistol, approached us from his hooch. He was my BAR man and had just received the pistol in a package from his dad. Walking up to PFC Ralph

E. Mead, Potter cocked the hammer. Mead was his best buddy as well as his assistant BAR man; they had left the States in the same draft after training together from boot camp.

Pointing the weapon at his buddy, Potter said, "Mead, this f———ing thing could go off." With that, he pulled the trigger and the pistol fired. Mead did not say anything immediately because of shock. Then he grabbed his knee, rolled on the ground, and began cursing Potter. Potter seemed to be in more shock than Mead.

Potter's game was Russian roulette. His prank backfired because he was confused about the rotation direction of the cylinder, putting the bullet on the wrong side. Mead took the bullet through his kneecap and shortly was hauled down the mountain, breaking up my new family.

Rumor had been circulating for some time that the division would be going in Corps Reserve. It happened. On 15 July, the 5th Marines were relieved in place by the 2nd Infantry Division. We walked off the ridge, boarded trucks, and headed south for Rest and Rehabilitation. Instead of R&R, the squad talk was of I&I. Most of us needed one, if not both, of the letter identifiers for intercourse and intoxication.

The 5th Marines received a Ready Reserve mission and set up camp along the Soyang-Gang near Inje. We dismounted the trucks, and turned-to making our new home. We had no more than erected our shelterhalves when the rain started.

I lay in that small, sweltering shelterhalf with the odor of my sweaty buddy for two days while the rain beat on the tent fabric. Of course, the good government material was only water repellent, not waterproof. Wherever we touched the tent, as with a shoulder in turning over, we had a major water leak. In spite of the discomfort, we considered ourselves lucky: we could have been on patrol or in the attack in that downpour.

The regiment held a memorial service for those who no longer answered the call. Purple Hearts were awarded, and then we became serious with this Marine thing. Training began. We were fighting a war, we had a chance for real rest, and somebody came up with a training plan. The idea was hard to accept, and our efforts at compliance were worse.

Conducting COD in the soft rice paddies did not provide the obedience, discipline, and motivation that it should have. Worse was the waste of our time and energy; we were not going to be more efficient at destroying the enemy or staying alive with one hour of drill each day. General military subjects went over just as sourly. Classes included the Uniform Code of Military Justice; function, care, and cleaning of the Cal

.30 M-1 Rifle, which we knew by heart; and first aid. Assault tactics or test firing and zeroing our rifles—something useful and necessary—was not presented.

To compound the problem, our teachers were not instructors but the lowest sergeants in the pecking order. With little experience, they were not prepared to present a period of instruction. We had no place suitable for a classroom, we sat on the ground until we grew tired, and (following the attention-getting joke) we lay back and slept in front of the instructor.

I took command of the 3rd Squad, which was not a popular position at Inje because of the training and personnel accountability. We rapidly became the bad guys as we rounded up our Marines from their many hideouts. Squad leaders, along with the platoon sergeants, were charged with making the training schedule work.

There were some good deals at Inje, and outpost duty was one. My first independent assignment as a leader was to man an OP. The location of the OP was on a mountain northeast of Inje, and it took two hours to get there because of the steepness and distance.

Relieving the squad in position, I set in with a perimeter defense. I loved it! A corpsman and a radio operator were attached; the three of us built a three-man hooch. A 25 percent watch at night provided our security, and our day activity amounted to a close-in fire team patrol. There was no training schedule! Chow, water, and radio batteries were carried up every other day by Korean laborers. We received PX supplies through the supply system to the OP, whereas we had to buy these items at Inje.

Our radio worked for the most part, and I reported directly to the S-3 watch. All of my Marines liked the assignment so much that I asked for and was given a second week. Our new platoon leader climbed up with a fire team escort for a visit; 2nd Lieutenant Arden R. Grover USMCR found everything to his satisfaction.

I grew on that mountain, as this was my first opportunity to exercise leadership on my own. Most of my squad members were fresh from the States, regular Marines who wanted and expected guidance and leadership. The earlier, salty reservists had served their purpose and were home or on their way. I might not be a Davis yet, but I was working at it.

Introduction to the air mattress and the heat tablet happened on the OP, and the supply trains carried the items. From the viewpoint of a rifleman who had been sleeping on the ground for six months and had gone without food rather than chip the frozen stuff out of a can, the two items revolutionized the infantry. The air mat, fondly called a rubber lady, made getting up from sleep a chore. Heat tablets worked despite the weather, were small with no weight, and allowed for heating rations after dark. Life for Marine infantry was becoming almost comfortable.

R&R ended, and on 27 August, we moved back to the front along the Punchbowl. On 1 September, 3rd Bn, 5th Marines relieved the 2nd KMC Bn on Line Kansas. A new offense began with the objective of straightening out the front. We jumped off on the 3rd and secured the northern rim of the Punchbowl, known as the Hayes Line.

Leading a rifle squad as a maneuver element of the platoon was great, but it lacked the freedom of individual thought and action that I enjoyed on the OP. I could not necessarily do my thing or do things my way. Despite that, I should add that I enjoyed an easy working relationship with my new platoon leader. He spent a lot of time in our squad area getting to know his Marines.

A big attack was planned for 8 September. Receiving the order on the 7th, I issued mine along with supplies and equipment. As we were behind the lines, we experienced a good night's sleep with only a 10 percent watch.

The next morning I committed my first mistake in leadership, one that probably set my career course for the next forty years in the Marines. The war was my purpose in joining the Marines, and I intended to return to the farm. Considering my one enlistment and one war, at this point I had not had enough. I was not ready to leave Korea or 3rd Squad. My mistake was in not doing a route reconnaissance to the Platoon Assembly Position. The first half of the route I knew, as I had been over it several times. The Assembly Position was a short distance beyond and should be easy to find in the dark.

At 0400 on 8 September, I led my squad to join 3rd Platoon. Some distance from our night position, Potter behind me stated, "I cannot see anything. How do you know where you're going?"

Feeling cocky, I responded with, "Just follow Hawkeye." With the words barely out of my mouth, I was falling. I had stepped off into space and had time to know it before I hit the ground. Pain shot through my body with fireworks exploding in my head. The fireworks did a repeat when Potter landed on me. Fortunately, the third Marine in the column heard us fall and stopped the squad's forward movement. I had stepped off the ridge into a cut for a roadway that had been dozed out by the engineers. The height was only twelve feet, but when you do not expect it, a belly flop hurts.

We collected ourselves, and I began to feel better. The squad climbed down while I found my gear, and we made ready to move out. My right hand hurt like the blazes; it felt as if a hot iron was pressed against my index finger and large knuckle. When I commented on it, Potter produced a flashlight for a closer look under a poncho. I was surprised to see the crooked shape of my finger. There was no doubt that it was broken, and the white knucklebone was bared. Taking out my battle dressing, I wrapped my hand with the obvious intention of continuing our movement to join the platoon.

Squad members insisted that I go by BAS to get the bone set and splinted. My first thoughts were that it was only a finger, and I really did not want to take a chance of losing the 3rd Platoon. My buddies reminded me that it would be some time yet before we jumped off, and that our platoon was in company reserve, so I could catch up. The pain in my hand convinced me; I walked down that same road to the Bn CP.

At BAS, the doctor did not listen to anything I said about wanting to remain with my squad and directed a corpsman to send me to the rear. He gave me some hope by saying that after my hand healed I would be returned to my unit. I banged around in a crackerbox, the Marine name for a field ambulance, on the ride to 1st Med Bn only to spend the night.

The next day I was flown to the hospital ship, *USS Repose.* Placed almost instantly into another world, I felt very much out of place and extremely uncomfortable in that environment of white sheets, soft beds, pillows, and American female nurses. Still encased in the grime and crud of the front lines, I was not ready to be in the presence of women.

I began to lose hope of getting returned to my squad. My wound was cleaned, I was given some shots, but nothing was done about the broken bone. On 18 September I flew to Japan and entered the Naval Hospital at Yokosuka. A few days later, I was seated on the opposite side of a table from a young man in white.

With a pair of pliers, this modern-day doctor began to bore a hole through the middle bone of my right index finger. His drill was a large hypodermic needle held by and twisted with the pliers. For two weeks, no one had paid any attention to my broken finger. Now that mending had started, they would put it in traction. If they would not re-break the bone, what good was the traction? The man in white did numb my finger but it took some time and several needles to drill through the bone.

Both ends of the last needle were cut off, and a small wire looped through the needle hole. A cast was molded on my hand, a stick extended from the cast, and the wire loop and stick were joined with a rubber band. I was mad; my finger was crooked then and it still is today.

The Korean War was over for me; on 29 October, I headed for the States. I adjusted to the idea and began to look forward to being with my family. The R5D route home was an eight-hour flight to Wake Island where we remained overnight. The next hop was to Hawaii with another eight-hour leg in the air and a two-day stay in the Trippler Army Hospital. A third eight-hour flight on 1 November put me in the Naval Hospital at Mare Island, California.

My stay at Mare Island allowed me to attend my first Marine Corps Birthday Ball. We patients wore greens or whatever portions of a uniform we had. Upon seeing the many Marines attending in Blues, I decided that I would have that uniform in time for next year's ball.

The last leg of my homeward flight took place on 18 November. That day ended with my assignment to Ward 107 of the National Naval Medical Center, Bethesda, Maryland. Since my seabag had not been located in Yokohama, I was in the process of receiving all new uniforms. Tailoring, cleaning, and pressing were needed, as well as the sewing-on of my rank insignia. Marines were squared away, and I would not go home without a proper uniform.

My uniforms and I were ready for Thanksgiving. I headed home on a thirty-day convalescent leave. The bus schedule to Round Hill was unsatisfactory so I hitchhiked. A young, squared-away Marine did not walk far along the Virginia roads in 1951. Those thirty days were great and I did so well that my doctor agreed to another thirty-day C-leave.

On 22 March 1952, I was found fit for duty at sea and in the field. A transfer to the 1st Guard Detachment, MB, Navy Gun Factory (NGF), 8th and M Street SE, Washington, DC followed. As a corporal, I stood post on the 8th and M (the longest continuously manned post in Marine Corps history) and 11th and O Street gates. A two-section guard gave me plenty of time off, which I spent on the farm. Then I caught mess duty. I had never pulled mess duty as a private and had only two weeks as a PFC; now as a corporal, it looked like I would be a permanent fixture in the mess hall. We served family style in 1st Guard, and it had to be the best chow in the Corps. We did not do any exercise, and we did not run in those days. Except for standing post, we did not do much to burn off the intake of good food.

Lessons Learned

1. Personal commitment in a firefight has to do with brotherhood and the Marine beside you, more so than Mom, apple pie, and the flag, which are far away.

2. Combat is tough enough without removing a fighter from the bond of his unit and his friends.

3. A tour of duty in a combat zone is one thing; a firefight is another.

4. One man attacking at a time is a tough way to take an objective.

5. A rifleman must know his rifle and his battle sights.

6. Elite troops are wasted in the line when flank units cannot maintain their pace.

7. Use and exercise all Troop Leading Steps.

4
Sergeant
1128290/0311/8511

1 March 1952

Sergeant's rank came as unexpectedly as had corporal; I was promoted on 19 April 1952 with date of rank of 1 March. The promotion ceremony doubled with a routine 0700 formation modified with individuals called forward to receive their warrants. I was an exception; my warrant was delivered to me on the mess deck.

Standing post as a gate sentry was acceptable infantryman work, but mess duty was something else. Just about everyone in the detachment was a sergeant, but I felt that three-stripers should not pull mess duty. Noon chow found me scrubbing pots and pans while expecting relief. I paid a visit to the 1st Sergeant who did not hide his contempt for a bitching Marine. Nevertheless, he had to face my question, "Were sergeants now going to pull mess duty?" After much puffing, cursing, and throwing papers around, he told me to secure and report to the guard chief. I did so and moved my gear into the sergeants' quarters, one end of the squadbay closed off with wall lockers. I had attained my goal of sergeant after eighteen months and twenty-seven days in the Corps.

I soon learned, however, that I was only a "slick-arm" sergeant. The term was used by all sergeants who had a service stripe, called a hashmark, representing four years of service. Marines are great about checking dates of rank and determining who is in charge. Old Corps and New Corps rumblings never cease, with the "Old Corps" including anything that took place before your time. As such, all Marines enjoy the position of being Old Corps.

I was pleased to be a sergeant, even with a slick-arm. I would qualify for my hashmark on the same day I finished my enlistment, so I would never join the Hashmark Club. However, I was becoming aware that the hashmark was a significant symbol of membership in a tight, select fraternity. Over the next eighteen months, the hashmark idea would continue to work on me.

Sergeants stood the post of Corporal of the Guard (COG) while staff sergeants performed the Sergeant of the Guard (SOG) duties. We had a two-section guard that placed individuals on guard duty every other day and every other weekend. Days not on guard were training and Corps business days, but liberty call sounded for the nights and every other weekend.

I was one of the sergeants serving as COG; while other sergeants stood post. Three sergeants stood the COG duty on any one day, which amounted to being on post four hours and off eight. Posting and relieving the sentries and manning the COG's desk in the guard shack, just inside the 8th and M Street gate, were the duties. The eight hours off-post were spent conducting guard school, feeding, and racking out in the Guard shack.

An important duty of the COG was sounding the time by ringing the admiral's bell every half-hour. The bell was positioned by the flagpole about fifty meters from the guard shack and the admiral's quarters. The admiral (I assumed that he was the Gun Factory CO and he may have held other naval positions) had not much more to do than listen for the Marines to mess up the bell-ringing: too early, too late, too many, or too few bells sounded. There were times that the COG was involved with other duty demands and the bell was forgotten. The admiral did not call the guard shack, he called the colonel, and we received the word through the chain of command.

The SOG and the Officer of the Day (OD) stood twenty-four-hour posts and usually had nothing more important to do than ensure that the bell rang correctly. The bell ringer, on the other hand, was at the working level and had other things to do than sit around waiting to ring the bell. Those directly involved were the COG, his supernumerary, and the sentry on the 8th and M Street gate known as Post 1. Either the COG or the Super rang the bell. Post 1 would signal the time as the big hand on the electric wall clock over his post jumped to the half-hour. The supernumerary was not always around, as his duties included courier runs and relieving other sentries for breaks. Post 1 would periodically get heavy automobile and pedestrian traffic, all of which were checked for ID and Liberty Cards. The COG spent half his time on the telephone with problems on the different posts and running the guard.

It never failed that most of the business happened on the half hour. All posts were required to check in by phone hourly, and problems and complaints constantly bombarded the first level of leadership in the security of the Gun Factory. Many were the times that my eyes would happen to catch the clock over Post 1 just as the next leap of the hands would place it on the half hour. I would tear out of the guard shack running for the bell, figuring how many rings to make as I ran.

Captain William F. Goggin was the Guard Officer and an inspiration to me. He was a professional in every sense of the word, and I liked the way he dealt with us on a daily basis. The Hashmarks liked to talk about Lt Goggin's long platoon patrol around the Chosin Reservoir in Korea two Novembers past while making contact with only a few Chinese. Several days later there was a Chinese soldier for each snowflake on the ridges. The captain wore the Silver Star Medal and was a hero to those of us who arrived in Korea too late for the Chosin fight.

Meanwhile, the Korean War moved into the stages of outpost fighting and trench warfare. Marines were still getting a big share of the action, although the 1st MarDiv had been fighting over two years in this war. Wanting to return to the division and Korea, I paid another visit to my 1st Sergeant with the intention of submitting a Letter of Request to CMC. He led me to believe he was handling my request and later told me that CMC had not approved it. While my record contains later correspondence requesting combat assignment (submitted after the master sergeant left us), there is no record of the request I made in the spring of 1952.

The squared-away Marine in the early 1950s was something less than regulation. We started with our rebuilt cordovan dress shoes. The cordovan did not show off a deep spit shine, so we dyed our shoes black. Shoe soles were doubled or tripled and capped with steel plates, and our heels were covered with full steel plates. The guard sounded like a herd of horses when we marched from Building 58 to the guard shack after Guard Mount. Pockets on our green and khaki trousers were sewed shut, as were the pocket flaps on the Vandegrift jacket. The extra material in the jacket that allowed it to blouse over the belt line was tailored out so that the jacket was more formfitting.

Barracks covers had great seagoing dips in their tops, and no one wore his garrison cap with a straight ridge. Some wore it with the center pushed down on the head and a fore and aft tip sticking up, doggie style. Most of us wore the cover with a Marine dip: the rear ridge broken and pushed down with a tip rising in the rear and the front half unbroken.

No one bothered us with regulations, probably because younger officers had their own uniform modifications and older ones did not even bother to shine their shoes. My green and khaki trousers had no hip pockets, and with my side pockets sewed shut, I carried my change and keys in my watch pocket. My ID, Liberty Card, and any bills that I might have (never a problem) were placed in one of my socks. It was not a practical uniform, but we thought we looked sharp.

On 17 June 1952 I was assigned to the Armed Services Police Detachment (ASPD) that worked out of the NGF barracks beside the 11th and O Street gate. Six Marine sergeants were assigned to the ASPD on a permanent basis. The senior Marine was CWO Bales, lovingly referred to by all as Pappy Bales. He was the first Marine whom I heard state, "I've got thirty years in the Corps today; think I'll make a career of it." He was quite a Marine and the first of the few thirty-year Marines whom I knew in my early years. He kept us together although we never patrolled with another Marine.

I worked with a member of the other services, and never the same one two weeks in a row. I liked working with a sailor because our uniforms matched better: we both wore white leggings and pistol belts. In addition, our mental approach to police work was closer, as we both were training on the job. Marines and sailors took the duty in addition to their occupational specialty. The Marine Corps would later return military police (MOS 5800) to our occupational fields.

I received no formal schooling in police work other than the two-week course conducted by the ASPD. We learned the Ten Code for radio transmissions and some dos and don'ts of the police business. Every day on the job was a learning experience; the work was interesting and an exposure to the world outside the Corps. Developing close relationships with other service members was a unique benefit. The real pros in the business were the Army and Air Force policemen; beyond the law enforcement schools that prepared them, police business was their only work.

About the time I started with the ASPD, both Goggin and Bales interviewed me for OCS. The idea had never crossed my mind, and when Bales first mentioned it, I thought he was joking. Reporting to Mr. Bales made the idea official. Next, I reported to Captain Goggin to explain why I was not interested. Both officers encouraged me to get busy with the High School and College General Education Development Test and start off-duty education, but it was too soon for me to want to be a student. What really turned me off about the officer idea was the reserve commission. Although most of my fellow squad members in Korea were reservists, I did not want to be one. Goggin tried to explain that most officers started with a reserve commission, but I did not hear anything after the word reservist and the issue died. Besides, I liked my downtown police duties.

This discussion of a commission served one good purpose. I had been thinking about getting a tattoo with the Corps's emblem and "Death before Dishonor." Most of my buddies were getting one, as we were in that age group. Upon learning that officers could not have tattoos, I reevaluated my desire for something so permanent. I decided to keep my options open, realizing that I needed no picture on my skin to remind me of my personal values.

The ASPD worked shifts, with the second shift from 1500 to 2300 being the best. Things were happening, the bars and nightclubs were busy, and people were on the streets. The first shift, 0700 to 1500, was easy and went fast. The least desirable was the 2300 to 0700 because the only people not asleep were the drunks. On weekends, the evening shift employed up to six foot-patrols and double that number of motorized patrols. The best patrols were the foot-patrols on 14th and H Streets, NW, where the night action was taking place. The downtown motor patrols were the next best for action.

The disadvantage of a motor patrol was that at least one patrolman was tied to the radio unless they checked off the net. Foot patrols called in hourly on a police call box; that meant the dispatcher could not task us between calls. We also manned ASPD booths in Union Station and the Greyhound Bus Station with roving foot patrols. Both of these posts offered a lot of exposure to the young people moving within the city, meaning dates with pretty girls.

An Army sergeant managed to park his government sedan beside Union Station; I found him slumped over his steering wheel with the motor running. He was so drunk that I had to carry him into our office located at one end of the concourse. Too drunk to be questioned, he slept until hauled to our brig at headquarters. At this stage in my training and education, I did not know much about the military legal system.

This sergeant's Army lawyer won his case on the drunk charge due to my inexperience with court-martial proceedings. This captain tore into me, asking, "How did you know he was drunk? Are you a medical officer? Do you have training in determining who is intoxicated? How could you be sure that he was not sick?" He kept up that attack while I was thinking, "Hey, Buddy, I don't really care, he is your problem. If you want to let him go, it is your business. You are his leader." The attack continued, and I started answering his questions with "I think so" and then "Maybe."

I did not realize this captain was the defense lawyer. I thought of him only as an officer in the staff sergeant's service, and whatever he wanted to do with the drunk, he could. I received my fill of that captain's stuff and wanted to leave the Army scene. Besides, my Korean War experiences had not given me a very high opinion of Army officers. Saluting them was difficult enough, and I certainly did not like this verbal abuse. When I returned to Headquarters, Mr. Bales helped me see the matter in a different light. In the future, all formal charges would be backed to the fullest. I never lost any more cases.

★ ★ ★

On 4 December 1952, I submitted a request to CMC for a transfer to the Fleet Marine Force with duty in a combat organization overseas. HQMC responded with a letter dated 15 December 1952 to my CO stating:

> Please inform the subject named Marine that his request for assignment to duty in a combat area is not approved at this time; however, the spirit with which his request is submitted is appreciated by this headquarters.

Professionalism and the Hashmark club were working; I loved everything about being a Marine. There was no way I could do all of the Marine things that I wanted to do during my four-year enlistment. I seriously intended to return to the 1st MarDiv, and a Med Cruise was on my wish list. Hashmarkers liked to talk of their experiences on a six-month deployment of an infantry battalion aboard ships to the Mediterranean Sea and nearby ports.

Accepting the fact that I could not do the Marine things on my list by August 1954, I started thinking of putting the farm off a few years and reenlisting. If I reenlisted for six, I would have ten in and only ten to go for retirement. Actually, a twenty-year retirement was awarded with nineteen years and six months active duty. In 1970 I could go back to the farm and draw a half pay pension for the rest of my life. However, that was a journey impossible to appreciate; 1970 was so far away. I began to accept the career idea; I would join the Hashmark Club.

On 25 June 1953, I again requested combat duty with the FMF overseas, and I agreed to extend my enlistment. This time the Commandant responded with a report date to El Toro, California, for further transportation beyond the seas. Checking out of the ASPD and the 1st Guard Detachment on 11 September 1953, I took a thirty-day leave on the farm; it was corn-cutting time.

Allowed eleven days' travel time, I hitchhiked to El Toro on US 40 and 66. Rides did not take me far, but a young, squared-away Marine sergeant did not stand very long on any road for the next lift. I did not thumb; I felt that was below the class of Marine NCOs. On my leather suitcase were the letters C A L I F in reflective tape. The letters and the uniform allowed few cars to pass me up.

My itinerary amounted to selecting the next major city about 500 miles' distance for that day's travel where I usually found a rack at the YMCA if it was not out of my way. I stayed two nights each in Wheeling, St. Louis, Oklahoma City, and Amarillo, which gave me a chance to see the sights. The start of each day saw me with a freshly pressed full green uniform, one day my battle jacket, the next my blouse. With no civilian clothes, whatever I did around town was done in uniform. My money held out well, as I was not spending much except for meals, lodging, and press-while-you-wait service.

My day's objective upon leaving Amarillo was Albuquerque. The day went well until late in the afternoon when a rancher dropped me at an intersection about thirty miles short of the city. Major roadwork caused the rerouting of traffic lanes, and driver attention seemed focused on the detour signs. The roadwork greatly reduced traffic speed (there was no speed limit on highways in the West in 1953) but that proved no help.

My luck had changed; no one was stopping. Storm clouds developed while I stood for hours in that dusty, hot spot wondering about my next move. My options were simple: stand or start walking with my suitcase. There was relief from the heat with the buildup of the storm. While I needed a drink of water, I did not look favorably on taking a shower in my uniform. Darkness came early with the storm clouds, and the rain started.

A car slowed while pulling out of the graveled detour lane. It started to move forward again while I ran toward it at high-port. The car stopped. Two young men my age told me to get in. They were driving through to Los Angeles, saw the reflection of their headlights on my taped C A L I F, and thinking that it was a reroute-road sign, pulled over in that direction.

No problem, I was welcome to ride all the way. They would be in Los Angeles in the morning. I thought quickly about my planned visit to Albuquerque and the long wait on US 66, and took the "bird in hand." I offered but was not asked to help with the driving, so with the entire back seat, I slept.

Reporting in at El Toro, I was assigned to the LTA (Lighter Than Air) Facility, the old Dirigible Station with huge hangars. The air wing portion of the 36th Replacement Draft was forming up and training at LTA. We lived in Quonset Huts and pulled liberty in Santa Ana. Other than a little COD, we did not do any training but did draw M-1 rifles and field gear to take overseas. With three formations a day to get the word, we were swinging with the wing.

On 10 November 1953, the 36th Replacement Draft boarded the *USS Mountrail* (APA-213) and sailed for Kobe, Japan. Another Marine Corps birthday passed for me with no celebration. The Pacific lived up to its name; the voyage was uneventful. A favorite pastime was making our new dungarees salty by dragging them behind the ship for a half hour. Finding spare rope and standing room on the ship's fantail were problems on pretty days.

The only other event of the day was the chow line, and being a sergeant did not make that any shorter than it was on my earlier crossing. Two weeks aboard a troop ship is simply wasted time in a Marine's life. Even writing letters became a chore. The sea-going routine ended on the 28th; we docked in Kobe, unloaded the ship, and moved to the Wing headquarters.

On 3 December, I reported to Marine Air Group 11 (MAG-11) based at the Naval Air Station, Atsugi, and assigned to the Provost Marshal's Office (PMO), Marine Air Base Squadron 11. My first taste of professionalism with a flair was experienced upon checking in with the PMO.

Master Sergeant Johnson (known to his fellow SNCOs as Caribou Johnson because of an affair he supposedly had with a female caribou many years earlier while stationed in Adak, Alaska) was the Provost Sergeant. He assigned the duty driver, PFC Carr, to drive me around in the PMOs weapons carrier, a 3/4-ton truck, for my check-in and to get me settled. Being taken around by the duty driver was a fine touch that immediately translated to, "Sergeants rank in this organization." There was no hassle in finding a particular office or someone with whom to check in. Carr knew where to go and whom to see.

Other personalities included the Provost Marshal, Captain Steve Bonora, who had worked in the ASPD, Washington, DC, when I first arrived at 1st Guard. Displaying a hard, sinister personality, he could always be counted on to come off with something like, "What did you do with the waffle iron, Marine?" The normal response was, "What waffle iron, Sir?", which Bonora followed with, "The one you pressed your uniform with, PFC." Another favorite of the captain was, "What did you comb your hair with, Marine, a Mixmaster?" We never quite knew how to take his deadpan face and serious attitude. Standing before Bonora to be relieved or assume the SOG duty was always stressful because some sharply pointed comment or question was expected. "Did you have a chicken do this writing for you, Sergeant?" He did tighten up the professional competency of his young sergeants.

Technical Sergeant James Nash was the Group Investigator, had his own office, did his own thing, and had a personal relationship with Bonora. They had served as sergeants together somewhere in their past. Nash was with the Drysdale relief convoy that was ambushed while trying to smash through to the Marines surrounded in the Chosin Reservoir. Consequently, he was a prisoner of war until he escaped.

MAG-11 was on the far side of the air station in an area known as East Camp, across the runway from the Navy side. It was a new camp; the barracks, offices, and hangars were under construction. We lived in tents and bathed and shaved in a wooden community head left over by the Japanese military from WW II.

The mess hall was the first building to be completed, followed by barracks for the different squadrons. The provost section was the last to get barracks. We lived well with wooden walkways and wooden decks in the tents. The distance to the head and shower on cold, rainy nights was the biggest drawback.

My first duty was a military police patrol in the two nearby towns of Yomato and Sugama-oska. These patrols were manned during liberty hours, which were evenings and weekends until the bars closed at midnight.

The atmosphere, if not the duty, was far different from that of the ASPD in DC. The streets were dirt, which meant mud during most of the winter months. Because of the dirt and mud, we wore boondockers with our green uniform. The brown, rough-side-out boondocker did not look right with the white-web gear worn. By the time we were on duty, however, it did not matter; the gear was difficult to keep white. Just riding out in a dusty field vehicle took the white out. We walked the streets, bar to bar, letting our presence be known.

On weeknights long after payday when business was slow, the girls would try to sell their wares to us. It was the same story, bar after bar. "You catch-ee short time with me, sarg-ee. Nobody know," she said as she rubbed up against me and grabbed my crotch. "You stay with me tonight. No cost-ee money cause I love you. You pay me payday. Okay, Hon-ee." The girls were all business-minded, doing their part to improve the Japanese economy from the war loss. I recognized it as such and chose to keep my meager funds for the attainment of my personal goals. They used their best phrase, however, on payday nights. "How can you speak of love when you have no yen?"

Town patrols worked for the Commander of the Guard (CmdrGd) located in East Camp while performing their duties in the nearby towns, which placed military police very much on their own. The CmdrGd, a staff sergeant, ran the daily business of the PMO. There were two of them with duty every other day and weekend. The OD was a junior squadron officer who caught the duty for a twenty-four-hour period every once in a great while. The lieutenant, usually a jet jockey, did not know and did not care about the guard; he just served his time. The East Camp fence line, the aircraft, and the flight line were secured by the two guard platoons working a two-section guard.

A job promotion came along on 5 January 1954, and I became a platoon sergeant. That also made me a SOG. My section had some great Marines who took their duty seriously, and we had some fun in the process. Duties started with a guard mount, which was a personnel and rifle inspection with emphasis on appearance and knowledge of duties. Sentries then left their rifles in the guardhouse and carried a shotgun on post. My primary duties included checking posts and supervising the three COGs. The posts were challenging at night, which added some excitement to an otherwise boring routine.

The OD and SOG were the only routine challenges, or at least the expected ones, as they checked all sentries on each relief. Sentries took advantage of the element of surprise by hiding somewhere close to where our vehicle would pass, trying to startle us with a thunderous command of "HALT" out of the darkness. They were usually successful, especially with the inexperienced OD. We all got a kick out of shaking up young lieutenants.

The fence on the perimeter was not an obstacle and could be walked through at almost any point. Most of the fence traffic was from those inside selling cigarettes, alcohol, and other Marine Exchange items to the Japanese on the black market. We prepared our security against the threats of communism and those outside that would do us harm. All of our action, however, involved those inside trying to get out with a load on their back and return undetected.

Sergeant William B. Donahoo from Brownwood, Texas, was my counterpart with the other platoon. In the year we served together, Wild Bill became one of my best buddies. We pulled some great liberty in Tokyo along with another gungy Marine, Sergeant Jack B. Shaw. Donahoo and I had a lot in common, including our love of country music and thoughts on manhood. I suppose being from the South contributed to this similarity.

One night, nothing would do but for the two of us to go out back of the barracks and see who was the better man. We fought until we were both sick with exhaustion and so weak that we could not raise a hand, let alone throw a fist. That satisfied what had to be proven. With the thought of "no one can beat me" ringing in each head, we walked into the barracks with arms around each other.

Wild Bill did not do so well in another fight, however. Shaw had his sights on a girl who worked in a certain bar that some sailors considered their private club in Sugama-oska. This girl was a steady with a sailor, meaning that he was keeping house with her when he rated liberty. Shaw's plan was to visit the bar when the Navy would not be around.

Two nights before payday was N-night; everyone would be broke. We had saved our money for the occasion, knowing that we would have exclusive use of the bar. As the night developed, we had the undivided attention of all of the girls. Whatever Donahoo and Shaw ordered to drink, they ordered for three. I did not drink alcohol, and as one of them emptied his glass, he placed his empty in front of me while taking the full one.

We were well into the night when ten sailors entered the bar, seated themselves on the opposite side of the room, and proceeded to drink. Both of my buddies were well-looped, and the sailors were beginning to show the effects of their drinking with loud talking.

A sailor came over, leaned over while gripping our table edge, and asked where we were stationed. To my surprise, Wild Bill wobbled to his feet, drew back, and released a haymaker against the side of the sailor's head. The man in white hit the floor, flat. There were a dozen sailors in the bar by this time and they attacked.

Shaw and Donahoo each grabbed a sailor and started wrestling. That left the remainder for me, and I was throwing fist with three, keeping them between the bunch and me. Thanks to that small bar, others could not get to me without pulling their buddies out of the way. Sailors who could not reach us retreated to their tables and started throwing bottles and glasses that mostly hit their buddies because they were between the two groups.

One little sailor of the three facing me had gotten under my swing and was working on my stomach. He might as well have been hitting me with a pillow, as his blows had no effect, and I had not given him much attention. He yelled out to no one in particular, "Hell, this son-of-a-bitch ain't drunk." Grabbing him by his neck-scarf, I concentrated one well-placed right that exploded his nose in red over both of us. His rapid departure took the fight out of the other two and they returned to their tables.

Looking around, I found Wild Bill on his back on the stairway leading up to private places. A sailor was seated on his chest with a death grip on his throat. Donahoo's face was white, and he had about ceased to struggle. I grabbed the sailor by his cute little knotted kerchief, jerked him up off Donahoo, and mashed his face. He returned to the other side of the room.

Shaw's sailor took off as I moved in his direction. Donahoo was coming to with much coughing and cursing. He later said that he could not break the sailor's grip. He was thinking that this was a hell of a way for a gungy Marine to die, drunk in a Japanese whorehouse at the hands of a sailor.

The sailors disappeared in a flash upon learning that Mama-san had called the Shore Patrol. We easily convinced the SP, with the girls' help, that the sailors had started the fight. We had a little professional recognition working for us as well; the SP mainside and MPs from East Camp had to get along. Shaw got the girl he came after.

Prices in those days were manageable, although my sergeant's pay was only $129.00 a month before deductions. (After income tax and the $50.00 allotment home, I drew $31.00 a payday.) Everything on the Japanese economy was negotiable. The girls normally asked $5.00 for a "short time." If business was slow and the Marine played his cards right, two or three dollars would get the same thing. An all-night stay started at ten dollars, but with a little experience, five dollars would buy the night. Japan's economy was not booming in 1954; however, there had been a noticeable price increase since 1951. Cigarettes were no longer acceptable tender for a young woman's favor. The quality and workmanship of Japanese goods were not yet respected, but prices were well below the US price for an equivalent item.

I was completing my first enlistment in the Marine Corps. In order to get my current assignment, I had signed an agreement to extend my enlistment. As planned and as I had been advised, I dropped my agreement to extend and reenlisted for six years. I understood that a transfer to the 1st MarDiv was part of my reenlistment package. The reenlistment bonus was $60.00 for each year reenlisted, plus pay for sixty days of unused leave and leave rations, and a state of Virginia Mustering Out payment for the Korean War of $300.00. The total was $1645.00, more money than I had ever hoped to have at one time.

Military personnel paid income tax while assigned to duty in Japan; those in Korea did not. The fighting had stopped in Korea, but the communists were still rattling the saber, and combat benefits continued for all personnel assigned in Korea. My leaders sent me TAD to MAG 33 in Korea to exempt my income from tax for the month, including the reenlistment money. Allowing a Marine to do something that would save him money impressed me, another point of professionalism while swinging with the wing.

My orders for the 1st MarDiv were slow in coming. The answer to my inquiry was always, "Give it time, just hang on, it will come one of these days. You know how slowly the military system moves on personnel issues."

I learned much later that my squadron commander went to CMC requesting duty in Korea for me upon completion of my current tour, not as a reenlistment option to be effective upon reenlisting. Therefore, in October, when I had completed my year in MAG-11 and they would lose me anyway, I received orders to report to the CG, 1st MarDiv. On 22 October 1954, I checked out of the wing.

The personnel assignment sections at both division and regiment treated me right and assigned me as requested to 3rd Bn, 5th Marines. Battalion would not go along with my choice, however, and instead of Item Company, assigned me to George. The change was softened by the fact that George was short on rifle platoon sergeants. As a buck sergeant, I would be a squad leader in Item but stood a good chance of being a platoon sergeant in George. On 26 October, I became the Platoon Sergeant of 2nd Platoon, George Company with Lt Parrish as the Platoon Leader.

Other strong personalities in the platoon included: Cpl John Hinson, who had been the PltSgt and now was the right guide, and PFCs John Christen and Hilton E. Boyd, squad leaders. Christen and I would serve together again on the drill field. Cpl Donald J. Myers was a MG section leader. I would next see him as Major Myers serving at MB, 8th and I, where he was my escort when I received the Medal of Honor from President Nixon. He retired as a colonel and the CO of 8th and I Barracks.

Sergeant Shelton Lee Eakin was the 3rd PltSgt. If I used his name on every page of this book, I could not tell the complete Eakin story. He was the perfect example of a gungy Marine and everything for which the Marine Corps stands. Eakin's platoon leader was 2nd Lt W. E. McKinstry. The three of us would serve together five years later in 1st Force Reconnaissance Company, and again they would work a platoon. Mc Kinstry and I served together a third time in 1967 as Advisors to the Vietnamese Marine Corps. Second Lieutenant James J. McMonagle was a platoon leader in How Company. I would next serve with him at the Basic School where he was the S-3. He retired as a MajGen.

Our battalion was set up in a valley behind the Baker Block position, the first defensive position on our side of the Demilitarized Zone. We lived in a tent city where we slept, ate chow, and showered. Drill and tactical training were conducted in the dried, graded rice paddies. Our mission was to man the blocking positions should the North Koreans attack and continue the war. While most of us secretly hoped for some trigger time, the prospects did not look good.

We were roused from warm sleeping bags at all hours of the night. Then with great haste we made the one-hour climb up the ridge into our fighting positions thinking that maybe this was it. There we learned that "it was just a drill." These drills became a pain, and after a while they had a negative effect upon our readiness. We came to know that an alert would only be another drill and ceased taking them seriously.

Home for my Marines was an airy, dark, dirty canvas tent, one for each squad. Two kerosene stoves "heated" the tents and provided some heat for those positioned next to them. Otherwise, the heat quickly dissipated with the cold air moving through the tent. I soon learned that the major bitch of my Marines was the cold, ugly tent in which they had to survive. They knew that the army had liners, wooden decks, and hard backs in all of their tents. We should at least have the tent liners to help hold in the heat.

I attempted to educate my young Marines on how the DOD's money pie was sliced. Marines always get a small piece of money, material, and creature-comfort items. This slight has always been corrected by giving us a much larger portion of the combat load. So it evens out; all is fair. Meanwhile, a plan was forming: somehow, I would get tent liners.

"Not available" was the official word. Other platoon sergeants and the company gunny allowed that if liners were available, we would have them. The only Marines who had liners were those in the division CP; there simply were not enough to go around to the infantry units. "Yes, the Army had plenty of tent liners; all Army units had them."

The following morning I paid a call on our 1st Sergeant. MSgt Horwich listened and followed by offering me the use of his jeep, trailer, and driver. He seemed amused at my expressed purpose of getting tent liners. His patronizing attitude was, "take the jeep but do not expect favorable results." As he did not need the jeep, I suppose he chose the easiest way to teach me a lesson in the way things were done in George 3/5. I took the jeep and headed toward Seoul for the rear areas and the big Army camps.

My first stop was with an Army artillery battery set up with guns deployed. Yes, they had tent liners but no extra; their regimental supply at headquarters kept the excess. If I were to visit their supply officer, I probably could get some used liners. With directions and a point of contact, I was back on the road.

After some wrong turns (the dirt road system was not well marked), I located the supply area and found the Army willing to help the less fortunate. The captain could not believe that the Marine Corps expected us to get through the winter without liners in our tents. I did not want to break his good will by telling him how life continued in a Marine rifle squad through these Korean winters without even a tent.

His men dug out four of the best liners from a survey pile for turn-in or burn. Apologizing for some liners that might have some small tears in them and explaining why he could not give me new ones, he escorted me to his gate. He might be kindhearted, but he was not dumb. He probably had learned the hard way not to let a Marine loose in his supply dump.

My mission accomplished, I returned to George in high spirits. Not only did I get three liners for my Marines, I added one for my patronizing 1st Sergeant. The company gunny and he shared a squad tent, living on one end with their office set up on the other.

All three liners were up before dark and 2nd Platoon was full of visitors checking out the facts. The liners really made a difference in the inner tent area. The white material reflected the light from the two bare light bulbs and the heat from the two small stoves. There was now an overall clean, warm atmosphere to the tent home.

The liners were not only a hit with my Marines, but the rest of George focused on the 2nd Platoon Sergeant who took care of his Marines. "If 2nd Platoon can have tent liners, why can't we," became the cry. The affair raised a problem for my buddies, the other platoon sergeants. Right off, they wanted to know who and where for the liners. Unfortunately, we moved to Baker Block as scheduled before daylight the following morning for a four-day field exercise. By the time the platoon sergeants were ready, there were no liners available. My captain had sent all used liners to the rear. The other platoons never did get liners, but we learned that the division was returning to the States, so the pressing need went away.

Eakin quickly took Donahoo's place as my buddy. We competed with our platoons and tried to outdo each other in all that came our way. Eakin was younger and still on his first enlistment, a slick-arm sergeant, but in all ways he was every bit as capable and gungy as I. He deeply regretted having been too young for the shooting part of the Korean War, and freely acknowledged his respect for those he considered more fortunate with the Marine Badge of Combat, the Purple Heart.

Eakin was the first Marine I knew who asked for the rifleman MOS as his first choice of duty, as I did. We shared the same thoughts and beliefs on the role of the US Marine while preparing our platoons for when "Luke jumps." Marines referred to the enemy as Gooks; therefore, the enemy became known as "Luke the Gook." We wanted Luke to jump over the 38th Parallel and cross the DMZ in the attack. Our platoons were ready for a realistic evaluation of our ability to conduct warfare.

Eakin had just finished the division's NCO school and was far ahead of me in infantry tactics, book leadership, and especially in the technique of military instruction. He was good at the business of being a Marine; I watched him and borrowed his manuals. NCO School was on my Do List; I needed and wanted that school. As it turned out, however, I would never get the opportunity.

Despite his smooth-faced, youthful appearance, Eakin was a born leader. He seemed to do easily and naturally what I worked to achieve. Because I was close in age to most of my platoon members, I maintained a distance. I did not chance familiarity, probably because of my unsatisfactory experience during the war when I was promoted above my squad members in Item Company. I wanted the title of sergeant to be used with my last name. In the early and mid fifties, salty PFCs seldom used rank when addressing NCOs with whom they had become familiar.

Familiarity was not a problem with Eakin, although he was the same age as his Marines. He played football with them, giving no quarter and expecting none. He was roughed up because he was always right in the middle of everything, carrying the ball or otherwise. I have a picture of him with his boots high in the air, sticking out of a fifty-five-gallon fire barrel of water, as his Marines dunked him headfirst in celebration of the word that we were returning stateside. His Marines always addressed him as Sergeant Eakin and they loved him.

After knowing Eakin for several months and realizing that I had met one of my kind, I made the mistake of addressing him as Shelton. He quickly informed me that I was not to use his given name and went into a tirade about having to listen to the officers as they used first names while calling to each other in company formation. He thought that was a poor example of leadership, and he was going to do his part to ensure that the platoon sergeants did not put on the same show. Years later, as gunnies and with our families, he remained Eakin and I, Fox.

Two other sergeants, Otis Guy and James McBride, joined George during December with one going to guns and the other to tubes (mortars). They provided a spark in the weapons platoon. With Corporal Myers, who was shortly promoted to sergeant, the big weapons platoon came on line to give us some competition. George was ready for Luke.

The 5th Marine Regiment, which was the first to come over four and a half years earlier, was the first to return home. My company moved aboard the *USS Renville*. With several other ships mounting the regiment, the 5th sailed for San Diego on 27 February 1955.

I caught duty as a member of the embarked guard, which occupied my time. SOG duties kept me moving when we hit rough seas two days out. While everyone but my guard was pasted to their racks, we, like the sailors, had to function. Activity and responsibility helped combat seasickness; I avoided the greasy things on the chow line but stayed on the job. After three days, the ship settled down to slow rolls. Going home by ship did not suit me; twelve knots' speed plus playing Navy games wore down my patience. As I leaned on the deck rail and watched the slow-moving water below, I realized that flying home the first time had spoiled me.

Eighteen long days and nights gave us plenty of time to get our boots, utilities, and equipment ready for the San Diego parade. We entered San Diego harbor with a welcome committee of beautiful girls on water skis. We were going to be right among these lovely "round eyes."

We disembarked on 17 March and formed up in company-mass-front formations at close interval for our march up Broadway to Balboa Park. We formed up according to height with the word, "If you are taller than the Marine in front of you, move up." The other platoon sergeants, being taller, were maintaining their front rank positions while I was being reluctantly pushed toward the center.

Our CO, 1st Lt Lloyd, saved my ego by pulling me out of ranks to march as company Right Guide. This placed me up front with and to the right of the platoon leader rank. There was not a better enlisted position in the formation. I was pleased, especially being ahead of my tall buddies who were now lost in the first solid rank of the company formation. Smartly turned out in utilities starched by the ship's laundry, we marched at sling arms with fixed bayonets and wore helmets, cartridge belts, and a light marching pack.

Broadway was full of people, with police holding the crowd on the sidewalks, leaving the street to our broad four-platoon, sixteen-man, company front. I moved on air and did not feel a thing as we moved up the wide avenue. My position put me near the gutter on the right side of the street causing near bodily contact as the crowd would surge forward between passing companies.

A cop was trying to get the people back so he could get out of my line of march. He was not forceful enough, so I and the Marine behind me provided the force. Prepared for contact, my right shoulder and arm sent him crashing into the crowd. He rebounded into Eakin marching behind me for a repeat performance.

A left turn off Broadway put us in a climb to the park with no strain or pain. We were all on such a high that we floated up that hill unaware of an effort. The crowd showed their appreciation, and even the platoon bitchers had nothing bad to say. At the park, we were given the commands "Halt" and "Fall Out." More beautiful round eyes were serving coffee and doughnuts. We helped ourselves to the refreshments while moving among the people and talking with the young ladies.

The people said things like, "Thank you, Marines, we never would have made it in Korea if it had not been for you." Something nagged at me, however. I finally realized that my problem revolved around getting recognition and praise while most of the recipients had never heard a shot fired in anger. We were not returning from bleeding in that war; the Marines from 1950 through 1953 had done that. They were the ones who deserved the thanks and this parade. The senior sergeants, SNCOs, and officers with the rank of captain and above had been there earlier, so maybe it fit.

The fun ended with the word to board busses for the trip north to Camp Pendleton. With much hooting and howling out of the windows at the young women, we headed up US 101. Our new home, Camp San Margarita, turned out to be badly in need of tenants with good housekeeping habits. The place had been closed for sometime, so we did our Marine thing. After squaring away the camp, we continued with a company training schedule while half the command went on leave. I elected to take leave during the second half, which would give me time to get myself and 2nd Platoon squared away.

I planned to pick up Eakin's car, as he had gone home to Texarkana in December on his reenlistment leave. Like most Marines, Eakin invested his reenlistment money in a new car: in his case a 1955 model 98 Oldsmobile with full power. Then he returned to Korea only to come stateside two months later. He did not plan to take leave and wanted me to bring his car back from Texarkana. Using his need to my benefit, he agreed that I should pick it up on my way to Virginia. What a deal and what a dream boat!

Daily company training during this leave and transition time was light. A short hike was scheduled for the few who could be collected while Marines checked in and out on leave. George Company (without me, as my leave had started) had just returned from a morning hike and went to chow.

In uniform and with suitcase in hand, I had almost reached the barracks door when a huge explosion rattled the windows. Rushing to the door, I looked out upon a street full of prone Marines in front of the mess hall. My company had been standing in the chow line; now they were all down. Fortunately, they were on the deck because that is where Marines go when explosions happen close to them.

I remained long enough to learn that about a half-dozen Marines were hurt, none seriously. Corpsmen were already on the scene, and there was no threat to the company, so I made my bird. I had been a Marine long enough to know that whatever happened would require an investigation, and no one would be going on leave. After I spent a few concerned minutes at the bus stop, the Oceanside bus arrived and I was on my way.

I learned later that one of our "not-too-smarts" while on the hike that morning had picked up and pocketed something like a 20mm round of ammunition. Playing with it in the chow line, he dropped it and it exploded. He received the most injuries, losing some toes.

Also hurt, though not physically, were those in positions of leadership. They were found responsible for the cause of the accident because they had not given a "Dud" lecture. Base standing orders required Marines to be given a safety brief on dud ammunition before going into the field. Sgt McBride, the sergeant in charge of the hike, took a hit; he was the senior sergeant because my leave had started. Both company and battalion commanders were relieved of command.

A hop in a Navy plane out of Long Beach placed me in Corpus Christi; from there, I hitchhiked to Texarkana. The most memorable thing about the trip was crossing Texas. An older Texan, giving me a ride in his dusty, old pickup truck, asserted that it was humanly impossible to cross Texas in one night. He almost had me believing him, as the night dragged on with short distance, local rides. Thanks to a big-rig truck driver with a load of logs bound for Shreveport, I made it. It was midmorning by the time I bussed into Texarkana. I spent the night with Eakin's folks and then hit the road for Virginia.

My dad had sold the farm when it became clear that I was not returning. I had to find our new home, now somewhere east of Aldie, a thirty-minute drive from the farm. Being home on leave, especially with a new 98 Oldsmobile, was great, and as always, it did not last long enough.

Sgt Don Myers, of our Gun Platoon, was on leave in Baltimore, and as planned, I picked him up for our return to Pendleton. I was surprised when Don informed me that he had never driven a car and of course had no driver's license. I was counting on his help at driving and planned my leave to allow for a straight-through drive on our return. Now our options were to call in for a leave extension, be absent-over-leave, or for me to drive straight through.

I drove that night, the next day until midnight, and gave the wheel to Don. (There were no interstate highways then; we traveled on US 40 and 66.) We had talked about driving all day, and Don learned fast. Moreover, that full-powered, automatic Oldsmobile only required a little guidance in direction, and it did all the rest. We made it to Camp Pendleton with him driving when I needed sleep, usually in the early morning hours when he had the highway to himself.

The regiment became serious about training after our leave cycle ended. Our battalion was the helo-assault force for an amphibious exercise that took place in May. The Marine Corps wanted data and experience with the vertical assault concept. At the time I wondered about the force buildup ashore, as the choppers, early model HUSs, could haul only two to three combat-loaded Marines, depending on the heat of the day. Nevertheless, we were developing a new assault technique and were excited to ride the choppers. After our air assault into the Case Springs area we reverted to the aggressor force role and took on the rest of the regiment.

Eakin had a particularly good time when he moved his platoon behind the good guy's line and ravaged a battalion CP. He captured that BnCmdr, but the LtCol would not play the game and pulled his rank. The only notable thing my platoon accomplished was a long, hot hike from Case Springs to San Margarita in record time at the close of the exercise.

The word came down that the Recruit Depots needed Drill Instructors (DIs), and I applied. On 5 August 1955, I transferred from the division and started DI School. Captain Frank R. Kothe was the OIC, and TSgt "Daddy" (I'll-unscrew-your-head-and-shit-in-it) Lyons was the Chief Drill Instructor.

Never having done well academically, I was motivated to learn in this school. I wanted to know the ins and outs of drill and to be a good

DI. To accomplish this goal, I became deeply involved with each subject as it was presented. For the first time, I took a seat in the front of the classroom.

Most of the thirty-plus students were corporals and sergeants; three were staff sergeants, and one was a technical sergeant. TSgt McGuire was our class leader by virtue of his rank. I worked hard to graduate first in that school but ended placing third behind Sgt Moore (who deserved to be first) and McGuire. Nevertheless, I was pleased: I handled the academic load, and I knew our LPM drill.

While in DI School, I applied for OCS as a result of the efforts of some officers in 3/5, primarily Lt Mazarov, my last platoon leader, who strongly encouraged me to seek a commission. My reasoning was that platoon sergeant was the last good job for an enlisted man in a rifle company. The role of company gunny and 1st sergeant did not interest me; they were too far removed from the action elements, the rifle squads. As a platoon leader, I would be right back with the heart of the word Marine. Several months later, in the 1st Recruit Training Battalion (RTB), my sergeant major delighted in informing me that I did not score high enough on the test to be competitive for officer rank.

Graduating from DI School on 16 September, I reported to the 1st RTB with further assignment to Company B. Upon checking into the company office, I received an eye-opening introduction to the way things would be in my new job. As I approached the Quonset Hut office, the door burst open, a recruit flew through the air, and landed on the sidewalk in front. Immediately behind him was a yelling Marine with many stripes on his sleeves. This TSgt proceeded to jump up and down on the recruit's chest while reminding him of the proper way to address DIs. My four weeks of training went down the tube. I had accepted the school's word that things had changed on the field, that DIs were not allowed to and did not touch a recruit.

Lt Earnest C. Cheatham Jr. was my company commander. He played football for the recruit depot, however, and I would not see him until the end of ball season. I was assigned as a second junior DI with a Sgt Richards who enjoyed the reputation of being the best on the field. Richards' fame came from the fact that his platoon usually took the honor flag upon graduation. He was obviously the man to beat, and after a few days with him, I decided that it would not be a problem.

Richards and I did not hit it off well. He made several comments about my appearance, ending with the point that after a little time on the field, the spit shine and creases would disappear. Maybe he saw me as a threat to his way of playing the Marine game; he seemed to lead the clique of scruffy boots and wrinkled uniforms.

Appearance is not all there is to being a Marine, but I was disappointed in the sloppy presentation of some DIs. They crapped out during the day and slept fully clothed on their duty racks, then rose and went about their business with a no fuss and no hassle personal appearance. Keeping a uniform squared away required a little more time, which I took from my sleeping time.

Later, my second company commander, 1st Lt Frank R. Pirman, would write the following comment on my Fitness Report for the period 1 October 1955 to 31 January 1956.

> Sgt Fox is one of the few NCOs that I have seen that maintains his appearance at the optimum 100% of the time. His bearing and leadership inspire the men under him to perform outstandingly.

Richards did not have to put up with me for very long. The recruit depot received its annual flood of recruits. DIs were in short supply, and I received my own platoon, a mere three weeks out of DI School.

I picked up Platoon 181 alone, and for the first three weeks, I worked it without a junior DI. While this was day-on-and-stay-on duty, I loved it. Actually, I probably would have been around as much even with a junior because this platoon was mine. It was going to be the best on the field, and my recruits would become the best Marines in the Corps. Only those deserving the title Marine would make it through the course.

Overall they were a good bunch of young men, but there were some who could not handle the stress. Those who could not think on their feet with me in their faces did not belong in my Corps. I set about getting rid of the unsuitables; recruit stress, both individually and collectively, was on a high. The first objective amounted to shocking the recruit out of his civilian habits, thoughts, needs, desires, and even his manner of speaking. First-week recruits understood that they were a failure in any and everything they attempted. Even their parents had done a miserable job in bringing them to this point in their young lives. As Cpl Reiser had so often reminded me, the recruit was lower than whale shit and that was on the bottom of the ocean.

Communicating was a big stress factor because the recruit was required to speak in the third person. The words "I" and "you" were strictly forbidden, which required a recruit to think closely before he spoke. A recruit wanting to speak to his DI first requested permission to do so: "Sir, Private Burke requests permission to speak to the Drill Instructor, Sir." Told to speak, he might continue with, "Sir, Private Burke has misplaced Private Burke's *Guidebook for Marines,* Sir."

Some recruits had a problem dropping the "I's" and "you's"—that added to their stress level. The DI's response would be something like, "YOU! You call me a EWE. Do I look like a female sheep to you, asshole? Are you plainly stupid? Can you not speak properly?" The DI's first objective of breaking down the civilian was reached quickly enough with all of the screaming and yelling, especially with physical enforcement.

Next was the slower process of building Marines from the civilian wrecks. Recruits' acceptance of the fact that they could not do anything right hindered the build up. Some recruits could not handle the transition, but the majority was being molded in steel. The eagle, globe, and anchor found its way into their hearts, and there it would be forever.

Long hours were spent teaching the elements of COD, and one man's voice is not equal to the task. Voice projection and the constant use of my voice caused me to lose it. After the first week, my screws had to strain to hear my bullfrog croaks, but there was no change in our schedule. (DIs called recruits screws in reference to their continuous screw-ups.)

I lived in my duty hut (the 1st Bn was billeted in Quonset Huts: my recruits filled six huts, and I shared another with other DIs for the duty hut) and ate my meals in the recruit mess. I put my screws to bed and I got them up. My personal time was while my recruits slept, which also was my sleep time. Taps usually went about 2200, or later, depending on what I wanted to do with my platoon.

Head facilities were limited. In order to make the morning chow schedule and get the day started right, I held reveille about 0330, never later than 0400. My interest was getting my screws in the heads before the other platoons. There was a constant problem of getting out of the heads so the platoon responsible for cleanup could get their work done and eat chow before the schedule started.

Other than chow time and academic classes, a platoon's schedule was left to the individual DI. As there was no higher authority among the DIs, I could not get anything done by suggesting that we all move our reveille two hours later. The Chief Drill Instructor was no help; he was of the opinion that nothing was broken, which was based upon his 0800 to 1630 involvement. Everyone would agree to start the day later, but the next morning, each DI tried to beat his buddy to the heads. So, recruits fought sleep and slept in the hot classrooms while DIs caught up on their sleep by crapping out on their duty rack in full uniform.

Help came. Sergeant J. H. Van Ness joined me to serve as my junior during the later part of the third week. He was with me two days when he was yanked to pick up his own platoon from the receiving barracks. I was promised help from the series graduating that week.

The Staff Sergeant Selection List had my name on it. I was a senior sergeant, which meant that I would put the rocker (the lower stripe) on shortly. I enjoyed my service as a sergeant but looked forward to joining the ranks of the real professionals, the backbone of the Corps.

Lessons Learned

1. Integrity, dedication, and enthusiasm pave the road of leadership.
2. Professionalism has a flavor; do all you can to improve the taste.
3. Most young people do better if left alone to accomplish their assigned task.

5
Staff Sergeant
1128290/0369/8511

1 October 1955

LtCol Ralph Wisner promoted me to staff sergeant in his office on 28 October 1955. This promotion brought a significant change in my Marine life as Staff NCOs lived in their own barracks, two to a cubicle. In addition, I was now not only knowledgeable and responsible enough to know if a uniform fit me, but I could determine the fit of uniforms for others. An officer or staff NCO was required to verify the fit of uniforms purchased by sergeants and below. That reenlistment money, which had been sitting in the bank for over a year, was ready for a fit also.

When the first 1956 automobiles hit the dealership, I bought my Korean War dream, although five years later. A Mercury Montclair convertible with full power became mine for $3600 cash through Fedmart in San Diego. Of course, a DI with a new car caused many eyeballs to roll with suggestions of recruit financial dealings. The inference really picked up a year later, when I traded the Merc in on a 1957 Super 88 Oldsmobile.

Another eye-catcher in the fifties was people running for no purpose. Running for physical fitness in this era was not a common practice among Marines. The little running that did take place happened during boot camp as punishment. Usually, the DI stood in one spot on the parade field and ran his platoon in a large circle around him.

Drill gets boring after hours of the same routine, but I could always get heel rhythm and a snap in the step from my screws with a suggestion that I was ready for a run. They knew what to expect when I marched them west toward the 3rd RTB. There was nothing for us in the area, and the sand flats lay beyond. After the first introduction to the sand run, my recruits were motivated not to return. I liked to run along the Convair fence where it did not take long to drop the entire platoon. The sand flats were isolated from prying eyes, just my screws and me. I differed from the norm in that I ran with my platoon.

DIs had special methods of getting a recruit's attention in 1955. One way was to close a thumb and forefinger on the recruit's throat. Any type of screw-up had the DI in the recruit's face with his throat the target. Discipline could be measured by whether a recruit would pass out before he raised his hands to resist the grip. Seldom did a recruit hit the deck, but just as seldom did a recruit attempt to raise his hands.

When a recruit screwed up in a major way, his DI might bring him into the duty hut for a special treat. The recruit stood on a field desk with a ten quart, sand-filled, iron fire bucket placed at his feet. He was told to drop his trousers and drawers and was provided with a short strong cord. Next, he was directed to tie one end of the cord securely to the fire bucket bail. For the recruit's benefit, the DI would place the bucket on the deck, stretch the cord up, and cut it at the recruit's feet. With the bucket back on the table, the recruit was told to tie the free end of the cord securely around his scrotum. The DI jerked the cord to ensure a good knot, causing the recruit to get the picture. A tight, secure blindfold was next, then instructions to kick the bucket off the table when ordered.

Apologies and pleadings usually followed the order to kick. No one ever kicked the bucket off the first time despite much yelling of the command "Kick" by the DI. Some recruits pleaded before each kick, as the bucket moved closer to the edge. Others would give the bucket a mighty kick as they sought relief from the DI's verbal attack. After applying the blindfold, the DI cut the string to the bucket, ensuring that no harm came to the recruit. The expression on the recruit's face as the bucket crashed onto the deck told the whole story. The power that a DI enjoyed in the early fifties was not healthy for the Marine Corps. We were to find out just how unhealthy within the year.

Help came; after three weeks alone, Cpl Coleman and his dog, Freto, joined me for our move to the rifle range at Camp Matthews and were with me for the remainder of Platoon 181's time. The duty now demanded less effort from a DI than in the first three weeks. At the range the Primary Marksmanship Instructor (PMI) took over during working hours and gave the DIs some slack. The later weeks were also easier because the recruits knew the routine and what was expected of them.

Eakin and John Christen followed me to the drill field and were enrolled in DI School while I had Platoon 181. Knowing that Eakin would visit me, I prepared his welcome. A recruit named Burke was from Arkansas; I instructed Burke that anytime and anywhere he heard the word Arkansas, he was to crow like a rooster. Further, if there was anything upon which he could climb, he was to break ranks, climb up, flap his arms like wings, and crow. I gave him plenty of rehearsal time, and redheaded Burke became good at sounding like a rooster.

Burke's rooster instruction came during the third week of training, and it was the first occasion that my screws saw anything other than serious Marine business from me. As such, the event served as a relief valve for all; occasionally, I heard and ignored a snicker among the platoon members. Burke seemed to enjoy the attention, and he knew my purpose for the game.

Eakin visited me at the rifle range on a Sunday and my screws were busy in their tents cleaning rifles and working on their gear. Showing Eakin through my area, I sounded off with "Arkansas." Burke did a first-rate job of mounting his tent's wooden strong back, flapping, and crowing. Eakin, however, always dead serious, did not seem to appreciate my attempt at humor and made no comment.

Platoon 181 became known at the Range for having a rooster in its ranks; our PMI used the Arkansas command quite often. On our qualification day, it all came home to bite me. While Burke was firing a slow-fire string, someone, and I am sure it was one of my DI competitors, yelled "Arkansas." I did not want to believe what I was seeing as Burke, with his rifle strapped to his arm, rose from his firing position, flapped his arms, and crowed. He lost firing time getting back into position and messed up his concentration. While he fired a qualifying score, he could have done much better. The platoon that did better at the range was well on its way to being the honor platoon, thus the DI's interest in the interruption of concentration along my firing line. Burke's reaction no doubt affected other recruits firing next to him. I never played the game again.

Platoon 181 dropped three at the range: Three recruits failed to fire a qualifying score with the M-1 rifle. They had one chance to qualify but could graduate from recruit training anyway. Dropping only three was good, as most platoons dropped twice that number. However, we placed second within our three competing platoons.

Naturally, I had the answer for our placement of second: platoons with easy DIs did well at the range because they had little discipline. DIs in general did not stress their screws at the range so that they would fire better rifle scores. Strict, hammer-hand discipline, and the relaxed, confident atmosphere of shooting a rifle did not go well together.

This relaxed discipline sometimes allowed odd things to happen. I learned from Burke that a recruit must buy toilet paper if he wanted to use any while making a head call. The going price was twenty-five cents for five wraps around the hand. Looking into the matter, I found that certain recruits in another platoon owned the toilet paper and were making a large profit. Several platoons were assigned the same head for use; the cleaning responsibility rotated between the users. Toilet paper would be in the holders for the DI's morning inspection, but afterwards it would disappear. I went to the Range Officer with a plan to flood the area with toilet paper. Besides having a roll replaced the instant it was missed in the heads, we issued a roll to each squad to keep in their tents. The problem went away.

Upon completing DI School, Eakin went to the 3rd RTB, and Christen joined me. We worked together for most of my two years on the field. Christen's assignment to my team meant that Platoon 181 recruits were oversupervised. All three of us were single and work-oriented; we spent most of our time with the platoon and in the duty hut. As such, it was a good time to revisit DI School.

The officers leading the Marine Corps the year before had decided to change our COD. Instead of the current drill known as the Landing Party Manual (LPM) Drill that had been around since the buildup for World War II, we would do the 8-Man Squad Drill referred to as Squads Right Drill. The LPM Drill is column, flanking, and to-the-rear movements, causing the ranks and files to face in the different directions of march with different Marines in the front on each movement. Less complicated, LPM Drill is more easily taught and learned. The Squads Right Drill was old Corps stuff, dating back to the time when men fought standing in ranks. This drill includes squad turns, right or left, squads right or left front into line, and squads right or left about for a movement to the rear. Squad drill always has the same rank of Marines facing forward or in the direction of march and squad members' positions never change in relation to each other.

The Drill Manual was rewritten, and eighteen months later DIs went back to school for one week to learn the new drill. My week came during 181's ninth week of training. The new drill proved more difficult for recruits to learn, which was probably a big reason it did not stay. Soldiering today is more involved than merely filling a rifleman position within the rank and file. There is more to learn besides COD: weapons, tactics, employment of supporting arms, individual protective measures, land navigation, and first aid are a few that make time a key factor. If a Marine has to be proficient in all areas, at what point is he overloaded?

Platoon 181 did not have to learn the new drill; they would get it at their next command. I worked hard with my platoon in COD, and my screws performed well on the drill field. They marched so well and looked so sharp that I, upon occasion, enjoyed catching other DIs watching us march to chow or to class. We won the drill competition easily, which made 181 the Honor Platoon. Sixty-three of the original seventy-five members of Platoon 181 graduated as Marines.

The platoon had departed MCRD when I found a paper bag containing money known as flight pay in my car. I divided the bag's contents three ways; that gave each of us close to a hundred dollars. It was obvious that if a DI's screws liked him or at least respected him, he did not have to work the financial dealings and stage gimmicks such as fake weddings.

Platoon 107, which Christen and I picked up immediately upon 181's departure, was my next challenge. It was normal in that era to pick up a new platoon a week or more before graduating the old; the pick-up timing was a break in itself. Two platoons allowed no breaks with a DI working each.

All DIs were now teaching the Squads Right Drill, eight men in two ranks. The front rank execution movements were turns right or left as in LPM drill. The rear rank individual steps, however, were a problem. Each of the rear rank members had specific steps to take, including obliques, turns, and mark time, depending upon the movement. When the movement initiates, the rear rank looks like a fire drill but quickly comes on line behind the front rank that is marking time.

Some recruits were slow in learning the specific rear rank steps. Compounding this difficulty was the requirement that each member of the squad know the steps in all positions for each movement. An absence required a position move from the two center-rear-rank positions. Fewer than six squad members made the drill impractical. Platoon 107 screws worked hard learning the new drill.

While at the rifle range, word came that Capt G. C. Koontz, the Bn S-3, would be up the following day to look into an allegation that I had made a recruit eat his vomit. Pvt Gresehammer had written home to impress a friend with what he was going through. His friend thought that Mrs. Gresehammer ought to know; she in turn passed her concern to her congressman. Therefore, my first of two congressional inquiries was underway.

The facts were that a DI caught another recruit, Colburn, at the poggy bait machines filling his pockets with candy bars. The area was off limits to recruits, who were not to have candy. Because Colburn wanted candy, I ordered him to eat it. The usual routine was to eat the complete bar, paper, and all with a canteen of warm water to help get it down. He did vomit and I did order him to lick it up and eat it right. But, when he went down, and I was satisfied that he was about to do so, I pulled him back to his feet. He did not eat any vomit, but he must have enjoyed telling the story.

Upon getting the phone call, Christen brought Gresehammer to the duty hut. He admitted to wanting to impress his friend with the Colburn story. Gresehammer's letter conveyed the fact that he experienced the event rather than Colburn. Koontz talked with Gresehammer and other members of his squad, and found that Gresehammer had dreamed up the whole affair to impress his friend back home. I was cleared of any wrongdoing.

Colonel Henry P. (Jim) Crowe, the base Chief of Staff, provided some duties not covered by DI School. The premier of *Hold Back the Night,* a Korean War movie starring William Holden, was to take place in Oceanside. In addition to showing the movie, Camp Pendleton's Commanding General invited Hollywood down for an Open House and an all-day Dog and Pony show. Among the movie stars were two young starlets who would have personal escorts and be given the red carpet treatment. Two NCOs would be the escorts, Pendleton providing one and Diego the other. Crowe appointed a board of WMs[16] to select the DI for Diego's escort from the candidates submitted by the three battalions. From the three finalists, one of whom was Eakin, I was selected for the extra duty.

I reported in khakis and carried my blues for the evening affair. Pendleton assigned a corporal to escort Cleo Moore; my starlet was Joi Lansing. We were a foursome for the entire day and evening. Senior Marines made way upon our approach, which added to our feeling of importance. This was my first time with a celebrity or as part of a special group, and it was pure enjoyment. I played the role, and Joi and I hit it off well. She invited me to her place in Hollywood two weekends away.

One should not make an idle invitation to a Marine; I kept our date. We were both surprised: me in catching her with her hair down and in a bathing suit while cleaning her apartment and she in my showing up. She had said the words and forgotten the affair but handled it like a Marine and gave me her day.

First, she took me to her mother's home, then to a male friend's apartment to cancel their evening plans. A sightseeing tour of Hollywood followed, including a walk through some movie studios and lunch in a place well above my pay grade. We walked, looked, and talked, and I got the picture. Joi was repaying me for what I had done for her. She also helped me see that I wanted no part of her lifestyle. Joi convinced me that there were no real men in Hollywood, including John Wayne; she related a personal experience with my Hollywood hero that would not help sell movie tickets. According to her, Hollywood males had no respect for females, and again Wayne received the brunt of her criticism. I enjoyed a full day in Hollywood but was relieved to be southbound on 101 later that night. As it would not do for me to return to my barracks on the same day that I left for my big Hollywood weekend, I spent the night in a motel on 101.

DIs had a free hand to do their thing, their way, but the DI and recruit life was about to change. On 8 April 1956 Staff Sergeant Matthew C. McKeon took his mob of recruits on a night march through a tidal body of water near the Parris Island Rifle Range.[17] Six recruits drowned that night, some while heroically saving others. What followed in the next six months changed the way the Corps would do business at the two recruit depots forever. McKeon screwed it up for all of us on the field (my thoughts at the time). I was convinced that without our DI brand of discipline, Marines would never perform in combat as they had throughout history. They would lack the will to hang onto the hill, to take the beach, or stick with any other difficult mission that placed them in harm's way. I was to learn differently in the Vietnam War, but that was some eleven years away.

The New Corps, if there ever was such a thing, surely received its start with the McKeon shakeup. The rite of passage from civilian to Marine continued to happen at the recruit depots; the DIs had to learn another way of performing the rite. The new way was not much different from what was already taught in DI School; the application of training at the platoon and company level saw a major overhaul. It has been aptly stated that, old breed or new breed, it does not matter as long as they are the Marine breed. The big question was, were we turning out the Marine breed?

McKeon suffered his court martial and paid his dues, but he was no more responsible for Ribbon Creek than the leadership at all levels. The DIs' working environment and our individual mental attitudes set the stage. Something equally as bad and deadly could have happened to any number of us, as there were no limits to our power over recruits. Many DIs exercised that power in unacceptable ways, unacceptable not only to our society but equally ill-suited for those who profess to be leaders of men. DIs needed guidance, direction, and boundaries, someone on hand to say, "NO!" The Commandant, General Randolph Mc-Call Pate, provided just that.

Brigadier General Alan Shapley, with a flood of company and field grades officers, was ordered to MCRD, San Diego, to set up and command the new Recruit Training Command (RTC). He reported to the CG MCRD with the sole duty of supervising recruit training and leading DIs. The old Raider met his challenge head-on, meeting all DIs in the base theater. Just as he had handled the enemy in the Pacific during WW II, he laid it on the line; there would be no compromise of his objective.

There was a new set of rules for this old game, and those of us who could not accept that fact and play by his rules were transferred as of that moment. Shapley cautioned us to think seriously about his words because we could leave now with a good record and move on to a good job. Stay and violate his rules, and he would ensure a court martial with no second chances.

The general continued with his requirements: There would be recruit rights forthcoming, and if necessary, an entirely new way of making Marines. There would be no abuse of any recruit, in any manner, physically or mentally, including his name or his money. If necessary, all DIs would be replaced and an entirely new group of Marine NCOs brought in to do the job. He would go to the Army for help if he had to; that threat really caught our attention. Either way was suitable to him; this depot would make Marines his way. I heard his message; there was a change.

A company-grade officer was assigned as Series Officer over several DI teams, with responsibility to ensure compliance with regulations and schedules. After the shock of having an officer looking over my shoulder, I learned that the addition was not all bad. He got things done. Instead of the usual excuses regarding something needed, we received the goods.

The RTC staff conducted studies to determine how to make the DI's job easier and reduce DI stress. All bitches and complaints were considered; consequently, we received free uniforms, laundry, dry cleaning, and a unique DI uniform.

Initially the DI uniform was the green uniform scarf worn around the neck under an open shirt collar. This changed within the year to the campaign hat, known as the Smoky Bear. Special DI incentive pay followed a year later. Three DIs assigned to each platoon (requiring a twenty-four-hour duty only every third day) provided the greatest help, especially for married Marines.

The current staffing level of two DIs per platoon was unacceptable; however, there were not enough DIs. Until DI School could train the number needed, Staff NCOs from throughout the Corps were ordered TAD to the two MCRDs as the third members of the DI teams. Many of these Staff NCOs had the 8511 MOS from an earlier DI tour, but just as many had never been on the drill field.

One DI gripe was that we now had no manner of punishing deserving recruits, which caused a morale problem when others observed that nothing was done to non-performers. RTC's answer was to establish a Disciplinary Platoon at the RTC level.

DIs could award recruits up to three days with the Disciplinary Platoon. A side benefit for the DI was that a three-day loss in training set the recruit back a week; DIs shed their unwanted people. The negative side was that they picked up trash from the series ahead. The idea worked well under the watchful eyes of Captain James L. Day, who worked out of the RTC G-3 section.

SSgt James Giles and I were selected to run the Disciplinary Platoon. Our daily routine was one hour of calisthenics and one hour on the obstacle course, repeated throughout the eight-hour day. Three days of that routine made believers out of the screw-ups. Giles and I split the day with one leading for a four-hour session and doing everything with the recruits, while the other corrected and ensured that all recruits did the events properly. Four hours of that routine was all I wanted! The word on the platoon got around; recruits would do anything to avoid it. The DIs had some clout for a short time.

The San Diego Tribune received word of this special platoon and sent a reporter out to do a story. Giles and I gave him some good background pictures under the watchful eyes of Capt Day. The story was never printed, however, as the platoon became history the day after the reporter's visit. Jim and I returned to our companies with Day's explanation that higher leadership had decided that the Corps did not need the publicity. The DI's clout had lasted less than a month.

About this time, the Marine Corps came out with its first Physical Fitness Test. Along with pull-ups, push-ups, sit-ups, and other events were the 440- and 880-yard runs. Marines under thirty years of age had to run the 440 within a specified time; those over thirty merely had to get around the track two times, walking or running. It was a pass or fail event and nothing much came of it, as we were not motivated to do more.

With national attention focused on Marine boot camp, it followed that Hollywood would capitalize on the public interest. Jack Webb and staff appeared at MCRD with the stated purpose of learning the DI role and duty. Webb would select DIs to play parts in his upcoming movie, *The DI*. The Marine Corps supported this effort; DIs not on duty were told to report to the base theater.

Webb talked to us, saying that he wanted to tell our story. His staff took over and directed all DIs from the South to collect in one corner of the theater. Directions followed for other groups, breaking the mass down into a manageable size. From the Southerners, one DI was needed to play the role of a recruit named Hillbilly.

We each took a small screen test in front of a group of selectors that included Webb. TSgt Love of Company C landed the part of Hillbilly. Sgt Peter J. O'Neill of my company received the role of Rodriguez. (O'Neill was with me in MAG-11 in 1954.) Several other Marines were selected; they spent six weeks in Hollywood and each received an engraved wristwatch from Jack Webb.

After the Ribbon Creek incident my recruits probably received as much constructive time from me as my earlier recruits, but the duty hours alone made a difference. Full twenty-four-hour duty every third day provided the only evenings with my recruits. Evening hours are DI time; this is when the little things pass between a DI and his recruits. However, off-duty DIs were not allowed in the recruit area after the normal workday. We had the day off following night duty and the other day of the three we worked eight to ten hours. Compared to Platoon 181, this was a major change. How could I make Marines out of these screws when I was never around them? When officers asked, I told them: we were not making Marines. Captain John B. Harris, my CO, spelled it out in his change of reporting senior report. This report for the period 1 February 1957 to 1 April 1957 stated in section D:

> S/Sgt Fox is a shining example of what every Marine should
> be in military bearing and neatness. He is an excellent drill
> instructor and outstanding NCO. Almost two years on the drill
> field has taken its toll and although now excellent, he was
> once outstanding.

The Series Officer's assistant was a Technical or Master Sergeant and called the Series Gunny. My Series Gunny was Technical Sergeant John Bell, an older, experienced Marine of the motor transport field. Bell understood me and appreciated may manner and method of work. We would later serve together in 1st Force Recon Company.

The drill field had lost its glamour in spite of media presentations about DIs and recruit training; two years on the field was enough. Wanting to see the other side, to be the one sending these potential Marines to the DI, I applied for Recruiters School. Orders came and on 16 August

1957, my Super 88 was eastbound on US Route 66. I stopped in Brownwood, Texas, to visit with Wild Bill Donahoo, now a town policeman. Bill had calmed down, married, and he and Boots had started their family.

Following leave, I reported to Recruiters School at Parris Island on 6 September 1957. This was my first visit to this hellhole since I graduated from boot camp, but now I saw it in a different light, and got even with the sand fleas. Recruiters School was less demanding than DI school. For starters, it was a bigger class; it would graduate fifty as compared to twenty-seven in DI School. Seventy Marines reported, but attrition started on day one because of individual financial problems. Drill and clothing inspections were a snap for an ex-DI, but public speaking and typing captured my full attention.

Ex-DIs had a problem with public speaking because of their stiff military manner of presentation. Capt John Elm Smith, the OIC, wanted us to appear relaxed, "to put a hand in a pocket, and let it all hang out." That took some adjustment, as my training had been that Marines never place their hands in uniform pockets. SSgt Duke Miller, who had been a DI with me at San Diego, and I worked at it and became better at presenting what the captain wanted to see. To graduate, one also had to have a twenty-words-a-minute proficiency in typing, a requirement that took some work for those of us starting with a zero capability. Six weeks of school passed; on 19 October 1957, I graduated with a standing of 14 of 50.

One recruiter billet was open in each recruiting district, so the honor man could be assigned to the area of his choice. The needs of the Corps determined the assignment of others. The graduates with the higher class standings had the first choices of the districts still available. There was one opening in the 5th District that included Virginia. Fortunately for me, none of the thirteen ranked above me wanted it, so I got my first choice. My recruiting station was Baltimore, Maryland, with substations in DC and Northern Virginia.

Checking in on 23 October was a new experience. First, I had to fight the downtown traffic, and, while doing that, find the city post office, my new CP. Then came the search for a place to park my Olds and stay somewhere near.

Major Rayford K. "Scoop" Adams was the OIC, and the chief recruiter was MSgt William H. Ewing. My recruiting job was that of a canvasser, meaning that I was out beating the bushes. My area was all of southwest Baltimore, including Catonsville and Arbutus.

I planned to rent an apartment, but the chief suggested that initially I move into Marine House, the home of a Mrs. Dodd. She ran a boarding house; four Marines lived with her. The cost of a room and two meals a day was $100.00 per month, exactly what I was getting for that purpose, except that it was one meal per day short. A phone call confirmed that she had room, and I accepted for the quick fix.

Given a 1949 Chevy sedan that also served as my office, I was on my own. The station's four canvassers did not have a specific quota but contributed their share to the station's quota. MSgt Talbert was the walk-in recruiter at the main station, and as might be expected, his name appeared with the most applicants shipped. The Top asked the walk-in if he had talked with another recruiter; if he did not come up with a name, the Top's shipped-list grew by one more name.

I quickly accomplished my first objective of locating an apartment. Finding one in Arbutus that fit my needs and cost, I offered the second bedroom to SSgt Thomas G. Roberts. Tom and I set up housekeeping in a furnished second-floor apartment in a modified row house. Our cost was half what we had been paying Mrs. Dodd. Now, though, we had to cook, and this was before electric crockpots.

Locating the hangouts of young people was not difficult; acceptance by them was the challenge. I had to get involved in young men's activities. The ice cream parlor across the road from the Catonsville High School was a hangout for juniors and seniors. Hotrods, pretty girls, and young men who needed to experience Parris Island made up the scene.

My Marine dress blues became a regular addition to the happenings at the parlor, but what really broke the ice was my car. Young male interest at the time was in hotrods, souped-up cars, and hitting the speed of sixty in the shortest time. I usually parked my recruiting sedan and drove up in my Super 88 Oldsmobile with the owner-installed Mercury fender skirts and continental kit. Super 88s the year before had made a name for themselves in the quarter mile; the 57s were no slackers, even with nothing extra under the hood. All red-blooded young men wanted to see under my hood; I was in.

My sales approach was a subtle one to this high school crowd. Several voiced their surprise that I was not trying to recruit them and exhibited disbelief when I informed them that I would not let them enter my Corps without a high school education. I did not directly seek those attending school but let the overall environment of the blue uniform, the cool car, and acceptance by the crowd of young people do the selling. Past graduates and dropouts were fair game.

I was selling the Corps for the recruiter one and two years away, who might be me. At the time, I was not shipping anyone, but I was kindling an interest and building a pool of applicants. Names, addresses, and phone numbers were adding to my prospect list. Christmas was coming up; the young men whom I wanted in my Corps had the kind of family love, devotion, and loyalty to want to spend it at home. I understood that need, but my boss had other thoughts.

In December, Ewing informed me that I was to report to the Major. Adams was concerned because I had not shipped anyone during my two months on the street. Top Ewing spoke up for me, but the Major read me the act, anyway. His bottom line was, "Either you start shipping bodies (I really am not concerned about quality, as the district commander only knows if I did or did not fill my station quota) or I am shipping you. Moreover, you will be headed for the FMF."

Well, the FMF was nothing with which to threaten me. I would gladly change this downtown work for duty in the field, anywhere. He also did not seem to put much stock in my response that my applicants wanted to spend Christmas at home. Belief in me was the difference between the major and Ewing. My semiannual fitness report of 31 January 1958 for a three-month period reflected the major's opinion of me with a General Value to the Service mark of Average. He allowed in section D that I was new to the business and trying hard.

My young guys and gals came through for me as expected with a steady stream moving to Parris Island after the first of the year. The 5th Recruiting District selected me as their Outstanding Recruiter for the month of May. The write-up acknowledged my shipment of twelve male applicants during February. Although it was not identified officially, I noted with satisfaction that none of my applicants were sent home as unsuitable.

In spite of my evening work, I decided to get serious with my formal education. I had taken the High School GED Test at the NGF in 1952. The long winter nights of 1954–55 in Korea had motivated me to take high school English and math courses from the Marine Corps Institute, which offered academic as well as technical courses. I enrolled in the University of Maryland and started night classes at Fort Meade. At six credit hours per semester, the 120 hours required for a degree was to be a long, slow process.

Recruiters caught extra duty with details in dress blues throughout the state of Maryland. We did it all, from a rifle firing detail at funerals to a color guard for social events. One of the big ones at the time was the grand opening of the Baltimore Harbor Tunnel. Carrying the colors in full blues under the hot summer sun brought out the juice, but

Marines did not mind. We were front and center and the heart of the show. There were always many good contacts made at these events, with both the guys and the gals.

My free weekends were spent on the farm in Virginia, and that did not allow me to become attached to the Baltimore area. I continued to hope for a substation in Virginia. Initially the chances did not look good; all of those recruiters had most of their tours ahead of them. Then SSgt Dutton was removed from the substation in Alexandria. It was perfect for me, and I jumped at the chance.

On 20 September 1958, I became the Alexandria recruiter, covering six counties in Northern Virginia. I worked alone but directly for MSgt Joe Florence, who was the NCOIC of the Washington Substation. GySgt Dave Blanco worked with Florence, SSgt Rayburn worked the substation in Hyattsville, and SSgt Prichett was in Winchester.

Moving in with my folks near Aldie allowed me to beat my rent cost in Baltimore, but the commute was long. What really caught my attention was loss of sleep. I usually got home around midnight or later and was on the way to my office by seven. Our uniforms were not maintenance free; in addition to a steam press, the buttons on my blues were polished and shoes, spitshined. That averaged a minimum of forty-five minutes each night.

I set up my schedule to be in the post office each Monday, Wednesday, and Friday. Tuesdays I spent visiting the post offices in the major towns in my area as scheduled. Thursdays I kept open for house calls, running down contacts, and the like.

The four service recruiters were located on the second deck of the main post office in Alexandria. Our desks were lined up with the Air Force at the head of the stairs, the Army next, followed with Navy, then me, the farthest back. I handled the question about that position arrangement with the response, "An ideal place for the Marine Recruiter—if a young man makes it all the way back to me, he really wants to be a Marine."

The other service recruiters would respond to an applicant's question of, "What do you have to offer me?" with promises and a long laundry list of schools and technical jobs. My response was always simply, "If you make it through boot camp, you will be a Marine." My answer did not appeal to the technically oriented, but it did strike a spark in the gungy ones who sought a challenge.

RS Baltimore received a new OIC: Major Robert J. Norton relieved Scoop Adams. The change was a plus for us as Norton, a tanker, got down into the trenches with us. Adam's last fitness report moved me into the excellent category with the following statement:

Fox is the most improved recruiter at this station. He is extremely hard working and loyal and has increased his productivity. His personal appearance and bearing are outstanding.

Once each quarter I saw both DC recruiters when we replaced the recruiting signs known as A-frames located by post offices and other prominent places. Pasting and replacing A-frames, and preparing the high school graduating class mail-outs were the only real chores of recruiting duty.

The demand for new Marines decreased, and I could not ship those few good men whom I wanted in my Corps. HQMC established a 120-day delayed enlistment program that helped. For the rest of my tour, I had my quota filled four months in advance. I could ship a deserving young man who insisted on leaving right away by having Top Florence ask Baltimore for a quota. Shipping only those with whom I wanted to serve became easy. I saved a quota for my cousin Charles, and he went off for a four-year enlistment. Clifton N. (Buddy) Simpson Jr., a neighborhood farm boy, was another of my hand-picked enlistees; I actually reenlisted him. Buddy played a lot of good baseball as a top hitter and center fielder for Marines during his Corps career.

An embarrassing situation happened on recruiting duty that equaled my accidental discharge in the Korean War. In observance of Veteran's Day, I spoke to the students and faculty in the auditorium of Washington and Lee High School, the largest high school in my area. The day was Friday, 10 November, and my presentation on our Corp's history and the importance to Marines of 10 November, the Corps's birthday, was well received. My trouble started as the program was ending and the attending Air Force Band played the Marines Hymn. I had heard barracks talk about standing for our hymn; until this day, however, I had never experienced a formal recognition. I was in front of a thousand students and faculty and decided not to make a Marine issue of it. I remained seated.

The Air Force Hymn followed. Because the band stood, so did everyone else, everyone except the Marine. I sat there burning with embarrassment, regret, and yes, maybe pride. Why did I not stand for my hymn? I felt that hymn would never end so that I could disappear. The gaze of one thousand eyes bore upon the single seated figure on the stage while everyone else was on their feet, including a dozen on the stage with me. That was a hard lesson, but one that will last me a lifetime. I cleared the area fast and headed for Baltimore and our Marine Corps Birthday Ball. My date and the Ball helped me forget my humiliation.

Another day, I had completed business at HQMC and was headed for the front hatch and my car. The staff sergeant on duty in the reception and locator booth, positioned just inside the main entrance, called to me. He had the new Technical Sergeant Selection List; was I on it? I surely did not expect to be; I had only been a staff sergeant three years. He responded with, "There are many surprises; many were selected who did not expect it." Getting my name, he checked his list. Sure enough, I was selected to be a technical sergeant before wearing the starch out of my staff sergeant rockers.

While recruiting was enjoyable, I missed FMF duty. To help keep me Marine-qualified, I scheduled a hike on a Sunday, just for me. In utilities, boots, helmet, light marching pack with cartridge belt and canteen, and my 1903 bolt-action Springfield rifle, I headed for Leesburg. The back route was eleven miles, which would make a fair hump by the time I returned. It was a fair hump for an infantryman, and I would shortly learn that a recruiter was not an infantryman. Too much time had passed from the last time I wore boots on the trail.

A lone Marine in combat gear moving along that country road was an uncommon sight. Just about every farmer on his way to town asked, "Son, are the damn Yankees acting up again?" It was a beautiful day that added to my enjoyment of the exercise. Arriving at my march objective, which was a small park on the south side of Leesburg, I chowed down and took a half-hour break. Returning home, however, was another story after the blisters started.

Night arrived with three miles to go and feet that were just one big blister. I sincerely hoped that someone at home would come looking for me; however, my family would never dream that their Marine would accept a ride. I finished what I started, but while my march rate out was four miles per hour, I was lucky to log two miles per hour on return. That was my last long hike on recruiting duty. What really hurt was having to walk in dress shoes for the remainder of the week. On the plus side, I did provide the other recruiters with a good round of laughs.

★ ★ ★

Boatswain Mate 1st Class Robert McGowan took over the Navy Recruiting desk, and Bob was a skier. I had always wanted to ski, but the sport belonged to the few with the means. The opportunity had never presented itself until Bob took me in tow. Rental gear and a weekend with Bob on the slopes at Davis, West Virginia, got me started. I committed with ski clothing and equipment purchases, which at the time was well over two month's pay. I loved the slopes, the outdoors, and the sport for which the weather never became too cold or too bad. Fridays now included getting the snow-condition reports and deciding where we would ski the weekend—Seven Springs or Ligonier in Pennsylvania, Deep Creek, Maryland, or go back to Davis.

Technical sergeants were in short supply so my name came up fast on the promotion list. Top Florence and I drove to Baltimore where Major Norton gave me my second rocker in an office ceremony on 7 January 1959. My new date of rank was 1 December 1958.

Lessons Learned

1. Spirited and well-meaning individuals also need checks and balances, someone on hand to say no.
2. Seek followers with pride and commitment.

6
Technical Sergeant
1128290/0369/8511/8411

1 December 1958

My recruiting experiences were routine throughout 1959, and then I was on my last year. There was a shortage of recruiters, and we were encouraged to extend for a year. While I enjoyed the duty and the time with my family, I also missed doing Marine things. I was in the home stretch of my recruiting duty; there would not be another year.

My enlistment would also end in 1960, and I would be halfway to retirement. I was still having fun and had not begun to do all the Marine things available. Reenlisting was not a question; I loved the Marines. There would be some reenlistment money also, which, along with selling back sixty days' leave and rations, would be a noticeable amount.

My '57 Olds was holding up fine; I would not blow my reenlistment money on another car. I bought three acres of land from my dad and started building a house. Becoming a property owner was one of my better investments. Renting the house later provided a steady source of additional income.

I took a five-day leave in June, and met Eakin in Texarkana. He had married while we were on the drill field; now, he and Deanna were visiting their folks to show off their son, Mark. We spent the week on Lake Ouachita, living on the family's houseboat, water skiing and skin diving. Visiting with my buddy was great, and I also wanted to get the scoop on 1st Force Reconnaissance Company. Force Recon was a new organization and my first choice for a duty assignment. Parachute jumping and SCUBA diving were their means of going to work and that appealed to me. Eakin had joined Force Recon following assignment as an instructor at Sea School. His recommendation of the best way to get into the company was to knock the door down with desire and determination. The plan was that I visit 1st Force before checking in with division. Should I pass their physical fitness test and make a favorable impression on the leadership, they would request Division to assign me to the company.

Marines did not do much running in the fifties, and that bodily abuse was unheard of among recruiters. My morning routine changed to include a fifteen-minute run to a farm pond, a ten-minute swim, and the run home. The exertion really knocked me initially, but slowly I came around to what I thought would be acceptable. I would later learn that I greatly underestimated what would be expected.

Something was on the horizon to give me mixed emotions about my decision to not take another year of recruiting. In early August, I was enjoying a sandwich in the Waffle Shop at King and Washington when a beautiful, blonde nurse caught my attention. She was seated across the counter, and I could not look anywhere except into her lovely green eyes. I was interested immediately, but something warned me that this situation should be handled differently from my norm. Deciding to move slowly, I let her leave the diner ahead of me; my intention was to learn where she worked. That idea was blown when she entered a 1949 Chevrolet and drove away.

Her eye message satisfied me that she would again be in the Waffle Shop. As I was in Alexandria every other day, I made a mental note to be there at the same time Wednesday. She was not in the diner when I arrived, but my disappointment did not last long before she appeared in her white uniform.

The diner was crowded, but my biggest problem was that she was with someone. It all figured: a young woman this pretty would be involved with some lucky guy. They seated themselves together across the curved counter from me. After my initial loss of hope, I was encouraged by her smiling, acknowledging face and again those lovely green eyes. She nodded her head with the biggest smile in response to my over-the-counter greeting. Obviously, her relationship with this guy was not interfering with her meeting someone. Not knowing the situation, I decided to keep it cool, paid for my sandwich and departed.

Entering the diner at noon on Friday, I found her seated at the lunch counter, and as luck would have it, there was a vacant seat beside her. In the attack, I took the seat, placed my order, and then introduced myself. She was Dotti Lu Bossinger from Mattawana, Pennsylvania, and she was a dental nurse in Alexandria. That was the beginning of the love of my life. I secured a date for the following Wednesday night and walked this classy young lady to her car. That was the start of our courtship; I lost interest in other girls.

October saw me answering the call of the wild with a week of bow hunting for deer in the mountains. The George Washington National

Forest lies along the Virginia and West Virginia border and runs from Strasburg in the north to Roanoke in the south. Camping out for the week, I never saw another human being in that forest, but I was not alone. A constant vision of Dotti Lu was before me; on a deer stand or by my campfire at night, I would see her. I asked and answered all sorts of questions regarding that girl on that hunting trip. Out there in the wilderness, I found my answer. I was in love. Miss Right had come along; I had found the woman of my dreams.

My last day with the recruiting service was 31 October 1960. The captain's Fitness Report remarks were:

> Given my choice of any Marine in the Corps for a company gunnery sergeant, I would pick Fox. He is thoroughly professional, forceful, intelligent, resourceful, and literally "gung-ho." His potential as a leader of men is tremendous, and I would trust him to do the right thing under almost any circumstance.

A thirty-day leave followed in which I gave my full attention to pressing issues. Though I worked hard on my house, my dad would have to finish it for me. Dotti Lu had become very important in my life, and I wanted to make her a permanent part of it. I asked her father for her hand in marriage after she agreed to marry me. She did not intend the marriage to happen soon, but she would be my wife. Those thirty days passed, and I found leaving home not easy for this Marine: I had become too involved in the daily family activities. Above all, my heart was now in Alexandria. However, I had made my choice, so I packed the Olds and headed for Camp Pendleton.

En route, I visited with Tom Roberts in Danville, Virginia, and Donahoo in Texas. Before checking in with the Division on 9 December, I went by 1st Force Reconnaissance Company located in Camp Delmar just north of Oceanside. The company first sergeant had responded to a letter from me with an invitation: bring boots and utilities.

Presenting myself in Winter Service Alpha, I was told to get into boots and utes. Force Recon did not talk with anyone until they had a feel for his physical condition and his quitting level. Their PFT was a big up-front eliminator. In addition, it was a tool used in deciding the bigger questions: How badly do you want to be a Recon Marine? Where is your stopping point? What is the depth of your guts?

The Recon and Pathfinder platoons were in the field, so the 1st sergeant called the communication's shack in his attempt to locate someone to give me the test. A lance corporal reported for the duty. That was part of the test, I later learned: to see how the technical sergeant would respond to the demands of a lance corporal. Eakin had informed me that the company was more interested in what one did after reaching his stop point than in mere numbers of repetitions; this was the gut measurement. A hundred repetitions of an event did not help if you quit without trying to get more.

After my normal twelve pull-ups and with the lance corporal's urging, I grunted and squeezed out two more slow, painful ones. The third never counted as I could not get my chin over the bar, but I strained for it. The same routine occurred for the sit-ups, squat jumpers, and other company favorites. Next was the run.

I understood from Eakin that one must do well on the Army Airborne test: three repetitions of running four minutes with walking two minutes between the runs. I assumed incorrectly that I had only to pass the Army test as we ran to the beach and through the soft sand. After a while, I wondered if the lance corporal had forgotten his watch. Finally, I asked, "Are we not supposed to run four and walk two?"

"Run until you drop or quit, Gunny" was the response. (I must have been distracted when Eakin covered that point.) The lance corporal told me that I could stop anytime that I wanted. There would be no stopping on my account, but I was not ready for that run. I had never run forever in my life. I hurt like the blazes from overexerting myself on the first part of the test, and I was running on something that I have had to draw on a very few times. In spite of the hurt, it would be a run forever; I was neither going to quit, nor drop.

A thirty-minute hard run satisfied the lance corporal, and we returned to the company area. Told to shower and dress, I made ready for my appearance before the board and hopefully the CO. Major Robert G. Hunt was the CO, and I later locked my heels in front of his desk. The board had agreed to give me a chance, but there was a problem.

My overseas control date showed that I was past due for a tour on Okinawa. Division was required to put me in a trans-placement battalion bound for that little island and my time on the rock. Captain Burhans, the XO, suggested that I go to Okinawa with the next deploying Pathfinder team. That would satisfy the overseas requirement, and it suited me. Burhans fixed it up with the division personnel officer; I checked in and was assigned to the company.

The company consisted of three operational platoons: two reconnaissance and one Pathfinder. A headquarters platoon that included administration, supply, motor transport, paraloft, and SCUBA locker completed the company. Recon platoons conducted deep reconnaissance missions while the Pathfinders provided terminal guidance for helicopter assault forces.

The Pathfinder Platoon consisted of three teams of ten men each. A team broke down into three Landing Site Teams consisting of a Landing Site NCO (LSNCO), normally a corporal, and a Fieldmaster, a PFC or lance corporal. Pathfinder Team Leaders were captains, with the assistant being a staff or technical sergeant (both E-6[18]). A radioman and a machine gunner completed the team.

Another recent addition was the Pathfinder Platoon Commander, Captain Wise.[19] First Lieutenants Patrick E. Duffy and Richard (Dick) Culver were Pathfinder Team Leaders. The Platoon was short one team leader. I was assigned as the Team Leader of Pathfinder Team 44 until another officer joined. I would be the assistant team leader upon deployment to WestPac (Western Pacific Command). Sgt (E-5) Robert E. Happy was my assistant team leader. Team 44 was manned and being trained for a thirteen-month deployment to the 3rd MarDiv.

The team leader position gave me a slow start in learning my new role. I assumed that my duties were the same as the other team leaders; no one told me differently. Initially that amounted to sitting around in the platoon office telling sea stories. Happy had Team 44 in the palm of his hand and needed no help in the barracks. December moved along with little Pathfinder work; everyone took off on holiday leave.

Leave did not fit into my plans for several reasons: I had just left home, Virginia was a long way from California, and my cash flow was low because of a short payoff plan on the bank loan to finish my house. Dotti Lu's diamond purchased on an installment plan further reduced my cash. While I would love to place the ring on her finger, going home was not an option. I mailed her diamond with the request that her father place it on her finger for me on Christmas day.

Gunnery Sergeant John Bell, from my DI days, was the motor transport chief. He suggested that I take a jeep over the holidays and learn the Pendleton training areas. The jeep would get me out of the barracks. That turned out to be a great plan, or I would have had a more miserable holiday existence.

Saturday, two days before Christmas, someone entered my room and stole my wallet while I was in the community shower across the passageway. I did not miss it until evening chow when I tore the room apart searching for it. Gradually the facts began to sink in; my wallet was not in my room. All the money I had in the world, over $70.00, and my ID card and driver's license were gone.

I drew commuted rations and paid to eat in the mess hall, so I would not be eating for the next three days. Until friends returned from their holidays and the disbursing office opened for a special pay, no money was available. I have never seen any base as empty as Pendleton was over the holidays in 1960. I found some discarded fruit behind the Staff NCO mess; otherwise I did without.

Thanks to Gunny Bell and his jeep idea, I could get my mind off my hunger. He later chastised me for checking out the jeep without a driver's license (I felt sorry for his duty dispatcher) and for not calling him down in El Cajon. Heck, I did not even have a dime for a collect call.

My first clue that things were not going well for me in the company came before the workday started one morning in early January. The company operations officer was a Major Davis who found me one morning the first to arrive in the Pathfinder Office. I followed him into the vacant XO's office where he raved in general terms about what the company needed from its staff NCOs. He spoke of the efforts of others and seemed to be saying that I was not doing what was expected of me. As no one had told me specifically what to do, he probably was correct. Standing at attention, I wondered how he had gotten into my chain of command. He finished and I took my leave with a "Will that be all, Sir?"

I was applying myself in the manner of the other team leaders and there had not been a hint of dissatisfaction or job guidance from my platoon leader. True enough, I did not do much because of the holiday schedule, but no one in Pathfinders did otherwise. Confronting Wise and seeking insight on Davis's motive was no help. Later that day, Lt Culver provided the best advice: "Consider the source and take it with a grain of salt."

During ParaOps I rode out to the drop zone (DZ) with the DZ controller and others who were not jump qualified, referred to as Legs. Following the jump, the Legs joined their teams on the ground and continued with whatever operation or training was scheduled. Hanging over each Leg was the dreaded one-week Junior Jump School (known as JJ). This course prepared the Marine for the US Army Airborne School and assured the command that he would not wash out at Benning. Until one had been through JJ, he was a bastard child. He had not made the elusive Rite of Passage into this exclusive organization. A JJ was scheduled in January, and my name was on the list. Meanwhile, I learned more about my fellow staff NCOs.

GySgt Bobby Joe Patterson was our Company Gunnery Sergeant and a reconner who knew the business inside and out. In the spring of 1961, he was assigned a top-secret mission in some distant part of the world. His departure was sudden and silent, here one day and gone the next. GySgt John R. Massaro (later Sergeant Major of the Marine Corps), who had just returned for another tour with recon, replaced Patterson.

SSgt (E-6) Eakin was the platoon sergeant of a recon platoon. Moreover, as I expected, he was "Sergeant Recon." Knowing the business to an immeasurable depth, he also had his own solid ideas about how things ought to be. Force Reconnaissance had been in existence now for two years. The Company's current task was not only testing and evaluating but also writing up everything from the Company SOPs to the FMF Manuals on the many reconnaissance tasks and missions. Eakin was always busy, in the field or at his desk.

Eakin had earlier received the Navy and Marine Corps Medal for a life-saving action during a night ParaOp on 29 September 1960. Out and open under his canopy, he grabbed the malfunctioned chute of another jumper who was falling past him in the dark. Holding on to the collapsed chute, he yelled for the jumper to deploy his reserve parachute. LCpl Thomas McNulty deployed his reserve as his suspension lines slipped through Eakin's fingers.

One of my favorite stories of the Force Recon Marines involved a recon platoon on a cross-country Escape and Evasion (E & E) exercise from Yuma, Arizona, to Camp Pendleton. Law enforcement officials and the National Guard were notified and asked to be on the lookout for Ronnie Recon. Knowing this, the platoon members separated and played the game. They stayed in rough country and off roads as they moved individually toward Pendleton.

One Marine went too deep into the desert where he used up his water and fell from exhaustion and dehydration. Realizing that he could not continue, he loaded his grease gun with his fading strength. (Some reconners and Pathfinders carried one 45-caliber round of ammunition, known as a survival round, in their survival pouch.) As he was down under an electric power line, he fired his M3-A1 at—and broke—a pole insulator. The line crew found him hours later while looking for the break in their line. We all carried a survival round thereafter, though the SOP and regulations forbade it. Survival was soon to become a major concern of mine.

JJ started on the second Monday in January with a briefing of the rules. We could quit anytime we wanted, but if we quit, we were out of the company. Happy ran the JJ with two Cpls (E-4) assisting him. The students numbered fifteen and included Wise and myself.

JJ kicked off with a personnel inspection. Each discrepancy noted by Happy, as he inspected the ranks, cost the student ten recon push-ups. The captain and I formed the third rank of the small formation, and I felt confident in my starched utilities and spit-shined boots. I was not concerned about the sergeant's inspection; after all, rank had its privileges, and Happy would be working for us afterwards.

When Happy finished with the captain to my right, giving him three discrepancies for thirty push-ups, I received the message. He managed to find something that he called an Irish pennant on my pistol belt and something under a fingernail. I owed him twenty. Then I learned the difference between a push-up and a recon push-up. I was awarded ten more because I did not dive for the ground to get into the push-up position. Back on my feet to do it right, I dove for California. While doing my first push-up, Happy stated, "I did not hear 'RECON!' as you went down, Gunny. Back on your feet. You owe me ten more." As I worked out forty push-ups, which was about ten over what I would normally do, I had the picture loud and clear: Students had no rank, and anything that they did was wrong. This was boot camp with a different flavor, all over again.

We moved next to the pull-up bars for the company PFT. I had no time to recover from my push-ups, which was why Cpl (E-4) Robert N. Justus invited me to the bar. Mounting, I gave my all for the twelve counted and followed with much straining and pulling. I gained different heights but no more chin over the bar.

Told to dismount, I dropped and experienced a complete vision blur. On the verge of being sick, I also needed to make an urgent, heavy-duty headcall. Unable to focus, I sought permission from a source of authoritative noise, and found my way into the nearby barracks and a head. I recovered and completed the rest of the test.

The following long run in the Del Mar beach sand lost all but three before Happy turned us around far up the beach. Our turnaround found the others scattered all along the shore with the corporals trying to herd them into some kind of formation. They entered our ranks as we returned down the beach.

The morning set the stage for the rest of the day and the week. There were some classes on parachutes and related equipment, parachute landing falls (PLFs) and canopy control. Throughout it all was the dreaded command, "Drop, give me ten." Any slight hint of a violation such as allowing one's eyes to wander off the instructor was just cause.

Lunchtime came, but I could not eat; I did manage to down a little ice cream. After a one-hour break, we were back at it, only our ranks had decreased, including the loss of the captain. The routine continued and somehow 1700 arrived. Food was important for energy and strength, but I felt that I could not keep it in my stomach. Too exhausted to eat, all I wanted to do was pass out on my rack. Somehow, I made the half-mile to my barracks.

I got out of my sweat-soaked uniform and fell onto my rack. Time passed while I faded in and out of consciousness. I had a gigantic dread of the morrow and going through another day of the same stuff. An inspection would start the day; I had to press a uniform and shine my boots. Worrying did not help; I would doze off again before gathering the strength or motivation to get up. I had spent some miserable nights in the Korean War hoping that I would be around to see the light of day. This night I did not want to end. I dreaded the coming of day because I felt that I could not do again what I had just done. Somehow though, I came around, prepared my uniform, made morning chow, and even ate some of it.

Day 2 was a repeat of the first except there was no PFT. Wise was back in ranks; he apparently had a legitimate visit to sickbay the previous afternoon. No such breaks for the enlisted that quit; our numbers would continue to decline. My arms were completely useless for push-ups by the afternoon of Day 2. We were now allowed to pay for infractions with squat jumpers that I used for the remainder of the week. My body adjusted to the demands upon it, and I managed to eat proper meals. The remaining nights were not as bad as the first one.

I experienced a new low in mid-afternoon of Day 4 while working on the swing-landing trainer. Literally exhausted, I was just plain worn out with no drive or motivation left. It no doubt showed, as Wise offered help. During a ten-minute break, he gave me an unidentified pill, telling me that it would make me feel better. It did and I did. Feeling great, I buzzed through the next hour as though I was a new man.

Payback was a bitch, however. A run on the beach ended our day, and the benefit of that pill wore off shortly after starting the run. For a while I wondered if I could hang in for the completion of the run. I later could hardly drag myself to chow and to my room. Never again have I taken that kind of help. JJ finished but several weeks passed before my body recovered.

There were no recovery breaks, as each day the company fell out for PT and a company run. All hands, from the CO down to the corpsmen, made the last event of the day. The daily dozens were usually led by the company gunny or his designate, and were followed by a three-mile or greater run.

Recon's organization and approach to PT appealed to me. We had tried to do PT in the 5th Marines but our approach was wrong. We did it in full field uniform after reveille and before chow. The problems included: the uniform and boots lost their sharpness for the rest of the day, the fitted uniform restricted movement, there was no time for a shower after working up a sweat, and most people do not like to wake up their bodies so violently. 1st Force dressed for PT, sometimes in boots and utes with skivvy shirt, and other times in shorts. PT was the last event of the day and allowed a shower and dress for evening chow or return to quarters. A big plus is that the body is awake and ready for exertion in the afternoon.

On 31 January 1961 another "new guy" fitness report covering three months, which included my thirty-day leave, fifteen days of travel, Christmas Holidays, and breaking in on a new job, entered my file. My platoon leader gave me the only "Be Glad to Have" in my entire record of forty-three years. One peer was marked between Excellent and Outstanding to the right of me. Extracts of his comments:

> . . . a complete evaluation of his growth and career potential cannot be made. He readily learns and adapts to varied assignments and it is felt that his overall performance and value will increase.

Our company commander as the reviewing officer felt the need to add the following remark:

> . . . [Fox] is new to this work and he has had no opportunity to learn it before he came. The marking officer was TAD during much of January.

First Lieutenants Gerald F. Reczek and John W. Phillips joined the Pathfinder Platoon from the Division. (Reczek retired as a colonel and Phillips was killed while serving as a captain in Vietnam.) They took the new guy heat off me.

On 4 March 1961, I reported to Fort Benning, Georgia, for a week of air mobility school followed by airborne training. Three other 1st Force Marines, Cpls Billy T. Branch and Robert F. Boland and LCpl Frank M. Goulaillier, joined me for the jump course. After our JJ, we were ready for the real thing. The course began with six repetitions of the Daily Dozen. And, true enough, the run was four minutes with a two-minute walk, repeated three times.

On the command to fall in for the run following PT, we Marines rushed to fill the leading rank positions, thinking that we would set the pace. We did for thirty seconds, until the instructor ordered the leading rank to peel off and fall in on the rear. The mornings thereafter, Marines took the first four right file positions (one behind the other) in the fourth file. Guide was normally right, which allowed a Marine pace through four commands to peel off and fall in on the rear. Most of the Army students were 2nd lieutenants, and enough of them picked up the spirit so that we managed to keep a good pace going for several minutes. Our Army friends picked up the right guide positions behind us.

We did not get anything by the instructors, however. There was always the cry, "Marine, Drop. Give me ten!" Though we knew that the command was for the one closest to the bark, because he said Marine we all four broke ranks and dove for the Georgia dirt. We quickly knocked out ten, then raced to catch the formation. Next, we found ourselves running circles around the moving student formation for further punishment; we loved it.

The instructors took issue with our yell of "RECON" as we dove into the push-up position; they wanted us to shout "AIRBORNE." Because we yelled "RECON," we were usually awarded ten more push-ups or told to run around the formation. We had a no-win situation as we dove for Georgia again yelling "RECON" or "AR-RUG-G-GA-A-A", Force Recon's motivational response.

During the evening formation of the second training day, the senior instructor ordered the Marines to report to SFC Hadley, behind the building to our front. We were collected by a big sergeant first class who had never been involved with us up to this point. He informed us that we were going to do push-ups, since we liked to do them so well.

Since he presented the picture of Mister Physical Fitness, I expected him to lead us in push-ups until we quit. Instead, he ordered us down into position, commanded "UP" and "DOWN" for a set of ten push-ups, and then ordered us to stand.

The SFC stood with folded arms barking the commands as he repeated the push-up sets. About ten repetitions of this game were enough for me; he surely could stand there longer than we could do push-ups.

While grunting out ten, I challenged him with, "I will give the Corps ten for every one that you do for the Army." That did it.

There were two more commands: "On your feet. Dismissed."

The victory, however, was for the battle and not the war. Next morning, we Marines were told to report to the OIC. The major laid it on the line. He liked our spirit, but we seemed to miss the school's point. This was airborne training, not Marine training. We either did things the airborne way or we packed and went home. Specifically, if we could not yell "AIRBORNE" on our way into the push-up position, we were dropped from the course as of the moment. His position was clear; we became airborne.

Tower week followed with doing events in the air, and I found the thirty-four-foot tower unnerving. For some reason that leap at thirty-four feet, though we were caught by a cable for a slide to the ground, was most difficult for me. Almost to the point of being overcome by fear, I went out the door like a robot. An instructor under the tower who observed each door-exit body position and evaluated the student performance was in stitches with laughter as I reported. I had screwed up so badly that he did not even bother awarding me push-ups. Never very good at hiding my feelings, I guess I let it all hang out on my exit. I got back in line to do it again. A student had to have two good body positions off the thirty-four-foot tower before he was cleared for Jump Week. Cpl Branch made two jumps from that tower; I do not know how many I made to qualify.

The 250-foot tower was enjoyable. For this I was attached to a cable under an open canopy and pulled up to 250 feet. When ready, I released for a slow descent under the canopy. I only had to do two of these but wanted more. Next were Jump Week and a visitor.

Our first jump took place on Friday of our tower week. No one is likely to forget his first parachute jump; even simple things like drawing a parachute from a stack has stressful tones. I wanted and looked for a special parachute: one with a personal bonding to me. Just any chute would not do, especially the older-looking ones. Who packed it? What shape was it in, and how often had it been jumped? The chute I drew looked well used, and the rigger-packing card showed that it had been. Jump master (JM) checks were followed by detail rigger checks, so it must be all right.

All went well in our C-123 jump plane while I was seated. The unnaturalness started with my stick standing up and going through the jump commands. There was, however, still the chance that the jump would be called off for wind or something of the like.

"Stand in the Door." The line moved forward as Number one took position in the doorway. This whole business was crazy, dumb. The JM yelled, "GO"; students ahead of me began disappearing out the door. I moved forward with a weak and very negative feeling. Thinking of how great my life had been up to this point, why was I up here trying to end it? Out that door was a black hole, and right now, I had no desire to learn of it, but I kept moving.

Suddenly the parachutist in front of me was gone and there was that door showing the world passing below me. Grabbing both sides of the doorway, I sprang outward. Bringing feet together, I entered the prop-blast as both hands moved to cover my reserve parachute. A giant was tugging on my risers. I realized that I had forgotten to count, and four seconds surely had passed. Pushing my helmeted head back through my risers, I watched my chute blossom directly on a horizontal line with me. Then I began to swing down under that beautiful canopy. What a thriller! I was ready to do it again.

Jump altitude of 1,000 feet does not give much canopy time; the ground was approaching fast. Preparing for my PLF, I wanted to pull up my feet to delay hitting the ground. My rate of descent looked as if ground contact was going to hurt, and I rolled through the points of contact with surprise at the pain. They were only minute pains as I rolled over the rough-plowed ground, but they did take some fun out of the experience. Motivation was high as we students collected at the trucks with our field-rolled chutes for the return to mainside. Now we each had a jump story for the telling.

Dotti Lu and I could not pass up the opportunity for some togetherness during my month back east. My sister Betty, her husband K. Lee, and Dotti Lu drove down one weekend, and Dotti Lu flew down for my last weekend. Those beautiful Georgia spring days worked their magic; we started talking of her quitting her job and moving to Oceanside.

I was thinking of marriage, but it was difficult to plan with my immediate deployment to Okinawa. Being married and leaving a new wife did not make much sense, and leaving this beautiful girl free for thirteen months made even less. We decided to take it one step at a time; she would come to Oceanside as soon as the dentist could replace her. Jump week went smoothly, and we graduated as Airborne Marines with Cpl Branch as the class Honor Man.

Our return to 1st Force was in time for an R4D jump that gave me my blood jump (first Marine jump following school). Officers, staff NCOs, and selected sergeants were JM qualified for both free fall (FF) and static line ParaOps; I needed that qualification before deploying. During the JM-training course we jumped every type of aircraft available, into all kinds of DZs, including water, and carrying every possible load.

Personnel reassignments had taken place: Wise was now the S-3; Duffy was the Pathfinder Plt Leader and the leader of Team 44. My new positions were those of the Pathfinder Platoon Sergeant and the Assistant Team Leader of 44. Platoon leadership required little of our time because we trained and operated as teams in an independent mode. There were four teams in the platoon counting the one currently on Okinawa. Duffy and I trained and operated with Team 44, getting ready for our deployment.

The Navy's carrier utility plane, TF-1, was our primary insertion aircraft. With all seats removed, a full team could be seated on the deck. Besides being carrier launched and recovered, it was fast for a propeller-driven plane. Most of our jumps were from the TF-1. When a larger plane, such as the R4D or the GV1, was scheduled, the entire platoon and sometimes the company would jump.

Pathfinders had a jump scheduled on a Monday night; this was my first night jump and the apprehension level was high. At day's end, we were on the Pendleton airfield chuting-up. After JM and rigger checks, we sat propped up by our gear on the parking apron. Full darkness fell with no jump aircraft.

Finally the jump was canceled; we turned in our chutes, boarded the trucks, and headed for the DZ. I assumed that we would truck out, pick up Duffy who was DZ Control and carry out the training schedule. We were scheduled to E & E back to camp following the jump. Told to keep everyone on the trucks at the DZ, we sat with typical military unquestioning acceptance of such things. After a long wait, we were again moving.

Seated by the tailgate of the covered six-by, I soon realized that we were off the base and headed east. This would be a long E & E. Then I remembered the blank training schedule for Tuesday through Friday back in the platoon office. I had visited GySgt Julian W. Parrish, the S-3 Chief, seeking the full schedule but was put off with an explanation of a printing problem. Now I began to wonder, as the two trucks, with grinding gears, began climbing a mountain several hours from our DZ.

Well up into mountain country in a forest of big firs, we turned off the highway onto a dirt road. Pulling into a camp, Duffy dismounted his jeep to our front, and yelled for me to keep the Marines aboard the trucks. Time was past midnight, and keeping the Pathfinders aboard was not a problem. Most were asleep, in all shapes and forms, lying against each other on the bench and on the deck of the truck bed.

Shortly, four strange Marines with leveled rifles ordered the nearest two Marines to dismount; I climbed over the tailgate. With a rifle muzzle pressed into my back, we moved a hundred meters forward of the trucks. I could see that we were in some kind of camp with several small, rustic cabins nearest to us and an area beyond them lighted brilliantly with flood lights.

Our legs were spread while we were searched, and the leader informed us that we were prisoners of the Peoples Army. I assumed that a POW Exercise was the reason for no training schedule for the remainder of the week. Looking again to my direct front and the lighted area, I recognized a high fenced stockade with guard towers on two sides. I had been taught that one's best chance of escape is before he enters a stockade or prison. As the game was starting with the stockade only 200 meters away, I would not get many options.

As though he could read my mind, the leader spoke. "PFC, place your muzzle against this Gunny's back, and if he even as much as moves an eyelid, blast him." Then he said to me, "Gunny, you are supposed to play the game, and you might know that the blank ammo in that rifle will burn the hell out of your back through your jacket." I would play their game; however, I did not intend ever to be a prisoner.

The guards took us into one of the cabins near the stockade where we were searched again. Interrogators told us how sorry we should feel about murdering women and children and how happy we should be with our liberation by the Peoples Army. There were more discussions promised for the future.

I was reminded that I was the senior Marine in the compound and held responsible for my Marines' actions. Desperately, I looked for anything or anyway that I could make a break for the nearby woods as we were led to the compound. Two other Pathfinders moved with us but they were not going along with the game. They cursed the guards, resisted the guard's action of moving them, and for the most part had to be physically placed in the compound. Once inside, one ran screaming at a cluster of guards and leaped high upon the fence that separated them.

I took a different approach. Head down with shoulders slumped and hands in pockets, I hoped to present a whipped, give-up attitude. My eyes were closely and carefully checking out the fence as I slumped around the perimeter. Meanwhile, more Pathfinders were placed in the compound.

The pedestrian gate through which we entered was on the west fence. Three-quarters of the way along the north fence was a wooden truck gate containing a smaller manhole-size door. I moved closer for a better look. It was big enough for a man to get through quickly, and the hinges and hasp were not strong. A check of the guard tower on the north fence showed it unmanned, although a light, 30-caliber machine gun was in full view.

Confusion and noise erupted around the south guard tower. The guards' attention was drawn toward the commotion Pathfinders were making throughout the compound. One or two Pathfinders would run at the fence, jump high, and try to climb over. The fence was too high, and the wire was too closely woven to allow foot and hand holds. In addition, things were not going well in getting the remainder of the Pathfinders out of the two six-bys.

Pathfinders in the trucks were now awake; they had heard the Peoples Army talk and realized what was happening. Our captors, although US Marines, were now the bad guys, and Pathfinders acted accordingly. They closed the back flaps of the covered trucks, and when next told to send out two, sounded off with "Come in and get us." Naturally, the Peoples Army personnel, being Marines, did just that and suffered some casualties.

A Pathfinder in one truck shoved an ignited "day and night" flare into the face of the first man to come through the flaps. Another "not too smart" Pathfinder hit a Marine in the face with a camp ax when he tried to mount the other truck. All of this action caused the leaders to pull guards off the compound.

This was my break; already near the small gate, I moved. Placing my fingers through the cracks on the hasp side of the gate, I gave a tug that confirmed my suspicions that it would tear loose. Before I could give a serious tug, PFC Grossiano's fingers also appeared in the crack. With a mighty heave, the door tore free; I was through the hole and running hard for the darkness.

I expected to hear the MGs fire at any second, but I was not stopping. Upon reaching the ring of darkness, I looked over my shoulder to see Pathfinders following, strung out from me to the compound. I was well into the darkness when someone placed a gun in action. Realizing that we needed to separate and that all were following me across the level ground, I turned right and headed for high ground. Rattlesnakes sounded off as I sped through the high sagebrush. Moving too fast to be concerned unless I stepped upon one, I considered getting away worth the chance.

My thoughts were, better alone than in a group, stay in the bush and off roads, and patrols will be heaviest near camp. Therefore, make haste in getting away from camp. I would not make much distance on foot; mobility was the answer. My plan seemed to take me in a mental circle: stay off the roads, yet roads provided the only means of mobilization.

A Pathfinder was crashing through the brush behind me; I allowed him to catch up. Grossiano joined me and we continued toward a community of several houses. We approached a highway when two shadows moved out of the sage; Boland and Goudaillier joined us.

I told the three of the blank training schedule, suggesting that the POW exercise was probably the reason. I saw it my duty to return to the Company. They each said that they would like to stay with me; I considered a team of four about right and agreed. Goudaillier's boots had been taken in the search shack so we gave him our socks.

We moved south on the road away from the little community. Highway signs provided information: we were on Route 76 and forty-seven miles from Oceanside. Headlights and traffic noise gave us warning; we moved off the road and took cover whenever a vehicle passed.

After taking cover for one set of oncoming lights, the gear noise indicated that it was a big truck; it would not contain the Peoples Army. I told the others to stay hidden until I had the truck stopped, then come running. We did not consider how four of us might get into a truck cab.

The tractor with double trailers came on slow with much down shifting. Seeing me in the road, the driver stopped. This driver was the first person to whom I could brag about breaking out of the POW camp. I managed to say, "I have escaped," when simultaneously his window went up and he got the big truck moving. He shook his head negatively to my shouts through his closed window while he moved past me. I realized that it was now or never, and with a shout to the other Pathfinders to mount up, I caught the ladder on the rear of the first trailer.

Climbing to the top, I hoped to see the others on the road racing for the rear trailer. The road was clear; they were on their own. The wind over the trailer top was strong as the driver got up his speed; I climbed halfway down the ladder and hung on. This was what I wanted; it was ideal for putting fast distance between me and that compound with no questions asked and leaving no trail. Time passed, we were off the mountain and speeding along level ground when the trailer's turn signals came on.

Moving up the ladder, I saw an intersection ahead where the truck would turn left. The intersection was isolated, but it was lighted, and a car was parked on the near-left. Road signs showed Oceanside straight ahead; I would dismount. Assuming that the car held the Peoples Army, I swung off on the right side as the long truck made a slow left turn. I kept the truck between the car and me while I raced for the darkness again. I was pleasantly surprised when the other three Pathfinders came abreast of me, also moving fast. They had mounted the rear trailer upon seeing the small cab.

Keeping an eye on the car in the lighted intersection, we continued to run on the dark road. After about two miles with no traffic, we slowed to a walk. We had a long hike to Delmar. Our watches had been taken in the search shack, but not much darkness remained. I had planned to move at night and rest during daytime, but we were wearing down. Goudaillier was not complaining, but he was limping from stone bruises and cuts to his feet.

We started looking for a barn. A close check of a home did not provide a barn or any outbuilding that we could use. Moving past several such non-helpful homes, we finally came upon an old pump shack on an orchard-covered hillside, just as the sky lightened in the east. Entering, we lay down for some much needed sleep, which came quickly, but it did not last long. We had been comfortable while moving; now we were cold, compounded with sweaty clothing and only skivvy shirts. Sleeping like buddies, we pressed tightly together, back to chest, with all of us lying on the same side for warmth.

Laying up all day, especially in that little eight-by-eight-foot shack, did not sound so good in daylight. Our sleep satisfied, we needed to pacify our hunger and decided to move. We helped ourselves to oranges in an orchard with signs that read "No trespassing. Do not take any fruit. Violators will be prosecuted."

Our hunger, stiffness, and Goudaillier's sore feet helped us decide that we were probably well out of the area patrolled by the Peoples Army. We returned to the road in two-man teams for a better chance of catching a ride to Oceanside. A hero's welcome with the rest of the week off awaited us.

After many short farmer-supplied rides, we reported to the 1st Sergeant. He conferred with the S-3 and the CO, then gave us the bad news. We were not getting any POW compound training; we must return to Warner Springs, a Navy Air Survival, Evasion, Resistance, and Escape training school run by NAS Mirmar. As the Navy was not using the compound that week, Duffy locked it on with certain Navy staff as actors for our benefit. The supporting Marines were a rifle company of the 7th Marines, who were also locked on for the week. Duffy's original plan was for two Pathfinders to jump at a time on the night ParaOps. They would be grabbed by the infantry immediately upon hitting the ground, tied up, and then trucked up to Warner Springs for the exercise. Cancellation of the jump had messed up the plan.

We enjoyed our evening meal, stuffing ourselves because we knew that the next meal was three days away. The 1st Sergeant ensured that we had transportation; we were received by the Peoples Army with open arms and led immediately to the punishment boxes.

Duffy was in the search shack, which also doubled as the CP for the Peoples Army. He did not have anything to say and avoided my gaze when I was brought in for some thoughts of "The People." He was our leader. I felt that Duffy ought to be involved with us: to hurt, hunger, and bleed with us. I greatly resented his being on the outside while his Marines were catching it on the inside. Worse, he provided some of the hassle and discomfort that his Marines endured. (Duffy and I became good friends over the next two years with our Team 44 experiences in the 3rd MarDiv. I was deeply saddened seven years later to learn of his death in Vietnam. He was struck in the throat by a piece of shrapnel while standing in a bunker entranceway during an artillery barrage.)

The compound breakout, the flare, and the camp ax incident of the night before caused Duffy to realize Pathfinders were going to be difficult for the infantry to handle; he had to regain order. With a bullhorn, he ordered all Pathfinders out of the six-bys and the escapees hiding in the dark to report. This was POW compound training, not an escape and evasion exercise. Most Pathfinders had not considered moving from that place; they hid in the dark locally where Duffy collected them. His order to return did not affect my team; we were long gone. Two other Pathfinders traveled to Delmar and were returned; a third spent the entire week walking to Delmar.

Payback for breaking out was going to be rough and I expected the worst. Taken to the torture box area, I was placed in a box similar in shape and size to a footlocker. I had to cross my shins, placing each foot in the corner on the opposite side from the knee. With this X foundation, I was forced down while guards closed the lid by standing on it. Yes! This was going to be rough!

The pain in my shins and ankles caused me almost to scream. The hasp locked the lid shut, and I held a meeting with my mind. I would take this thing one second at a time; nothing would be allowed to get to me. I tried mentally to remove myself from the box; I tried to think of things that required close, detailed concentration. If others could take it, I could also. My legs became numb, and the pain less sharp. However, I found it extremely difficult to concentrate on anything else. After what seemed an eternity, but was probably about thirty minutes, the lid opened. Told to get out, I started with a crawl as I had lost control of my legs.

Next, I was placed in something like a wall locker requiring me to stand, only it was not high enough to stand erect and too narrow to sit. There was no way to support the body weight (as with bone on bone). Letting the knees bend forward until they touched the hatch was painful to the kneecaps, but that was the only alternative to supporting the bent knees with muscles. Next was a smaller locker box and others followed of different sizes. Time moved well into the night and the games ceased.

Our utility jackets were taken; a skivvy shirt was all we had to ward off the cold mountain air. The early morning hours were cold, forcing us to sleep tightly back to chest from one bulkhead to the other. Pathfinders on the ends either had a cold back or front; it was important to have only one row of sleepers, and we changed the two end positions periodically.

The major problem beyond the obvious of end positions and a cold top, was a turn to the other side. Some could not lie on one side very long. It did not matter, if one had to turn, we all had to turn. Usually we did the turn over and rotated the ends at the same time, but little sleep was gained.

Each day was a repeat with each of us getting an opportunity to learn about ourselves in the boxes followed by sessions with the interrogators. Military and personal information was sought, but anything was used to get one talking. The Navy had some real experts with foreign accents who lent their services at Warner Springs. As the senior Marine in the compound, I had more than my share of time under their hot light.

The Camp Commander ordered me to conduct PT for the POWs. PT was not a problem for Pathfinders, we wanted and needed it, but the enemy ordering me to do it, was something else. We were getting one thousand calories (one C-ration meal) per day and that did not provide much energy. Therefore, I filled the PT requirement with some light stretching exercises, making a mockery out of the camp authorities. The Pathfinders enjoyed the break in the routine, but it was the punishment box again for me.

Captors lose their threat of fear tactics over prisoners who have gone the distance, know of, and have taken the worst the captors have to offer. With the loss of fear of the unknown, everything takes its place in a routine. In the case of the boxes, most ceased to be a problem, while better ways were learned to handle the few that were difficult.

Friday arrived. We knew this thing would end before the weekend, and several guards had passed information through the fence. After a few remarks from big, burly Pathfinders about a promised liberty meeting in town and a settlement of the score, most of the guards went out of their way to be nice as early as Thursday.

Word came over the compound loudspeaker Friday morning for the Pathfinders to assemble in the compound yard. We were all standing around, as were many of the infantry Marines, when Duffy came out of camp headquarters and mounted a guard box.

"Gunny, fall in the Pathfinders."

"Whose side are you on now, Lieutenant?"

"God-damn it, Gunnery Sergeant, I said fall the Pathfinders in! NOW!"

Still bothered by the fact that our leader was not with us, but worse, with his being on the other side of the fence, I had asked upon impulse. His hot, immediate response was all that was needed to get my Marine mind back in battery. I fell the platoon in and reported to my platoon leader.

★ ★ ★

My life was moving toward a major change in style and routine. Dotti Lu would fly out the first week of June. My plan was marriage, while hers, I was to learn later, was to get a job where she could be near me. Immediate problem: I was scheduled to go through the E & E School at Bridgeport, California, from 5 to 20 June. The timing for the school 400 miles north was not of my choosing; I would not be able to help her get settled.

Locating a suitable, small, two-room cottage one block off the Oceanside beach, I signed a three-month lease with Mr. Fishe, the owner. He had four cute cottages at 205 South Myers Street and one should suit Dotti Lu. She immediately fell in love with the freshly painted white cottage. She looked for employment while I and Team 44 headed for Bridgeport.

Two days of classroom work at Bridgeport mixed with physical training helped us acclimatize. Nothing new was learned over what we had already suffered at Warner Springs. The big difference was that this was official; a course graduation entry would be made in our Service Record Book. We went hiking under the ruse of terrain appreciation the morning of the third day. We knew from graduates of the course that this was the entry point of the Peoples Army and the start of the POW compound exercise. We were ambushed and taken prisoner but not without incident. Other students in the class accepted the capture as part of the course, but not the Pathfinders. Having no weapons, we scattered like rabbits with the opening rounds of the ambush. In open country, we had no cover or concealment other than a few sage bushes. Partially hidden, I realized that my efforts were fruitless as the class members were lined up and counted. No one would be left behind.

After a full body search, we were placed in the compound. Team 44 rallied inside the bunker and compared notes and ideas. Noticing my Marine Corps ring, I removed it, and hid it on a ledge in the bunker. The enemy did not need to know that I was a Marine. Later, my interrogator noticed the non-weathered skin on my ring finger and went in the attack.

"I see that you are not proud of your marriage," he said with a heavy East European accent.

There was no comment from me.

"I do not blame you, if I were married to a woman who was sleeping around with sailors and even soldiers, I would be ashamed to wear my wedding ring also," he stated.

My thoughts, which I kept to my self, were how wrong he was. His mistake gave me a feeling of mastery of the interview. However, I was close enough to having a wife that I considered the difference if I had been married. I might not have remained so cool.

The June night air in the high Sierras was cold, causing us to sleep like buddies again, only there was not much sleeping, as the blaring loudspeaker music was interrupted throughout the night with a command for someone to report. My turn came in the middle of the first night. Guards took me inside and seated me on the deck with several waiting POWs, too close to a red-hot stove. With the lack of sleep and the change from cold to hot, we could not stay awake.

Sleep overcame us in spite of the discomfort of sitting at attention on the deck. We constantly fell over, for which we received verbal abuse from the guards. Naturally, we were not allowed to place our backs against the bulkheads or any other support. That torture lasted for almost an hour, until the interrogator was ready for his next brainwashing victim.

This POW camp had boxes, but they were not as small and therefore not as torturous as those at Warner Springs. In the afternoon of the second day, I received my box time for not providing the requested information. My first torture box was buried in the ground; other than total blackness and silt and slime in the bottom with crawling things in it, the size was not unbearable. Another good thing about this box exercise was that a log was kept on when a POW entered a box and exactly twenty minutes later he was let out. Knowing where the end is helps greatly.

My second box was a coffin type, comfortable in size, and placed on the ground surface. The lid closed me in darkness and the sun heated up the inside area and me. This was perfect bliss, not torture, I thought as I drifted into a much-needed sleep. So warm, so comfortable, stretched out at full length, I went into a deep sleep. A brilliant light filled the box, a flood of ice water dashed over me, and the box lid slammed shut. Drenched into total shock by the icy water, I managed to regain my senses.

One Marine had quietly unlocked the lid. The instant he raised it, allowing in the sunshine, his buddy dumped five gallons of the coldest water in the world on me. Of course, they immediately slammed the box lid shut and locked it. Such shock would kill one with a weak heart, and if I could have gotten out, I would have done some hurting. Those outside heard not a word from me; I hoped to rob them of their sick fun.

The biggest threat was the Peoples Pool, a pond of water made by damming up the small mountain stream behind the interrogation hut. The water was five feet deep and POWs were forced to walk into that icy water and stand for a time with water armpit high. There were no dry clothes to put on later, which allowed the hurt to last longer.

As time wore on, I lived in fear that the next loudspeaker blast would be for me to report to the People's Pool. Most had experienced it early in the exercise and were now going again, especially Pathfinders. My time had to be next, and after that bucket drench, I really dreaded it. However, my turn never came; the exercise ended without me learning the horrors of the pool.

A critique followed our POW experience with the school's instructors making the following points: Why did we go into the water as directed, especially as deep as we were told to go? Why not just wait for someone to put us into the water, and as guards do not like cold water either, maybe they would not. At the most, just walk in beyond arm's reach; no guard was going to get in to push a POW deeper.

Those points were valid in our training situation. As I saw it, however, the threat in a real situation would include bullets, which allowed the guards to keep their feet dry. The same rationale could be applied to the boxes: make the guards put you in them.

Next on the agenda was a drop off in the wild country for a three-day exercise in living off the land. The fourth day would be a movement back to base camp with enemy forces looking for us. We organized into four-man teams; each man was issued a K-Bar knife, half a parachute canopy, one fishhook, a compass, a map of the area, and a book of matches. Each team was issued a number ten can. After trucking into a distant area, we dismounted and moved as a class by foot for about an hour before the instructors started breaking us into sections.

My section moved down a valley, dropping off four-man teams thirty minutes apart. The last and deepest insertion into Fly Valley was my team; we were on our own. There was a sizable creek, sparse timber, grassy meadows, and a well-used dirt trail in the valley. The People Army patrols would be active here, expecting to find us taking advantage of the easier life.

My map study showed Fish Valley about 2,000 feet above us with a small stream, and the name implied that food was available. The stream would feed us, and the remoteness and difficulty in getting there would keep the patrols off us. We started climbing; rock cliffs, cuts, diagonally running draws, and small valleys made the climb difficult even without packs. Climbing took so long that darkness was close when we arrived in Fish Valley.

Stuffing with chow that morning was helpful, but the long day and the energy spent in the climb had long since burned off the benefit. We were hungry, tired, and de-motivated upon seeing the small stream. While the blue lines on the map were the same size for Fish and Fly Valleys, the real thing was different in a major way. It was not big enough to expect fish; the little creek could be stepped over at any point. We separated, moving in both directions, looking for a pool of water offering fish. Full darkness caused us to give up; we found only a fast-moving small stream of water.

Our dinner entrees were three frogs and one crawfish. These were put in the can and placed over a fire. Making beds of leaves, we wrapped in our parachute canopies to wait for the feast. Almost immediately, we were asleep from exhaustion. The cold awakened me sometime during the night; the fire was out. Burrowing deeper into my bed of leaves, I placed my parachute over me for more warmth. My hunger pangs had subsided, and I really did not have a taste for cold frog legs.

The cold gray dawn had us awake with a big fire. Water had evaporated from our cooking can during the night causing our frogs and crawfish to be a black burnt mess. Even Zeorb, who would eat anything, alive or dead, did not care for our meal. We had to have food. We had spent our energy on the climb in the thin atmosphere; now we were physically and mentally weak. I decided, and the others agreed, that we should return to Fly Valley and take our chances with the enemy patrols.

Arriving in the meadows in early afternoon, I split the team with two assigned to collect fish bait while two prepared fishing poles. Using the inner strings within the parachute shroud lines, we attached our hooks and cut long poles. After almost an hour, the bait hunters returned with no suitable bait, only a few mashed bugs. They had dug into the ground but could find no worms.

There had to be earthworms here; I entered the meadow for a look. Almost immediately, I spotted cow dung in the grass from the rancher's cattle and turned over the first one knowing there would be worms. There were big, juicy worms, and with a handful, I returned to the fishing task. Again splitting into teams with a fisherman and a security lookout, we went to work. Almost immediately I had a nice brook trout on the bank; in a half-hour, we had enough to feed us.

Selecting a campsite, we built a cook fire and roasted the trout over the coals. At this main camp, we prepared food, ate, and sat around. For sleeping, we split into two-man teams, separating about 200 yards and making our beds. This way if the enemy chanced upon us, at least two of us stood a good chance of getting away. Also, bedding down alone (even the two of us kept twenty-five yards apart), we could build shelters against and within fallen trees, taking advantage of nature's shelters, cover, and concealment (we actually had a problem in finding each other once we bedded down). Our beds included enough dry leaves to keep out the morning cold.

With full stomachs, we began to fuss about the lack of salt on our fish. The team on patrol during our third day found an old cow camp and returned with salt, boxes of Jell-O, and an iron grill. Now our trout would not only have salt but also be roasted on a grill with all meat edible. The real blessing was the Jell-O; when mixed with the cold creek water, tiny particles gelled, making a delicious drink.

Directed to expect a partisan visitor at the end of the third day, we had a big fire burning. The partisan appeared as promised. He gave us a time of departure with directions on our E & E route to free-world forces and departed as silently as he had appeared. As we were not to leave camp until midmorning, we received a good night's rest, followed by a fish brunch.

I studied our assigned return route with emphasis on danger areas, especially choke points through which the enemy could expect us to move. We had to stay within one click (1,000 meters) of the assigned route. One major ridgeline with only one way over it spelled trouble. The pass was clear of timber, so we would have no concealment. If the enemy was there, we did not have a chance.

We moved out and shortly arrived on the long incline to the pass. Once we reached the timberline, I put my plan into effect. We would cross one man at a time; that way, three ought to have a chance of getting away. As the enemy would not fire on one Pathfinder, but wait until the group appeared, the first guy would have it made.

The second man did not start up from the timberline until the first was about to enter the pass. Number one would be through the pass and gone by the time the second man came into the enemy's reach. The same plan applied to three and four; I was last and expected to be caught. The enemy would realize how we had duped them.

Reaching the pass, I ran through it without being jumped or fired upon. I could not believe our good luck. Either the enemy was not in the pass or maybe another team was close behind us, and they were waiting for numbers, not caring for individuals. I moved down on the double and joined my waiting team.

It was well after dark when we reached camp. After debriefing, we had steak and eggs in the chow hall, then a critique of the entire E & E exercise. The Pathfinders had done well. The next day we boarded a GV1 at Norton AFB for our return to 1st Force.

My first interest on return was to join my bride-to-be. I did not expect to find her in the cottage, and I figured that Mrs. Fishe could tell me where Dotti Lu had found work. I had mixed feelings upon learning that I could find her on the beach. It was great to be able to enjoy her immediate attention but with what was she going to pay her rent?

I found Dotti Lu and a neighbor lady enjoying the sun, sand, and surf. There were no dental or medical jobs available so she had taken a job in a laundry. The work amounted to shaking wet sheets with a large Somoan woman on the other side of a pile that never became smaller. I got the picture that the woman shook my Dotti Lu as much as the sheets, and she never went back. The employer had made it easy with his opening statement that he did not think she was right for the job. After one day, Dotti Lu agreed with him.

We received the marriage preliminaries (chaplain's talk, marriage license, etc.) and the wedding was set for Friday, 23 June 1961. On the 22nd, after returning with the marriage license, Dotti Lu seemed hesitant about going through with the ceremony. In the years since, I have learned that the dream of every young lady is the splendor of her wedding day, and Dotti Lu is a proper lady. That day, I initially took her hesitation personally, but we worked it out. It was straightforward for me: I wanted to be with the love of my life, and with a thirteen-month deployment staring at us, we did not have much time.

Friday, 23 June 1961, was a workday, but I left the barracks with my gear packed. There was an envelope containing two ten-dollar bills on my desk from Lieutenants Reczek and Phillips. This was a lot of money in 1961; we would have a honeymoon after all. I had the afternoon through Sunday off, and we had planned to spend the time in our cottage and on the local beach. Now plans included a honeymoon in La Jolla, which I knew Dotti Lu would enjoy.

Chaplain Plank performed the ceremony in the Ranch House Chapel. GySgt John Bell, Sgt Robert Happy, and his wife Barbara were present. Thanks to John, we have pictures of the wedding. He also set up a reception at the Mirmar Restaurant in Oceanside for our small group. I am forever indebted to John Bell for his foresight, guidance, and care in providing these amenities to our wedding. Without his contributions, ours would have been the simplest of weddings, and Dotti Lu deserved more.

My bride and I headed for La Jolla following the reception. We found a nice motel two blocks off the beach and the management sent up a bottle of champagne. The next morning, I learned that during my haste of the evening before, I had locked my keys in the car. We had a wonderful weekend, swimming, walking, lying on the beach, and enjoying the thought that we belonged to each other and were now one. The only missing ingredient of a perfect honeymoon was a longer time together.

Sunday afternoon found me eager to move my stuff from the barracks before the start of another Pathfinder week. Mondays through Thursdays were usually filled with heavy schedules containing much night work if not continually in the field. On the other hand, the company was good about make-up time on Fridays; the routine was to be on liberty by mid-morning, early afternoon at the latest. I had to get my new home set up and functioning.

Our cash flow was a problem until my quarters allowance started. The Olds was out of gas so I ran to and from work. The Del Mar work location was a blessing; I simply had to run about two miles straight up the beach. Force Recon had me in shape for the running, but the commute run was compounded by all of the running and physical work done during the workday. The three-to-six (occasionally ten) mile runs with the company following the 1500 PT session were enough. Adding on the four-mile commute should have had me in super shape, but I did not feel strong.

Heavy physical work burned up calories, highlighting our second problem: our pantry was empty. Like the gas tank, there was no money for a refill. We managed until payday by rationing, rabbit hunting, doing without, and inventory. During the close inventory of our assets, we discovered that Dotti Lu had not closed out her Alexandria checking account, which had a balance of $1.87. We immediately headed for the neighborhood grocery store.

The company, assigned to the 1st MarDiv for administrative control, was required to participate in a division parade. We stole the show with three platoons in jump boots, the Vandegrift green jackets with jump wings, garrison caps, and M-3A1s. The M-3A1 grease guns made the difference as we passed in review at sling arms with barrels slanted forward and right hands gripping the slings at the same position. All other units wore the blouse, barracks cover, and carried the M-14 rifle at Right Shoulder. Our egos, in spite of us having to stand a parade, were not hurt by the awareness of our smart appearance.

In garrison we kept our jump boots encased in a deep spit shine, our utilities starched with razor-sharp creases, and a blocked, squared-away cover. I have never seen Marines of another unit, including 8th and I Barracks, the drill field, or Marine Security Guard come close to the everyday routine personal appearance and display of pride and esprit as did 1st Force personnel in 1961. Many Marines would like something different in their uniform such as a symbol (shoulder patch, beret, etc.) to make them stand out. First Force personnel broke the code: when every man in the unit spends a little time and attention on appearance, the unit readily stands out.

Another people event in which the entire company was involved was a mass parachute jump. While calling a small company jump a mass jump would bring laughter from Army types, our jumps were in line with our mission, insertion of small teams. We conducted a surprise jump for our CO, Major McAlister, who had replaced Hunt.

Major James S. McAlister had been a Para-Marine in WW II; he was coming up on twenty years' service to Corps and Country and was again a jumping Marine. Gunny Parish lined up two R4Ds and an R4Q for the big event to take place on the major's twenty-year anniversary. Short of the safety personnel required on the ground, the entire company was airborne.

Our DZ was the Pendleton airfield; jump day was 18 July 1961. The Division CG, BGen F. E. Leek, escorted Major Mac to the airfield. Whatever the pretense was to get him to the field, he knew of the jump only when the Margaretta sky filled with parachutes. The three planes in a tight formation dropped us all around him. He loved it, and so did his Marines!

An R4D was scheduled for FF ParaOps on 24 July and an A3D jet bomber was on for the 26th. Free Fall was the only way out of the A3D, and company policy required a FF jump from a slower aircraft before jumping the jet; the R4D qualified us for the big one. Other than the high-stress factors, my first Hop and Pop (three-second FF jump) came off without a hitch.

Free-fall parachuting in Force Recon, I was shortly to learn, was a stressful experience for two reasons: the body position for three-second delays upon exit of the aircraft was the airborne static-line tuck, and no Delayed Opening Device was employed to slow the canopy opening. Sport jumpers were using sleeves or bags to slow their canopy openings.

Captain Jacques Andre Istell, a Marine reservist, brought the sport over from France several years earlier. The Corps brought Istell on active duty for ten days in 1958 to train Test Unit 1 Marines in FF parachuting. Two years later, Force Recon had a long way to go.

A new jumper's first FF in the company was a three-second delay before pulling the ripcord. Three seconds in the slipstream of the R4D in the required static-line body tuck left one to the mercy of luck. There was no stabilizing effect against the blast of air other then the bent torso, similar to sitting in a lawn chair with feet together, elbows tucked into sides, and hands grasping the reserve parachute. We were allowed fully flared body positions (arms and legs extended and spread) for longer delays.

The company FF parachute was a T-10, thirty-five-foot-diameter troop canopy, packed into a twenty-eight-foot aviator-emergency-parachute container. Closing the smaller container over the larger canopy required arm strength in our riggers; this tight fit created greater tension between the pack closing cones and the ripcord pins that held the container closed. A hefty tug on the ripcord opened the container, and many pulls required the use of both hands. Gunny Patterson once noted, "Hard pull—it doesn't matter. If a bull elephant were beside me, my pull would crush his skull. My chute is coming open."

Opening the container released a pilot chute that pulled out the canopy and the other problem. The rushing air opened the canopy instantly, and then the suspension lines played out causing the body at the end of the lines to stop suddenly. The opening shock was unforgettable; worse, it hurt. Man does not like to do things that punish him so severely, but when pull time came, we always did it with gritted teeth and a prayer. It was not uncommon to see a jumper hanging limp in his harness after opening shock until he regained consciousness or the hurt subsided. On quiet, windless nights, screams of agony were sometimes heard on the DZ 2,000 feet below.

While I never blacked out on one of those opening shocks, I never had one that did not cause a thousand bubbles to appear in my vision, called the "sperm count." The worst opening shocks were on the ten-second delays, which allowed the falling body to almost reach maximum velocity. The three-second-delay-opening shock did not hurt, but the bad body position increased the probability of a canopy malfunction.

On 26 July, we headed for Mirmar NAS to jump the A3D jet bomber, the recon-team-insertion aircraft. We chuted up, received our JM and rigger checks, and waited our turn. This particular plane could only carry a two-man team by replacing the bombardier and crew chief.

On jump run, we would start our slow movement (caused by the bulky, cramping parachutes) toward the bomb bay. We scooted on our rears through the small escape tunnel leading from the cockpit back through the fuselage to the bomb bay. The pilot performed the duties of the JM. On his call, the signal was passed rearward by jumper number two with a slap on the helmet of the jumper in the bomb bay. "GO!" The jumper in the escape tunnel had to scoot fast to get out and still have a chance of making the DZ.

Company procedure later changed to include the use of a four-by-twelve-inch oak board fastened to each side of the bomb bay. A four-man team strapped to the board for take off and flight. The JM, also on the board, was on the intercom with the pilot. On jump run, after the clear to drop was passed by the pilot, the JM replaced the earphones with his helmet. When he saw his exit point come under the aircraft, he dropped off the board with the others following. Problem: Once the JM removed his earphones, there was no communication with the pilot.

On a night jump the JM received clear-to-drop and removed his earphones in preparation. Observing the JM's actions, other jumpers edged forward with their legs extended downward in anticipation. At the last moment on jump run, the pilot received a "NO JUMP" from DZ Control. Not able to pass the word verbally, the pilot closed the bomb bay doors to ensure that no one jumped. The clam shell doors closed with two jumpers' feet caught between them. One managed to free himself, but the other remained clamped for the return to Mirmar. He suffered physical damage to his ankles and feet that caused the plank idea to be put on hold.

I was second in our A3D stick. When number one dropped out, it seemed to take me forever to fill his spot. The jet would be in the next county by the time I exited. Again my system was on automatic; I was simply doing things because I had been trained to do them, not because the action was wise, smart, or in my best interest.

My feet dropped and I pushed off. Going out facing aft caused the wind speed to hit my bent back, which helped stabilize me for my five-second FF. I flared back into a good arch and was almost facing the ground when I pulled my ripcord. The flat-wrapped canopy opened instantly with a murderous shock leaving me with a heavy sperm count to look through while confirming a good canopy.

Exit was at 3,000 and we were open at 2,500 feet. Initially I felt good about the long ride down. I looked the area over around the Ysidora DZ and watched the base traffic on the nearby Vandegrift Boulevard. The wind was strong, however, and I soon became concerned about an electric power line on my descent path.

My only canopy control was the riser slip. Pulling down a riser dumped air out of the opposite side of the canopy causing movement in the direction of the pulled riser. Should I try to stay on the DZ side of the power line, or go over high to be safe and sure? Trying to read my glide path, I decided to stay on the DZ and began pulling huge double-arm diagonal riser slips.

Slips helped me lose altitude, and the power line ceased to be a concern. I was not noticeably moving toward the line but seemed to be holding while descending another 500 feet. Then the wind shifted and started moving me toward the boulevard, an obstacle that I had not earlier considered. In spite of major slips of the canopy to keep me away, I was going to hit dead center of the boulevard. Raising my feet to clear the many small telephone wires lining the roadside, I decided to take the shock on my feet.

Two cars and I would hit my landing point at the same instant. I will never know what caused the driver of the lead car to look up. She stopped and I smashed in on the road in front of her. Landing on my feet, I did a cartwheel, feet to head due to my lateral speed. The impact was hard with my canopy still full of wind.

Instantly, I was off the road, across Vandegrift from the DZ, with the canopy dragging me at twenty miles per hour. I hurt so badly that it took me a few seconds to get my senses together. There was no way that I could get on my feet and collapse my chute. Fortunately, some Marines were in the field doing that very thing, and before I could remove my K-Bar to cut a riser, they collapsed my chute. The soles of my feet turned black the next day from the impact, and I received a large gash on the top of my left shoulder.

The other jumper was blown out of the zone and received help collapsing his chute. Parachuting was canceled but as the old gunny says,

"Any jump you walk away from is a good one." I logged my A3D jump while others made the trip to Mirmar for nothing.

Our Salton Sea water jump on the following day was uneventful at the unit level, but several events stood out for me. My three-second FF appeared to go okay; I went into the required body tuck, and pulled on three. We exited at 5,000 feet, and although we used the Navy's smaller twenty-eight-foot chutes, this was my first experience of so much time under the canopy. Initially, I felt that the extra canopy time would be enjoyable.

Harness straps cut into and reduced the blood circulation in my legs, and the long ride down was not the fun I expected. Several times, I prepared to enter the water because I was looking down and I could not judge the distance. The only way to tell how far I was from the water surface was to look off at the safety boats or to the distant shoreline.

We were directed not to prepare for a normal water landing (sitting deeply in the saddle and releasing our harness snaps while in the air). After feet-wet we were to activate the navy canopy releases. Once clear of the canopy, the jumper was to remove his harness and reserve parachute.

Splash down was enjoyable and the soft water refreshing. I was so buoyant, the boat so close and moving toward me, that I decided there was no need to get out of my harness. Recon's rub of non-swimming Pathfinders was on my mind. I would show them.

Well, the boat stopped to pick up another jumper, and my reserve parachute attached to my harness quickly became waterlogged. By the time the boat moved to me, the water line was at my eyes. I was getting a breath of air only with a mighty scissors kick and arm push. Ronnie Recon was not impressed with my aquatic abilities as he extended me a boat hook.

The company received movie film of the water jump, and I was shocked to watch my parachute opening in slow motion. On my back in that basic airborne-tuck position placed my parachute under me for ripcord pull. My pilot chute with the canopy apex started up one side of me as the force of air pushed more canopy up the other side. This was a perfect setup for falling all the way, rolled up and bound in a parachute canopy. The canopy rolled up my legs as my body become more head down. Finally, the canopy rolled free from under my feet. I could not believe that was me as I had not felt the canopy against me.

The summer moved rapidly toward our departure for WestPac. Dotti Lu was working for an OB/GYN physician. Our purchasing power increased with her income and the housing allowance. By 27 August, we had enough money to go east when the team was given its pre-deployment leave. A household and personal-effects move by the government was not authorized, as this was not a permanent change of station. Our possessions were packed in the Olds, and we headed home. Our plan was that Dotti Lu would stay with her folks and work in her hometown.

Two days before my leave was up, I called Naval Air at Andrew AFB and learned that a Marine GV1 with open seats was departing the following morning for El Toro, California. In order to save two months pay for airfare, I took it.

Team 44 members returned from leave, ready for deployment. While detached from the company and working with the 3rd MarDiv, Team 44 would be known as Sub-unit One, 1st Force Reconnaissance Company. In addition to our T/O Pathfinder Team, we took a parachute rigger and an extra Pathfinder.

Team members were Lt Duffy, team leader (killed in Vietnam, rank: Maj); Fox, assistant team leader; Cpl James Capers, radioman (retired as Maj and CO of 2nd Force Recon); Sgt Dennis R. Zoerb, 1st LSNCO (retired as Capt); PFC Thomas J. Vallario, Zoerb's FM (retired as GySgt with Silver Star); Cpl William E. Martin, 2nd LSNCO (killed in Vietnam, rank: Lt); PFC Patrick G. Hall, Martin's FM (non-career); Cpl Robert F. Boland, 3rd LSNCO (retired as MgySgt); PFC Frank M. Goudaillier, Boland's FM (later injured in an accidental explosion at Pendleton); PFC Edsel Ford Young, machine gunner (retired as GySgt); Sgt Carl D. Hinkle, rigger (retired as SgtMaj) and Sgt Happy, training NCO and extra hand (retired as Maj).

Team 43 returned two Marines to the States for personal reasons, leaving them short-handed. We were going prepared; we also would pick up the replacement rigger from Team 43 who wanted to stay on Okinawa to make it count for an overseas tour. In that manner, we received our thirteenth member, Cpl Edwin D. Miller, rigger. Later released from active duty, he jumped with the TV series "Rip Cord." Miller came back in the Corps for the Vietnam War and was awarded the Silver Star. He retired as a LtCol in September 1994 and was the last member of Team 44 to leave the Corps.

Team 44 members were the cream of the Corps and the best of the few good men. However, the team was only an example of the quality of the Marines in 1st Force in 1960–61. All who stayed in the Corps for a career, which was a majority, rose to the top Staff NCO ranks or received a commission by 1967, six years later. They served our Corps well in combat leadership billets during the Vietnam War.

First Force Marines of the 1960–62 era later killed in Vietnam, besides Duffy, Phillips, and Martin, were SSgt Shelton L. Eakin serving as a lieutenant, 1st Lt Walter J. Spainhour, Sgt Roy Fryman serving as Gunnery Sergeant, Cpl J. A. Rosas serving as a Staff Sergeant, Cpl Lavoy D. McVey serving as a captain and CO of a recon company, LCpl Wilbur G. Kirchoff serving as a sergeant, PFC Lowell H. Merrill serving as a corporal. The last two were killed early in that war. This roster would no doubt be much longer with good research. Our Corps has probably never had a better selection of its best serving simultaneously in a small unit.

Operation Silver Sword was scheduled for 27 October 1961 on the Hawaiian big island of Maui, and the CG FMFPAC directed 1st Force participation. Team 44 would cover the Pathfinder work en route to Okinawa, which would add to our deployment time.

We went aboard the USS Stone County, LST 1141, at San Diego on 4 October. Eakin's platoon was the company's reconnaissance commitment. We made the most of the flat bottom LST, with PT conducted daily on deck and on ropework from the ship's bridge to different masts. The Stone County arrived in Hawaii on the 17th and unloaded at Kaneohe Bay, Oahu. We trained and enjoyed some liberty before the operation kicked off. The squadron that would insert us on the operation flew us for ParaOps.

D–day was the 27th; we went in during the night of the 26th. A TF–1 Trader was not available as our jump plane so we used two HRS helicopters. On an azimuth from a coastal point, our pilots flew east for a predetermined number of minutes calculated to place us over our DZ.

The night was black with no illumination, which was good for getting on the ground unseen. However, I had to wonder how the pilots could see the terrain features necessary to place us over the DZ and how Duffy, the JM, could recognize it when he was over it. Happy was to lead my planeload out after he saw Duffy exit the chopper forward; how could he see that much? We went through the jump commands with equipment and parachute checks, then waited. After an eternity, Happy shouted, "STANDBY" and disappeared through the black hole.

The next thing I knew, I was swinging gently under an open canopy, the outline of which I could just make out above me. After the noise of the chopper engine beating my eardrums for so long, I found the quietness unreal. I was part of the blackness of the night sky; only the ground looked darker.

Keeping the play tactical, there was no talking with other jumpers to find out how close we were to each other. We had gone out in a tight Pathfinder stick; they would be in the air around me. Because of the quietness and the darkness, I felt completely alone.

I could not see, let alone focus on, the ground until I hit it with a poor PLF over volcanic rocks. Fortunately, there was no wind to cause lateral movement or we would have had some hurt Pathfinders. The entire area was one big rock pile, I learned as I rolled up my chute. I wondered how many Pathfinders might be hurt; I heard no one moving.

In total darkness, I moved on a precalculated compass azimuth to our Team Rally Point. If we landed as planned, my azimuth should work. Moving a short distance, I was challenged by a chipper, a small tin noise-maker that sounds like a big cricket. The challenge was three chirps to which I responded with the countersign of two. The two of us moved on to the rally point where we found another Pathfinder.

After waiting an hour, I decided that we must get on with the mission. I had two hours to set up the zone; the first wave of the landing force would arrive at dawn. Along the way and at the zone, I gathered three more Pathfinders; that gave me six-tenths of the team. I now had the radio and enough air panels to do the job; we started to work.

Radio silence was maintained until broken by the inbound flight leader when he passed over the Initial Point. "Lone Ranger, Lone Ranger, this is Blue Duck. I am over the IP with a flight of four. Over."

"Blue Duck, this is Lone Ranger. Azimuth is 095 degrees, no obstacles near the zone, ground is covered with big rocks, no enemy activity. Over," I responded.

"Lone Ranger, I copy 095 degrees from the IP, no obstacles, and no enemy. Over."

"Roger, Blue Duck, Wind is 285 at three knots, landing approach 285 degrees. Land in Sites Red. Over."

"Roger, three knots wind and approach at 285 on Red. Out."

The assault was on time, and we were ready. We cleared the grass and brush camouflage from our panels (a precaution against enemy patrol activity) after the check-in by the flight leader. Now it did not matter; the combat force buildup would be fast. Helicopter Support Team personnel came in on the sixth flight to relieve us of our terminal guidance mission. Our job was finished, and we were ready for sleep.

All team members had found their way to the HLZ by daylight except Duffy. He had landed against the rough side of a canyon wall and hurt his leg badly. Barely able to walk and in extreme pain, he managed to get to DZ Control. He was taken out by vehicle during the night for medical attention.

After almost a month in the Islands, Eakin returned with his platoon to California. Pathfinders went aboard the *USS Lenawee,* APA 195 on 14 November to complete our journey and relieve Team 43. Duffy went with us, although he was on crutches. We sailed on the 15th and arrived at Okinawa on the 28th. We had a short turnover with Team 43, which was headed by 1st Lt R. J. Rigg and Gunny Curt Stacy. They boarded the *Lenawee* for their return to 1st Force.

Pathfinders were located at Camp Sukiran and attached to Force Troops for billeting and administrative purposes. Supplies such as field rations, ammo, six-bys, jeeps, and training areas were ours for the asking. Operationally we were assigned to the CG, 3rd MarDiv, and worked directly for the G-3. No commander was responsible for us on a daily basis. Duffy had a free hand.

After settling into camp, we headed for the Northern Training Area (NTA) for a week. We trained hard and went into the field, either in the NTA or the Central Training Area (CTA), one week each month. In addition to terminal guidance training, we honed our skills in observing and reporting as well as entry and recovery techniques. As the division had no organic deep reconnaissance assets, we assumed that mission. There was a rumor that all Force Recon platoons would be dual-qualified, reconnaissance and Pathfinder. There would be no Pathfinder Platoons; we would be ready should the rumor be true.

A ParaOp was scheduled weekly with any aircraft that we could get from the Marines or the Navy. The old Japanese airfield, Yomitan, was our DZ. Other good DZs were nonexistent due to the island's inhabitants crowding the more level areas and the extreme roughness of the remaining land. Yomitan is on the west coast with a 300-foot cliff on the ocean side. Also of concern to parachutists were the concrete runway and parking aprons. These were rough on skin and bones while one was being dragged by a parachute filled with a strong wind. The land between the runways was tilled by the native farmers and made for soft landings. The entire field was suitable for jumping, and we only needed a small part of it. Therefore, we oriented ourselves inland and initially paid little attention to the cliff, almost a mile away.

Because of other training requirements, cancellations due to weather, and availability of jump aircraft, our first jump on The Rock was not until 3 January 1962. Jump aircraft was a HUS chopper, Duffy was the JM, and I sat in the door as his wind dummy. Duffy placed the bird over his exit spot and tapped me out at 1,500 feet; that was chopper jump altitude. Under open canopy, I quickly learned that we had a much stronger wind aloft than reported. In addition, this wind was blowing toward the cliff and ocean. I was moving rapidly across the field, but the cliff was some distance away.

The wind dummy is supposed to be that: a dummy who does nothing to steer his chute. Thus, the JM gets a true reading of how he might want to alter his exit point to put the jump sticks center DZ. I did nothing until I felt that the cliff was a threat; then I pulled heavy diagonal riser slips into the wind. Besides reducing the wind's movement of my canopy, dumping the air was increasing my rate of descent. I wanted to get down fast; the cliff was coming up.

I began to wonder if I was going to make it. Maybe I should have slipped earlier with the wind, passed safely over the cliff, and tried for a landing in the paddies along the ocean beach. Too late for a change, I placed my riser connector link under my boot, while I pulled suspension lines to dump more air. Any more and my chute would have collapsed.

I landed fifty yards from the cliff, but my relief was short lived. The wind was blowing my inflated canopy toward the cliff. This parachute did not have Capewell releases on the risers. My best chance was to run around the canopy while pulling in lines to deflate it. Getting my K-Bar off my reserve would take too long. These thoughts raced through my mind as I rolled through my PLF and back to my feet running hard for the cliff while pulling in suspension lines.

I did not make it; my chute beat me to the cliff and went over. Expecting the worst, I wondered if I could get airborne again with my canopy in the rocks. Suddenly the giant pulling me stopped. The wind flow over the cliff was such that my canopy blew over, deflated, and lay against the rocks. Pulling in one side of my canopy lines while running no doubt helped. I very quickly removed my harness before trying to pull up my chute. Duffy brought the plane down and secured the ParaOp.

Operation Tulungan was scheduled in the Philippines 26–31 March 1962. Our team and two recon platoons were assigned support missions. First Force flew over from Pendleton, and we joined them at Subic Bay. Native Negritos taught us how to live off the land before the operation started, followed with parachuting, rubber-boat work, and open-ocean swims. Closer to D-day, Team 44 went aboard a carrier in preparation for our insert.

We boarded the *USS Hancock*, CVA-19 on 19 March and for the next seven days made the most of a lack of billet planning. We made do with canvas fold-up cots in the only space available out of the weather:

in the bow-forward anchor compartment just under the flight deck. At first, we appreciated having our private area. Flight quarters, however, made our new home something else. The steam catapult that launched the aircraft was immediately over us. This arrangement caused two problems: no sleep during night launches, and vacating the compartment to preserve hearing and sanity.

At 0200 on D-day, we boarded a TF-1 for insertion on the island of Mindoro. Pathfinders forward placed their backs against the forward bulkhead. Following jumpers sat with their parachutes against the men forward; we all sat facing aft. Ten parachutists with equipment filled the small plane until I, pushing the stick, was partially in the pilot's cabin. That was better than Duffy's location; being first as JM, he was by the open hatch.

Our plane's catapult off the carrier deck was a new experience for most of us and only served to heighten our anxiety level. Planes have been known to fall into the sea at the end of the deck run. They hit the water in front of the speeding carrier, are sliced by the ship's bow, and chewed up by the ship's screws, leaving no survivors. With my entire team between the door and me, I would drink much seawater before my way out was clear, if the carrier did not plow us under. Duffy's position did not look so bad now. However, I had no influence on the situation so I tried to put it out of mind.

Our plane moved onto the cat and raced its engines, causing several Pathfinders to make the sign of the Cross. I was relieved to see that I was not the only one concerned but did not find comfort in noting that my JM was one of those making the sign. Brakes and the cat were released simultaneously causing me to feel like I was being unloaded and left on the spot. If we had not been strapped down, we would have been against the rear bulkhead or out the hatch. The short run down the deck was over before I recovered from the cat force and took a breath of air.

Going off the deck at the end of the cat gave me a moment of fright. I have since learned that it is routine for the plane to sink after it loses the cat power and before its propellers get a good bite into the air. Not expecting that drop caused a few more gray hairs to get an early start.

Instantly, our realization that the plane was flying caused a release of pent-up energy. Ten pairs of lungs expelled an "AR–RUG–GA–A–A!" heard clearly over the heavy engine roar through the open hatch. A habit of company jumpers was to hold a thumbs-down signal while the jump aircraft is rolling down the runway for takeoff. A high thumbs-up is given the second there is a feel of wheel lift-off. I saw no thumbs-down as we rolled up the deck under the cat, but there were ten thumbs up after we were airborne.

Thirty minutes of flight time put us over the coastline. Duffy, with his head out the hatch, tried to pick up landmarks. All of the plane's lights were out, which helped me note that daylight was arriving in the east. Shortly, the JM shouted, "Stand By!" Duffy followed with his jump command, "Stand Up!" The overhead was less than five feet at its highest point. Somehow, while packed like sardines, we got on our knees or squatted to do what had to be done.

"Hook Up!" was another command not easily carried out, as the anchor line cable (ALC) ran along the starboard bulkhead opposite the hatch. Parachutists nearest the cable hooked up those on the port side. A jumper is taught to hook and close his own static-line snap fastener and insert his safety wire. Jumpers on this plane had to trust their buddies to do these things.

"Check Static Line!" Again, more trust in one's buddy.

"Check Equipment!" Performance was quick and not serious as discomfort and pain took over.

"Sound Off Equipment Check!" I slapped the parachute nearest me, sounding off with, "Ten Okay!" The count with a slap was carried down to "One Okay."

Misery does not describe my feelings at this stage in that cramped space with my load. My muscles were cramped from the weight on my body, but there was no relief short of going out the door. The bumpy plane ride, the early morning hour, and the apprehension all added up to an ill feeling. I hoped the JM had not gotten us up too soon; this stooped, cramped position was next to unbearable. All I wanted to do was get out, regardless of the circumstances. JUMP!

Some minutes later the plane began to empty; I never heard Duffy's "Stand By" and "Go." Nevertheless, there was no doubt what I was about to do. In a hurting crouch caused by my tight parachute straps, I pushed against the Pathfinder to my front. As one body, ten Pathfinders passed through that little hatch, one at a time, pushing the man in front and being pushed by the man behind. For a brief second out of the hatch, I received a whiff of the rank exhaust fumes from the huge, overpowered engines.

Nine Pathfinders were in a descending line before me in the gray dawn sky with their parachutes in different stages of deployment, from Duffy, at the bottom already under a full canopy, to the man in front of me whose canopy was just breaking free of its deployment bag. We had a tight stick that would put us on the ground together.

My canopy filled with air, giving me a solid tug that meant that I had a good one in the same instant I counted "four thousand." After checking my canopy, I looked over the ground below to get oriented with my mission requirements. Parachutes were in stair-step fashion from me to the ground with Duffy going through his PLF. In the next second, I was floating down onto rolling grassland.

L-Hour for the airborne force and H-Hour for the surface force were both 0500. Arriving at dawn, we had thirty minutes to set up and be ready for the assault force. We had jumped directly into our HLZ so there was plenty of time.

Another plus for this mission was that our jump loads were lighter with the nylon air panels used for setting up day zones as compared to the heavy lights and batteries used for night zones. Once on the ground, the three LSNCOs collected their fieldmasters and moved out smartly. My job was organizing our Zone Control; that included placing Young with his A-6 MG in a commanding position in some rocks forming a high point in the terrain. Capers made his radio operational. After a short wait, the birds were over the IP wanting a vector to our zone and the enemy situation. It was a beautiful day; the landing force rapidly grew in strength.

The operation ended for us after the landing force was ashore. We flew up to Cubi Point, NAS, Subic for a few more training days and liberty, including Manila. On the training side, the company conducted a ParaOp on 6 April 1962 that drew national attention.

A Navy camera crew was in a plane taking pictures of the jump, which made every detail a matter of record. Jump aircraft was a Navy TF-1 Trader, and LCpl Dennis Boyle was caught outside the aircraft and dragged along through the air. The film shows a tight stick with Boyle pushing against the jumper ahead of him. When the deployment bag on the static line of the preceding jumper broke away from the canopy, Boyle's leg was there for it to wrap around.

Normally, when the deployment bags break away, they blow high and to the aircraft's rear. They are towed behind the plane connected by static lines. Deployment bags have probably slapped every Pathfinder jumping the Trader. This one was different, as it made a half hitch around Boyle's leg. He was caught fast with his weight binding the knot, pulling him in the slipstream of the plane.

Once a stick moves, nothing stops it; the jumpers behind Boyle did not know of his situation until they were outside the plane. Their bags and static lines slapped at Boyle, fortunately none hanging up on his equipment. Boyle and the company were again fortunate that this was an administrative jump; the JM, Lt Jack Phillips, stayed aboard to return for another load of parachutists. When Jack reached out to pull in the deployment bags, he saw Boyle flying feet first behind the plane.

Jack could not shake Boyle free so he directed the pilot to climb to 2,000 feet and return over the DZ. Boyle's training also was in play, as the JM would cut a hung-up jumper loose only if he were conscious. Boyle had been taught to signal that he was conscious by placing one or both hands on his helmet. He kept both hands on his helmet. The fouled static line held Boyle close enough to the aircraft that he had not reached the end of his own static-line-canopy-deployment cycle. His deployment bag closing strings did not break so his canopy remained safely inside the bag. Passing over the DZ, Jack cut the retaining static line and Boyle's chute deployed normally as he fell away from the plane. He landed safely with nothing more than a strained leg.

Back on Okee, we enjoyed two weeks of garrison life before returning to the field. Then we jumped on a small airstrip in the NTA to kick off Operation Habu, conducted from 23 to 28 April. Movement from the airstrip to the separate helicopter landing sites was uneventful. Each flight leader checked in with Zone Control where I vectored him to his colored site.

After the landing on D-day, Pathfinders became the aggressors and took on the good guys. The Corps' training was moving toward counter-guerrilla warfare so our small team fit the enemy scenario. The good guys had to find us.

The operation was non-eventful through Day 2. On Day 3, the last day of the operation, Duffy and I went to Camp Schwab for an administrative matter. We replaced our khaki shirts that marked us as bad guys and drove down the narrow, winding, dirt road to do our business. We were in a six-by and I was driving. At a sharp turn in the narrow road, four Marines sprang from the woods on Duffy's side, and one threw a smoke grenade into our cab.

A sharp edge of the grenade hit my forehead causing a gash and a gush of blood. Stopping the truck in heavy smoke, we both exploded through the truck doors bent on getting a handful of young, dumb Marines. They, on the other hand, saw the blood running down my face as I rounded the truck and were smart enough to clear the area. After stopping my blood flow, we continued the rest of our journey through enemy territory without incident. Operation Habu ended with no further excitement.

Pathfinders were now scheduled to be history. We would have to be dual-qualified, long-range reconnaissance and Pathfinder, if we wanted to stay with Force. While we were all Marine Corps swim qualified, some were not strong enough swimmers to suit Force Reconnaissance needs. We were fortunate in that Goudaillier was a certified Red Cross Water Safety Instructor.

I locked on the Camp Sukiran swimming pool for the entire day, every day, every other week for the month of May. Duffy did not join us as he was SCUBA qualified, but every other Pathfinder spent so much time in the water that we felt webs growing between our fingers and toes.

Frenchy, as we were allowed to call Goudaillier, was a lance corporal and, despite most of his students being in command positions over him, did not cut us any slack. While being respectful, he made and laid down the rules. With pain and occasional thoughts of near-drowning, we stayed in the water. If we wanted a certificate, we had to impress him with the fact that we were qualified.

Our first week was Pre-SCUBA School, which amounted to much hassle and harassment, similar to Junior Jump. Besides the flutter kicks and hello darlings (leg spreads) conducted on the poolside (replacing push-ups for infractions), the week was full of swim strokes and swimmer endurance. We entered the water and were not allowed to touch the sides or the bottom of the pool for a given period, usually one hour.

We learned to relax and rest in the water. Other pool weeks followed with instruction and training in the Red Cross Swimming Program. We went through all the qualifications from Swimmer to Senior Life Saving; a few of us continued to become certified as Expert Swimmers.

The weeks between our pool workouts were spent camped out on one of the Okinawa beaches. Day and night, we conducted distant open-ocean swims and rubber-boat work. We were on the beaches for so long that we could have been considered beach bums except that we kept ourselves clean and hair-free. Moreover, we were paid for having all of this fun!

Subic Bay Naval Base in the Philippines was starting up a SCUBA School and Pathfinders received one quota. I locked onto it and caught a GV-1 flight to Cubi Point on 1 July. Eleven Marines from the 3rd Recon Bn, twelve sailors, one civilian, and I checked into the Ship Repair Facility (SRF) for training. We were the first SCUBA class for the SRF, so we all learned together, instructors and students. The only physical exercise in our schedule was early morning when I would fall out the Marines. The school had no PT program; if I wanted one, I had to conduct it. Marines started each day with the Daily Dozens followed by a run before we ate chow and started our class day.

The school was easy compared to Goudaillier's pre-SCUBA training and my expectations of a good underwater-swim school. There lay the problem: the school was set up as a ship bottom repair facility. When a bunch of Marines showed up wanting an underwater-swim course, something had to be added.

Most of our dives were under the ship-loaded piers at Subic Bay with the solely stated mission of picking up coffee cups and tableware. What I did not like, and was surprised that the Navy allowed, was swimming in that filth as though there were no health concern. It was nothing to have a big brown turd hit your facemask and rub against your ear while swimming under those ships. That was our training, breathing air underwater and working with our hands.

School officials came up with a three-mile open-water surface swim that Marines would have to complete in order to graduate. Navy students did not have to do the swim. Swim time would count for 50 percent of the course grade in determining class standing among Marines, with separate standards for the Navy.

Some of the sailors went along for the boat ride as we headed for the bay in Mike boats. Two boats took their position three miles apart, and all we had to do was swim from one to the other. We hit the water as a gaggle but soon started lining out due to swim strength and speed.

My swim buddy was Sergeant Moore; we were well matched as swimmers besides being the senior enlisted Marines in the class. We took the lead early and the rest dropped quickly behind. I had shot a compass azimuth to our target boat while still in our launch boat knowing that once in the water, it would be a while before we could see the swim objective.

After about forty-five minutes, Moore began slowing with cramps. The safety boat took him aboard and remained with me so that I could complete the swim. Shortly, I could see the objective, small in the distance. The range slowly narrowed. I was the first swimmer in but only by a few minutes. The safety boat provided guidance for those without good azimuths, so all swimmers zeroed in on it to get back on course. Graduation was 27 July with me taking the honor position.

I arrived back on Okinawa in time for some ParaOps, but several weeks went by before I could exercise my latest skill. Duffy, the only other qualified diver in the team, had other business, so I lacked a dive buddy on the official side. Goudaillier and Vallario were both sport qualified on the island. Pathfinder teams did not have SCUBA gear in their T/O so I checked out diving gear from Special Services for recreational diving.

I scheduled IBS (Inflatable Boat, Small) work on the west coast at Onna Point. The island had a big storm the day before, and the surf was still up. We planned to gain some experience in getting the IBS in and out of a rough-surf zone, to include capsized drill.

Vallario and I planned to dive on the in-shore reefs while the rest of the team worked the boat. First, I wanted to test my gear in shallow water, as things like no air, not enough air, leaking mouth piece, leaking face mask, and so on are normal with Special Service gear. Adjustment and repairs are better made on land.

Stepping off a rock into waist-deep water, I submerged for my equipment test. Instantly, I was aware of rocks and jagged coral flying by my facemask. In a flash, I realized that I was being swept out to sea and that I was powerless to do anything about it. I was grateful that my regulator and tank were working well; I was breathing good air. Remembering what to do if caught in a riptide, I did not fight it. The current force slackened, and I began moving upward. Breaking surface about 300 meters offshore, I waved and yelled; I did not want Vallario to enter the water. With the surf noise, no one could understand my message. Vallario was not near the water, which was a good sign.

I headed for shore swimming on the surface, but the water was so rough that I was underwater most of the time. My strokes did not appear to move me toward the nearest point of land, a big rock. I seemed to be losing, if I were moving at all. (Unknowingly, I had surfaced on one side of the riptide, then swam back through it for the rock.) I started slow breathing to conserve air. That ready source of air was my lifesaver; without it, I would not have made it.

Meanwhile, the IBS crew launched, made it to the first breaker, were capsized, and washed up on the beach. They kept trying, and I kept flutter kicking. By this time, the IBS crew had identified the area of the riptide along the rocks on the left of the surf.

Finally getting on the other side of the riptide, I closed on the rock that I was about to learn was a poor swim objective. The waves and breakers, which did not look so bad from landward earlier, all but murdered me on that rock. I was flung crashing onto the rock and in spite of the pain, felt relief thinking I had made it, only to be washed off with the returning water.

Now the SCUBA bottle was a hazard as different parts of my body, including my head, cushioned its impact upon the rock. Not wanting to pay for it, and dearly loving its air, I hung on to the bottle. Finally, with help from those ashore, I made it. The IBS and crew were ashore. All was well.

"Where is Vallario?" I asked, when I caught my breath.

"He was with you, Gunny. He followed you into the water and was right behind you," was the dreaded response.

I was completely exhausted, and the news made me feel even worse. It was pure luck that one survived; it was too much to expect a second Marine to miss the jagged coral on the washout. Looking seaward, we found Vallario. He was a small speck out beyond the surf zone, waving a hand. He did not try to come shoreward; we would have to get him.

After many attempts, the IBS crew finally made it through the surf zone. The boat crew stayed well on the right side of the beach for the return. All was looking well; Vallario was aboard and they were inbound for the surf.

The first big breaker caught the IBS in the stern, raised it like a leaf, dumping its cargo and passengers to the winds. I could not believe what followed. Crewmembers swam shoreward; Vallario alone swam seaward. He had to work at it, but he was swimming out to sea. Of all the dumb acts! In addition, now we would pay for a SCUBA rig as Vallario had placed his in the boat after getting aboard.

The IBS crew was completely exhausted upon getting ashore. All were disgusted to see Vallario out in the water, waving for help. Nothing to do but put myself on report; I sent our truck driver to the nearest phone to call SAR (SeaAirRescue). A half-hour later, a Marine helicopter arrived, dropped a line, and hoisted Vallario aboard. SAR saved him just so I could tear into him. It ended well, and we secured our day in the surf. The only fallout was a piece in the newspaper about the SAR bird saving one of the "Great Pathfinders" from the sea.

Vallario thought he had misunderstood me saying that I was only going to test my regulator in the shallow water. Seeing me disappear seaward and knowing the place of the dive buddy, he entered the water to catch me. He was less fortunate passing through the jagged coral reef; after losing some skin, he was not ready to reenter that surf zone. He knew that there was an easier way to get ashore and waited for it. The IBS crew had tied his SCUBA rig to the boat after picking him up, so all personnel and gear were present.

Parachuting was Pathfinders' means of going to work; we made many jumps in Sub Unit 1 after leaving the company at Del Mar. I logged thirty-nine jumps with Sub Unit 1, fifty-nine upon leaving 1st Force Recon. In that number, I became JM qualified, both FF and static line. While Team 44 mounted out with only two FF rigs, I was able to get five more FFs on Okinawa.

Team 44 members' future did not include continued duty with 1st Force. Each of us received individual orders to different commands. The name Pathfinder was going into the Corps's history along with the Raiders and the Para-Marines.

Our first concern was our relief; Team 41 was trained and ready for the task. However, the entire company, including 41, was on the East Coast. President Kennedy had ordered a naval blockade of Cuba; the missile crisis was in full swing. Until that issue was settled, there would be no relief for Team 44. It mattered not that Fox had been married now for sixteen months and had spent all of three months with his bride. Hinkle, Zoerb, Capers, and I were the married Pathfinders; time really began to drag when our return looked so uncertain.

Dotti Lu was not any more enthused with my orders to Marine Aviation Detachment, NAS, Jacksonville, Florida, than I. We had no connection in Jacksonville. Worse, what was I, an infantryman, to do in a Marine Aviation Detachment? Nothing was right: no relief, going beyond our scheduled deployment time, losing Force Recon, and lousy orders. There sure was no warm glow in the future other than Dotti Lu and I being together whenever the missile crisis ended. Family togetherness was the only plus in not returning to 1st Force, where deployments, training, and field time would surely have us apart many nights. A job in an aviation-training unit, on the other hand, ought to have me home every night; it would be great getting to know the lady, my wife.

Lt Gould and SSgt Dozer with Team 41 finally arrived. We briefed the relievers and turned over our mission and equipment. Team 44 members departed Okinawa by MAC flights on 19 November, fourteen months after leaving our families. A leave followed that included Christmas in Pennsylvania and Virginia.

On 27 December 1962, I checked into Marine Aviation Detachment, Jacksonville, Florida, known as MAD, JAX. Part of the Naval Air Technical Training Command, MAD served as the housekeeper for the Marines undergoing aviation training.

The two captains in the S-3 Office were 03s, as were the enlisted. Staff NCO Troop handlers were also 03s. Marine students, some NCOs but mostly privates directly from the Infantry Training Regiment following boot camp, were assigned to one of three schools. Aviation Electronics was the big school; there was also Aviation Ordnance, and Aviation Fundamentals. My first duty assignment was as the Training NCO within the S-3 Office.

During our drive south, Dotti Lu and I talked of buying a house, but with only several hundred dollars in our pockets, that was a distant dream. However, as we drove through Jacksonville neighborhoods, we realized that our dream was within reach. Each street had several empty houses with "For Sale" signs in the yard, reading, "Nothing Down, $100.00 Closing Cost." Major naval units had moved out, causing a housing dump on the market. The Veterans Administration had foreclosed on the homes and was selling them to anyone wanting a house for the monthly payments.

We selected a six-room, masonry house with hardwood floors at 6300 Bartoff Avenue in Cedar Hills. The purchase price was $11,500.00, nothing down, $68.00 monthly payments, and $100.00 dollars closing cost. My tour of duty was for three years; surely, we would make some money on this house when we transferred in 1965. Dotti Lu and I set up housekeeping; I became a Brown Bagger.

Duty in MAD was light, which allowed time on the Detachment Rifle and Pistol Team. With the exception of Sgt Hodgson in supply, all shooters were 03s. We were out of the office from 1100 to 1400 "busting caps." Military and police units conducted the NRA-sponsored matches in which we competed, individually and as a team.

On the family side, Dotti Lu accepted a position with a doctor; that helped us furnish our home. With easy payment plans on our furniture, money was available for fun things like SCUBA gear. We bought two sets of double seventy-two-cubic-inch tanks and regulators as well as other gear needed for diving. I was the trainer and my wife the student. We did the classroom work at home and trained in the base pool (including harassment swims—I gave her the full course.) When ready for real diving, we moved to the deep wells for which northern Florida is well known. Dotti Lu, always athletic and a good swimmer, really took to SCUBA diving.

JAX had an active sport parachute club. Lt Hagen, a Navy doctor and president of the club, invited me to attend a meeting and I became a member. Based on my jump logs, the club safety officer approved my going directly into FF with the first one a three-second delay. Club requirements included membership in the Parachute Club of America.[20]

My fifth jump with the club on 31 March 1963 was not a good one. Ground wind was fifteen knots; Hagen secured jumping for all but the experienced. I should have stayed on the ground for two good reasons: First, my Double-L modified canopy had little effect on wind speed compared to the TU modification that had all of the material cut away across the bottom of a LL modification. All other jumpers on this day had TU modifications in their surplus canopies; they handled the wind better. Second, I did not have Capewell canopy releases should I be dragged and unable to deflate my chute. As it turned out, the Capewell releases would not have helped me.

We chuted up, boarded the HRS-3, and climbed to jump altitude. At 3,600 feet I exited on a ten-second delay, pulled my ripcord, and had a good canopy. Moving rapidly over the Whitehouse airfield, our DZ, I felt relief as I passed over the runway. Because of the high wind, this would be a bad time to smash in on it and be dragged over its abrasive surface. The wind line was almost down the runway. I was off the runway and about 400 feet in the air facing into the wind and backing up fast, about twenty miles per hour.

Closer to the ground, I cautioned myself to make a good PLF, not feet, ass, and head, as is habit with a backward PLF. I remember being about twenty feet off the deck but nothing else, including ground contact. I gained consciousness in the Naval Hospital, hours later, looking into the lovely face of a very concerned young lady. (I am told that I was some time in recognizing her.)

Dotti Lu was on the DZ, saw me crash and burn, and watched as the wind pushed my canopy and me across the field. The ground impact from my backward PLF knocked me unconscious. A barbed-wire fence stopped my canopy from dragging me; my head also helped when it hit a fence post. I never knew if the blood in my helmet was caused by contact with the ground or the post. Both, no doubt, contributed to my brain concussion. I had double vision throughout my ten days in the hospital. My vision slowly cleared, but the double vision bothered me while running up to six weeks later. That incident secured my jumping for a while.

On 5 May I moved from the S-3 and became the troop handler for Aviation Electronics School. An entire barracks was my responsibility, including 200 students. My duty involved maintaining the barracks, policing the daily routine, and mothering the students after classroom hours. My work took place before and after class, which gave me plenty of time in between for the pistol range and working in the parachute club.

Due to difficulties with weather, acquiring aircraft, and volunteer pilots, I was slow getting airborne after my injury. Our club worked an agreement with the JAX Navy Flying Club; we bought the gas and rented the plane, and the pilot received free flying hours. To add to my apprehension, my first jump after the injury would be out of a strange aircraft, a Cessna 170. The big difference, in addition to it being small and slow, was that the exit required climbing out on the landing gear while hanging on to the wing strut. My exit on 15 June turned out to be easier than expected; the slipstream was soft, and the slow fall away was pleasant. By 30 June, we were back in business with Naval Air; we had an R4D all day.

Dotti Lu had progressed through her ground training for parachuting when we learned that we were starting our family. While this was not a planned happening, we were pleased. She would work as long as she could, then become a full-time mommy. However, her parachuting would have to wait. We continued SCUBA diving until Dotti Lu's six-month check-up, when her doctor commented on how well she looked. Her response of SCUBA diving to his question of what she did to keep in such good shape terminated diving.

The Saturday evening of 9 November 1963 started out to be a quiet one at home. The MAD Marine Birthday Ball was taking place that night, but we were not going because the baby would arrive any day. Dotti Lu had worked up to the day before, but she was very uncomfortable. About 2200, she announced that she thought her labor had started, and we should go to the hospital. She packed and we got underway when it dawned on me that in less than an hour it would be 10 November, the Marine Corp's birthday.

Until this moment, I had not cared about the sex of our child. We had a name for either sex. Actually, I had decided at a young age that I wanted a daughter named Dixie Lee. Now, I wanted my boy born on the Corp's birthday. We talked about it on the way in, but I had the feeling that my wife did not share my enthusiasm.

I checked Dotti Lu in at 2345; the child had twenty-four hours in which to arrive on the 10th. The hospital staff shooed me away, telling me to go somewhere for coffee, or go home for some sleep. Several nurses assured me that it would be a while, and there was no way I could help. I kissed Dotti Lu and left. My Marines would be returning to the barracks after the Ball; it would be good to be on hand to ensure that I had a barracks in the morning. I stayed until all students were in and lights out. Returning to the hospital at 0130, I was surprised to learn that Dixie Lee had checked in at 0050 on 10 November.

My emotional level was pegging at an extreme high as I gazed upon my baby, that little life that was my doing, my responsibility. All parents go through it, and I have twice since, but the first time is different. This was a miracle, such a wonderful thing to have happened to me. I left that hospital feeling very important and worthwhile; my purpose on this earth was clear. I had contributed to the world.

Our world gained one personality and lost one. Twelve days later while I was driving away from the base service station, a voice on my car radio informed me that my Commander in Chief, President Kennedy, had been shot. What a crude joke: a president shot in our day and time? Later came the confirmation; our president was dead. That fact was difficult to accept; I was convinced that the Soviet Union was behind the murder.

I was selected for Gunnery Sergeant. Dixie Lee's first Christmas came and went while I waited for my promotion. We had been in JAX a year. Despite my expectations of this tour with the air Marines, it had been a good year.

Lessons Learned

1. The stress caused by a beginner's early parachute jumps is not that different from the stress of a firefight in combat.

2. Physically and mentally demanding experiences bond those who share them.

3. A special uniform or device is not necessary to identify truly elite Marines or troops.

4. The tougher and more demanding the training, the closer the bond between the individuals who share it.

7
Gunnery Sergeant
1128290/0369/8511/8411
1 February 1964

Marine Aviation Detachment held a special promotion formation; this advancement gave me only the crossed rifles, not another stripe. My rank title was cleaner, however, without the Acting word, and the pay increase replaced the jump pay that I no longer received. At that, I was well paid for the work done.

My midday routine at the pistol range improved my scores by a large margin. Team goals were to keep our qualifications as Marksmen so we would bring home more team trophies. To avoid getting a higher classification in line with our shooting abilities, we were directed to "throw away rounds." This means to miss the ten-ring purposely during official NRA matches, but intentionally losing points tends to instill bad habits. Regardless, I moved into the NRA Expert category.

Our big shooting circuit started each March with the Jacksonville Police Department's JAX Annual Dixie Pistol Matches. Tampa followed for six days with the National Mid-Winter Pistol Championships, then on to Coral Gables for seven days of shooting in the Flamingo Pistol Tournament. The big guns from all over the nation attended these meets, and I enjoyed shooting beside the Marine Corps Red and Gold Teams from Quantico. My best shooting took place at a Parris Island match where I won practically every event in my class. I did not hold back or throw away, and I moved into a higher classification. The awards were in cash coupons that I traded for a vendor's merchandise.

One other match stands out because of the high scores I received despite my intentions for the opposite. We fired at a NRA-sponsored big-bore rifle match at Camp Blanning, Florida, where I was told to hold my shooting to a Marksman classification. My M-1 and I were together that day because I could not get out of the black. Rather than practice bad habits, I held my sight picture, trigger squeeze, and timing as though I was shooting for the X-ring with each round. I planned to avoid the point buildup by moving my rear-sight windage and elevation knobs enough to place my bullet strike out of the black. My sight movements were neither bold nor soon enough; I moved from the center but remained in the black. A rapid-fire string of ten rounds hitting at nine o'-clock in the bullring was not dropping points. Too many ten-round matches ended with similar results, and I fired an Expert score.

During this time, the Corps instituted a semiannual Physical Readiness Test (PRT). As it was a pass or fail evaluation and passing was easy enough, few Marines worked up a sweat outside of the actual test. There was no incentive to do better than the minimum for passing, and Marines did no more. The PRT was conducted in boots, utilities, cartridge belt with full canteen, helmet, and individual weapon. Events of the PRT were Step-ups, Rope Climb, Buddy Carry, Advance by Fire and Maneuver, Broad Jump, and Forced March. While the rope climb with combat equipment was tough, knots were placed in the rope for foot assists.

I ran the three-mile forced march in the twenty-four-minute range, but it was not easy with a full canteen bouncing on my hip. Helmets were not made for distance running either, as they turned on your head, covering your eyes. Running with the equipment was a pure hassle, but it was combat dress the Marine Corps way. Most Marines could complete the three miles in the thirty-six minutes allowed (depending on age) with very little running. There was no follow-through on those who failed the test, which did not help the motivational level.

★ ★ ★

A Warrant Officer Gunner rate in the infantry MOS was established in 1964. This program offered me the chance to stay active in the field while working squads and platoons of infantry. I applied. Time in the Corps was against me, however, as the prerequisites specified a maximum of twelve years' service time. A waiver could be requested up to my fourteen years, but this would be my last application for the program. Now that I wanted to start over as an officer, my service time was held against me. My package went to the Board where I would later learn that I was considered but not selected. Commanding a rifle platoon became a dream. I wanted a commission, and I knew that I could handle the task. That goal was dead-ended, as I no longer met the maximum age requirement. Looking on the positive side, I was still a Marine.

The parachute club took more and more of my time; I was a member of our demonstration team, the Vapor Trails. We were not rated as high as the Navy's Shooting Stars, but we did not cost the taxpayer money either. Our show included the same events performed with the same precision in spite of our part-time, in comparison to their full-time, duty status. We jumped for all occasions in the states of Florida and Georgia.

Highlights of our in-state jumps were air shows at Boca Chica, Key West, and St. Petersburg. We flew to Meridian, Mississippi, for a big show on 24 October 1964 and performed from a C-117 at 15,000 feet. On 24 and 25 July 1965, we jumped the Flying Boxcar, the C-119, for our part in the Minneapolis, Minnesota, Air Show. Getting that crate to 15,000 feet for our jump run was a feat in itself. With smoke grenades attached to our boots, we made three passes with sub-teams doing the Diamond Star Burst, a Variable Fall, and Baton Pass. These events would not be spectacular today, but we were performing on the edge for the early sixties.

Our jump pilot, Cmdr John C. Brown USN, had a personal interest in our demonstration team, and was our secret to success. Brown, a naval aviator, was our pilot and the Navy Recruiting Officer for the Jacksonville area. If we could get a jump plane, our preference was a C-47; he could fly it or any other aircraft at Navy JAX. Brown could get a plane when we could not. He not only flew us as our Vapor Trails pilot, but his recruiting service set up many of our demonstration jumps. A Master Blaster (one who loves to jump) could not ask for a better jump situation. With our own pilot, a C-47, and plenty of fuel, we made few jumps under 15,000 feet.

Another benefit of having a team pilot was being able to make a jump from 19,000 feet, which we did on 11 April 1964. After a Sunday of jumping on our Whitehouse DZ, we planned to make the last one of the day at Deland, Florida, one hundred miles south. Naval aircraft had not been available to us for over a month, causing some of our members to drive to Deland and pay for jumps. Deland club members had ribbed our guys, saying in effect that we should belong to a club with aircraft support.

This special jump was our way of saying that we were back in business with Naval Air. Our plan was to arrive over the Deland Field unannounced at 15,000 feet, and Deland members would know of our presence when their sky filled with our parachutes. Safe jump procedures were modified for the surprise effect. Brown kept the C-47 in climb for the entire trip. We were also surprised as our altimeters continued to rise above 15,000 feet. There is an oxygen requirement for jumps over 15,000, including jumping from that altitude if much time is spent in the climb. Our mass exit over the field was at 19,000; that gave us ninety-six seconds of free-fall time down to opening altitude of 2,500 feet. Yes, we surprised the Deland Club members.

After less than a year in the club, I was elected president. In addition to being president for the remainder of my time at JAX, I was also the PCA's Area Safety Officer. I took a course in emergency parachute maintenance and packing that qualified me as a FAA Parachute Rigger. Packing my own reserve parachute appealed to me; it would save me money, and I would know that it was done correctly. (Sport parachutists pack their main parachute, but a qualified, licensed rigger must pack the reserve.)

Receiving my C License (C-2014) from PCA qualified me as a JM for all jump activities, including student training and jumps. Our club was constantly losing the more qualified members and replacements were needed for continuity. Several members had joined the club in my time, and we progressed together through the ratings, qualifications, and club leadership. Our goal was the D License, the ultimate recognition in sport parachuting at the time.

We worked hard for each requirement of the license: jump numbers, distance to target, speed in performing a series of aerial body movements in FF, and an intentional water jump. Boatswain Mate 1st Class Red Holden, Airman 1st Class Dan Asplund USAF, and I were having a problem meeting our last requirement, a night FF of twenty seconds or longer.

After several night jumps had been canceled because of weather, loss of jump aircraft, or other reasons, the three of us became obsessed with logging a qualifying night jump. On a weeknight, 22 December 1964, I had a C-45J scheduled with Brown flying. We left NAS JAX early enough to jump in on Whitehouse for a twilight jump from 9,600 feet, and a forty-five-second delay. We chuted up again while Brown landed on the airstrip, and darkness fell. There was no wind, and we were all but logging that elusive night jump.

We took off after dark, Brown climbed to 9,600 feet, and approached the DZ. Clouds had moved in and I could not see the field. There was no intercom between me (as the JM) and Brown. Motioning Dan forward, Brown sent word that he would go down to 6,000 feet, the minimum to satisfy our jump requirement, and make another run. As the JM and pilot were not talking to each other, things could go wrong and they did.

Six thousand feet put us at the base of the clouds, but a haze was moving in under the clouds. I could see the ground well enough to pick up the general trace of major terrain features like roads, wooded areas, and open fields. Thinking that Brown was inbound for our DZ, I studied hard to pick up landmarks in the approach to our DZ. Open fields relative to woods looked right, the railroad track was where I expected to find it, and the DZ must be the lighter area coming up. An automobile's headlights came on and off three times. That would be our DZ Control helping us with his position and a visible clear to drop signal.

Looking back into the aircraft, I yelled, "Stand By," as I got to my feet. Over the engine roar, I warned Red and Dan that I was not sure of my exit point, but that I was going anyway. They could do as they liked; I dove out the hatch.

Flaring, I settled into a slow fall, then did a figure eight while looking over the dark ground below. A vehicle's headlights were now on so I oriented upon them. My stopwatch read twenty seconds and my altimeter 2,500 feet; I pulled. Setting in the saddle after a good opening, I turned toward the headlights. I could not make out any detail on the ground below; the night had really gotten dark.

Those headlights started to move. Thinking that our DZ Controller had given up on us and was going home, I yelled. This caused the vehicle to depart the area quickly. Now I was truly confused but there was more to come.

The dark mass below me became trees. I raised my feet to clear treetops bordering a clearing where the vehicle had been. That clearing turned out to be a high-voltage-power-line right-of-way that I recognized too late. Luckily, my descent angle was such that I cleared the tree line and hit the ground before my canopy carried me into the wires. My canopy hit and folded over at least one wire, but fell to the ground as I stood up.

From where did this power line come, and what was this heavy forest around me? I hoped Red and Dan were as lucky as I had been. I could have been fried in the high-tension wires. I had obviously missed the DZ; where was I? The vehicle had probably headed out of the woods; I walked in the direction it had taken. The vehicle probably contained deer poachers, and my shout out of the darkness must have concerned them. An hour's walk on several dirt roads with all of my gear brought me to a hardtop. A young man in a pickup was the first driver to come along; he stopped. I was eight miles from our DZ.

Calling the club from NAS, Cecil Field, I learned that Brown had reported us off the DZ and maybe lost. No one was excited about our venture and outcome; they took the wait-and-see attitude. I called Dotti Lu to come for me, Red checked in later by phone, and Dan did not get in until daylight.

Dan and Red also earned jump stories. Dan had followed me out the aircraft hatch. Red had moved to the hatch, but at the last minute decided that he would not jump. He was not comfortable with what I had said before leaving, and he could not make out anything on the ground. As he turned to move away from the hatch, he was snatched violently out of the aircraft.

His reserve had deployed accidentally, blew out the hatch and pulled him with it. Red was fortunate that he did not make a new hatch in the bulkhead of that small plane, break any bones, or lose any limbs. He landed in a tall tree and was able to get out of his harness and climb down.

Dan did not land near the power line, but spent most of the night getting out of the forest with his gear. The word that he was okay came with the last hour of darkness and his call for a ride. That ended our drive to become D License qualified, and it came soon enough that we got three-digit numbers. My D-833 was worth the effort, but luck was also a player; that night jump could have caused deep regret and a lifetime of sorrow.

On the marksmanship side, my pistol scores had improved to the point where I would shoot for MAD at the USMC Annual Eastern Division Rifle and Pistol Matches. These matches take place each year at Camp Lejeune during April and May. I checked out on leave along with my TAD orders to the matches.

Leave was spent in Virginia and Pennsylvania, and my family stayed with Dotti Lu's parents when I headed for Lejeune. Part of my scheme included visiting my monitor at HQMC where I hoped to influence my next duty assignment. My tour was up that December, and I expected a move. The Vietnam situation was heating up, and it looked as if America would become involved in the land war. The 9th Marines were ashore and spreading out from Danang. Newspapers were full of combat actions, and there was talk of a further ground commitment beyond guarding the airfields and planes. As I had just returned from an unaccompanied tour overseas, I would not be ordered back for several years. I needed to talk with my monitor like a buddy.

Finding the correct gunnery sergeant in the Ground Staff NCO Monitor Section was not a problem. He and I made progress until we reached the point where his captain needed to sign off on waiving my overseas control date. The captain wanted to see me, after which he directed the gunny to get my record. The result of that record check and interview was that the captain wanted to send me to Paris, France. He needed the right gunnery sergeant to fill a new billet just accepted by

HQMC in Supreme Headquarters Allied Powers Europe (SHAPE). The job was Security and Honor Guard Platoon Sergeant, and the Commandant wanted it filled by the sharpest gunnery sergeant with the best record in our Corps. Well, I was flattered but not interested.

SHAPE was a three-year duty assignment that would cause me to miss the Vietnam action. The duty in Europe appealed to me, however, and I could not help thinking about the lousy timing. Any other time I would have jumped at the chance, with or without the ego buildup. Now, I only wanted a waiver and a combat assignment. I have never been a warmonger but I was a Marine trained to fight my country's battles. If there was a war, my countrymen had paid me all of those easy years to step forward and handle the war. As Marine infantry, I belonged at the cutting edge. Like in 1950, I did not want to be told how it was; I wanted to do my share and now.

The captain said that he was considering two other gunnery sergeants, and that I should submit a formal request for an overseas waiver and a combat assignment when I returned to JAX. He would consider my request and give the SHAPE assignment to a gunny who wanted the job. I headed for the matches feeling confident that Vietnam was in my near future.

Each shooting day started with rifle rounds going down range at first light. Our afternoons were spent on the pistol range firing the National Match course. We also received detailed instruction on firing the different infantry weapons. Part of a command's interest in sending a shooter to the Division Matches was to receive a qualified weapons instructor in return for the six weeks lost from duty.

My six weeks passed with me never getting a secure grip on that little monkey on the end of my rifle and pistol barrels. Timing was my weak area. A shooter must get all of his rounds off in the time allowed, yet he must concentrate totally on sight alignment and trigger squeeze, nothing else. Too often, the thought would enter my mind that the targets were about to turn, and I had a few more rounds to fire. (Timing had not been a concern when we wanted to throw rounds away.) Concentration on alignment and squeeze weakened with concern for time.

I did not shoot well enough to go to the Marine Corps Matches. Placing in the top of the second quarter of 200 pistol shooters was not bad, but I should have done better than place in the top of the third quarter of 400 rifle shooters.

We also fired both weapons for our annual Marine Corps qualification. I fired the best scores of my entire career at this time: 390 with the 45-caliber pistol, dropping ten points; and 230 with the M-1 Rifle, dropping twenty. Our Marine pistol course was easy to score well on after working so long on the National Match course. The biggest difference between the two courses was that the Marine slow-fire string of ten rounds was fired from twenty-five yards compared to the NRA fifty-yard distance. A slight misalignment of a five-inch barrel is very unforgiving at fifty yards.

I joined Dotti Lu and Dixie in Pennsylvania and we returned to JAX. Checking in off leave that Sunday night, I received the bad news. The Staff Duty Officer thought I would be ecstatic with the word that I had orders for Paris, France. "Not when there is a war going on, buddy," I said. I never learned if the captain in the Monitor Section intended all along to fill his Paris quota with me regardless of my request. My failure to inform him that I was TAD to the matches and would be six weeks before submitting the waiver request could have been a factor. Now, I did not have a chance of duty in Vietnam; the war surely would not last more than three years. My time at JAX was ending; it had been a good tour of duty except for our house situation. The market had not improved and we had to give our first home away.

Leave time fits well with transfers; we headed home to say good-bye for three years. Eakin was stationed at Marine Barracks where he was the Color Sergeant. Dotti Lu, Dixie, and I visited with Eakin, Deanna, and Mark in their Maryland apartment. Always the tall, skinny kid, Eakin had finally arrived at one of his objectives. Still with a small thirty-inch waist, his arms and shoulders were next to massive, topped with a muscular 16½–inch neck. He really looked great and was enjoying his tour of duty. We talked about Vietnam and our chances of becoming involved; he was in a much better position to see action. Little did I know that I was talking with my gungy buddy for the last time.

On 29 September 1965, we took a MAC flight out of McGuire AFB to Orly Field, Paris. Dixie, not yet two years old, slept for most of the flight. Neither Dotti Lu nor I had any rest, and we were ready for the hotel when our sponsor met us at the airport. GySgt Joseph P. McCartney, our sponsor, delivered us to a hotel off the Champs-Elysees. Joe, who was assigned to the European Command, picked me up the following day and took me to SHAPE for an orientation and check-in.

SHAPE was outside the western edge of the city proper. A hotel on SHAPE's side of the city would suit my commute better; I found one in Versailles and we moved. Our transportation problem was settled by buying a used Volkswagen.

The Security and Honor Guard Platoon was in the process of forming with three men from each NATO member country. The plan called
for each service from each country to be represented, but some countries,
such as Norway, sent three soldiers. Security for SHAPE had been provided by Army personnel from the US, the UK, and France. This force
would be reduced by the numbers arriving for the new organization.

International Police Supervisor was my secondary job title and primary functional role. I replaced a US Army MSgt and joined an UK Army
WO and a French Gendarme WO in supervising the security force concerned with all of SHAPE property. As such, we worked a twenty-four-
hour duty every third day. The two days between were truly days off.

We rented a two-bedroom apartment in a recent high-rise development in Parc St Cyr, Fontenay-le-Fleury, close to SHAPE. The lack of
our household goods, however, kept us in the hotel for the full sixty days
at government expense.

The Stars and Stripes newspaper was now full of Marine action in
Vietnam. Keeping up with what was happening in Vietnam did not make
my great duty any easier to accept. A ray of hope appeared in late October 1965 in the form of ALMAR 23: subject was a new Temporary 2nd
Lt and WO Program.[21] A Board would screen all SNCOs for selection
to temporary 2nd lieutenant and warrant officer ranks. Selectees would
retain their permanent enlisted ranks; there would be no OCS or TBS.
Commissioning would be direct and into the field for which qualified
and serving.

That the commission was temporary did not concern me because
I felt that once I had it, I would keep it. Much can happen in four years,
including my having enough time to retire. I thought of SgtMaj Daniel
J. Daly, an old Corps legend who received two Medals of Honor. He was
credited with rallying his Marines to attack the Germans in WW I with
the cry, "Come on you sons-of-bitches, do you want to live forever?"
Daly's answer to the question of why he never became an officer is said
to have been: "I had rather be an outstanding sergeant than just another
officer."

I never understood why Daly felt that he would not make an outstanding officer. I had been an outstanding sergeant, and I was going to
work at being an outstanding officer. I felt confident in my future performance as a rifle platoon leader; I had experienced that level of responsibility at times as a sergeant and enjoyed the challenge. Outstanding sergeants can be outstanding officers; I personally knew many such
Mustangs.

Not leaving my chance solely to the Selection Board, I immediately applied for consideration. On my application dated 3 November 1965, I again requested the infantry MOS. A second choice was required on the application: Armored Vehicles would do. I did not worry about getting tanks; the Corps needed infantry platoon leaders.

LtCol J. F. Holzbauer, the Senior Marine Officer at SHAPE, signed the second endorsement of my application. He recommended me with enthusiasm and followed with:

> Despite the fact that I have had the opportunity to observe Fox for a limited period of time, I consider him outstandingly qualified for the subject program. I have been most favorably impressed with his enthusiastic attitude, initiative, aggressiveness, and his ability to get along with people. The latter characteristic has been most evident in his association with the many nationalities represented at SHAPE.
>
> Fox's recent assignment to this Headquarters should not be considered as an impediment for his selection. The Marine Corps would be remiss in overlooking Fox's outstanding potential for this vital program. In time of hostilities, I would particularly desire to have Fox serve in my command as a commissioned or warrant officer.

With my application on the way, I settled down to making the most of my European assignment and surviving among the French. Paris rush-hour traffic was something else; I had never seen such driver behavior. My duty hours allowed me to miss the worst, and driving an older and smaller car helped. I soon learned that one could not move very far driving defensively. Driving in Paris is one great bluff game; the faster you drive and the more careless you appear to be, the better you move. The only rule seemed to be "Watch the car on your right; it has the right-of-way."

Germany, Norway, Denmark, and Italy sent their contingent of honor guards. Along with the three countries' troops already in place, my platoon began taking on an international flavor. The US Army provided 2nd Lt A. J. Ridolfi as the Security Honor Guard Platoon Commander.

My assignment gave me plenty of time off, and Marine opportunities to visit Europe did not come around often. Skiing the Alps was high on our priority list. My work schedule allowed us to ski in France and Switzerland for two days just about anytime we wanted. Toward the end of February 1966, we enjoyed a ski week at Berchtesgaden, Germany. We used the US Army facilities, everything from the hotel to the ski slope with a ski-week package. Skiing occupied our days while the evenings were spent enjoying good food and checking out the local merchandise.

Shopping in Berchtesgaden was great; the deutsche mark was four to the dollar, which made good German products affordable. We visited the Schober's Crystal factory and invested in our family crystal. We were able to appreciate the price better six years later when we returned to add to our selection. The German mark was much more closely valued to the dollar, and Schober had become big business. Increasing our place settings, we paid more for the four of each setting than we did for the original eight.

With all of the skiing and shopping taking place, there was yet time for parachuting. The US Army had an aviation unit at Bricy, France, located below Orleans. While not handy, the unit did have an active sport parachute club, and I added Army Beavers and Otters to my growing list of aircraft jumped. Several jumps with a French parachute club added the French Albert Goulordt, but I did not make enough money to afford many jumps with the French.

Officer selection was now foremost in my mind; I read all message traffic arriving in the Naval Admin Section. I wanted selection as a 2nd lieutenant in a big way; I had never wanted anything more. *The Navy Times* and *The Stars and Stripes* were helpful in keeping me abreast of what the Marine Corps was doing in getting ready for the war in Vietnam. We were growing to three full divisions with supporting air wings.

A message from HQMC provided the results of the 1st Sergeant and Master Sergeant Selection Board. I had not paid any attention to the Board meeting as I considered myself years away from that rank. Because of the buildup for the war, however, both Eakin and I were selected for promotion to 1st Sergeant. Although Eakin was far down on the list, he was closing the gap on me; we were now on the same list. While I had only been a gunnery sergeant for two years, Eakin was *on* his first year. Neither of us would ever wear any more stripes.

Finally, the list for which I had been waiting was published. I was selected for commissioning to the rank of 2nd Lt, Temporary, with MOS 0302, Infantry. Great! Naturally, Eakin was also selected; he had more than closed the gap between us. His name was now several hundred numbers ahead of mine. Our date of rank would be the same but technically he would be senior. Lineal placement showed just how well the selection board members had done their work. Eakin's gungy attitude, approach to duties, and job performances were measurable and deserved this recognition.

The first commissioning of staff NCOs would be on 27 May 1966; the end was in sight. I would be commissioned out of my job, and "Mark Time" became the order in my life. The Marine Corps, in my case anyway, did not move fast enough with the buildup of the force. Time was available for a leave that included a ferry ride and visit to London and a timely visit to the tulip fields in Holland. While seeing Europe, we also began preparations for our return to the States by ordering two cars to take with us, a Volkswagen Fastback and a Triumph Spitfire.

President Charles DeGaulle was making my departure easy. While the military clause would have gotten me out of my three-year apartment lease, DeGaulle was kicking SHAPE out of France. Our family move would be ahead of the mass exodus. My landlord expected my departure and returned my full security deposit.

While I never wore the stripes of 1st Sergeant, my record shows that I was one from 16 May until 27 May 1966. My 1st Sergeant warrant must have come over by boat because it arrived after my commissioning date. I was a lieutenant when it caught up with me, my second promotion within the month.

Lesson Learned

Regardless of the barriers before you, if you want something strongly enough, continue to work hard for it.

8
2nd Lieutenant
096702/0302/9953

27 May 1966

Brigadier General John W. Antonelli commissioned three gunnery sergeants to lieutenant on 27 May 1966. Antonelli, the Senior Marine in Europe, and two of the gunnies, Joe McCartney and Richard E. Farlee, were assigned to the US European Command located near the SHAPE Headquarters. I was the third; the only enlisted US Marine assigned to SHAPE. Our ceremony took place in the general's office, and Dotti Lu assisted with pinning on my bars.

The first thing I noticed with my commission was that I did not meet anyone without saluting. Enlisted personnel salute all officers, but I had never thought of the officer's position. Now it hit home; most of the people encountered are enlisted, and enlisted do not salute each other. A 2nd lieutenant salutes everyone except 2nd lieutenants, and there was only one other in SHAPE. Later, I learned that the encounters not requiring return salutes get fewer with the rise in rank: generals exchange salutes with everyone. Saluting was never a problem for me; my point is that I gained a different perspective on this military formality as a lieutenant.

Rather than receiving orders directly to Vietnam, I would be assigned stateside to settle my family. I requested duty with 2nd Force Recon at Camp Lejeune. The transition from SHAPE would take a month. Sergeant Hertner of the German Army assumed my platoon sergeant duties, and I became the assistant platoon commander. Ridolfi and Hertner did not need help running the platoon, and I no longer worked as Police Supervisor. My name was on the OD duty roster for two days each week, which required me to be reachable by phone should the supervisor need me.

By trading OD duty days, I had a week's leave and we toured Europe. On 31 May, we drove through Switzerland to Italy, climbed the Leaning Tower of Pisa, enjoyed the sand and surf at the US Army Base at Leghorn, and shopped. Our travel plans originally included Rome, but we were forced to give that up after three days in Livorno. Shopping ended our travel because our car was overloaded with alabaster. We returned to Paris, with much of Europe yet to visit and on our "Do List."

I signed my family up for a West Berlin visit, and on 21 June, we made the unforgettable trip that provided our first exposure to the Soviet routine. The train ride was uneventful, other than the delays through the checkpoints that took all night. We had a sleeping car so that was no problem; our train pulled into Berlin early on the 22nd.

The difference between West and East Berlin was like night and day. With thriving communities, the West was all business, and the city was rebuilt from the war damage. We visited the East through Checkpoint Charlie and found a different story. The streets were empty, very few people and vehicles were seen, and there was little repair of the war damage from twenty-plus years earlier. Communism was not going to make it. We returned to the West feeling fortunate to enjoy the free world's way of life.

On 24 July, with less than eleven months served on this three-year assignment, we returned to the States for fifteen days of leave before heading to Camp Lejeune. Our first visit with Dotti Lu's family gave me a few more days before my beliefs were shattered. Soon after arriving at my home, my mother gave me my mail. In that stack was a letter from Captain Bob Reed at Marine Barracks, 8th and I, that should have been rimmed in black. I did not immediately connect him to the Sergeant Bob Reed of my Drill Instructor days, a skin-diving buddy of Eakin's and mine. The letter read:

2 August 1966

Dear Lieutenant Fox:

It is my unpleasant task to inform you that Lieutenant Shelton L. Eakin was killed in Vietnam on 27 July. Details are sketchy, but we do know that he left Okinawa on 7 July for Chu Lai with Recon Company, 1st Marine Division. He participated in only two missions, capturing two prisoners. He was commencing his third, when he stepped out of the helicopter directly onto a mine. Death was officially caused by multiple shrapnel wounds in the legs, stomach, and chest. He held on for about 12 hours before dying in the field hospital.

Deanna has asked that I be the escort officer when he arrives in the States. As yet, he has not left Saigon. He is to be buried in Texarkana. I talked to her by telephone today, and she and Mark are taking it as well as to be expected. Since he left them only a month ago tomorrow, the shock was probably compounded. She asked that I write you, as she doubted you might already know.

While here at 8th and Eye, Shelton continued to be the totally outstanding Marine everyone knew him to be. He was first the Color Sergeant of the Marine Corps, before being commissioned a 2nd Lieutenant in June. This entire command feels the loss—as he was unquestionably one of the finest Marines any of us shall ever know.

If there is any information I can provide to you, please don't hesitate to ask. Deanna is living with her parents at the following address: 1030 Linden Street, Texarkana, Arkansas.

I'm sure she'd appreciate hearing from you.

Sincerely,
R. M. Reed
Captain, US Marine Corps
Adjutant

Nothing registered. There had to be a mistake! I read Bob's letter repeatedly, expecting the words to change their message. They had to change. Eakin was at the Barracks; I planned to visit him within the next few days. This letter placed him in Vietnam, in combat, dead, KIA. Nothing fit; nothing was right. How did he get there so quickly? Not only did he get into combat quickly, he died too soon. Eakin did not have a chance to do all the great things of which he was so capable. I could not accept the message this letter conveyed!

In spite of knowing firsthand that combat is unforgiving and merciless, I was severely shaken by Eakin's death. A Marine is an optimist and must be in order to move forward with what he is expected to accomplish. The one person he knows will come through the fight is himself. I had accepted the fact that I might go down but not for the long count. My problem with Eakin's death, I have since realized, was that I had placed him in that hands-off position with me. He would never be killed doing his Marine duty. Eakin's death proved that theory wrong. His death was such a waste to his young family, his Corps, and his country. I would be a long time getting over this black letter. Though my faith was deeply shaken, my dedication and resolve to take on the communist was strengthened. I had to go to Texarkana. I called Deanna and learned that Eakin's body was home; the funeral would be in three days.

Our Volkswagen was somewhere at sea, but the Triumph Spitfire arrived in New York in time for my need. Picking up the car, I drove straight through to Texarkana, arriving the night before the funeral service. For sixteen hours each way (before the interstate highway system), I asked and tried to reason why. Why Eakin? Beating myself up on the highway and saluting Eakin during the rifle volley and taps helped.

Three years later I would meet Eakin's Company Commander and learn of my buddy's last hours. Captain Timothy Geraghty headed for the hospital ship when he learned of Eakin's situation. Eakin was the leader of a reconnaissance patrol that had been inserted by helicopter. Before the chopper had lifted off, Eakin tripped a mine while leading his team from the LZ. The team immediately reembarked the chopper with their wounded, carrying Eakin to the hospital ship.

Eakin lost everything below his upper torso. The doctors were shocked that a man could be alive in such condition, let alone be conscious. Eakin hung on for twelve hours, gaining consciousness and speaking of his family. Typical of this gungy Marine, he would not give in to death. It had to take him. Losing Eakin to a mine hurt even worse because he was capable of so many great actions. Even Geraghty, who had known Eakin less than a month, was deeply affected by his loss.

Marine activity would help pull my focus toward center so I headed for Camp Lejeune. Until our furniture arrived from France and we were assigned quarters, my girls would stay in Pennsylvania. On 16 August I checked in for duty with 2nd Force Reconnaissance Company and received a room in the Camp Geiger BOQ. (A month later, we were assigned quarters in Tarawa Terrace, our furniture was delivered, and we were back into housekeeping.)

I assumed command of the 2nd Platoon from 1st Lieutenant John Walter Ripley, who was departing for Vietnam. John's orders did not give him much slack, and our command turnover was brief. He fell the platoon in, thanked each Marine for his support, wished them all well, and introduced me as their new commander. John departed immediately.[22]

Getting back into Recon's way of doing things helped my mental state. Eakin was less than a constant thought; I was beginning to function.

Learning the officer's role on the job was easy enough, but my adjustment to officer status had a glitch. For some reason, the 1st Sergeant seemed to resent me. His words and actions were barely on the proper side of respectful. His "sirs," as few as they were, were borderline mockery but not enough to nail him. Being the new guy on the team, I hesitated to call him down. He no doubt resented my temporary lieutenant status; otherwise, we were of equal rank.

After several weeks, his problem came into the open. A Marine developed a domestic situation that deserved his taking emergency leave. I signed his leave request and put it in the admin office for the CO's signature. The following morning I was surprised to see this Marine in formation. His answer to my question was, "The 1st Sergeant disapproved my leave."

Telling Jefferson to get ready to depart on leave and to come by my office for his leave paper, I headed for that 1st Sgt's office. Finding him seated behind his desk, I slammed his hatch shut and let him have it. "Who do you think you are to disapprove a leave that I have approved? Once a platoon leader has approved an action, you are merely a paper carrier, or at best an advisor to the commander. The CO is the only person in this company who can override my decision." I was ready to take the issue to the Major; it was the 1st Sgt's move. The tiger disappeared with an apology and statement that he had failed to notice my signature on the leave request. He thought the platoon sergeant had sent the request up the chain. I had no more staff NCO problems.

Second Force deployed to Roosevelt Roads, Puerto Rico, on 15 October for training and preparation for a ReconEx on Trinidad. Planning and conducting the exercise offered excellent training opportunities, as the area, the people, and the island were all different from our normal operating routine. Submarine and aircraft insertions of our teams added a realistic flavor. The local people were never to see our Ronnie Recons, and they did not.

R–Day was 31 October, with teams swimming ashore following their underway-submerged-lockouts from the *USS Sea Lion,* APSS-315. Other teams entered the objective area by parachute from C1As[23] the same night. For safety reasons, the naval base golf course was used as the DZ; teams moved out silently while keeping realism in their play.

After four days, teams recovered by swimming out to the *Sea Lion* or walking out to a safe area. Fresh teams were again inserted for additional information. We did the full package from beach reconnaissance and hydrographic surveys to road, bridge, and facility reconnaissance.

After eight days and nights at work, we enjoyed liberty on the island. We loaded aboard the *Sea Lion* on 13 November for a three-day return trip to Puerto Rico with a liberty stop in St. Thomas and returned to Camp Lejeune and our families on the 17th by C-130s.

Marine leaders in Vietnam were learning the value of reconnaissance forces. The commander needed to know where the enemy was and in what force, but lack of information about the enemy was a constant problem. Saturating an area with small, four-man recon teams was better than deploying larger combat units for the same information-gathering missions. Our Corps, however, was short on reconnaissance personnel. To help with this shortfall, 3rd Force Reconnaisance Company had formed and trained at Camp Geiger; it was deploying to Vietnam as I reported aboard.

Our company became a training source for replacements to 1st and 3rd Force Reconnaissance Companies. Individual orders came daily, directing our more experienced Marines to Vietnam. On the plus side, we began to get some returns from Vietnam who provided first-hand information on what was expected of Ronnie Recon in this war. My Platoon Sergeant, SSgt Jess Giles was one of the returnees. Jess is the brother of Jim, with whom I served in the Disciplinary Platoon on the Drill Field in 1956.

On 19 January 1967, we traveled to the Submarine Base, New London, Connecticut, for Buoyant Ascent Training. Our purpose was certification for submarine lockout after making the required ascents under supervision in the submarine escape-training tower. Known as Blow and Go, the swimmer slowly flutter-kicks upward at the speed of his rising bubbles. The 110-foot ascent was easy while blowing out air the entire distance. Buoyant ascent training educates one about the laws of gravity and pressure. The point of the training is not concern for having enough breath to allow you to make the long movement upward, but the realization that you have so much air compressed in your lungs that you must continually blow it out on your ascent. Pressure at the 110-foot level equals the weight of the water placement above and must be released as you move upward, or your lungs simply explode. We were getting ready for SUBOPS with the *Sea Lion*.

Second Force went aboard the *Sea Lion* on 23 January 1967 at Roosevelt Roads, and got underway for St. Thomas and St. Croix. For the next two days we lay on the bottom of Perseverance Bay and practiced getting out of and back into the sub. Known as Lockout and Lockin, the escape trunk provided the means for submerged exit and entry. Water depth for the first day was forty feet over the deck.

The escape trunk on a submarine is the emergency exit while submerged. If the sub cannot rise to the surface, the crew can get out if they are not too deep. Reconnaissance Marines use this trunk as a doorway to work, to get out of the submarine undetected and move into their objective area. Other services use this method with SCUBA gear; to my knowledge, Marines are the only ones who do it the bare-balls way.

Submarines are built to withstand the pressure against them for the depths in which they operate. Their hull strength allows the crew to live and work at surface pressure, despite their depth. Different pressures inside and out are the reasons for the escape trunk. With the trunk at the inside pressure, the inner hatch can be opened. One enters the trunk, dogs the hatch, and turns on the water and pressure. When the water level rises above the outside hatch and the trunk pressure equals the outside water pressure, the outside hatch can be opened.

The *Sea Lion's* escape trunk is located above the forward torpedo room. With torpedoes unloaded, the torpedo room is used for troop berthing. The escape-trunk hatch is located in the compartment overhead and serves as the bottom or deck of the escape trunk. Besides that small, twenty-one-by-twenty-seven-inch hatch, the rest of the escape trunk deck is a narrow ring around the hatch extending to the circular bulkhead. The internal size of the trunk is forty-four inches in diameter and seventy-two inches in height. Four Marines can squeeze into the trunk.

Teams have four members, and they must lock out simultaneously if they are to swim together. Otherwise, two have to lock out with SCUBA gear and hang onto the deck structure for up to fifteen minutes until the other pair gets out. No more than two Marines can lock out with SCUBA gear consisting of double seventy-two-cubic-inch tanks. Locking out with four men was tight and tough. However, it was the better way if the entry was a surface swim and SCUBA was not needed for the mission.

"Team One, enter the tank," came the voice over the 31-MC. I was first up the ladder and placed my feet, duck fashion, along the border around the hatch opening. By the time number three crowded upward, I wondered if it would work. We had already filled the small space, facing each other with life jackets (deflated), face masks over our foreheads, and swim fins hanging from our arms. Number four had yet to enter, and with the hatch sticking up in his space, he had no room. A place was made, however, as I maneuvered behind and onto the hatch. Number four squeezed in, and we managed to get the hatch down while suspending ourselves in space, one at a time. Fortunately, dogging the hatch is done from below.

"Secure vent. Open flood," barked the 31-MC. As the Escape Trunk Operator, I pressed the talk switch on the 31-MC and repeated the commands while doing as told. The vents had been set on drain and de-pressurize; I closed the vent and opened the water valve.

While the tank filled with water, we took turns putting on our swim fins. It was next to impossible to bend over or raise a leg to get the flippers on, but we could not put them on sooner because of having to climb the ladder and lower that hatch. With much work and cursing, flippers were placed while the water continued to rise until it reached a mark about two inches above the top of the thirty-inch diameter side hatch. That placed the water line at my chin.

"Secure flood. Open blow," I said for the benefit of the 31-MC. The message was repeated back to me. Turning off the water, I opened the pressure valve called the blow. With a loud noise, pressurized air began filling the small space left between the water line and the top of the tank, known as the bubble, which contained our heads.[24]

"Undogging outside hatch." With the repeat from control, I un-dogged the hatch. As the pressure built, we began working our jaws or holding our noses and blowing to equalize the pressure within our ears. The buildup continued until the outside hatch cracked open. With the flood of daylight into our tank, I pushed the talk button, stating, "Securing the blow. Team departing." Following the repeat, we pushed out through the hatch into a beautiful underwater world.

At forty feet in that clear bay water, the sub was bathed in filtered sunlight. The scene was that of a giant sleeping in the sun's warmth. Everything took its place in a Technicolor picture with schools of fish of all sizes and colors darting about. However, we could not hang around and enjoy the sights; we had to blow and go. Normally the last man out closes and dogs the hatch so that it can be used again from inside. We would return in a few minutes so it was left open.

Each of us blew air from our lungs and started upward at the speed of our rising bubbles while continuing to blow out air. Reaching the surface, we lay on our backs while working our flippers lazily in the sun and warm water. After about two minutes, we started down. This was a different animal. We started down one behind the other, but that order was broken as one, and then another, could not equalize (clear) the pressure building in their inner ears. They stopped in order to relieve the severe pain. A lung full of surface air is no air in the lungs below fifteen feet; if one could not clear his ears, he went back to the surface in need of air.

Although I had filled my lungs, I was not halfway to the tank when my body demanded a breath. I had to fight the impulse to breathe although I was deep in the water. Clearing my ears became a lower priority in spite of a sharp pain in my right ear. My lungs felt flat as I bore-sighted on the open escape-trunk hatch. Maybe I would make it, but I would have nothing to spare.

Grabbing the edges of the hatch, I heaved myself bodily in and upward into the small tank. Smashing into the body already in the tank, I had but one thought: get my head into that air bubble. The simple task of breathing takes on the highest priority when we do not have air.

The third swimmer entered the tank, demanding and taking his share of space. After about a minute, number four entered like a bull, making a hole where there was none. The three of us pretty much filled the small space, each using a third while taking off our flippers, without any thoughts of preparation for the fourth swimmer. Not to worry, number four knew where the air bubble was, and ten Marines in that space would not have kept him out of it.

I pushed the talk button, "Team One aboard. Outside hatch dogged. Coming up." Coming up referred to pressure; we were going to surface pressure. I continued with "Opening the drain. Opening the vent." The water line started down while we started adjusting to the change from the pressure of depth. Next was the problem of pulling one end of our deck, the only little space upon which we stood, up through our midst. Clinging to the sides of the tank, we raised the hatch, and climbed down for our critique and debrief.

Other teams took their turns at locking out, then we all did the Lockout and In again during darkness. The next day the *Sea Lion* moved into deeper water where we again did a day and night lockout with the sub on the bottom. Then the real fun started.

We moved into underway Lockout and In with the *Sea Lion* in open water. The sub moved at periscope depth at one-knot speed and dropped off teams as quickly as the escape trunk could be operated. Even with the best team trunk-operating times, teams were scattered ten minutes and more apart. No action was wasted or done without a purpose; the hour in the water waiting on the returning sub was training time: learning to rest in the ocean.

Recon teams recovering aboard a submarine are prepared for a long wait at sea. After a four-day mission ashore, the team and the sub expect to meet at a specified distance and azimuth from a shore landmark at a specified time. Unknown factors that influence this meeting engagement are enemy activities, wind and current drifts, casualties among team members, and team strength. Individual strength weakens after four days ashore with little to eat.

While sub commanders have tidal charts and can plan pickup times to give swim teams favorable tidal flows, execution is seldom the way it is planned. Teams have experienced an all-night wait in the water 6,000 yards offshore while floating on their backs. (Life vests are no help; that descent is tough enough without carrying an air bubble down with you. Once the sub snags the pickup line, there is no time to get the air out of the vest.) Occasionally, subs are unsuccessful with their recovery attempt, causing a team to return ashore, hide during daylight, and swim out the following night for pickup.

Team members play an active role in helping the sub find them after they arrive in the pickup area. Three members rest while the fourth strikes two K-Bars or brass rods, known as calypso sticks, together underwater. The sub's sonar searches for and homes in on this sound. Although the team members swim on a compass azimuth for the calculated time it should take their team to swim to the pickup point, they seldom are close. Wind and tidal currents move them if they wait very long for the sub, as the sea is a live, moving stage. Without something for the submarine to home in on, pickup of teams is a hit or miss situation. At pickup time, the sub simply tracks up and down the coast on 500-meter slices, working its sonar for the signal.

Two safety divers with SCUBA gear lock out in preparation for the pickup. They ensure the trunk is ready for the team, the outside hatch open, and send up a buoy with a descent line. They hang on to the sub's bridge where they can observe and help anyone who gets in trouble.

The buoy rope is attached to the escape-trunk hatch and is long enough to allow the buoy to ride on the water surface. The buoy alerts the team to the sub's location and its direction of movement. It snags the climbing rope, pulling the team along with the sub. Swimmers use the buoy rope as a guide to the escape trunk and as a means to pull themselves down, hand over hand.

Once the sub has a lock on the calypso signal, it approaches the team, running parallel with the coast. The team members have been waiting with a 120-foot climbing rope strung out between them, perpendicular to the coastline. One member is on each end of the rope with the others in the center trading off on the calypso sticks.

When the buoy is sighted coming toward them, team members swim right or left so that it catches the climbing rope center. The sub

movement continues and the two end members are brought together by
the rope action. Though the sub is moving at only about one-knot speed,
pulling hand over hand forward along the climbing rope is not easy because of the push of the water. Both center men reach the buoy first and
start down.

Packs, with all land gear including boots, clothing, communication
equipment, and weapons, have been waterproofed and towed by the
swimmers. As each swimmer reaches the buoy, he attaches his pack for
recovery by the safety swimmers. It is impossible to pull that buoyant
pack down the rope on a free dive, even for Marines. Most of us are lucky
to get ourselves down.

Underway recoveries do not allow a swimmer having difficulty
clearing his ears to go up for pressure relief. Unless he is the last man, others on the rope behind him must keep moving to make the air bubble.
Anyone stopping the movement is knocked off and out of the way. Without a hold on the moving submarine, the swimmer is behind the boat.

Safety divers are on towropes that allow them to move up and
down the swimmer descent line. Should a swimmer have clearing problems, he signals the safety and grabs the safety's towrope. The safety then
gives his mouthpiece to the swimmer, allowing him to suck in air while
equalizing the pressure buildup in his ears. Once the swimmer clears, he
is back on the rope in descent.

After an hour wait, the buoy and periscope were bearing in on us.
The buoy caught our rope center, and I quickly joined the swimmer on
the other end. Things were happening faster than I expected. The big difference was that this was positive forward action; lose the rope and you
were left alone in the sea.

As I moved forward on the rope, I was grateful that I was not
pulling an equipment pack. Breathing through my snorkel tube was not
constant as now and then I would be towed under a wave, requiring
heavy outward blowing to clear the tube before my next inhale. I tried
to determine when a wave would wash over me so that I would have
my lungs full of air. No air in my lungs and a water-filled snorkel created a major problem. Face mask and snorkel were helpful, but at this
stage, swim fins did not offer much help. Movement was primarily by
pulling along on the rope; fins would be essential for going down, even
with the rope.

Arriving at the buoy, I paused, trying to suck up the whole atmosphere of air. I was number three going down; receiving a thumbs–up from
number four, I took a final huge gulp of air, and went under. Underway

was a far different task from stationary descent. The wash, or resistance, of the water was unbelievable.

I immediately started my ear-clearing, hoping to stay ahead of the squeeze. There would be no time for anything other than getting into that air bubble. The safety divers were on station, one high and the other low, holding on to their towropes. They did not appear handy, and as I was almost down when I received an ear squeeze, I continued for the bubble. I was to learn later that this was not the smart thing to do. Number four stopped off for some air while he equalized the pressure buildup. My squeeze, with sharp pain, stayed until we were almost to surface pressure in the trunk. The pain went away and I forgot it.

Our graduation exercise was a night, underway lockout with a mission on a small island. The following night, we locked out underway. Surfacing 4,000 yards offshore, my team's swim-to-shore azimuth of 060 degrees put us on our target beach, a point of land jutting seaward on the west side.

A limited beach survey followed our swim, and we had time to kill before our 0330 pickup. We lay in the warm sand for a while, then elected to do some of our waiting on the other end of our swim. Based upon the swim speed of our slowest swimmer and considering the tide and wind effect, we calculated an hour-and-twenty-minute swim.

Entering the surf at the point we came ashore, we started outward on a 240-degree azimuth. My compass man was half a length ahead, and the other members swam closely behind me. Too close, actually: a hard bump made me think that a shark had hit me. My instant turn to confront the shark caused a collision with my buddy, which was a great relief. There were sharks in these waters, we had seen one in the distance during the day.

Completing our swim, we took our stations on the rope and rested on our backs with a slow flutter kick. Pickup time was forty-five minutes away. In the center this time, I started my calypso sticks ten minutes before pickup time.

The buoy was almost on me before I saw the submarine. The phosphorescent action of the water sliding over the boat's superstructure gave it an eerie appearance, like something from another world. Seeing the boat come under me, I felt the buoy snag our line and take off with us. Again, things happened too fast; the boat arrived ahead of expectation and I was hanging on the buoy. The next action was down the rope.

I was not ready mentally and could not be sure about my physical readiness. What I wanted to do was hang on and breathe air, forever.

Below the surface were all the comforts of home, and there was only one way to get there, down the rope. I sucked in air and dove. Visibility underwater was good; the entire boat was clearly outlined, including the safety divers. However, the rope disappeared in the dark distance before it reached my immediate objective, the trunk. Blowing air against my nose ring and face mask, I tried to stay ahead of the ear squeeze. Johnson behind me was bumping my flippers; I could not slow down or stop.

The water pressure halfway down was crushing my lungs; I felt as though they had collapsed. I needed air and the ear squeeze was painful. Just as I thought that I would seek help from the lower Safety, he swam to a swimmer behind me. My pain instantly became so great that air lost its position of importance. Continuing for the trunk hatch with excruciating ear pain, I pulled into the bubble.

Removing my mask, I held my nose and blew hard, trying to equalize the pressure. I now had a blockage; there would be no relief until I moved into lower pressure. I could not take the trunk up until the others were aboard. Fortunately, they were right behind me; I dogged the hatch and started up.

The severe pain eased off as we came up from depth, but it did not go away. The boat doctor informed me that I had perforated an eardrum. My diving was over for this exercise; I was stuck on the boat. The exercise was about over anyway, and I had accomplished my purpose. Certified as a qualified Escape Trunk Operator, I also gained firsthand submarine experience. Force Recon officers normally do not go on missions as members of four-man teams; they insert and recover their teams. Personally going through the recon-team basics, however, gives the leader a deeper appreciation of his team member's tasks.

Liberty call in St. Thomas for two days preceded our return to Puerto Rico where we disembarked the sub. A C-130 flew us back to Cherry Point on 31 January 1967.

Most, maybe 90 percent, of the company personnel had less than a year in the Corps, having joined Force Recon out of the Infantry Training Regiment. They had no infantry battalion experience, but they were doing well. They had much to learn in the reconnaissance field, as well as picking up what they should already know from an infantry tour. Reconnaissance's needs in Vietnam, however, never let us arrive at a stable training level. As the more experienced began to get a hold on the business, they received individual orders for Vietnam.

On 13 March, I attended a ten-day top-secret school that fits the criterion of, "If I tell you, I must dispose of you," so I will not write about the school. During my absence, the company conducted a night jump in which our communication officer and my good friend, Captain Brad Collins, was killed.

Brad was the JM for his planeload, and he elected and briefed that he would follow the stick out rather than lead. The jump plane was a C1A; each load had its JM. The jump appeared to go as planned until the plane returned to the air station for another load. That stick boarded the plane to find the anchor line cable (ALC) torn out along with some aircraft bulkhead. The jump was canceled; everyone moved to the Fountain DZ for an accountability check. Brad was missing; no one had seen him on the DZ.

Collins's stick was collected to determine who last saw him. He was standing by the hatch while the stick exited down to the seventh of nine jumpers. As number seven moved toward the hatch pressed tightly against six, Collins crowded between them and instantly went out the hatch. Number seven assumed that the JM had changed his mind, electing to jump in the middle of the stick, something a JM would never do. The others followed him.

Jumpers number eight and nine provided a bit of startling information; their static lines and deployment bags were attached to their canopies. How were their canopies pulled from their deployment bags if the bags were not attached to the plane? Somehow, this information tied to the missing ALC. The area where the last three jumpers landed was searched closely, but nothing was found. All personnel got on line for a close search of the entire DZ area and found Collins's body impacted in the mud.

The ensuing investigation determined that Brad's reserve parachute had accidentally deployed, blew out the hatch, and he followed it as taught or was jerked out between parachutists. No one saw the canopy of his reserve chute in the dark. The worst was yet to come.

A jumper-free deployment bag whipping around at the end of a static line outside the aircraft did a half hitch around the suspension lines of Brad's reserve chute. The friction of nylon on nylon burned and broke these suspension lines. At the same instant, braking energy from the open canopy was transferred inside the plane by the half-hitched static line that tore out the ALC.

Brad had no options. His reserve canopy was a white flag flying above him with all but five suspension lines severed. His main parachute, which he had hooked to the ALC for his jump, would not work; that ALC was falling with him.

Brad's angel was off duty, but those of the last three jumpers were working. Their main parachutes deployed from the ALC that was now attached to Brad's reserve. In addition, they had their reserve parachutes on their chest, providing they used them soon enough. They were never aware of the need, and felt they had a normal jump until rolling up their chutes. I returned in time for the memorial service.

May came along with my platoon catching the parachuting portion of a big demonstration put on by Division and Force Troops. Known as SPEX, it was the Corps's way of showing Marines in action to congressmen, politicians, foreign dignitaries, and others. The demo ran from 2 to 5 May, the same act at the same time each day.

A Pathfinder stick opened the show by jumping in, supposedly from a carrier-launched C1A. We were followed shortly by helicopters carrying the air-assault waves into our supposedly Pathfinder-controlled zone. The surface landing force rolled up on Onslow Beach, and the entire amphibious operation took place in full view of the spectators in the viewing stands near the water's edge.

My role was to put Pathfinder canopies in the air at the exact time over Bluebird DZ, which was inland from the assault beach. There would be no fly-around or second pass if the first did not look good for putting jumpers on the DZ. We had to go out the hatch. During our first jump, the wind on the coast was different from what we had been informed of by the air station, making things a little hairy as four of us landed deep in tall trees. I prepared for my tree landing, suffered some skin loss, and climbed down.

The requirement of one pass over the DZ with an exit that might not put us near the zone increased the pucker factor. The first day's tree landings increased my concern; I had given the Navy pilot corrections to his flight path on our approach, but he was slow and weak in making them. Jump run corrections were covered in detail during my pilot brief, but execution was another story.

Marginal to high winds were forecast for the next three days, and I had to put parachutes in the air, no matter the wind speed. Four dummies were rigged with parachutes; for wind over fifteen knots, I would kick out the dummy stick. The idea sounded good but did not hold up in practice. Unless the wind was steady over fifteen knots before starting jump run, I did not have time to unhook my jumpers and hook up the dummies. We made the jump runs on marginal winds, and all landed on the DZ each day.

My year in the States was winding down and Vietnam was near. I no longer worried about the war ending before I could get to it. US force buildup in Vietnam continued with more combat forces justified by the military leadership and the White House.

I received orders to attend the US Army Military Assistance Training Advisor (MATA) Course at Fort Bragg, North Carolina. My orders further indicated that I would later be assigned as a Military Advisor to the Vietnamese Marine Corps. On 22 May, I drove over to Bragg and checked in for the five-week course.

Professionally presented, the MATA Course prepared me well for my future duties. The biggest help was in learning some of the Vietnamese language. Besides the language, we learned what was currently being done in that country and what should be done to accomplish our national objective. We learned how to organize and train the local militia, how to get along with the village chief, and what to look for as indicators of booby traps. We fired all the weapons available to us, including many communist types, and we did some physical fitness training. Studying language, however, soaked up most of my time.

We learned twenty-five words a day, Tuesday through Friday. Each morning, we had language class for three hours and used the new words. Our Vietnamese teacher did not cut us any slack; she expected instant recall and proper pronunciation. My days were very long as I grappled with the new-word list, sometimes until 0200 before memorizing it. The language requirement upon graduation was a five-hundred-word vocabulary, which would help us get started in country.

Five nights of the week I lived in the BOQ, drove to Lejeune Friday night to be with my family, and returned Sunday night. Lieutenant Robert C. Zwiener was the other Marine in the class, and we shared rides on weekends. While driving back Sunday nights, the non-driver would review our class notes of material presented. Mondays were test days.

The MATA Mile was a three-mile path through the sandy, scrubby backwoods that we ran each Thursday for time. As the path was wide enough for only one person, we ran according to speed potential and started according to age. The younger (up to age twenty-four) officers were first, followed by a middle group, then my group of older guys. That did not work well; I had to pass almost the entire class or plod along at too-slow pace. Passing someone required getting into the brush, and in some places that was not possible. For the remaining MATA Miles, I moved up with the young bucks, making my energy output considerably less.

MATA School ended, and on 29 June, I returned to 2nd Force. The war was magnifying the normal summer rotation; there were many new faces and the loss of familiar ones. Captain John J. Clancy III had been our S-3 until Major Don Norris received orders. John did a tour in Vietnam before joining 2nd Force; he now moved up to the CO position. This Change of Command was my first parade as an officer, and for this one I served as the Parade Adjutant. It was different from standing in the ranks, and I had to admit liking the extra visibility. For many years, I had wanted to give the command, "SOUND OFF."

★ ★ ★

Dotti Lu and I wanted a brother for Dixie; we planned to have two children. Dixie was almost four, and we were past due for our second child. For the last two years, the uncertainties about where and what I would be doing because of Vietnam caused us to delay our family addition plans. Discussing the situation, we decided that waiting until after my Vietnam tour would put too much of an age difference between our children. Dotti Lu allowed that she could handle things at home; caring for a new baby would help time pass. My boy was expected in October. We sold our home (built while I was on recruiting duty) and bought a bigger house that my dad had just finished in his Foxtrail Subdivision.

Orders arrived assigning me to the Marine Advisory Unit within the Naval Advisory Group, Military Assistance Command, Vietnam (MACV). I liked those orders and what the duty had to offer, especially after completing the MATA course. However, I was torn between carrying them out and leaving Dotti Lu, who now was in her eighth month of pregnancy. She would be alone in an involved, demanding environment, while I would be off doing my thing, having fun. Dotti Lu, who always knows what is going on in my mind, made the decision easier for me. She reasoned that as I had to go, the sooner I left, the quicker I would return.

I checked out of 2nd Force on 26 August 1967. The next day marked my fifteenth month as a 2nd lieutenant; that was the time in grade required for promotion. The company had no authorization to promote; once I arrived at my new command, I would be promoted and everything backdated.

We moved into our first new home with a door-to-door move. My thirty-day leave was used in getting our new house and large yard organized and set up to do without me for a year. We loved the home, and being in the middle of Foxtrail Subdivision had great benefits; Ray lived on one side and my parents on the other. The family environment gave me a comfortable feeling about leaving my loved ones.

My port call arrived, putting a definite end to all the fun I was having on the farm. September 30, my 36th birthday, was my flight date out of Travis AFB. Dotti Lu was uncomfortable in pregnancy, and I wanted her to rest rather than go to Dulles Airport with me in the early morning hours of the 29th. The disadvantage of having to get Dixie Lee up so early for my 0530 show time was the only way I convinced her to stay home.

Probably the most difficult thing I have ever had to do was kiss Dotti Lu good-bye while she was so heavy with child and walk out of our bedroom. Darkness that morning was not limited to the outside atmosphere; my world was small, confused, and confounding. At that moment, things were not right; what I was doing could not be right. I knew that my mom and dad would look after and help Dotti Lu, but my place was here with her—to share what she would be going through very shortly. However, it was too late to change; I flew to San Francisco and checked in at Travis AFB for a military airlift flight to Saigon.

Going into Saigon received my full attention. The pilot took us down in a steep descent—I assumed to avoid giving the communists a target out over the countryside. Looking out my porthole, I saw flares in the night sky. That fact surprised me; was Saigon under attack? I later learned that the flares were routine.

My promotion came up while checking in with the Marine Corps Personnel Section of MACV. A message was on hand stating, ". . . promote to the rank of 1st Lieutenant, Temporary, to rank from 27 August and pay to accrue from date of acceptance." Capt Vera M. Jones, the OIC of the Personnel Section located in the Koepler Compound, promoted me. Seniority and effective date of rank was 27 August, but my pay increase did not start until 2 October. I also learned that promotion from 2nd to 1st lieutenant is the only grade change where pay is not retroactive.

While on leave, I should have driven to HQMC and found someone to promote me. Better yet, I could have checked out of 2nd Force one day later as a 1st Lieutenant. So went my luck; I was counting every penny with a new house and a new baby on the way.

Lessons Learned

1. You are never too old to start over.
2. Seemingly superhuman tasks can be accomplished with a motivated team effort.

9

1st Lieutenant
096702/0302/9953

27 August 1967
Section 1

Saigon did not appear to me as a city with a war: the streets were crowded with people going about their business and merchants were well stocked and busy. The only war indicators were uniformed personnel and a few sandbagged emplacements near government buildings. Our Army was everywhere, from the hotels used for billeting and messing to vehicles in the streets. Vietnamese small taxis, motorbikes, and bicycles filled the streets.

New arrivals assigned to the Saigon area received a two-day indoctrination that was mostly a repeat of issues covered in the MATA Course. Now, however, I was a wise, knowledgeable 1st lieutenant, full of abilities and on-the-job know-how, qualities gained automatically upon shedding the gold bar of 2nd lieutenant.

On 4 October, I was assigned to the Marine Advisory Unit and issued uniforms and equipment. The Vietnamese Marine uniform was a tiger-stripe camouflage field uniform, which we were expected to wear. My tiger-stripes suggested that I might not be long in the city, though I was assigned a hotel. My room served as a place to store my seabag and equipment that I did not want to hump. My bunkie, an Army lieutenant, had a room to himself. I used the Vietnamese buses for travel to and from the Thuy Quan Luc Chien Bo Thu Lien (Vietnamese Marine Corps [VNMC] Headquarters) where the Advisory Unit was located

The Senior Marine Advisor and his staff—consisting of administrative, supply, medical, and engineer advisors—were located at the VNMC Hqrs. Our colonel advised the VNMC Commandant and the other combat support advisors were near their MOS counterparts. The field portion of the Advisory Unit included the combat arms majors and captains who worked with the operational forces.

There were six infantry battalions and two artillery batteries in the

Boot Camp portrait of the author, taken at Parris Island, South Carolina, in September 1950. *Wesley Fox*

The author is Platoon 88's high shooter. 1950, Parris Island, South Carolina. *Official USMC photo*

Corporal Fox, as a squad leader, on a Korean ridgeline in 1951. *Wesley Fox*

Two Armed Service Police Detachment patrolmen (author and Buz Burnell) about to begin their motor patrol in Washington, DC in 1952. *Wesley Fox*

Author, William (Wild Bill) Donahoo, and Edward Maschoni on liberty in Tokyo, 1955. Note the Marine dip in author's cover (Garrison Cap). *Wesley Fox*

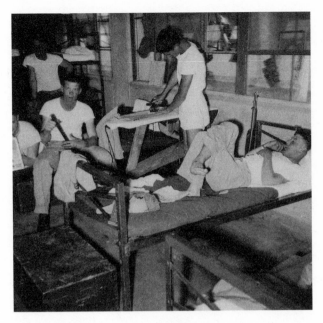

Sergeants' quarters in George Company 3/5 on Camp San Margarita, Camp Pendleton, California, in 1955. Shelton Eakin is on the ironing board. Other sergeants' names lost to memory. *Wesley Fox*

Drill Instructor Fox with Platoon 181 on the San Diego Recruit Depot drill field in 1955. *Wesley Fox*

Major Rayford K. Adams and the author sign up another Marine (unidentified) in Baltimore, Maryland, in 1958. *Official USMC Photo*

The author is chuted up and ready for a jet bomber jump. Miramar Naval Air Station, California, 1961. *Wesley Fox*

Pathfinder Team 44 members on Operation Silver Sword in Hawaii, 1961. From right are Robert Happy, Thomas Vallario, Frank Goudaillier, Robert Boland, Dennis Zoerb, and the author. *Official USMC photo*

The author as a Pathfinder on Operation Tulungan, Mindora Island, Philippines in spring of 1962. *Wesley Fox*

LCpl Dennis Boyle hung up outside the C1-A jump plane in the Philippines, 1962. *Official US Navy photo*

Pathfinders conducting rubber boat work on an Okinawa beach in 1962. From left are the author, Frank Goudallier, Edward Miller, Dennis Zoerb, and William Martin. *Wesley Fox*

The author returns
from a successful
effort at a Parris
Island, South Carolina,
Pistol Match in 1964.
Official USMC photo

The author briefs
platoon members
(2nd Platoon, 2nd
Force Recon) on
their Submarine
Operation.
USS Sea Lion,
APSS–315 at the
Naval Station,
Trinidad, West
Indies, in 1966.
*Official USMC
photo*

Diwe (Captain) Hein and the author eating rice on an operation in 3rd Corps Tactical Zone, Vietnam, in 1967. *Wesley Fox*

A walk in the sun with Captain Hein, outside of Saigon in 1967. *Wesley Fox*

1st Lieutenant Fox, Infantry Advisor with Vietnam Marines in 1968. *Wesley Fox*

Private Hi (Vietnamese Marine) and the author do some body cleaning near Saigon in 1967. *Wesley Fox*

The author's cowboy, Hi; his jeep driver, Hasi; and the author near Saigon in 1967. *Wesley Fox*

The author enjoying a Christmas break in 1968 at Vandegrift Combat Base, IV Corps Tactical Zone, Vietnam. *Wesley Fox*

Doc Charles Hudson pointing out a target to the author on Operation Dewey Canyon in the A Shau Valley, Vietnam. (Marine with rifle unidentified) 1969. *Official USMC negative*

Members of Alpha Co., 1st Bn, 9th Marines on Operation Dewey Canyon in the A Shau Valley, Vietnam. Front row from left are the author and GySgt Ronald Duerr. Standing on far right is Lt William Christman. The rest remain unidentified. *Wesley Fox*

The author catches up on the happenings with the "Stars and Stripes" while on Operation Dewey Canyon, A Shau Valley, Vietnam in 1969. Note the lack of a barber. *Official USMC photo*

From left: sitting, the author, and GySgt Ronald Duerr, standing, an unidentified Marine, and Doc Charles Hudson pose for an official USMC photo in the A Shau Valley, Vietnam, 1969. *Official USMC photo*

The author leaping high off the ramp of a CH-46 helicopter with the Quantico Skydivers. Quantico, Virginia, 1971. *Wesley Fox*

Buddies of the author's Basic School experience and Company Tactics Instructors, from left are Phil Torrey, author, Ed Riley, Bob Happy, and Nick Grosz. Quantico, Virginia, 1972. *Wesley Fox*

President Nixon presents the author with the Medal of Honor. Dotti Lu, Dixie Lee, and Amy are immediately behind the author with brothers and sisters behind them. The White House, Washington, DC, 1972. *Official White House photo*

Dotti Lu and the author on liberty in Budapest, Hungary, in 1973. *Wesley Fox*

SgtMaj Homer Hunt and the author on 1st Bn, 6th Marines' Combined Arms Exercise at 29 Palms, California, in 1982. *Wesley Fox*

A Saturday battalion hump on Okinawa, 1983. From left are Ken Harbin behind the author, Johnny Johnson, and Mike Whitten. *Wesley Fox*

The author's family in 1983; from left are Amy Lu, Dixie Lee, Dotti Lu, and Nicole Lyn. *Wesley Fox*

General Carl Mundy retired the author. Front row: Mundy, author, Dotti Lu, and Nicole Fox. Second row, from left: General Jack Sheehan and wife Peggy, General George Smith, General Stanton Musser. Third row, from left: General Joe Knots and wife Jo, Tex Donahoo and wife Boots, and Cousin Nelson. Quantico, 1993. *Official USMC photo*

The author in a 1987 portrait. *Official USMC photo*

VNMC. Each had two US advisors—a major for the CO, and a captain for the XO. Battalions typically operated with two maneuver elements, two rifle companies with each, the CO heading one and the XO the other. Sometimes the two US advisors would not see each other for weeks at a time.

Two headquarters field units known as Task Forces A and B controlled the battalions and were task-organized according to their mission. The Task Force advisors (co-vans) were a lieutenant colonel and a major. Like other Marine commands, the Advisory Unit was not up to T/O in rank, and it was routine for an advisor to work the job of a higher rank.

Colonel Richard L. Michael Jr. was the Senior Marine Advisor and briefed me on my new duties. He concluded with the following: Vietnamese officers resented the idea that an American lieutenant could in any way advise them on how to fight their war. Our counterparts were at least one rank higher, most had been through our Basic School, and they had been fighting this war for many years.

Advisors were not staying long with the 6th Bn, the newest battalion and yet to be blooded by the enemy. Captain Hein, the XO, had a reputation for not getting along with Americans. The battalion was turning over advisors in terms of weeks rather than months or tours of duty. Hein had just asked his seniors to replace the lieutenant who had been with him two weeks. His reasons were always frivolous, never anything concerning the abilities of the young officer.

Michael allowed that he was not giving me a fair start by sending me to the 6th. However, that battalion was now short one advisor, and I was his only option. He stated that I might come across better to Hein because I was ten years older than the average lieutenant and had another war under my belt.

The 6th Bn was assigned to TF-A and to Operation Song Than 704-67 taking place at Tan Uyen, III Corps Tactical Zone. Major Talman C. Budd was the TF Advisor with Major William E. McKinstry as the assistant. (This was my third assignment with McKinstry.) On 11 October, I flew by chopper to get directly involved in the effort to keep communism as far from home as possible.

The name of this operation suggested how the war was going: there had been 704 Song Than operations to date, and yet the enemy was still around. Over the next year, I would become frustrated by the awareness that I was involved in a one-sided show. My counterpart and his people did not do much to stop communism. Tan Uyen was no more involved in the war than the city of Saigon. Farmers worked their paddies, and the marketplace was full of people.

The Bn Advisor was Captain Gordon,[25] a USNA graduate; he took me to his bunk area for a get-acquainted talk. He did most of the talking, repeating what Michael had covered. Higher commanders were slow to commit their newest battalion to an area promising enemy contact, but that attitude was changing. His first-hand assessment of my counterpart was detailed and beneficial. Hein was an intelligent, highly educated (including several US military schools), pompous ass who did not like Americans. Small, even for a Vietnamese, he was youthful and always striking in his uniform. I could expect to stay in the battalion one to two weeks depending on Hein's mood. Major Chung was almost as bad, but Gordon thought he was making progress with his counterpart. Gordon was on his second month in Vietnam and spoke favorably of his duty expectation.

An introduction to the two leaders followed; Chung kept his seat, extended his hand, and grunted. His porky appearance suggested that he did not like to be on his feet. Hein at least stood, though he did not say much. Smooth, good-looking, a young man with fine features, he no doubt considered himself one of the blue bloods of his country. The message was clear: why bother; this lieutenant will not be here long enough to matter.

A young Marine with an open, smiling face appeared. Hein issued some orders, then gestured me away saying, "Go with him." The Marine was my cowboy, meaning bodyguard and servant; he would set up a cot and get me situated for the night. His name was Hi, of Chinese ancestry; he did not speak English. We would get along well. Right away, I started exercising my meager vocabulary of Vietnamese, and I was pleased that Hi responded. He settled me on the porch of a house across from where Hein had taken a private room.

Shortly, Hein's cowboy appeared saying "Chop Chop" while working his hand to and from his mouth. I followed him around the house to a table in the yard. Hein was seated, beckoned me to the chair across from him, and motioned me to help myself.

Our meal was rice with a small saucer of split cucumbers in a sauce. The rice had no salt or seasoning, but I put away two bowls while not doing badly in handling my chopsticks. The sauce on the cucumbers smelled like rotten fish; I went light on that. Hein smacked his lips but otherwise ate in silence; I did not offer any conversation. I could play his game; being a loner was easy and usually preferable. Having finished my rice, I excused myself and departed.

Hi awoke me the next morning with a glass of coffee; he had found the small jar of instant coffee in my pack. There was something lacking or not quite right about drinking coffee from a water glass. I also wondered about his water source, and how clean the glass was. These important considerations today became unworthy of thought on the morrow. Making my own coffee suited me better, but my manservant must do his job. Hi started each of my days with that glass of coffee.

Coffee was the extent of my breakfast; Hein did not serve lunch either. I would live on one rice meal a day unless I walked into the village. My evening meal increased to four bowls of rice, but I was still starving. Hein did serve three meals a day while on operations.

On 20 October, the battalion conducted a Search and Destroy operation. We did not search for or destroy anything. A better operational name would have been "A Walk in the Sun." We walked in two long columns, 1,000 yards apart; the enemy had fair warning to avoid us.

On the plus side, eating three meals a day with Hein, walking behind him, and talking operational matters were softening him. My professional, take-it-as-it-goes attitude also might have helped. He initiated all communication between us, and I did not go beyond answers to his questions. His casual remarks drew no response.

On the third day out, I received a radio message from TF-A. He had a personal telegram from the States to me. Did I want him to read it over the radio?

"Leatherneck Alpha, this is Leatherneck Six-Alpha. Read your traffic. Over."

"Six-Alpha, Leatherneck Alpha, message follows: Dear Wes. Our Amy Lu arrived at 0420 on 22 October weighing seven pounds and six ounces. We are both doing fine. With all my love. Dotti Lu. End of message, congratulations, Six-Alpha."

"Leatherneck Alpha, Six-Alpha, roger, thanks much. Out."

Dotti Lu and I had referred to our coming baby as my boy. I wanted a boy, and Dotti Lu felt that because she was carrying the baby differently than Dixie, it would be a boy. Amy Lu sounded as though I had a second daughter, but the important thing was that they were both doing fine. Meanwhile, we moved back into our position at Tan Uyen for a couple of days.

We trucked out on the 25th to an assignment on the Saigon security ring, known as the CMD for "Command Military District." Vietnamese Marine, Ranger, Airborne, and other special Army units formed this ring. We would stay in one place a week, then flip-flop positions with another battalion. Some of these assignments stood out while others were routine.

The best part of the CMD assignment was the opportunity to go into the city for an American meal in one of the hotel BOQs, to visit the PX and commissary, and to stop by the Bo Tu Lien. The Headquarters visit allowed me to catch up on the other battalions and the war. Gordon decided that one of us could go in each day unless we had an active mission. For survival, I picked up items in the commissary for my morning and noon meals in camp. By this time, Hein and I were getting along well. His evening meal had improved to include meat; however, breakfast and lunch remained missing.

Communication with Hein had to be in English, as he put an early stop to my use of Vietnamese. During my first week's attempt to talk with him in his language, he interrupted me with a harsh "Stop! Speak English so that I can understand you." I used my Vietnamese with my cowboy, my driver, and my radioman; they understood me.

Gordon and I had a satisfactory working relationship. Beyond the fact that we were the only two Americans, he was a captain. He sometimes managed to rub his rank on me the wrong way, however. Being the junior no doubt influenced my thinking, but I saw our situation as two officers doing a tough job as a team. The senior was responsible; nevertheless, for one to exercise rank over the other in our two-man daily routine was on the chicken-shit side of leadership.

I took his now-and-then condescending tone, though it grated me; I carried the bags. Example: upon getting the CMD assignment we went by MACV Hqrs for a briefing, maps, and operation orders. Afterwards, while walking to our jeep, he grunted and handed me the paperwork he had collected. I was not carrying anything and a few papers would not overload me. However, the way that he did it, stating, "Here, Lieutenant, why am I carrying these?" did not sit right. Other, similar, incidents happened along the way, like loading and unloading his personal gear from our jeep, until I called enough.

Gordon developed an intestinal problem and on one of his days in the city sought medical help. The fallout was that he had to provide stool specimens over the next several days. The problem was that the next day I was scheduled to help our battalion's base camp commander get lumber. Because Chung wanted lumber, it had a high priority on Gordon's list. Talking over the next day's plan, he stated, "No problem, I have a morning habit. You can leave right after and drop the little box by the medical facility on your way."

"I don't carry other people's shit, Captain. You can have the jeep."

"Well, it is in a box. It's not like you have to handle it."

I did not respond but let my position stand. The captain did not push the issue, spun on his heels, and departed with the words, "We'll see."

If it had not been for the earlier incidents, I would have dropped off the specimen. Marines will do anything for their buddies; buddies also do their share of the little things. Any Marine leader would be embarrassed to press charges against a subordinate with the specification, "He refused to take my shit." On second thought, some might not, but I felt comfortable that I had the captain on this one.

An ammunition ship was unloading at the naval port, and good framing lumber was available for the hauling. The lumber was dunnage used to hold ammunition in place for the sea voyage. One ship used many truckloads of new lumber, and it was left in Vietnam for the benefit of the people. Our battalion needed lumber to build up our base camp for Marine barracks and dependent housing. The base camp was located near Thu Duc, north of Saigon and not far from the port.

I had earlier checked out the lumber situation, made some contacts, and acquired some lumber that had been picked over. Promised first grabs on the next shipment, I had WO Thoan, the Base Camp Commander, with all of his trucks ready to roll. A stool specimen stood in the way.

The following morning Gordon said, "Take the jeep; I will get my specimen to the lab." With our driver Hasi (Vietnamese for corporal) behind the wheel, I headed for Thu Duc and a convoy of trucks.

Thoan did not have enough trucks to haul the available lumber. There would be no second chance, so Thoan directed his Marines to continue stacking on the trucks. We had eight normal truckloads on four six-bys while other trucks waited at the gate for the remaining lumber. These were American military six-bys, built stoutly, but one broke a spring, dumping part of its load, before we were halfway to Thu Duc.

Both Hein and Chung were now very warm towards their co-vans with far more than rice for our evening meal. Two weeks later Hein informed me that another ammo ship was in port; the word also came from Chung through Gordon—could I get four more truckloads? Their request surprised me, as I had assumed the last haul would hold the carpenters for a while, but I would look into it.

Without a word to Hein about my intentions, I headed for the 6th Bn Base Camp and Thoan's office. Thoan was not at work. I looked around and asked questions without getting any answers. What I did get was the feeling that Thoan was on a drunk. His Marines seemed embarrassed to talk about him except for one who made a drinking sign.

Hasi, though he knew no English, knew my purpose and tried to help. He seemed surprised and disappointed that there was no building going on and worse, no lumber. Hasi was married with two children, and no doubt thought that his family would have a chance of getting out of the cardboard shack in which they existed. The facts jumped out at me: Thoan, probably at Chung's direction, sold that lumber on the black market, and there was little doubt about who pocketed the total profit. My lumber dealing stopped, and so did the warm, friendly commander and advisor relationship.

The 6th Bn received orders to move into another section of the CMD. An immediate sweep operation helped soften Hein's reaction to my refusal to do what he asked. He was cordial enough but not as talkative. Several days after that operation, the 3rd Co was assigned a sweep mission. Did I want to go? I preferred a walk in the sun any day to sitting around camp. This sweep started out to be routine, one long column moving out four miles and returning by another route. In that flat, open country, the Vietcong had plenty of warning to avoid the government force. However, even the Cong screwed up sometimes.

Shortly after starting our return track, we came into a grassy grove full of trees with a well of cold water. The grove was surrounded with rice paddies and may have been a farm hamlet before the war. The commander, 1st Lt Hugen, decided to take a break; his Marines crapped out and ate their rice. I noticed that the area had been in use; there were cook pots by the well and ashes from recent campfires. Hugen explained that the farmers ate their noon rice there.

We were not there long before an older, well-worked, and weathered woman walked among us. Marines spoke to her, but no one paid her much attention. She struck me as uncomfortable, concerned, and seeming to be looking for something. I assumed that we were on her property, but such things normally do not bother the Vietnamese. She seemed relieved at not finding what she expected and left.

We were saddling up to move out when an explosion vibrated the air to my left, followed by rifle fire. We took cover while the firing moved to the rice paddies to my left front. I moved forward to the tree line where I could get a feel for what was happening.

Hugen moved with me while talking on his radio to learn that we had four VC out in the paddy. One black-dressed individual ran down a paddy dike, stopped, and took cover on our side of the dike. The VC's concern was the platoon of Marines in the direction from which he had run; he was under cover now from their fire. Hugen pointed to the black pajamas saying, "VC, VC," while Hi placed himself between the VC and me. The VC was unaware that we were behind him; however, he was in a good position, as neither side could fire at him for fear of hitting Marines.

Helicopter gunships would be helpful; their bullet impact would be into the ground under and around the target. Raising TF-A on my radio, I learned that they had choppers in the area. Shortly a light fire team, two US Army Huey gunships, reported overhead.

I was briefing the flight leader on our situation when one Huey made a rocket run on the lone black figure. The pilot had spied the prone VC and reacted on his own volition. His run was shallow and both rockets were high, exploding against the dike and wounding several Marines. Hugen's demand, "No gunships, No gunships," was unnecessary; I was already berating the flight leader for firing into our force. I directed him to stay above and make sure none of the black pajamas escaped. They were not authorized to fire.

A Marine near me opened fire with his M-16 and received heated words from Hugen. I had taken Hi's M-16, figuring to put a round or two into that black suit. The 1st Platoon was behind a dike further away; I would have to shoot two feet over the VC to endanger them. Looking at Hugen, I received his smiling approval and the motion to shoot.

Not knowing the zero of Hi's rifle, I set the elevation on 200 yards; sighted on the black shoulder and squeezed. The VC moved but did not go still. Other rifles were cracking as I fired my second shot. We all seemed to be hitting the VC who reacted as though he was swatting flies. Finally, he lay still; he was the last of the four VC to die.

These were young boys about eighteen years of age. One or more were probably sons of the woman showing the earlier concern; she must have thought that we had her sons. The boys had seen us coming and went underground into their hideaway, which was a huge mound of dirt covered with grass and a small tree growing on top. The tree was set cleverly in a removable box that covered the bunker entrance. Marines had crapped out on the mound, lying back on the slope. The cool air in the shade of the trees was enjoyable after the hot hump, and we had not rushed our lunch. These VC were within four feet of those Marines on the mound.

For whatever reason, the VC decided they had to make a fighting break for it. They dumped their tree, rolled out a grenade, and came out with AKs blazing. Two died on the mound, one a short way into the paddies, and number four might have made it, if he had not sought cover behind the dike. The old woman did not come back to see what all the shooting was about. Her war had become very personal and heavy upon her. Four for Eakin.

About the middle of November, we set up in a small farming community. Gordon and I slept under a shed roof attached to a small house where Hein had commandeered one of the two rooms. Chung moved into a house nearby; the farm families moved over and made do.

One evening I was aware of the farmwoman's unusual activity but did not realize until the next morning that a party was in the making. The yard was filled with tables of food, enough to feed several hundred people. Moving closer to the tables while the woman carried out more food, I saw that the blackness over the many dishes was a solid cover of houseflies, black and green ones. Just looking at that squirming mess was bad, but thinking that someone would eat it was unbelievable. There was neither an attempt to cover the food nor to shoo off the flies.

Returning to my cot, I entertained a frightening thought: Gordon had gone into the city, and neither Hein nor Chung was around. I was the only command representative. Maybe the old farmer, whom I had spoken with several times, would feel that he should invite me to chow. Refusing to eat his food would be an insult, and I could not eat what I had just seen. I had to take a walk with my radio.

It was a good idea, but while I was putting the radio on the backpack, the old, weathered farmer approached with his open, toothless grin. In a country manner, he invited me to eat. I tried to decline, but he insisted with, "Beaucoup, Beaucoup," probably the only foreign word that he knew, while pumping his hand to his mouth as in eating. Putting him off as though I was working with the radio, I indicated acceptance. That pleased him and he departed; his guests were beginning to arrive. I was already sick; how could I do what needed doing?

Waiting until all the people seemed to have arrived, I decided to get the dreaded obligation behind me. If I waited long enough, maybe the food would be eaten. I could not decline the old man's extension of kindness, sharing the little that he had with a stranger, as if his best were not good enough for me. He saw me coming, met me warmly, and introduced me around. Good, with all the bowing and hand shaking, maybe the food would be forgotten.

Food time came, but thankfully, the farmer was occupied. Feeling guilty, I took food that guests immediately uncovered while taking their portions. I had no idea what I was eating, but it was tasty. Kids came to a table and cleaned off the top of the dish, never bothering with the flies. I immediately had a bite of that sample. After a decent time, with more fuss and make-believe than eating, I thanked the old couple and departed feeling that I still had a chance to live.

Our Bn CP set up in a schoolhouse on the southwest quadrant of the CMD for our next assignment. VC activity was nonexistent during the month of November; the war was all but forgotten. Our sweeps netted only questionable suspects and a grenade or booby trap now and then. For something to do and to further my education in this war, I decided to accompany an ambush patrol periodically. A co-van ought to know how the squads conducted themselves and how effective the squad leaders were.

After dark on 30 November, I moved out with a squad from 2nd Company. The leader exercised good principles and his men responded well. Instead of an ambush posture when he arrived at the position, however, he circled the wagons. While it was good for overall security, the circle position did not allow maximum fire on any kill zone. After two hours in the position, I thought everyone was asleep, but learned that there was a watch. Few VC would be hurt walking into this ambush. My biggest disappointment was at 0500, return time. There had been coughing throughout the night, now everyone cleaned out the stale nicotine as they talked and lighted up their first cigarette of the day. We returned on the same path used to arrive at the position. The VC had to be weak not to take advantage of this shooting gallery.

A week later, I went out with a squad from 3rd Co and again was not pleased. Arriving short of the ambush position, the leader properly sent a scout forward to check out the position. However, once he had scouted the area, he simply shouted through the darkness, "The position is safe, come forward." Another ambush was positioned so close to us that several times during the night, individuals shouted back and forth. The leader took first watch while his squad members rolled up in their blankets and slept.

There was a curfew in effect after dark, restricting people movement. At 0400 singles and pairs moved on the dirt road 200 meters to our front. They each carried a torch or flashlight and according to the squad leader, they were people going to work. Like the VC would not be smart enough to use a light to walk by, especially if it kept them from getting shot! The nearby squad joined us for the return, talking, coughing, and smoking. This time we had a transistor radio, on and loud.

After hearing what I had to say about the night activities, Gordon decided to see for himself and went out with a squad on 8 December.

Toward morning, rifle fire roused me from sleep. I knew that it was an M-16 firing and was immediately concerned for Gordon. His voice with my call sign coming over my radio loudspeaker brought me wide awake. I responded with "Six. Six Alpha, Go."

"Six-Alpha, there has been a shooting here, and I think some Marines are hurt. Get a Dustoff. Over."

"Roger, Six. How many and nature of wounds? Are you hit? Anything for the SitRpt? Over."

"Six-Alpha, I am not hurt, I did the shooting, and I am now with the other squad. Looks like only one hit and he needs a MedEvac. I'll make the SitRpt. Over."

Shortly, I had a Dustoff (MedEvac) on the way. The pilot checked in on our radio net, and Gordon brought him in. The wounded was on his way for medical help, but there was no help for the co-vans of 6th Battalion. The shooting had occurred when a nearby squad approached Gordon's squad for the return as had been done on my last night. The captain did not know of this plan; what he did know was that all were asleep in his position.

Gordon suddenly saw people carrying flashlights coming directly toward him and in a minute would be on him. Thinking they were VC, he opened fire with his M-16. That one twenty-round magazine held reveille on the sleepers and wounded one member of the approaching squad.

Gordon would drive into MACV and make his report after talking with Chung. The captain was not long with the major. Their voices were heard over the firing of the 105-artillery battery beside us. Gordon stormed away, collected Hasi, and was gone. Hein came in to talk buddy-buddy as he always did when the captain and the major had their differences. There was a good chance, Hein said, that the captain would not be back. The major was mad. December 9 was not a good day, and it was far from over.

At 1330, gunfire erupted in a hamlet across a canal three quarters of a mile away. Shortly, old men carried a little girl to me using a door as a litter. The side of her head had been torn away by a bullet, but she was alive. Could I fly her to the hospital? I called for a Dustoff while Chung deployed several rifle platoons in the immediate area and sorted out the facts.

The hamlet chief had hosted a dinner for his relatives. He ran his hamlet according to what was good for his people and he was well liked. The VC could not buy him, scare him, or kill him—up to now. They had tried for years, but he was always one step ahead because his people loved and protected him. Hosting a family reunion was typical of him.

During the meal, three of his nephews left the gathering and returned immediately with AK-47s. They fired at the chief, their uncle; two men and three children were in the way, but that did not stop the communists. Innocent people stood in the way of their goals. The three-year-old girl on the door was the only one alive. My Dixie was that age, and I burned with a deep rage. These facts added to my earlier commitment to balance the score for Eakin.

The killers were not found. A helicopter would have helped, but I could not get one for the mission. MACV had a new deal: turn the war over to the Vietnamese, who must make their assets work. Short of life emergencies, like the Dustoffs requested earlier, the US would respond to a request for combat support only when the Vietnamese declared that they could not provide it themselves. By then, the VC had departed the area. Our reaction force, with a late start and no idea of direction, did not have a chance of catching the young men.

Despite Hein's words to the contrary, Gordon returned. Christmas and the start of the New Year came with us positioned on the CMD. New terrain was in our future, however, and on 11 January, we moved to Bong Son-Duong Lieu in II CTZ. (Map, page 248) Our base camp included a huge underground bunker where all advisors lived and worked. We had our own cooking facilities and, with US A-rations, lived well. We also became acquainted with each other for the first time; it was great working among my people.

TF-A was the senior command with three infantry battalions and one artillery battery. We joined in time for Operation Son Ha-3 that had us sweeping the ridgelines. The operation ended on the 18th and we returned to our bunker where I became feverish. A Dustoff delivered me to the 15th MedBn where I was diagnosed with dehydration. The cause was not determined, but I now suspect that it was a mosquito bite, as I had malaria much later. After two days on the needle, I returned to duty.

We moved up on the ridges for Song Than 38-68, or Operation Pershing for the US units involved. While moving on a ridge, Hein and I saw a figure in white run into a thicket, far down a draw. To my question, Hein raised his hand for silence while he talked with Chung and followed with "Just a wood cutter." Like using lights at night, VC would not be smart enough to put on white and go about their guerrilla business. US Marines would have given the runner a chance to explain. Again, I was reminded of our mission: Search and Avoid. Do nothing to shorten the war.

The Vietnamese did not have prepared field rations. They carried and boiled rice for their evening meal, cooking enough for the following two meals. Cold leftover rice was served for breakfast and lunch the following day. Canned foods, like sardines, were carried to support the rice. Of course, anything collected along the way, in the field or otherwise, went into the pot.

On an operation with 4th Co, the commander saw fit to explain his cowboy's action of shooting and carrying a big rat. This was a field rat, fattened on rice, the captain explained; he would not eat a city rat because of the filth. I satisfied my hunger that evening with rice, eating little of the meat.

One other Vietnamese meal ought to go on record. Before we left Saigon, Hein recognized a national day with a traditional meal to celebrate Vietnamese manhood. I had heard about the Duck's Blood and Peanuts ceremonial meal. Passing it off as more talk than real, I expected a little blood sprinkled on peanuts. I found out differently.

The meal was special: eight courses with candlelight. Then came the climax: the duck's blood and peanuts. I had it all backward; there was a little peanut dust sprinkled on the congealed blood that stood up like a pudding.

"Let me serve you, Thungwe. How much would you like?" asked Hein.

"Thank you Diwe, I would like half a bowl," I answered, trying to appear considerate and nonchalant.

"You are a big man. You meet your wife on R&R soon. You need much of what the duck can give you," he stated with a chuckle as he filled my bowl. I really hated him at that moment. I did not know how I would do it, but I would eat that crap just to keep Hein from getting pleasure from my discomfort. He watched closely as the first spoonful went to my mouth—and I did not die. Like soft Jell-O, it required no chewing; there was no requirement to dwell on the matter. Put it in, swallow, and be done with it. There was little taste, and I was pleased with pulling it off. I put on a show of eating heartily at first and then slowed as though getting full. Hein obviously wanted to save some; he did not push my taking more.

We were in the Bong Son bunker when Tet hit on 30 January 1968. The village had a flare-up of the local VC that was handled by the Popular Forces. The PF lined the streets with VC bodies so that everyone could see who the bad guys had been all along. We were on standby but not immediately involved in the enemy's latest offensive action.

On 2 February the 6th Bn was detached and readied for a mission in Saigon. Movement would be by helicopters to LZ English and from there to Ton Son Nhut by C-130s. While waiting for our choppers, we lost Marines in our LZ. All Marines have need for a metal ammo box, which is great for holding rifle-cleaning gear, tools, and just about anything else as long as you do not have to hump it. A young Marine spied an ammo box off the trail and broke ranks to retrieve it. He shook it as he lifted the box; good, it even had something in it. At that instant, this young man had four seconds of life remaining. As he joined his buddies, the grenade inside exploded with "TIME'S UP."

The VC scored with that booby trap: a hand grenade with the pin pulled, lying on the spoon handle waiting for a slight jar. Results: One killed and eleven wounded. Cost to the enemy: Nothing; the grenade and ammo box were made in the USA.

Hein had gone on leave for the Tet Holidays. His home was in Da Lat and the communists now claimed that city. In Hein's absence, the 4th Co Cmdr, Diwe Khanh, was my counterpart, the second in command of the battalion. He kept his company and commanded the second maneuver element. Khanh was a lady's man; he lived the role, taking full advantage of his rank and position. On several occasions, I had seen a particular woman with him. She could not be lost in a Vietnamese crowd, as she was different from most Oriental women: blessed with a breast size that would do honors to any race. While she was not the only woman to share Khanh's favors, she was a regular visitor.

Seeing this woman with another girl in the line of Marines boarding our C-130s was, however, a surprise. Both were in tiger-stripes, their hair up inside their helmets, and though they carried no gear, they fit into the picture. Marines had gear shoved in their own jackets so she did not look out of the ordinary. I noticed her because she looked at me with a big smile while turning to the other girl and saying something. They continued toward the aircraft for their ride home.

Civilians were not authorized on these flights, and public transportation was at a standstill. She probably came up the same way as she was going back to Saigon. I had to work with the guy, so I did nothing but report the incident to Gordon. Khanh was another Vietnamese making the most of his war.

Upon arriving in Saigon, the 6th Bn was assigned a reserve mission and remained overnight in the CMD Hqrs area. At 1000 on the 3rd, we moved by trucks to Thu Duc with the mission of relieving enemy pressure on that district. We dismounted north of the Bien Hoa Bridge and moved by foot into the town at 1330, encountering light sniper fire.

The companies pushed out in separate directions from the town, with the 4th moving to clear the northern portion. We ran into stiff resistance resulting in 13 WIA; then we came under fire from three sides.

Air support was available sporadically throughout the afternoon; everyone wanted gunships, but there were not enough to go around. With the enemy nearly surrounding us, I was finally able to get a light fire team. Marking the enemy positions with smoke rounds, I directed the gunships' attacks.

My first day of the heavy war was exhausting; besides the hurry-up-and-wait action, there was a real chance of collecting a round, stray or intentional. Though our command group was usually positioned behind the lead platoon, the exact enemy location and strength were unknown. We were all in the fight. In spite of the heat, I zipped up my flak jacket for the first time in Vietnam and wished that it covered more of me. Two hours before darkness, Khanh broke contact, and we returned to the 3rd Battalion's base camp, which had been cleared of the enemy earlier.

Like morning commuters going in for a day's work, the following morning we moved toward the enemy located the day before. I worked gunships on our left flank after a platoon contact. First Company was in hot contact with the major VC element while my company advanced against light sniper fire along our street. Following a radio call Khanh took me in tow as though he had something important to show me. We entered a house through a yard stacked full of firewood.

The entire family had been slaughtered and scattered all over that little cottage. Nearest the door was a woman large with child. Between her and the man, who was more to the rear of the single large room, were six others, aged from two to adult, male and female. Their faces were frozen in terror; they lay as they fell with bodies now swollen to twice their normal size.

I felt that they had been dead several days, but exactly how long was hard to tell. They were killed by gunfire that sprayed and plastered the room with blood, bone, and flesh. I read the scene: The woman answered a knock at the door. She was greeted by intruders with AK-47s who sprayed the room, killing and destroying. Besides the bodies being full of bullet holes, the walls and doors were shot up, and there was no glass in any window. Khanh pointed to the carnage, looked at me, and stated, "Gunships."

I questioned his accusation by saying that I thought this a communist act. He answered with, "I know. Gunships did this."

I did not agree. The firing appeared to be horizontal rather than on an angle from the air. The bodies were torn up by hand-held-weapon-sized bullets, not the bigger rounds used by aircraft. My question was "Why was this family here?" Everyone else, families especially, had vacated the area when the VC came. That scene ruined my day, and it took a while to get the stench out of my nostrils.

The communist offensive played itself out with our battalion not becoming involved in heavy combat. Our companies patrolled through new areas each day with the VC/NVA forces staying just beyond reach. Government forces did nothing to upset the routine that was known and expected of them by the enemy.

Although their initial attack was a complete surprise, the enemy force had run out of options. Theirs was now a game of survival. They had shot their bolt on the first day, and now for the most part were trying to get out of the cities and disappear. Their bold move for a checkmate was too open; their losses were not merely in numbers but included essential VC leaders from all communities who had long been underground. Communities were shocked by the identification of the dead in their streets; the trusted figurehead who had been so helpful was also a communist. While streets were barricaded to stop and reroute traffic through checkpoints, and official buildings were surrounded with barbed wire and guards, the war soon took on its old face of business as usual for private enterprise. Six days into the communists' offensive, we had to search hard to find any bad guys.

My counterpart and I lived in the Thu Duc Hotel, returning each evening after clearing an area. Truly a commuting force, we enjoyed beer and dinner upon our return. At this time I drank my first bottle of beer. Hi brought me a warm bottle and a glass of crushed ice our first evening. The heat, hot flak jacket, and warm canteen water of the day made the iced beer tasty and pleasant. Ice and beer became our return routine without our giving much thought to the source of the water for the ice.

Within a week, we were ready to take on a more aggressive mode of searching out the enemy—looking for him where we might find him. This was not normal, and I wondered who and what was behind it. On 8 February, 4th Co conducted an operation with another battalion on The Loop, also called VC Island. The Saigon River makes a big loop around this piece of ground, making it almost an island. Because the river is so deep and wide and flows so fast in this area, The Loop is isolated except for a narrow piece of land serving as the entry point. Land traffic on and off The Loop was easily controlled, and because it was so isolated, it was ideal enemy country.

We were optimistic about enemy contact; our company was the

blocking force, and the enemy would be pushed into our position on the connecting piece of land. Actually, enemy soldiers had three options: fight the battalion force (the hammer) that landed by boat on the far side from the connecting land, take to the water and try to escape, or run into our smaller force (the anvil). The hammer received most of the action that day with a tally of sixteen enemy KIA, two POWs, and twenty-nine held as VC suspects. Seven Sampans (small boats) were also destroyed.

On 9 February, 6th Battalion relieved the 1st at Gia Dinh, in the northeast section of Saigon. After several routine patrol days, I was again assigned to a mission on VC Island with 1st Co and the anvil mission. Second Bn was the hammer. This operation did not turn out so well: the battalion lost two Marines to booby traps and counted only one VC in return.

Fourth Company platoons patrolled on 19 February while the CP remained in camp. Traffic on our Leatherneck net picked up with a conversation between Leatherneck 3 and his 3-Alpha about mid-afternoon. Major Doug Ward was with the 3rd Bn CO and two companies at the Binh Loi railroad bridge. Captain John A. Williams was with the XO and two companies some distance from the bridge. Our battalion was on the right of the 3rd with my 4th Co nearest.

A 3rd Bn patrol had made contact with an enemy force dug in south of the bridge. Ward was attempting to get Williams to move so that he could control air strikes on the enemy position. Both advisors had reasons (mostly amounting to their counterparts' desires) why they could not leave their current positions. Which one could best control from his present location was unclear; neither could see the enemy position from his bunker.

Placing the grid coordinates on my map, I realized that the enemy was not far from me. They were near our battalion boundary and beside the village covered earlier that day by our patrols. Maybe I could control the air strike. Informing Khanh of the situation and my intentions, I moved down the road with Hi, my cowboy, and Bong, my radio bearer.

"Leatherneck Three, Leatherneck Six-Alpha, Over."

"Go, Six-Alpha."

"Three, I am moving forward to an area where I might control your air strike. When I'm in position, I'll let you know. Over."

"Great, Six-Alpha, we can use the help as we are both tied up. Fixed wing is on station; I'll turn them over to you. Out."

The village lay spread out before me as I moved down the hill. The tallest building, a small hotel under construction, offered the best observation into the enemy position. I figured the enemy to be in the paddies and bushy area about a thousand meters to my left front.

Reaching the hotel, we climbed the stairway. Built of concrete, including the roof, the four-story structure was only a shell with holes for windows and doors. The fourth floor structure did not cover the entire floor but opened into what probably would later be a patio area with a three-foot wall around the outside. It was perfect, and on the enemy side of the building.

"Leatherneck Three, Six-Alpha. Over."

"Go, Six-Alpha."

"Three, I am in a good position and looking down the throats of the bad guys. Bring on your air. Over."

"Roger, Six-Alpha, bird-dog push is 77.55 and call sign is Sir Galahad. He has a flight of four Phantoms loaded with snake and nape. They are getting low in fuel and need to dump now. I'll request more flights to work that position over. This is a suspected company-size unit, maybe a battalion. Over."

"Roger, Three. I'll be on 77.55. Out." Quickly, I rolled my radio dial to the air frequency.

"Sir Galahad, Leatherneck Six-Alpha. Over."

"Roger, Six-Alpha. Understand you have a little work down there for us. I have everything needed from Leatherneck Three except exact positions of the bad guys and yours. Can you mark? Over."

" Galahad, Six-Alpha, I see you. I am on tallest building in village southeast of bridge, about one mile from bridge on 138 degrees magnetic. When you call for it, I'll pop a smoke. The target is one thousand meters from me on my 289 magnetic. I cannot mark target. Over."

"Roger your last, Six-Alpha. Think I see your building, give me a smoke. Over."

"Got your green, Six-Alpha, and I see you. I am going to roll in and mark the target for the jet jocks." With that, the light observer aircraft made a slow descent toward the target. At 1,000 feet, Galahad fired a pair of rocket smokes that landed within the area I had designated.

"Good, Galahad. You are on target. Go for it."

The F-4s began their runs, making three passes each, while dropping their ordnance and firing their cannons. Smoke from the napalm billowed high above the greenery, blackening everything it touched. Sound waves of the exploding rockets vibrated off our building and through the village. With my radio seated on the low wall, I had a ringside seat for the air show. Hi and Bong were excited by the action and expressed the only English they knew: "Kill many-many VC!" The jet jocks dipped their wings following their last strike, leaving word with

Galahad that they would return. Galahad drove off for some different scenery while waiting for the next flight.

SPAT! SPAT! SPAT! Hearing what sounded like big angry bugs flying into a window, I realized that we were under rifle fire. Bullets hit the concrete, one on the wall below the radio, and the other two into the wall behind us. There was no rifle crack to emphasize that we were under fire. Several more rounds hit behind us as we dove for cover behind the low wall. I reached up and lowered the radio to safety.

Some enemy positions were obviously closer than I expected. I also realized that the rifle fire could be coming from inside a bunker, which would greatly muffle the sound. In addition, the wind was a steady fifteen knots, blowing from me to the enemy, which would carry the sound away. I realized that the enemy could be moving a squad to eliminate my little team under cover of the rifle fire.

Grabbing Hi's M-16, I extended my helmeted head over the wall; this time only my helmet and eyeballs showed. To my relief, the paddies, dikes, and canals were clear; I was satisfied that there was no movement. Enemy rounds smacked into the wall below and behind me. The enemy force extended from my earlier targets to within 500 meters of us.

"Leatherneck Six-Alpha, Sir Galahad. Over."

"Go, Galahad."

"Six-Alpha, there are fighting holes and bunkers in the area hit and you have a good-size unit before you. I am low on fuel. Red Rover will be on station in about zero-five and in time to work the inbound carrier strike flight. He will contact you when in the area. It's been good working with you. Over."

" Galahad, thanks for the help. You did well, boy. Good luck. Out."
Rifle fire continued and I kept an eye out for enemy movement. After five minutes my radio spoke: "Leatherneck Six-Alpha, Red Rover. Over."

"Red Rover, Six-Alpha. Do you have my position? Over."

"In general Six-Alpha. Galahad briefed me on what has taken place, but give me a smoke to be sure. The carrier flight is zero three mikes out. Over."

"Roger, Rover. My smoke is out."

"I see your red, Six-Alpha. Where is the enemy?"

"Rover, the enemy extends closer to me than the area worked over by Galahad. He is 500 meters from me on 283 magnetic. I want you to put it right in my backyard; I am under fire from this area. Over."

While giving Rover my last message and looking into the enemy area, I realized that I was seeing red smoke. The enemy in my new target area had popped two red smoke grenades. They were obviously listening to our radio conversation and heard Rover identify my red smoke as friendly. Before I could key my handset, Rover was on the air.

"Six-Alpha, I see two more red smokes. What does that mean? Over."

"Rover, that is the enemy position. They monitored your identification of red smoke as friendly. They have marked the boundaries of their unit hoping that you would leave them alone. Put your stuff right between those two smokes. Over."

"Roger, Six-Alpha, that's the way I read it; just wanted to make sure. The carrier flight is on station and I'm bringing them in."

While the carrier jets worked over the position, we received a good volume of fire from the enemy against our building. I wanted to ensure that the strike was on target, so I had to look over the wall. However, I did not rest up there. The enemy (we later learned that this was part of a regular NVA Bn) knew that my team was the cause of their problems and tried to do something about it with their rifle fire. That commander did not know that we numbered only three. A small reconnaissance team sent to check us out would have paid him back handsomely. If they had gotten into our building, their chances would have been as good as mine.

After the carrier jets, I brought in two different Army flights of helicopter gunships to work over the area. The spring evening dragged on with light finally beginning to fail. Ward wanted me to remain, as he had a C-47 Gunship locked on. Someone had to control, guide, and direct; with nothing better to do, I was game. We had no chow or bedding, but this was combat. Some rice would surely hit the spot. Just as I began preparations for the night, allowing for the fact that the bad guys might do something about me in the dark, we received company.

Khanh and company joined us. His cowboy moved the captain's stuff into the hotel, setting up his cot with mosquito netting. Meanwhile the cook produced hot rice. While I was happy for the company, the captain was dry; he had not wanted to leave his plush quarters of the last two days. Chung directed that Khanh join me, and Gordon was the push behind Chung with the question, "Who was protecting the co-van?"

Snoopy the Dragon provided great fireworks throughout the night while repeatedly working over the position. Their flares kept the paddies covered with light almost as bright as day. We received no more rifle fire.

The next afternoon, 3rd Bn sent a company in to check the area. The NVA had left, taking many of their dead and wounded. There were bloody clothing and bandages to tell the story, as well as many fresh mounds in the ground. Concern for booby traps prevented digging into the mounds to determine what was buried there. The Saigon side of the river was now free of the bad guys.

Ward worked up an award recommendation for my day of help. This would be my second combat decoration, counting the Purple Heart from the Korean War. He allowed that I deserved the Navy Commendation Medal. Following are excerpts from his write-up:

> The enemy position was in the vicinity of a company of the 6th Bn, advised and accompanied by Lt Fox.
>
> Lt Fox, realizing he was located in the only area that afforded visual observation into the enemy's defensive position, moved into an exposed observation post located only two hundred meters from the enemy. From this position, he accurately directed and adjusted the machine gun and rocket fire from gunships on the target area for a period of twelve hours. Lt Fox's superior judgment and professionalism contributed to the operational effectiveness of the 3rd Bn and greatly contributed to the rout of the enemy forces.
>
> Lt Fox's actions during this period inflicted heavy casualties and material losses on the enemy. He was instrumental in the saving of many Marine casualties and his courage under fire and exemplary performance of duty were in keeping with the highest traditions of the US Naval Service.

Organized enemy activity disappeared; neighborhoods were back to their pre-TET daily routine. In celebration, 4th Company held a party in one of the secure areas behind us. My presence was requested, and I found my counterpart well on his way to feeling good when I arrived.

Throughout the meal, Khanh demanded that I "bottoms up" with him. Initially I did; however, it became clear that the goal was to get me drunk. Each of the lieutenants approached me, one at a time, for the same purpose: bottoms up with him. For the reason of size alone, I could probably drink any one of these smaller guys under the table—but not all of them. Further, I had not the slightest intention of finding out.

I began spilling more than I drank as I raised my glass, letting the liquor run off my chin. Later Khanh became ugly; I assumed because I was not getting drunk and he surely was. I had never been drunk, and this would not be my first time. Khanh tried to get me on stage to sing with the entertainers. I would not; he did.

The next thing I knew, Khanh was out cold without a quiver. Immediately there was a big rush to get the co-van away from the party and back to camp, a face-saving move to protect the dignity of their commander. Marines tried to block his body from my view while escorting me to my jeep; I was not to see the great man down. Too late, Vietnam, I did!

The 6th Bn moved north of the Bien Hoa automobile bridge where Hein joined us early in March. He had survived in the mountains at Da Lat, afraid to go near anyone. He had no food. Always a small man, now there was nothing to him. His head looked like a skull, and the doctors told him to gain weight. He informed me that our mess cost would be higher because he needed to eat richer food. My weight was probably down forty pounds from my normal but that had not brought forth richer food.

"Yes, Diwe, I will give you more money when we leave this place. While we are here, I will eat with the Army. I need my country's meals." An Army artillery unit was set up two blocks down the road; I was eating two meals a day with them anyway.

Gordon, upon learning of my meal plans from Chung, paid me a visit. It was important for advisors to eat with their counterparts. Further, both he and Chung wanted me to eat with Hein. Explaining the situation as I saw it, I assured the captain that I intended to eat with Hein when there was no US alternative. Hein had not appeared concerned about my intentions. Anyway, I would be going on R&R within a few days, and when I returned, we would be in another area. The captain left me with the words, "You eat each evening meal with Hein." My R&R came up the next day.

On 24 April 1968, I was en route to Hawaii for four days with Dotti Lu and Dixie Lee. They arrived ahead of me to give us maximum time together. (Amy, only six months old, was with my mother.) We had a wonderful time, but shadowing it all was that very soon there would be another separation. After the first day, the end hung heavily over us; we knew that every minute brought us closer to that dreaded departure. We pretended that we were having fun and tried to enjoy our time to the fullest, lying on the beach, playing in the surf, and visiting the island sights.

My fun was also dampened by the realization that I was about to ruin Dotti Lu's chance for any remaining enjoyment. With her approval, I wanted a six-month combat extension. Justification of my wants paled beside the realization of my family duty and needs. Compounding my problem was learning that living alone in the country with our two babies was taking a toll upon Dotti Lu. Percentage-wise, she had lost as much weight as I and was getting very little sleep. While she had a new house, she was not comfortable alone in the country at night. Amy had been a colicky baby the first six months, which had allowed her mother no rest.

On the third day, I presented my desire and reasoning for my wife's understanding. My temporary commission was due to end shortly, and I liked the officer duties and responsibilities. I thought that I had a better chance of remaining an officer with extended duty in Vietnam.

Furthermore, my year as an advisor did not count for much. In short, I had not done enough against the communist effort. Moreover, what had been done was shadowed by too many events that had increased my hatred for all things under the banner of communism. I wanted to lead a Marine rifle company in combat, to show that I could handle the business end of the Green Machine. The war would not last long enough for me to return several years later for a second tour; it was now or never.

Dotti Lu listened to my desire and reasoning with no interruption, but her expression said it all. This was not an easy option for her and was farthest from her thoughts until that moment. We talked over the pros and cons of it, with her stating that she supported me in what I wanted to do. She could handle the home front, keeping things together until I returned. There were six months left on this tour, followed by a thirty-day leave and now another six months.

A Marine in her own right, Dotti Lu carried her burden well; she accepted another 180 days, another 4,320 hours of wondering and worrying about what was happening to me. All of her days and nights were filled with the dread of an official Marine Corps visit, a knock on her door that would stop her world. I knew what I was asking of her—six additional months of being a combat infantryman's wife. I did not feel good about that.

My girls went with me to the airport on the morning of day five. To say that this good-bye was more difficult than our parting six months earlier would not be right, but it surely was no easier. Dotti Lu would not relax her arms from around me for some minutes after the final boarding call. With huge tears filling her beautiful eyes, she gripped me as though she could stay my departure: "If I do not let go, he will not leave."

Breaking her hold on me broke my heart. The action required of me at that moment was so unnatural and difficult that I felt I was not doing right. The Marine part of me was now very small and silent. That last sight of my loved ones, as they tried to keep their eyes dry, was so pathetic that I almost lost control of my emotions. The long flight back to Vietnam allowed me to get it together again.

Checking in on 28 April, I learned that I would not be going back to the battalion; Gordon had won his war. Hein and I had made it for six months; considering his record on past advisors, my work was a breakthrough and a record. My position of eating American chow when convenient rather than pay Hein's inflated mess price was Gordon's justification for my reassignment.

Colonel Michael talked around the issue by addressing his desire to split the duties among his combat arms advisors. His aim was to give each advisor six months with a battalion and the remainder with a Force Headquarters. I had my time in the bush, now I deserved a job that was less stressful. On 1 May 1968, I became the Assistant Advisor to TF-A. While this was a major's billet, it did nothing for my lieutenant's ego. Michael's justification sounded good, but other advisors were spending their entire tour with battalions. This lieutenant was just not smart enough to take the captain's crap—literally.

TF-A was set up in the VNMC Hqrs compound. We manned our radios in an office, and I became better acquainted with the other advisors. Lt Col James T. Breckinridge replaced the Assistant Senior Marine Advisor, G. W. Rodney. Capt Cyril Kammeier replaced John Hainsworth as our Adjutant. Other headquarters personnel included Lt Joe Pratte, Admin, and Capt Pete McCarthy, Supply. Battalion Advisors, whom I got to know on their day into the city, were Lt Bill Fite and Capts Tom Taylor, Jack Sheehan, Mike McGowan, and Skip Sweetzer, all gungy Marines.

Major McAlove[26] was now the Senior Advisor to TF-A. His call sign was Leatherneck Alpha; I was Leatherneck Alpha-Alpha. One of us had to man the TF radios twenty-four hours, seven days a week. Besides our Leatherneck Advisor Net consisting of advisors with VNMC battalions assigned to TF-A, we monitored the Saigon CMD net, and those of any Regional or Popular Defense Force Hqrs and US Army units with which we might be involved.

The Task Force job amounted to directing and assisting the battalion advisors, handling radio traffic, maintaining logs of events, and making reports to higher headquarters, both US Marine and MACV. I had landed a rear echelon job, like it or not. My hotel room received some use, even if mostly for showers and uniform change. In addition, my chow situation improved, as all of my meals were taken at one of the hotel messes.

I spent my nights in the little office, monitoring the radios. Again, as in the field, when radio traffic died with the slowdown of operations, I slept. No one stayed awake monitoring the radio, as we did not have the personnel. At the same time, I never missed any radio traffic concerning me while asleep. A squawk on my radio loudspeaker would bring me awake enough to know whether to get with it or to disregard. Maybe a better way of putting it is that advisors never slept so soundly that they missed what was going on around them.

The Major was around most of the daytime hours so I had no problem getting away for meals. Evenings and nights on the radios were mine, however; there was keen night activity in the Saigon military officer society and McAlove did not miss much. He was involved with an Army nurse who saw more of him than I did. His absence was not a problem; I had nothing better to do.

VC forces were active on the night of 10 June; they set up and fired several rockets into Saigon at daylight on 11 June. Two rockets exploded near enough to awaken me. Pulling on my boots, I was on my feet when another rocket exploded against my building, hitting a tree limb twenty meters away. The explosive force blew out my office windows and door, knocking me to the deck where I caught and supported my weight on bare elbows and forearms. Glass from the windows covered the floor where I crawled on it, cutting both forearms.

There were no more explosions, so I made a quick tour of the second floor outside passageway, which encircled the building. There was nothing out of the ordinary. The city was yet asleep, as was the Bo Thu Lein. A shed roof under the tree limb was shredded; all the glass was blown out of that side of my building. As it was an office and supply building, it was too early for anyone to be in the other spaces. The headquarters personnel arrived from their hotels shortly to learn of the near miss of their workplace by a 122mm rocket.

On 25 July, TF-A with the 5th Bn moved to, and set up operations near, Can Tho within the IV CTZ. (Map, page 248) Heavily populated and the rice bowl of Indochina, this was not an easy area of operations. While the daily business of farming went on as usual, the bad guys had to be sorted from the good.

Sorting was the difficult part, and I had the opportunity to learn firsthand just how difficult. Nothing stands in the way of a Marine and his R&R, and Leatherneck 5-Alpha's time had come. I worked his position from 11 to 22 August.[27] During a four-day operation, I moved with the Bn XO's element and lived underwater. Even the solid ground (rice paddies) was underwater while the rivers, canals, and streams ran swift, wide, and deep. Clothes and gear never had a chance to dry and skin suffered with boils, blisters, and festering sores.

We started our ground movement from a highway after debarking from trucks. Moving through a forest was easy enough with water about boot-top level. Just when I had decided that this would be another walk in the sun, we hit a wide canal. My radio bearer (both he and my cowboy were provided by this battalion) moved up beside me and handed me the radio. Not understanding his intentions, I thought he was refusing to carry my radio. Then, with sign language and my limited Vietnamese, I learned that because he was so short, I needed to carry the radio to keep it out of the water. Feeling that this four-foot Marine was putting me on, I took the radio and entered the water. What a surprise!

I adjusted quickly enough to the cold temperature, but the force of the water current was something else. In addition, the silt on the bottom sucked at my boots, holding my feet while the current pushed me. Upon stepping into the water, I was immediately up to my armpits. With the radio resting on my helmet, I started across. My radio bearer hung on to me; his feet did not touch bottom and he could not swim. The routine was repeated often over the next few days. The swift flow of water caused many of the shorter Vietnamese to come ashore further down stream. The operation ended four days later without enemy contact, and I returned to TF-A.

From 30 July to 6 August, we did a Riverine Operation with 2nd Brigade, 9th US Infantry. TF-A went aboard the *USS Benewah* along with the Hqrs, Mobile Riverine Force. Our 5th Bn moved by water while the 2nd Brigade moved by water and helicopter. The operation worked smoothly with limited success, primarily in captured weapons and equipment, giving me my first SKS[28] war souvenir.

Riverine Operations were easy living with good Navy chow three times a day and at night if you desired. Lazing around on the boat was capped off with a bunk, no leeches, no wet feet, and no load on your back. We did another Riverine Operation (Operation Song Than 761–68) from 12 to 15 August with negative results.

Lazing around camp in midmorning on 23 August, I shaved with the radio speakers within earshot. McAlove had gone up the hill to the Army advisor building for breakfast and poker. We were set up with the Phong Dien Province Regional Force and were using their camp and advisor facilities. With no enemy activity, the compound security pushed the war far away. These are the times that guerrilla forces act.

Two heavy explosions racked the camp with the heavy whomp of mortar rounds. Smoke and dust drifted skyward from the advisor building on the hill above me. A VN Marine rushed toward me yelling "Co-van MedEvac, VC Mortar, VC Mortar." Was a co-van hurt or did he send for a MedEvac? Not able to raise the Army on their net, I took off on a run up the hill with my command radio.

An Army advisor met me halfway; they had taken a direct hit with an 82mm mortar. Two advisors were wounded; McAlove was the worst, bleeding heavily. I called for a Dust Off and worked up a SitRpt. There were enough advisors on the hill to care for the wounded. By the time my SitRpt was transmitted, the Dust Off was inbound. McAlove had taken a piece of shrapnel in the fleshy part of his buttocks. Not seriously injured, he would not return to duty during my remaining time with TF-A. Nothing exciting happened for the next two weeks; then it was time for my second R&R. I spent it on the ski slopes in Australia.

Several nights were spent in my Saigon hotel room after my return from my R&R. My year as an advisor was over. Colonel Michael had earlier written to his buddy in the 3rd MarDiv asking for assistance in getting me a rifle company. I would transfer to the 3rd MarDiv during October. Michael had completed his tour and turned the Advisory Unit over to Colonel L. V. Corbett on 27 July.

Michael's departing Fitness Report on me is typical of those I received for my year as an advisor. He rated me outstanding in all areas except Handling Officers, Cooperation, and Judgment. Those were marked excellent. (Corbett later marked me outstanding straight down the page, except for a couple not observes.). Section D excerpts:

> . . . His well-balanced qualities of professional enthusiasm, long infantry experience, superb motivation, unruffled disposition, and fine sense of humor have made him ideally suited for the demands and challenges of this assignment. In the field, under conditions of combat, Fox inspires immediate confidence by his aggressive actions, deliberate well-thought out decisions, and patient manner. . . .

With SKS in hand, I boarded a flight and was homeward bound. The CO MB USNS Treasure Island was responsible for my return and would send my return-flight port call. Thirty days back in Virginia with my girls was next, and I was excited to be with Amy, who was growing up without me.

My first sight of my second daughter was over the heads of passengers at some distance, as she was held closely and proudly by her mother for her daddy to see. Now almost a year old, Amy was slow to accept this heavy-voiced stranger who moved into her female-dominated life. I spent my days with my three lovely ladies and did little else. However, from day twenty, I started dreading that port call.

I visited my monitor at HQMC, as I would be assigned stateside in six months, and I wanted to influence the where. Officers assigned to HQMC wore civilian clothes four days a week, so I did not immediately recognize Captain John Ripley. He was onto me, however, wanting to know just how badly I had messed up his platoon in 2nd Force Recon. This was our first meeting since that morning in 1966 when he turned his platoon over to me on his way to Vietnam.

John was my monitor and suggested Amphibious Warfare School. "Save yourself a move and go to school while your family is situated here. That gives you six more months to decide where you want duty." AWS sounded professional; I accepted. If I could get that school, maybe there was a chance that I could become a regular officer. John had the privilege of access to my record; he obviously felt good about my officer potential.

Thirty days passed and I did not receive my port call; the extra time pleased me. At day forty-five, however, I called the number provided by the liaison section. A surprised captain said, "Wait, out. I'll call you back." Within the hour he called; my record had been misplaced; I should report by 2300 28 October, the following day. There was another tough good-bye and I was on my way.

My port call was 0300 on 29 October 1968. That hour is about as bad as they come for starting an eighteen to twenty-hour flight, but that is the military way. Another point jumped out at me: I was leaving the States on Dotti Lu's birthday; a year ago I flew out on my birthday. Was there a message in this? Flying to Vietnam was getting to be a commuter kind of thing. This was my fourth trip within the year and three of them were made with a heavy heart.

The Advisory Unit had begun to wonder what had happened to Fox. The day before my return, they sent a message to the CO MB Treasure Island requesting information on the stray lieutenant. I was to be transferred to the 3rd MarDiv during October; my return on the 31st did not allow that to happen. Turning in my field gear, checking out, and a farewell party soaked up a couple of days.

On 3 November 1968 I departed the Advisory Unit, and caught a C-130 flight north. My tour with the Vietnamese could have been better. They had their way of running their war, but I was responsible for some of the negative feelings I had about my tour. Spending my year with a battalion was preferable to splitting time in a headquarters. The cause was clearly my rub with Gordon, which was petty. Now, with it behind me, I could see that a better way would have been to zip up and take it. The 3rd MarDiv was a new start; from now on it would be, "Aye Aye, Sir. How high, how far, and what color?"

10
1st Lieutenant
Section 2

I checked in with Division Headquarters at the Quang Tri Marine Base. (Map, page 248) The personnel officer was a captain, and I reported to him in his tent. It was late evening, but this was war, and he had paperwork to move. Where did I want to go?

"Captain, my first choice is commander of a rifle company. If not that, then I want either 1st or 3rd Force Recon."

"One/Nine is short of captains, and I feel that as a senior 1st lieutenant you would get a company."

"I'll take 1/9."

He did some writing, pushed the papers aside and stated, "You are assigned to 1/9; they are on FSB (Fire Support Base) Ann. They have a rear headquarters here where you can draw your field gear, and they will get you on a resupply chopper out to Ann. You can't do anything else tonight; want a beer?"

Not wanting a beer, I nevertheless agreed. I had eaten chow and there was nothing else to do. Maybe the captain wanted to talk, and I might learn what was happening in the division's AO. Moving to his living area on the other side of his office tent, he produced two beers from an ice cooler. Handing me one, he asked, "Have you not heard of the Walking Dead?"

"No," I answered, expecting a sea story.

"One/Nine is known as the Walking Dead. They have had heavy contacts and taken many casualties. Several companies were all but annihilated on Khe Sanh. Did you never hear of that? A corporal was the commander for a while. No sir, it ain't no trouble to get a rifle company in 1/9. First off, no one wants to go to that battalion. Secondly, if you do—regardless of rank—stick around long enough, meaning stay alive, and you'll end up as the commander."

I responded with, "That name doesn't bother me, Captain; Walking Death might fit them better." If 1/9 was the unit most likely to have contact with the communists, then I could not have a better assignment.

The captain retrieved his guitar, and we moved outside for cooler air where he strummed and I listened. This was one way to fight a war. Nevertheless, all assignments count; each individual plays an essential part. Some assignments are tougher and more demanding of the individual and place him in harm's way. The infantry, those 20 percent who are on the cutting edge, cannot do their job without the 80 percent supporting them. All is fair for those who choose the infantry; those in the infantry against their choice find the difference in risk of life hard to take.

One/Nine supply was a revelation after my experience in the Advisory Group. Not only did I receive old, well-worn gear; supply was short in some items. No operable pistols were available. Battalion Forward had one from a casualty; I could get that as I went forward. Anything I was short and that was not available, I should take from casualties. Great! There was no doubt that I was back in my Marine Corps.

An H–34 delivered me to Ann; it contained an Army artillery battery and 1/9 Hqrs with Company A providing perimeter security. The other three companies were deployed elsewhere. I located the Adjutant, who escorted me to my new commander, Lieutenant Colonel George W. Smith. That day began what would become a lifelong friendship; Smith played a major role in developing me into a Marine officer in thought and deed.

Colonel Smith immediately made time for me; we sought shade with a breeze, and talked. He wanted to get to know this lieutenant who asked for command of one of his rifle companies. At issue was the responsibility for 240-plus Marines and corpsmen in his battalion, a responsibility that he did not pass along lightly. When we reached the family point, I wanted him to know that I was not one of those with a loveless marriage or a wife who made combat an easy option. It was important to me that he knew of my intimate, caring family relationship, so I talked family and career desires. I liked being a Marine officer and my heart was with the infantry. Smith gave me Alpha.

Alpha CP was in a bunker on the hillside just above the Bn CP. Captain John S. (Jack) Sirotniak came down and after a short talk with Smith escorted me to his command bunker. He was the Senior Captain in the battalion and would become the Bn S-3. Jack did not like giving up Alpha, but I was impressed with his manner of doing so.

Collecting his officers, he introduced me, told them of his new duties, and thanked them for their loyalty and support. He continued with, "I know that you will continue to do your duty for Lt Fox as you have for me. I would just remind you that although he is your rank, he is your commander. You are expected to address him by rank or position and not on a familiarity basis; he is your skipper. Any questions or problems with what I have said?" With that, Sirotniak walked off the hill, leaving me with a good feeling about this tour of duty. Albert V. Sheppard, also a 1st Lt, was my XO and the first black officer with whom I served. My PltLdrs, all 2nd lieutenants, would leave me shortly; they had put in their bush time.

Assuming command is more than moving into a CP. My Marines needed to know me and I them, and the FSB security mission offered me that opportunity. Chow time was a weakness: were enough alert Marines manning the positions? Darkness is a concern: Marines get tired, and sleep is always a problem. Who should know better than I? My rounds were not routine; they occurred at all hours.

On day three in command, I started just before daylight and was surprised with no challenge from a machine gun (MG) bunker. Walking through the gun pit to the crew's sleeping bunker, I wondered about a rifle propped against the bunker door. No one was around; who had placed the rifle against the door? I picked it up and opened the door to see a Marine sitting asleep on the step. Nudging him, I asked, "Who is on watch?"

He took a few seconds to awaken and then exploded into action. Charging out of the bunker, he tried to grab the rifle. He was bigger than I, but I had no problem fending him off with his rifle. I slapped his shoulders with the broad side of the weapon and repeated, "Who's on watch?"

"I am, Sir. Would you give me my rifle?" His words showed that he now recognized me, and he stood at attention. His concern about his rifle showed that he knew that my possession of his firearm would be solid evidence at a court martial of his sleeping on watch. Court martial proceedings were the furthest from my mind; Marines doing what was expected of them was my concern. During my roughest days in the Korean War, I never knew of a gun watch sleeping; there were more men to share the watch. If this were typical of Alpha, I would activate my old gunny group-tightener.

The gunner's attempt at retrieving his rifle had allowed me to expel my rage at finding him asleep. Already punished physically, he started rubbing his hurting places. I asked, "How did you get your rifle against the outside door?"

"The wind kept blowing the door open, Sir, and I reached out, placing my rifle as a prop."

"You stupid shit, suppose I had been the NVA? No loss with you, but where would your buddies be now? The enemy would be all over the artillery and the battalion CP. All because you got cold and sleepy. Hell, you don't stand watch in the bunker anyway; you're supposed to be in the gun pit."

"Sir, I know. I screwed up and deserve what I have coming. Please, Sir, go ahead and kick the shit out of me, here and now." This Marine might be lazily dumb, but he was thinking and he cared about his record. If I did the physical thing for which he asked, I probably would not bring charges against him.

The gun-squad leader appeared in the doorway to check on the noise. I responded with "Ask this dumb shit," gave the rifle to the squad leader, and walked away. They both needed time to worry about what would follow.

Later in the day, I visited Sirotniak to get his feelings on my sleeper. He felt that the gunner had potential and had never been a problem. Further, he seemed pleased that I handled the affair without pressing charges. That young man later came through for me in several tight enemy contacts. Months later, we would laugh together about his dumb act.

That incident helped me gain the attention of Alpha Marines; I had their minds, if not their hearts. The word was out: "The skipper checks the line. If he catches you sleeping, he kicks the shit out of you. No fancy court martial for this mustang." While that rumor was far from the truth, it would help Alpha do what had to be done.

The few days with Alpha on the FSB had given me a good feel for my company, and I was ready to get out on my own. Next was a mission to secure a ridgetop, build a FSB, and provide security while the artillery battery was emplaced. All I had to do was find this peak among many along a ridgeline, take it from the NVA if they wanted to claim it, and flatten the top for the emplacement of an artillery battery. A map study gave me movement azimuth, as well as a feel for the rough terrain over which we would move. I had it down cold; this was my chance to make a positive mark with my Marines. However, I did not allow for the proverbial "Hogan's Goat" factor.

As our choppers were landing, my radio operator received new grid coordinates for our insert zone. The birds were on the deck before I had a chance to talk with Sirotniak about the change; I had to go with my latest order, a different insert zone. Once airborne, I placed the spot on my map to learn that we would land on the opposite side of our objective, west of our ridge instead of east. The climb looked easier, maybe that was the reason.

We landed behind ground preparation by two gunships. Looking the terrain over, I did not like what was before me, considering our insertion west of our objective. A high peak rose west of us, a bit south of where I had pictured the objective from yesterday's insertion point. There were no peaks to my east, but I could not be sure because we were in deep-forested jungle. I tried to reach the S-3, but our radios were not making contact. Following the departure of the birds, I gathered my platoon leaders. They soon knew what I knew: we had landed west of our objective.

I moved the company eastward for high ground where I might study the landmarks and use the radio to confirm or dispel my suspicion that we had landed in the original zone. The high ridge behind bothered me; it was clearly the commanding ground. Our low ridge forked and I headed south for about thirty minutes without seeing any higher ground. After climbing a knoll with no high ground ahead, I called a halt.

My arty FO gained radio contact with his battery, and I called for an illumination round over our objective. High up in a tree when the round was fired, I looked toward the high peak behind us. Sure enough, the round burst over that peak with the flare burning under its slowly descending parachute.

The new skipper was off to a poor start. Marines are not fond of humping, especially under combat loads in high heat conditions. Our loads were heavy because there would be no resupply until we cut an HLZ. Bad weather was a factor that could delay the HLZ a few days. Having to walk over the same hills because we started in the wrong direction was plainly asking for a low popularity vote. Feelings showed plainly on faces as I doubled back along the sweaty, green line. It was clear that my platoon leaders had not had time to brief everyone on our change. For whatever reason, we had landed in the original HLZ.

Darkness arrived shortly after we passed our insert HLZ. The terrain was rough, with huge boulders that required a great effort to get over or around. Pulling Alpha into a perimeter, I set in with enough light to establish fields of fire and warm up some Cs.

The day's screw-up hung in my mind; what could I have done differently? I had no reason to doubt my latest orders. Why give me a change and then not execute it? The chopper flight leader probably did not get the change. Being out of radio contact also contributed to the mix-up. Except for exhausted Marines who must be wondering about the NDS (new dumb shit) leading them, nothing was lost. We would be on the objective early on the morrow.

Following a quiet night and a difficult climb over the rock ledges along the way, Alpha arrived on our objective in midday. I established a perimeter defense, and the combat engineers began clearing an HLZ. Few humans had been on this ground, and no timber had ever been harvested. We had some huge trees to displace.

Instead of chain saws, we carried C-4 explosives, and after dropping trees I called in a chopper with chain saws, gas, and axes that were lowered by line. The choppers could not land with the huge trees on the deck.

Riflemen and engineers had an HLZ early on day two. Next in was a small Case 450 bulldozer along with a supply of shape and cratering charges. Charges loosened the dirt and the tractor pushed it around as desired. Our mountaintop quickly changed its appearance, and with the explosions, chopper, and tractor noise, the bad guys had to know we were on it. That fact was not a concern because the peak was so difficult to get to that a squad could defend it. The position was selected well, and the selector was on the next chopper.

FSB Dick was the idea of our regimental commander, Colonel Robert H. Barrow. He liked the position so well after seeing how Dick was developing that he came to stay. With two radio operators to keep in touch with his forward command, he sent his chopper home. Later when Dick was ready, Barrow moved his staff to join him. For now, it was just he and I.

The colonel and I spent some time together, seated on a log in the shade—two old country boys passing the time of day while the building of Dick went on around us. I did not consider myself old, but I felt that this colonel met the qualification; he had served in the big war and in Korea. Barrow's slow drawl (with which I should have been familiar) probably helped influence my thinking that this old warrior had already served his best days in our Corps. These thoughts go to show that even older lieutenants do not know much: Barrow went on to be CMC.

An artillery battery arrived; the battery would provide their own security. Alpha was relieved and inserted into a new TAOR with a patrol mission. One/Nine was involved in Operation Scotland II/Afton from 5 to 12 November, followed by Gio Vin until the 17th. Enemy forces, if any, were staying low and avoiding contact; we had little success.

Operation Thuong-Xa began on 17 November with 1/9 involved in a two-battalion cordon and search. On the 23rd, Alpha's turn came to provide the defense for Vandegrift Combat Base. VCB was one of the good deals for the bush Marines and rifle companies who rotated through a four-day stay there. The duty company provided security for the base while also giving their Marines some of the benefits of the rear areas. Hot chow, showers, clean clothes, and tents with cots for sleeping were available, as well as facilities like post office, PX, barber shop, supply, and such. VCB was located between Dong Ha and Khe Sanh and served as a forward supply base, among other things. Marines stationed in Quang Tri and Danang considered Vandegrift to be in the bush; bush Marines enjoyed the comforts of a rear area at VCB.

Military units experienced racial and drug problems in Vietnam. For the most part, these problems happened within the huge rear area force, the 80 percent that were not concerned with the issue of staying alive. Alpha Company had no such problems, as we were always in the bush and living was enough of a challenge. Some individuals no doubt used drugs on R&R and in rear areas; if they did, they left it there. In the bush, we were Marines!

Companies maintained tents on VCB, including the companies of 1/9 except for Alpha. For this assignment, we moved into another company's area, which was not a problem—the tents were empty. Alpha Marines had no place to call home, which I learned was not a small issue with them. Why bother? Alpha Marines were not around long before they were hauled to the hospital or shipped home in body bags. I tasked my 1st Sergeant with getting tents, cots, and a company area for our next duty at VCB. Enemy weapons on hand were to be used for trade and more would be forthcoming.

VCB gave me an opportunity that I could not pass up. Day security required only 10 percent of my force on the perimeter. All other Marines were free to enjoy the good life found on the base, mostly sacking out. Days were free time for the individual and the unit.

Working with my leaders earlier had caused me to suspect a gap in what the Marine Corps teaches and what was actually taking place in the bush. My squad ambushes were not getting any kills, although the patrols were calling in that enemy was observed. Some of our tactics seemed rusty at best. My company, platoons, and squads had not trained together in how to make war. Using football as an analogy, my players knew how to play the game, but they had no team plays, much less any rehearsal of these plays. Who does what? When? School started now.

My platoon sergeants collected grumbling, complaining Marines on an embankment leading down to a wide path. I offered the ground upon which they stood: "Take a seat, Marines."

"What is a good way to trigger an ambush?" I asked. There were no answers and no hands to my question. Plenty of sour looks expressed the thought, "This is why this gungy SOB got me up?" That message was plain on most faces. I continued.

"What is usually the best formation for a squad ambush?" I paused to allow that thought to work. "Where is the position of the squad leader? Who triggers the ambush?" Pause. "Where do you place your Claymores?

"We are not doing the best that we can in the bush, and I feel the reason is that Smith isn't sure what Jones knows and how he will do a certain task. You have all been trained; hell, you're combat Marines. My purpose is not to teach you anything but to pull our collective knowledge together, to get our purpose, our plays, our timing down to a razor edge. I want Smith and Jones each to know what is inside the head of the other when something unexpected happens.

"My goal is that we operate as a team, not as a group of individuals. I also recognize that this is your chance to take your pack off and get much-deserved rest, to write letters, to enjoy a beer. What I am doing won't interfere with your time. We will spend two hours each day here talking and walking ourselves through some offensive tactics that I feel are needed. You might feel better about these hours that I'm taking, if you consider our effort as assurance that the body going home in a bag is the enemy's, not yours. This effort is insurance that you catch the big bird back to the World."

Ambushes were first; I talked about them, then had a squad come forward and take position in an L-shaped ambush on the path. We talked about placement of weapons and individuals, including all the whys. Good comments began coming out of the ranks. Another squad was assigned the enemy role and moved off to walk into the ambush. We talked that action through, including reversing the roles—good guys walking into an enemy ambush. Who does what and when?

Everyone got so involved with the class issues that we far exceeded my two hours and almost missed chow. Class was held easily afterwards, and each day Alpha spent at VCB included these sessions. The turnover of personnel demanded nothing less if Alpha was to be the cutting edge.

One/Nine was involved in Operation Dawson River/Afton from 28 November to 24 December. Alpha moved from VCB to a low hill called Pusan where I worked a patrol base but we had no enemy contact. Major D. N. Kennon replaced Sirotniak as the operations officer; he gave me a warning order of a mission on the battalion's flank. Alpha would insert by chopper on a low hill mass and move by foot up a ridge some distance to a mountain pass. Once in position, I would operate a CPB. For starters, we would carry a three-day supply of ordnance, food, and water, as an HLZ had to be cut before I could be resupplied. A section of 81mm mortars, a squad of engineers, and a sniper team were attached. The heavier mortar pleased me, but the section did not carry many rounds. Wanting to use it if I needed it, we each carried an additional mortar round.

The hump up the ridge was uneventful on 14 December, just a long steady climb with a load on our backs. Arriving in position, platoon sectors were assigned, fields of fire prepared, and we were set in by darkness. An HLZ was cleared the next day, which made humping the extra gear unnecessary. Each day, one platoon caught a long, full-day patrol while another sent out squads on shorter patrols.

We enjoyed our mission and position until the cold rain started. Once wet, there was no chance of getting dry, and after three days of rain, everyone was wet. Fighting holes collected water and became mud holes, causing Marines to look as though we lived underground. Resupply became limited due to clouds and low ceilings; tempers became short.

Patrols continued to go out with limited success. One patrol observed an enemy force on the move but lost contact before getting into position to take it under fire. Artillery was called on the last observed position and direction of movement.

Another patrol, AP1-3 (Alpha Patrol, 1st Plt, 3rd Sq) while moving on a trail, came face to face with an enemy squad. Just topping a hill, our point man saw the enemy first as they moved toward him. The enemy soldiers under heavy loads moved with heads down only twenty meters from him. Armed with an M-79, he attempted to fire two beehive rounds. When the second round followed the first with a failure to fire, he shouted a warning to his squad that caused the enemy to scatter.

Patrol routes were determined by map study. Our maps were not accurate and what appeared as passable terrain on paper was not necessarily so. I assigned 1st Platoon a patrol on the south side of our ridge. The map offered promise: this could be where the enemy was hiding. Instead of a day patrol, they made a day and night out of it.

Darkness caught them halfway along their route, and because of the difficult terrain and underbrush they had pushed through, 2nd Lt George Malone elected to continue instead of turning back. Compounded by darkness, movement became more difficult. They could not rest or sleep in the rain on the steep incline so the patrol pushed onward. I fired illumination rounds to give them light; the vines and brush were so thick that they would not have made it otherwise. Artillery covered for us when my 81s ran out of rounds. That patrol cost the taxpayer some money, but we brought everyone back safely. Enemy forces were not on that side of us; they had better sense.

The rain continued for several days with my heart pouring out for my riflemen. Vietnam does not get cold as we knew it in Korea. However, when one is wet and living in the open with no chance to get dry, he is cold and miserable. My muddy, wet Marines were miserable, but as we had no assurance that the enemy was in time-out, the war continued. We all looked forward to getting off that mountain.

Colonel Smith planned to fly us from our HLZ when the weather cleared. The rain and clouds left, but the word changed. Choppers would pick us up at our insertion zone; we had a hump before us. I fired off mortar rounds to reduce our load, and we started down. Everything went well at first with my lead platoon clearing the trail and moving fast. My point Marines, however, missed a turn that would have kept us on our descending route. Instead, following a slight trace of a trail, they led the company into an old abandoned enemy camp. Calling a halt, I turned the company around for a backtrack. Half a mile up the trail, a left turn placed us on our correct descending ridge, and we let off the brakes.

Major Kennon had choppers on standby, and with my call, he would have them in the zone. Alpha would celebrate the next day, 25 December 1968, at VCB. Passing this word to my platoon leaders, I was brought up to date. Someone in the attached mortar section had let a gap develop between himself and the mortarman to his front. The gap was so wide that the rear had not caught up by the time we backtracked from the enemy camp. The human 81-dud continued on the trail to the old enemy camp instead of turning right at the correct descending trail. There was simply no excuse to be that far behind the Marine walking to his front. The mortarman to his front, now the last one in my formation, never passed the word forward of a break in my column. Now that I was preparing to lift out, I learned that I was short one platoon plus.

With our zone in sight, I talked with Kennon. He had the birds only during daylight; we had to be off the deck before dark. My choices were to fly out two-thirds of my company or hold for a total lift tomorrow. Talking with my XO at the rear of the company, I learned that their movement was slow. He wanted to make camp where he was and get choppers the next day.

That did it. If they could not join me at my position for the night, I would not wait. The majority of my Marines could get hot chow, showers, clean clothes, and sleep in a tent on Christmas Eve. Major Kennon agreed that there was no enemy threat to a Marine platoon-size element reinforced with 81s. He had the birds on the way, and we lifted out before dark. While leaving the platoon was no different from sending them out on a night mission, I did not enjoy my night at Vandegrift; my Marines were still in the bush. All was well at 1000 the next day when I walked from our LZ with the late arrivals.

Christmas Day was a lazy one, used for cleaning both self and gear. The other company commanders became personalities rather than radio call signs. Captain George Meerdink Jr. was the commander of Bravo; Captain John (Jack) Kelly had Charlie; and Captain Edward Riley had Delta. Later in the evening, we all collected at Ed's tent for Christmas cheer.

Major Kennon proved to be the Marine I pictured during our radio transmissions, and Major C. D. Foreman, our XO, became a personality instead of a call sign. A better collection of talent, professionalism, and gungy spirit has probably never been collected in one battalion. George Smith was getting his team together. The price of war for the gungies, however, was that not all would live through our next big operation.

One day for Christmas, then I repeated and built on what I had started earlier: getting Alpha Marines to think alike when an action or reaction was required against enemy forces. A replacement draft arrived, and Alpha received its share of the FNGs (the last two letters stand for new guys). These FNGs were combat trained, but they had to get a feel for running the plays with the first team. It was pleasing to observe salty lance-corporal squad leaders explain the rules and roles to their new Marines.

Three 2nd Lieutenants also checked in for duty. William J. (Bill) Christman III and James H. Davis impressed me favorably and received rifle platoons. The third, whom I will call Rutland, did not fare as well. Not only did he talk too much, what he said did not need saying. I gave him the weapons platoon. As my guns were normally attached to the rifle platoons, all Rutland had to do was run the mortar section that was always near me; I could keep an eye on him. In addition, my weapons platoon sergeant, SSgt Talley, was an old mortar hand and could handle any lieutenant. If I were wrong about Rutland, he would get a rifle platoon later.

We enjoyed our new home, our own area with tents and cots; there truly was a Santa Claus. Individual spirit was on a high and I pushed it a notch higher. I wrapped up one of my training sessions with the suggestion that a good way to salute, as it was required aboard VCB, was to greet the senior by informing him of who you were: "Alpha One/Nine, Sir." That evening at chow Colonel Smith commented favorably on his salute exchange with one of my Marines.

I had an administrative requirement at our rear in Quang Tri. Depending upon truck convoy traffic, road-mine clearance, road repairs, and enemy action, the trip was usually under two hours. As I would be gone most of the day, I checked out with my commander. During our conversation, Smith lightly mentioned that if I had the time and could find one, he needed a gung-ho cap. I was about to learn an important lesson in priorities.

There was no enemy action, but military personnel's unquestioning acceptance of routines, lines, and happenings did interfere. After sitting in a line of traffic with periodic vehicle movement, I walked forward for the answer. "Why?" An Army jeep was stalled on a small bridge; the driver was directing traffic, one way at a time. With all of this manpower, why not push the jeep off the bridge? Several Marines joined me, and we easily pushed the jeep off and to the side of the road. Traffic immediately started in both directions. What the hell?

Finishing my business with the 1st Sergeant, I just happened to think of the utility cover. Where would I find one in this tent jungle? Battalion Supply seemed like a good place to start. "Sure," the lieutenant responded, "I have two covers for the colonel, but I haven't had a chance to get them up to him." That mission was completed easily; my driver and I headed home.

Colonel Smith was genuinely appreciative of the covers. He responded to my statement that the S-4 had them and all I did was deliver with, "I asked you to bring me a cover, and you did. The Four might have had them, but he did not get them to me. There are those who get things done and those who think about getting things done."

The idea that a commander's desire, expressed or otherwise, is an order to act became clear to me. I realized just how close I had come to a blunder with this commander whom I wanted to continue serving. His mentioning of a cover came across as an afterthought, if I had nothing better to do. Utility covers never crossed my mind until the moment that I thought to go to the S-4. After that, I paid closer attention to what he said, and to what he might be thinking.

Alpha received a new XO; 1st Lt Lee Roy Herron joined us, fresh from the States. Since graduating from TBS, Lee had studied Vietnamese language at Monterey. He would not use his language capability, but he would draw on his lessons learned at TBS. Although he had no line experience, he was a 1st Lt, and therefore second in command.

GySgt Ronald G. Duerr also joined me, giving Alpha a very capable and hard-working Company Gunny. Duerr had been promoted in

Delta Company, which had a Gunny, so Smith moved him to Alpha saying that he thought we would work well together. The colonel was correct as always; Duerr and I thought much alike.

One/Nine moved out on Operation Dawson River West from 2 to 19 January. We went back into the Khe Sanh area, looking for the enemy. (Map, page 248) We found no signs that they had returned after the Khe Sanh battles. The operation was a good training exercise for the recently joined Marines. We patrolled, ambushed, deployed, and roughed it in the bush but fired no rounds in anger. The war was over.

We returned to VCB to a rumor that a major operation was in line for the Walking Death Battalion and the entire 9th Regiment. Smith asked me to bring my platoon leaders to his tent for a talk about the operation. At the appointed hour we arrived to learn that it was not an operation brief but a Marine officer business social, George W. Smith style. He served drinks; the colonel talked, and we listened. We left our commander several hours later knowing the way his mind could be expected to work in a given enemy action, how he would respond, and what he would expect of us. This was combat philosophy, a lot of it crammed into little time, but my platoon leaders now felt as if they knew the man at the top. Colonel Smith reviewed TBS models for taking the fight to the enemy. (As a captain, he had taught tactics at TBS.) All of this preparation told me that we were going where the enemy was located; I was about to get what I had been looking for in this country.

Operation Dewey Canyon began for Alpha on 20 January 1969 with the mission of seizing Shiloh (an abandoned FSB), bringing in an artillery battery, and providing security for the battery. I worked directly for Regimental S-3, Major Joe Knotts.[29]

Shiloh was unoccupied, and our good luck continued with three weeks of rest and relaxation. There were limited day and night security patrols along with a daily platoon movement to the small river below Shiloh for bathing, swimming, clothes washing, and fishing. The last event of the day was fishing, done effortlessly with the toss of a grenade into one of the deep holes. Fresh fish were a welcome supplement to the regular diet of C-rations. Alpha enjoyed warm weather and a clear sky the first two weeks on Shiloh.

As the 9th Marines moved into jump-off positions and continued to open FSBs, the situation changed. Choppers lifted Captain Harvey C. Barnum's Hotel Battery out on 30 January, and we were to follow. Before the birds returned, a heavy mist and treetop-level clouds moved in. The rain and low ceiling remained for a week, preventing any chopper flights into the Da Krong and upper A Shau Valleys. We were not concerned, as C-rations had been stockpiled on Shiloh for forward movement, and water was plentiful.

About 0130 on 10 February, artillery rounds screaming over my shelterhalf awakened me. Four rounds of 105 landed in the center of our position. Marines on watch heard the battery fire in the distance; this had to be friendly fire. I quickly shouted for cease-fire over the command net.

One round landed in a MG team's position and at the feet of the gunner standing beside his fighting hole. We could not locate him in the dark, and he was unaccounted for until after daylight when we found his upper torso far down the hill. Also killed were two team members asleep in a dugout on the opposite side of the exploding round. Cpl J. T. Coleman, LCpl J. R. Phillips, and PFC S. J. Parrish were the first Alpha Marines to die on Dewey Canyon. An investigation determined that Fox Battery had fired an H&I mission two clicks north. One gun team had entered the wrong data on their gun, placing their rounds on our hill. The poncho-covered bodies lay in the rain as a dreadful reminder of the many faces of the Grim Reaper.

On 11 February the weather cleared and at 1330, choppers carried us to FSB Erskine. A burning CH-47, down beside Erskine's HLZ, caught my attention as our chopper flared in for landing. The downed chopper was a clear signal that our rest period had ended. Erskine was the Attack Position for 1/9 and located immediately north of the Da Krong River. The river served as the LOD for the battalion and as Phase Line Red for the regiment. The rest of 1/9 had just arrived on Erskine, having also been held up by weather.

The entire 1st Bn spent the night on a ridge extending from Erskine, in an area normally covered by one company. In this strength and in spite of security elements forward, Marines in the line became nervous at about midnight. An enemy probe in one sector caused the entire battalion to open up with automatic rifles, MGs, M-79s, and grenades. The sound caused by this massive eruption of fire was scary. While it made me feel good to know that we had such firepower, it also made the skin on the back of my neck crawl. The noise was deafening.

I had no chance to call in my LP, out about 300 meters. With all the lead going in their direction, I gave them up for lost when I could not raise them by radio. After a few minutes, leaders regained control and the firing stopped. My two Marines on the LP showed up, shaken but unharmed. They had not been concerned with monitoring their radio with that ordnance going over them. The line was so jumpy that I did not need another LP. Battalion casualties in that line probe were two KIA and nine WIA.

The weather was hot, close, and humid as we moved out the following morning. Although I expected heat casualties, I was surprised to hear over the battalion net that the chaplain was one before we were off the hill. Actually, three rifle companies had departed, and H&S Company moved out fourth, to be followed by Alpha. The route off the hill was by the HLZ. The Navy chaplain walked the 300 meters from his night position to the HLZ where he conveniently declared himself a heat casualty. As I led Alpha off the hill, we passed that faithless chaplain who would not look at us.

This was the first time US or South Vietnamese ground forces had been in the Da Krong Valley and the northern part of the A Shau. Intelligence reports from 3rd Force Recon indicated that the enemy was enjoying free use of this southwest section of Quang Tri Province. The area was known as the NVA Base Area 611, with Route 922 entering it from Laos.

Another factor influencing the expectation of positive contact with the enemy was the coming monsoon season and its effect on aircraft flights. All division operations in this part of I Corps had been by air assault. NVA commanders could reasonably expect the coming months to be quiet, a time to build up their force. They would not expect Marines to attack by foot and extend their lines of communication to where combat service support could only be provided by air—not in undependable flying weather.

Our battalion's zone of action included two major ridgelines running south from the Da Krong to the Laotian border. Alpha and Charlie with H&S Company continued east along the river after Bravo and Delta turned south to move up on their ridge. The day was running out before the second ridge was reached, so the three companies spent an uneasy night along the Da Krong.

Charlie again moved out in the lead the following morning. After an exhausting climb, the feeder ridge leveled out for a thousand meters before it became steep again for the climb to the main ridge. Moving along this broad, level ridge, Charlie's lead platoon was caught in an effective ambush. A natural cut lay in the ridge, as though a giant bulldozer had pushed part of the ridge over the side. This cut left a sharp canyon-like drop: about forty feet down, fifty yards across the floor, and then back up to the original level on the ridge.

Charlie's lead platoon was almost across the cut when the NVA opened fire with automatic weapons and RPGs from the other side. The ambush was effective with a perfect kill zone; it stopped our attack cold. By the time Charlie achieved fire superiority, it was late in the day. An HLZ had to be cleared for casualty evacuation and a night defensive position had to be established. Charlie set in for the night in a half-circle centered on the point of contact while Alpha moved up and tied in, completing the circle with H&S in the center.

About midnight the NVA moved again into position on the far side of the cut and placed grazing fire on Charlie, H&S, and part of Alpha. Marines were caught moving as well as sleeping above the ground. Major Kennon was killed as he rose from his sleeping position and several other H&S men were hit. More casualties were added to Charlie's list; they required evacuation before the battalion could move.

Smith had given me a verbal attack order before dark: Alpha would pass through Charlie and attack across the cut the following morning. The time of attack would be dependent upon completion of Charlie's MedEvacs. My preferred plan, an assault across the cut under cover of darkness, did not follow my commander's guidance not to weaken the perimeter defense until the MedEvac was completed. Because of the steep brush-covered slopes on both flanks, an envelopment was dropped. A frontal assault, supported by gunships and a base of fire, was my only course of action, and I expected it to be costly in Marines.

A low ceiling the following day caused the MedEvacs to go late morning. As the attack turned out, all of my worry was for nothing; the NVA had moved. I continued in the attack, moving toward a piece of high ground that appeared to wind its way to the top of the ridge at Hill 686, my intermediate objective. After two Marines were wounded by a booby trap on the trail, my lead platoon moved cautiously through the thick underbrush beside the trail.

Now fully deployed well off the trail, the platoon leader was taking no chances while checking out both flanks. In this manner, at 1530, he flanked an enemy ambush covering the trail, causing the NVA to withdraw leaving their dead and weapons. Clearing both flanks was time-consuming and the following companies were left waiting on the trail. Being closer to the probable point of action, I had not been concerned with the slow progress.

I received a call from Delmar Six who wanted to know what was holding up the advance. After my explanation, Smith had some comments. If I did not get moving, darkness would catch us in a lower night position and he wanted to be on high ground for a better night defense.

I called my platoon leader and told him to get on the trail, as the column behind us was using it anyway, and move out.

Some time later Delmar Three (the Three Alpha filled the position after Kennon's death) called, suggesting that I hold up; their H&S lead had lost contact with my rear. As I was approaching what appeared to be a good night position, I told the Three that I would like to continue to the position and check it out while the column caught up. This area was a plateau just below Hill 686, and the ground between was very steep, creating a concern for the following day. I pulled Alpha into a half-perimeter forward that allowed Charlie to position without interrupting our defense preparation.

Alpha began preparing positions while the rest of the column approached. A heavy explosion in the 3rd Platoon sector was followed by shouts of "Incoming!" and then rifle fire. Responding to incoming mortar rounds with rifle fire did not make sense. With no more explosions, I contacted Christman by radio while moving in his direction.

When I joined Bill, he repeated his radio transmission that they had fired at snipers, but he could not present any bodies. He thought that the snipers must be tied in the trees, but a closer search proved that reasoning incorrect. Everyone seemed baffled and embarrassed by the situation. Several Marines, including Christman, were wounded from shrapnel.

Putting the story together, I came up with the following facts: A squad was seated under a large tree when an explosion occurred where one Marine sat. Several Marines sounded off with "Incoming!" followed by someone yelling "Sniper!" which caused the nearby squad to fire into the trees. Hippie was missing; a search of the entire area did not turn up a trace of him, his rifle, or his helmet. He had been seated at the point of the explosion, and he was carrying the squad's Claymores wrapped around his body. Several squad members had known him to carry the mines without disarming them. There it was, no Hippie and several Marines wounded by shrapnel from his Claymores.

The following morning, I sent a rifle squad to the top of Hill 686 while we waited for a chopper to pick up water containers. Upon his return, the squad leader reported that the climb was tough, straight up in places over sheer rock. He found no enemy on the ridge, and felt that he could get the column up the rock wall with rope. Smith left the decision to me, up the rocks or find another way. The enemy did not seem to expect an approach from this direction, and time would be lost in looking for another route. Charlie and H&S provided climbing ropes, and we moved out.

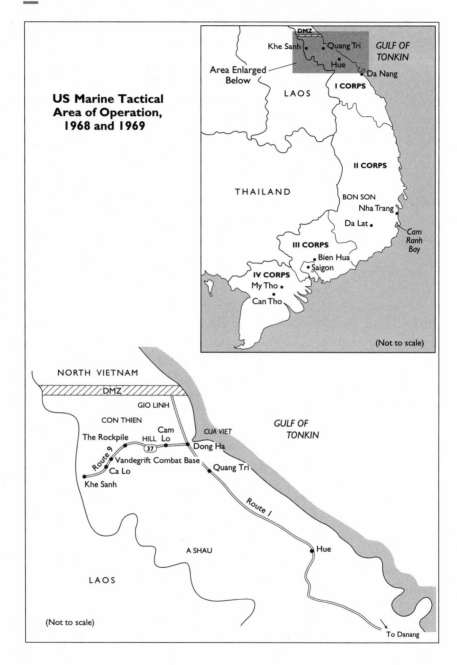

US Marine Tactical
Area of Operation,
1968 and 1969

First Platoon was first up to secure the ridge over the climbing area, and my command group followed. Movement amounted to going around or up-and-over the individual boulders. Last and most time-consuming were the sheer rock slopes or walls that required ropes to get heavily loaded Marines up and keep the column moving.

Climbers walked up the sloping rock wall with all of their back-mounted equipment, pulling themselves hand over hand on the nylon climbing ropes. It was not a difficult task except for the combat loads, the small-diameter ropes, and no gloves. Heavy crew-served weapons were pulled up individually.

Smith's concern was the time required in getting to the top. He did not want the cliff splitting his force, especially not knowing what the enemy had on the ridge. I positioned myself at the top of the largest wall that was the most difficult and most likely to cause problems. It was a choke point but the only place to climb without encountering more problems. Only four rope positions were established due to the narrowness of the sloping wall. Guides ensured order and provided assistance; a climber would start up as one was getting off at the top.

Alpha's climb went well, and it seemed no time before my platoons were deployed on the ridge, with one patrolling south. Next up was the battalion command with H&S, led by Smith. Finishing his climb, he paused at my position while I gave him a situation report on my action above. After some favorable comments on Alpha's work, he moved up the hill.

Because of the late start, movement up the ridge made a full day's work. Ropes became slick, and rocks worked loose from the wall as boots continued to dig into it. The narrowness of the wall placed Marines closely together, resulting in a rock dislodged by one being a threat to others below. Throughout the afternoon, there was a constant cry of "ROCKS!" as one would break loose and roll down the wall bouncing off Marines.

One heavily loaded Marine was halfway up the wall when he was hit and knocked into space. His fall brought the cry of "CORPSMAN UP!" Our surgeon, Lt Ray Pasker USNR, attended to the casualty who was hauled up the wall unconscious. Several other less serious casualties resulted from falling rocks.

As late evening approached, engineers began clearing trees with C-4 explosives for a MedEvac HLZ on the ridge. Pasker, not waiting for the HLZ, had the unconscious Marine pulled up by hoist into a hovering CH-46. Marking our location for the enemy, the chopper hovered five minutes before getting the Marine up through the tree limbs. We appreciated the situation and dug in, hoping to have our hole deep enough before the mortar fire fell. The rounds never came; what was the enemy doing?

Darkness caught one platoon of Charlie at the base of the wall and everyone else in a defensive perimeter at the top. The platoon's back was against the wall with good observation and fields of fire forward. They could hold off an army from their height, so no one was concerned. The night was uneventful, and the platoon joined us the next morning.

Rifle platoons patrolled into the valleys on both sides each day while the main column continued to move on the ridge toward Laos. These patrols had enemy contacts that amounted to exchange of rifle fire, followed by calls for artillery fire; as they were small contacts, further action was not pursued.

We were set in for the night of 19 February, and most men were eating their rations when tank sounds were heard. The murmur of diesel engines and the clank of steel tracks were just audible as darkness fell on the ridge. Tanks always get the infantry's attention, and this held true on our jungle ridgeline, although an armored attack was the furthest thought from my mind. Because of the terrain and what we knew of the enemy's order of battle, we had come light in AT weapons. I was not overly concerned, however, as Charlie was in the forward position and could handle tanks in a column on the narrow ridge trail.

I was visited shortly by Kelly with a request for my LAWS. Noting my reluctance to part with my tank killers, he made a casual observation. If he had them, I would not need them. I gave him some of my LAWS, and the night passed without any tank appearance.

The following morning, Kelly attacked down the ridgeline and discovered the explanation for the tank noise. His lead platoon under 2nd Lt Archie Biggers came upon two 122mm field guns in tow behind two half-track prime movers headed toward Laos on the ridge trail. While attempting to withdraw, the lead tractor had broken down on the narrow trail. Those engine sounds had been the NVA trying to get the second tractor around the breakdown, but it could not pull out of a deep gully crossing the ridgeline. Air strikes and artillery had discouraged any serious work on either project. After a quick firefight, 1/9 owned the guns in perfect working order. One of these guns ended up at Quantico and the other at Fort Sill.

The guns were a prize catch; Smith directed Kelly to secure the guns while working out their disposal. He told me to pass through Charlie and continue the attack for Objective Foxtrot, located on the Laotian Border with Route 922, the Ho Chi Minh Trail, passing through it.

I encountered light resistance on the movement to and the taking of Foxtrot. The objective, shown on Vietnamese maps as Lang Ha-Bn, was defended by service and support troops that withdrew under my assault. Artillery and small-arms ammo, medical supplies, an anti-aircraft gun, small gasoline engines, and other rear area gear were in sheds and bunkers on the hill.

That evening, the NVA fired mortars at Alpha, but they were not close. Probably concerned with rapid counter-battery fire, the NVA must have left their tubes in position for future use. The enemy gunners did note what sight changes were needed to place their rounds on Lang Ha-Bn, which would pay off for them two days later.

The following morning my 1st Platoon patrolled down the west side into the valley and found a hospital complex of bunkers, caves, and sheds with beds, abandoned medical supplies, and fresh evidence of use. The complex was destroyed. Delta moved east on 922 and joined me on Foxtrot while Bravo remained at their attack ridge junction with Laos.

A Charlie patrol made a heavy enemy contact east of their position causing Smith to suspect a force positioning for an attack to recapture the guns. All of Charlie was needed to secure the guns and H&S, so Smith directed me to chop a platoon to him for a reconnaissance-in-force mission. I directed Alpha-3 to return to battalion about midday on the 21st, and Christman was further directed to check out the valley eastward.

By late afternoon, Bill was locked in solid contact with an NVA force of unknown size. Smith directed me to return to his position, leaving Delta on Lang Ha-Bn. Arriving at dusk, I extended Charlie's position on the ridge while Christman remained in contact. He could break contact and withdraw, but he had two Marines down under the NVA's guns. Each time he tried to recover his men, the NVA increased their volume of fire. Finally, after dark the NVA either moved out or allowed the two bodies to be recovered, and the platoon joined me. At this point in the operation, Alpha had suffered seven KIA, seventeen WIA[E], and sixteen WIA but remaining with me. These numbers would more than double within the next twenty-four hours.

My orders for the following morning were to eliminate the threat. Artillery preparation and the enemy's habit of moving caused most of us to feel that we would find no enemy. Christman and some of his men did not share that feeling, however. If the area of contact on the 21st was clear, I was to continue down the mountain to the creek bed for Check-

Point 1. Then right, up the valley in a box pattern through two more checkpoints that would bring me back into the perimeter. If I arrived at CP 1 with no enemy contact, I was to alert battalion to send down a water detail. The weather had socked us in, and we were low on water.

In daylight of the 22nd, the jungle looked differently to Christman than his recollection of the previous night. Guiding the company, he selected the wrong trail to his place of contact. He then waited on the trail for his platoon, which was bringing up the rear.

As we closed on the creek at CP 1, NVA in a bunker killed my point rifleman and seriously wounded the second Marine. Without a pause in their forward movement, Jim Davis's leading squad assaulted, destroyed the bunker, and killed the NVA without further loss of Marines. I directed Davis to cross the creek, check out the area, and provide security from that side while the other two platoons deployed on the near side as they arrived. The bunker was the extent of enemy activity.

Christman approached me, saying that he had stopped at the wrong fork while guiding the company. He had later recognized the correct trail, further down; we had missed the NVA position, now on our right rear. We agreed that because we had not drawn fire, the enemy force must have pulled out leaving only the team encountered.

I informed battalion to send down the water detail; Alpha rested, ate a lunch of Cs, and enjoyed the water. The water detail of fifteen Marines from Charlie arrived a half-hour later and began filling their canteens.

A 82mm mortar began firing on our right rear (3rd Platoon's earlier contact location), with rounds exploding in the tall trees over us. Because of the jungle density and the tree heights, which provided many layers of limbs, the bursts were not effective. There was no further enemy action in the creek bed or anywhere near us, certainly not within my perimeter.

The water detail sergeant received a piece of shrapnel in his face and approached me crying that he could not see. I noted, however, that he had no problem in locating me. Hysterically, with unsightly mucus running from his nostrils, he cried that the enemy had us surrounded, and that it was my immediate responsibility to see him safely back into his perimeter. I did not want to believe what I was hearing from this big sergeant but realized that he was a basket case.[30] Not having the time to spend on him or to reorganize his demoralized water detail, I directed Davis to give me a squad. Cpl Randall B. Parnell reported, and I told him to take the water detail to battalion along with the one KIA and WIA from the earlier 2nd Platoon action. Parnell reported to me the next day that his return trip was uneventful and that the sergeant regained his composure as they entered the perimeter.

About this time, a MG began firing in our direction from the position of the mortar. Again, because of the thick jungle, the only effect of the gunfire was a crazy pattern of ricocheted, skyward-bound, tracer bullets high in the trees. No one was hit or felt threatened by the MG; the enemy was making sure that we found him. Alpha obliged and moved through the jungle in the attack, moving to the sound of the enemy's guns. Bill's platoon was closer to the enemy, so my movement was 1st Platoon, then 3rd, and 2nd Platoon bringing up the rear.

Shortly, I directed my two lead platoons to deploy on line and assault. Control and contact were maintained in the thick jungle by an initial formation of platoons on line while squads moved in column. As contact developed, fire teams and individuals came up on line; heavy rifle fire and MGs on both sides mowed down banana trees and jungle brush.

Initially my line moved well but began to slow as guns continued to chatter and Marines came up against a wall of lead. The jungle swallowed up my warriors, making it difficult for me to maintain a position behind and center of my assault line. Not seeing a line of Marines, I had only the sounds of weapons fire by which to guide. My battle-wise Marines were using the jungle for cover and concealment as they crawled from cover to cover.

A RPG exploded against a bush two feet behind me. Thanks to my helmet and flak jacket, I received shrapnel only in my left leg and shoulder. Recovering, I continued with my interrupted SitRpt to Delmar Six, agreeing that Delta should come to my aid. The enemy force was stronger than expected, and I was weak in numbers. Without my mortar section (I left them on the ridge as I could not use them in that jungle), my strength was ninety-nine men, and I was now minus Parnell's squad and the two earlier casualties. Alpha had taken casualties and would have more before the fight was over. I was concerned with carrying our casualties and providing for our security. I welcomed Delta's help. Because of the time-distance factor, I had no hope of Delta arriving in time to help with the fighting.

My assault stalled, and I moved forward to get a better feel for my tactical situation. I could see at the most only two Marines at a time as I moved along what I thought was my front. Rifle fire was greatly reduced.

A sniper fired and missed me by inches. I saw him as his rifle fired, and returned fire with an M-16 rifle that I had just picked up from a fallen Marine. Though the sniper was close, I did not take a chance with my strange battle sights and fired half a magazine. He slumped into a fork of the tree where his blood flowed down the trunk in a small stream. I moved more carefully along my battle line.

My estimate left me with two options: I did not like the one of breaking contact while recovering my Marines down under the enemy's guns. (Based upon Marines that I could see, I thought that I had more casualties than there actually were. Everyone was down and unless he was firing, the prone body appeared to me no different than a casualty.) I felt that I would lose more men just trying to withdraw and chose my other option: Attack! Moving back to my command group, I called Jim Davis forward.

Quickly briefing Jim on the situation, I told him to attack center front. A flanking action in that fluid situation and thick jungle would be difficult to control and risky. My decision, I realized, amounted to an all or nothing effort. If the 2nd Platoon did not make a difference in the balance of the forces, there would be no other source of help.

Before Jim could depart, a mortar round exploded within the command group, seriously wounding Davis. Shrapnel hit several supporting arms personnel, both of my radio operators, and me. Lee Herron was not hit and had heard my order to Jim. I told him to take the 2nd Platoon in the attack.

Moving upright and seemingly oblivious to the MG fire cutting down the brush around us, Lee immediately led the platoon forward in the classic Basic School style of "Follow Me!" I watched as the small eighteen-man platoon dissolved into the jungle, green into green. I did not feel good about 2nd Platoon's chances of making a difference; they were too small in number (minus Parnell's squad plus the two earlier casualties).

The day was dark with low clouds and fog down in the trees with patches of rain moving constantly through the jungle. It grew darker for me with the next three radio transmissions, one from each of my platoon sergeants as though they were reporting their post on a time schedule.

Less than five minutes after Lee moved the 2nd Platoon forward, Sgt David A. Beyerlein called to say that Lt Herron had been killed by MG fire. SSgt Lane followed: Christman was seriously wounded with MG bullets in his chest, and SSgt Jenson reported that George Malone was down with a second serious wound. All officers were now out of the action, but in Marine tradition, the platoon sergeants knew what had to be done, and Marines were doing it.

PFC Gary M. Winter, one of my snipers, observed me trying to handle three radios and crawled forward to help. Giving Mike my Bn Cmd radio, we positioned ourselves in a low place by a large tree. Less than two minutes in that position, MG bullets raked through us, missing me, hitting Mike in the leg, and nearly cutting down the tree. In extreme pain, Mike crawled to Doc Hudson[31] who was tending the earlier wounded.

That was my first moment of fear. All seemed hopeless; enemy gunners appeared to have every inch of the jungle floor covered. They were everywhere. I felt that we were losing the fight, and I was lost for ideas on how to improve our situation. A deep hole suited my needs, but I had to get my assault moving; I was now the one needing a spirit boost.

I realized that one MG had a commanding position that was key to the NVA defense. Somehow, I had to knock out that gun in spite of its excellent field of fire. Otherwise it would hold up my advance, but taking it would cost me Marines. I was saved from the undesirable task.

Seemingly all at once, the mist moved out, the jungle lighted up, and overhead were two Marine OV-10 Broncos. Colonel Smith had air on station in case the weather cleared. He gave me the air freq and call sign; I quickly changed channels on my radio. PltSgts marked their forward positions with smoke, and I directed the Broncos to the MG on an azimuth and distance from center of the line of smoke. The trial run looked good and I declared the strike hot. The Broncos followed with rocket and cannon strikes while I provided adjustments to place them on target. That did the job; the gun went silent.

With the Broncos' departure, the jungle was hushed with a deathly silence. Battalion called: Delta was coming down the mountain. To ensure that they did not take Christman's trail of the day before and approach into our guns, I sent guides around to meet them at the trail junction. The call meant that help was fifteen minutes or less away. As Alpha had not started moving after the air strike, I decided to let Delta have the remaining action. (A lucky decision as it turned out.) We were low in ammo at this stage of the fighting.

Earlier, Riley's Marines had heard the heavy battle going on in the valley beside them and knew from monitoring the radio that Alpha was in a fight. The fighting had been going on for some time when Riley received the call to help Alpha. His first thoughts were preparation and movement time; if Alpha needed help, they needed it now. He had to break camp, pack up, and make the foot march. Much to his surprise, he found his company packed and in march formation. Delta had sensed that Alpha might need help and took down their shelters, packed, and formed up on the trail. Ed grabbed his war belt and moved Delta out.

Meanwhile, Alpha was down and taking advantage of the rest and peaceful quiet. Watchful eyes scanned the jungle. What would the NVA do next? Suddenly, I saw movement ahead in a less dense portion of the jungle, near the position of the MG knocked out by the air strike. Men were coming toward us with weapons at the ready! While alarm raced through my body, I recognized US MARINES. "Don't fire, it's Delta!" Riley had missed my guides and come in on Christman's trail. It could have been a mess if Alpha had been moving also.

Delta's arrival at my front meant that there were no more NVA. We had assaulted through the bunker position! We gathered our casualties and went up the mountain. Riley cleared the area behind me with an enemy body count of 105 NVA.

Total count of Alpha's KIA on 22 February was twelve, with two of those being lieutenants (Christman died). Also killed were Cpl R. P. Hodges; LCpls J. R. Baird Jr. and D. A. Chacon; PFCs L. J. Boehm, F. Butler III, N. P. Chittester, J. F. Dedeck, A. L. Johnson, R. Pollard, and A. Thomas. Delta had a Marine killed when the unsafe rifle of the Marine walking behind him fired unintentionally.

Most of my men had been wounded, but if their wounds were not serious, they refused the MedEvac. Fifty-eight Marines and corpsmen had no choice on MedEvac; two of these were also lieutenants, Davis and Malone. Fortunately, the weather on the 23rd allowed the birds in with resupply and out with MedEvacs. Company A's strength now was two officers and sixty-three enlisted men that included Rutland and my mortar section plus attachments.

Doc Hudson's talk with Colonel Smith resulted in my Medal of Honor. My Colonel gathered supporting statements from Doc and my platoon sergeants and informed me of his intentions. Doc Hudson had been impressed with what he observed of me on the 22nd, but I have to state that I almost fell off of my helmet seat when Smith told me what he was doing. I do not feel that my actions were deserving of such recognition.

Alpha Company had several Marines who deserved that Medal on that day, but because of the lack of two eyewitnesses (due to deaths, MedEvacs, and thick jungle), no one was around to tell their story. I wrote Marines up for known deserved awards (three Navy Crosses, six Silver Stars, seventeen Bronze Stars, and thirteen Navy Commendation Medals) while continuing our attack; there was no time-out for administrative matters and no help by platoon leaders. I know that many platoon members deserving recognition with awards were missed due to loss of witnesses and lack of help with the write-up.

There was no rest for Alpha, as an NVA force estimated at twenty-five probed my lines at 2305 on the 23rd, causing four wounded. The enemy held a dawn reveille on us two mornings straight. They moved to a knoll the same height as ours, fired RPGs and automatic weapons for thirty seconds and departed before I could place fire on them.

The third morning, I acted on the recommendation of a platoon leader, who suggested that we fire first at that knoll. (Lts Aaron C. Burroughs, Michael V. Ziehmn, and Albert Sheppard had volunteered for more rifle platoon time and arrived in a chopper carrying out my casualties.) I doubted that the NVA would repeat their act a third time. For the lack of a better plan, however, I had all of Alpha's weapons aimed at the knoll before dark.

The third morning Alpha provided the crack-of-dawn as I gave the command "Fire" one minute before the beginning of daylight. I ceased fire after one minute and received no response from the knoll. An hour later, my patrol found enemy bodies and weapons on the hill; they were caught attempting to do their reveille act again.

Bravo Company moved to Lang Ha-Bn on the 22nd before Delta departed to help Alpha. Later, receiving mortar fire, Capt Meerdink and his FO moved from their bunker to shoot a compass azimuth on the tubes for counter-battery fire. The NVA had missed Alpha on the 20th, but this time they were on target: both Marines were killed as the mortar rounds impacted around them.

On 26 February, after lifting the 122mm guns out, Bn Cmd with H&S, Alpha, and Charlie moved to Lang Ha-Bn while Delta moved east on the Ho Chi Minh Trail. Riley's mission was to seize Obj G, Hill 1044. Delta took our final objective with 2nd Lt Gilbert E. (Gene) Smith's platoon in the assault.

After a hot firefight, one of the largest, if not the largest, caches of ordnance in the war was found along the Ho Chi Minh Trail bordering on Hill 1044. The cache included 629 rifles, 108 crew-served weapons, and well over 100 tons of munitions. These storage areas were located in the bottom of huge bomb craters made by B-52 strikes and covered with dirt. Alpha spent 28 February on 1044 assisting Delta with destroying this ordnance. Each Marine and corpsman carried an extra rifle upon our return to Lang Ha-Bn. These were new, blond-stock, semiautomatic, SKS rifles, greased and wrapped in waterproof oilcloth, packed three to a container with accessories.

The 9th Marines ran out of objectives at the Laotian border, and our thoughts turned to lifting out of the A Shau. LtCol E. R. (Sonny) Laine's 3rd Bn had taken their final objective, Tam Boi, overrunning six of the 122mm guns. LtCol George C. Fox and his 2nd Bn had cleared their zone and had started their withdrawal. The Walking Death Bn would be the last out of the A Shau.

February went out with 1/9 located on Hill 1044 minus Alpha, which remained on Lang Ha-Bn, operating a CPB. As there was no new ground to cover, we patrolled over old area. On 3 March, I went back into the bunker complex where we had fought on the 22nd. The experience was akin to placing one's hand back on a hot stove after being burned. Some bloated bodies were all we found.

On 4 March, LCpl McFarlane conducted his assigned squad patrol by moving through the brush, parallel to the ridge trail. The going was rough, but the price was right. His point detected an NVA ambush covering the trail when the enemy gunner stood up to stretch. The squad assaulted with favorable results: one Marine wounded while the enemy soldiers died in place.

Later, back in my perimeter, McFarlane reported that he inadvertently left his WIA's rifle at the ambush site. I told Rutland to send a squad for the rifle; he went with the patrol. (After losing all of my PltLdrs on the 22nd, I had given Rutland a platoon.) This squad moved on that trail and was ambushed in almost the same position as the morning experience. LCpl D. R. Sledge's fire team was leading; he and PFC C. L. Smith fell under the initial volley. Sledge died immediately and Smith later that day. LCpl William Northington was third in the fire team, and he immediately charged forward to cover his buddies with his M–16 blazing on full automatic. He fell under the NVA's withering fire. Other squad members took cover.

Rutland was on the radio immediately yelling for help. I was unable to make any sense out of what he was trying to pass; it was clear, however, that he could not handle the situation and had no idea of what to do. I sent LCpl Wisengarber's squad to help, which caused the enemy to break contact and withdraw. Both squads recovered the casualties and returned. Such were the small unit actions, day after day.

A CH-46 with blades turning was sitting in our HLZ unloading rations and ammo on 6 March. Two RPG rounds were fired at the chopper but missed. The pilot had been sitting there looking at the lower hill as the RPGs fired; he instantly had the CH-46 airborne and in the attack. Tail high, the 46 appeared to dive straight from launch to the RPG position with guns blazing. We watched in amazement as the chopper buzzed and blazed away at the small hill like an angry hornet. My mortar section was in action, and the pilot began giving me corrections to place rounds on target as he circled close on the knoll while working it over with his guns.

An impressive display of Marine ground and air teamwork, the violent participation in the attack by the CH-46 was a first in my experience and completely unexpected. Alpha Marines would talk about this event for days. The NVA surely did not expect to be pounced upon by a personnel/cargo carrier, either. After taking care of the NVA and in keeping with his positive attitude, the pilot landed back in our HLZ for an emergency MedEvac.

One RPG round had exploded beside an older rifleman known as Pappy, who appeared to be bleeding from every pore. He was completely soaked in blood and the only thing the corpsman could do was give him an IV and get him to an operating room. He was loaded aboard the chopper and en route to a field hospital within eight minutes of being hit.

Finally, I received word to join battalion. My Alpha-14 (Air Coordinator) worked his net for some birds to fly us to Hill 1044. Locating a CH-53 with fuel and a willing crew, he had them inbound while assuring me that the one chopper would carry my entire company, about ninety. If we flew, we all had to lift off together; there would be no shuttle runs. I did not want to walk because the enemy would have the trail covered.

With high hopes that the one chopper could lift all of us, I watched as the big bird, still far out, set up his approach on our zone. An automatic weapon fired in the distance and that bird made a hard left, departing the area with the words that our zone was too hot. Thanks, Air; I moved out with Alpha. Our only route to Hill 1044 was the Ho Chi Minh Trail, and I placed artillery fire on all areas that could conceal an ambush. A MG fired at us from such a distance that it was ineffective. A heat casualty following the gunfire did get my attention.

The heat case was in the rear platoon and the corpsman recommended an immediate MedEvac, which brought me to a halt while I sorted out the correct action. Gunny Duerr was bringing up the rear. Talking with Duerr, I learned that the heat case was one of our shit-birds. The attending corpsman was new and learning. Duerr was satisfied that the bird was faking in order to get out. We could be hours in getting a MedEvac because he clearly was no priority case.

I was frustrated with the circumstances and infuriated at the individual. The enemy fire had ceased for the time being, but what would be next? In addition, I had three-quarters of our movement ahead of us, and a holdup would cause us to arrive on 1044 after dark. Confident that the Gunny and I were reading this bird correctly, I took a chance.

"Alpha-Seven, Six. Over."

"Seven, Go."

"Seven, are you near the casualty? Over."

"Six, that is a neg-a-tory. Over."

"Seven, move close enough to him that he can hear my conversation. When ready, key your handset three times. Over."

Three clicks came over my handset, and I followed with, "Seven this is six. We are in a bad position to hold the company and no MedEvacs are available. The heat casualty can walk if he chooses and it is his call. For the safety of the many, I am moving the company. You are to leave the casualty on the road if that is his choice but take his rifle. I don't want the NVA using an M-16 against US Marines. Any questions? Over."

"Six, Neg-a-tory. Over."

"Roger. Move 'em out."

I stepped off with heavy reservations, hoping that I was correct. What was my next act if the bird did not catch up with us? I had not moved a hundred yards when I received a radio call.

"Six, Seven. Shit-bird-number-one just caught up. He is feeling OK now. Over." I responded by keying my handset. Encountering no more problems, we arrived on 1044 before dark.

Hill 1044 was hot with mortar barrages. The presence of many Marines and all the helicopter traffic bringing in supplies and VIPs while taking out captured weapons caused the enemy to focus on 1044. Chopper pilots turned off upon seeing mortar rounds impact on the hill during their approach.

Tam Boi would be the lift-out zone for 1/9's withdrawal, as Hill 1044 was too restricted by its proximity to Laos to allow suitable air cover. We would move to Tam Boi while 3/9 backtracked to Tiger Mountain. H&S, Charlie, and Delta moved to Tam Boi; Alpha and Bravo were to follow the next day. Instead, Capt Kenneth S. Junkins, the new CO of Bravo, and I were told to remain on 1044 for a Special Forces company. After the link up, we would move to Tam Boi.

During the wait, the enemy entertained us with mortar barrages and a futile, halfhearted, night ground attack that lasted fifteen minutes. The limited action cost me Marines; my dead and wounded list grew. I was dependent solely upon chopper flights for relief of my casualties, and both the weather and the enemy affected flights. I was given the SF's radio frequency and call sign; when contact was made, I was to direct them to my position. After two days of waiting, I monitored their broken SF radio traffic that amounted to their force maneuvering to avoid enemy personnel. PRC-25 radios did not reach far in those mountains; surely, we would make contact that day. That was not to be the case.

I finally made radio contact with the commander; Alpha waited, and 3/9 started their lift out of the A Shau. Two full days after radio contact, Capt Dick Meadows, US Army, brought his company[32] to 1044. Now 1/9 could lift out, except that the A Shau was socked in again.

Meadows approached me with his desire that his company be positioned inside the Marine perimeter; his troops did not stand line. Under normal conditions, his plan was acceptable because of language and coordination problems. At this time, however, the statement was ridiculous. Really! Who had stood line for them these past few days? We would have wall-to-wall bodies within our small perimeter. The SF had more men than either of the two rifle companies, and they surely were in better physical condition. I made it short: "Fill a sector of the line or move outside of it." He took a sector of the line.

Smith tasked me with moving the three-company force to Tam Boi. As there were connecting ridges with a trail between the two points and steep, rugged, heavily forested terrain in all other directions, there was not much choice of a route. Alpha and Bravo had stretcher cases (both KIAs and WIAs) from the incoming mortars and patrol actions over the past five days. We were trail-bound with our loads; I expected ambushes.

My order of movement was Alpha, SF, and Bravo as rear guard. Knowing that I would have to clear the ridges and be subject to ambush while the center company followed easily on the trail, I asked Meadows if his company would carry my stretchers.[33] He answered with, "NO, the contract with my people doesn't include carrying stretchers. They would lose face if asked to do such a thing."

I considered asking him to take the lead. However, they had been two days moving about the same distance after our radio contact; I wanted Alpha on Tam Boi that night. With half of my fighters carrying stretchers and crew-served weapons. I moved the column out on the morning of 13 March.

The backside of 1044 was steep, and movement was slow, as the ground and leaves were slick. Wounded were tied in their stretchers, as the thick underbrush caused the bearers, forward and aft, to hold the stretchers at a 45-degree angle or worse.

Alpha took a break while waiting for Bravo to get their loads down the hill; I looked for an HLZ in case the clouds cleared. Neither prospect was encouraging. Finally, all were on the trail where the clouds and fog had reduced visibility to about fifty yards. We moved out.

Two hundred meters down the trail, my point-fire team was wasted by an ambush consisting of a command-detonated mine, automatic weapons, and RPGs. (I had expected ambushes but not right under 1044. I also had moved alone to within a hundred meters of this ambush position while looking for a possible HLZ. Not smart!) Immediately, my forward observer was on the radio with a call for artillery fire.

SSgt Tally had a mortar in action even before the smoke cleared from the mine detonation. Tally and I were looking down on the ambush site from a position at a turn in the trail, fifty meters away. I was behind my lead platoon, and Tally had rushed forward with a mortar tube, baseplate, and an ammo bearer from his position farther back in the column.

Sighting the tube by eye through the openings in the tree limbs and holding the tube in his hand, free-gun style, Tally was dropping rounds as fast as they cleared his tube. MGs, rifles, and M-79s worked on the ambush position. Three Marines lay on the foggy trail below me.

By the time I walked artillery fire in, the NVA knew what to expect and some got away. After a short arty prep, I moved my lead platoon under Lt Burroughs against the position, resulting in the capture of a wounded NVA soldier. Seven bodies lay in the position and blood trails from the ambush site indicated that others also paid a price. It had not been a freebie for the ambushers, thanks to Sergeant Tally.

Alpha now had additional loads to carry; two Marines were killed and five wounded in the ambush. These Marines had to be carried in ponchos; we had no stretchers. Poncho litters require double effort for the bearers and are extremely rough on a seriously wounded Marine. Nothing new to Marines; we had no choice.

Meadows came forward upon learning that I had a prisoner. He wanted to talk to the prisoner and asked if he could have him. As I was already overloaded with litter cases, I had no options. The SF could not carry Americans, but they apparently had no problem with carrying a member of the enemy force. Garner writes that my Marines were eager to kill the prisoner; that is simply not true.[34] Killing was no novelty for us; we had done plenty. Someone may have expressed the thought: do we leave him here wounded or kill him? I surely was not about to saddle my few Marines with another load and an enemy at that.

As night arrived, Alpha moved on Tam Boi and into the battalion perimeter. The exhausted Marines and corpsmen who had carried the stretchers and cleared the ridges of the enemy needed rest, but we took our place in the perimeter defense. Meadows's SF unit bivouacked within our battalion perimeter,[35] and flew out behind the wounded during a break in the weather the following day.[36] Alpha was on Tam Boi several days, taking their share of the patrols, night ambushes, and incoming mortar rounds.

Alpha's combat casualty totals for Dewey Canyon were 24 KIA,[37] 89 WIA(E), and 129 WIA who continued to serve. These figures, however, do not tell the whole story: e.g., Christman is counted as a WIA and later as a KIA. Malone was hit twice in one fight but is counted as one WIA(E). Far fewer than 129 Marines and corpsmen shared the number of WIAs listed because of separate wounds in different times or actions. Alpha also suffered its share of heat and jungle rot casualty evacuations. Two months is a long time to exist on C-rations, the same unwashed clothes soaked daily with sweat, and with never enough drinking water.

Then, on 18 March, it was lift-out! The day opened with clear skies and Marine CH-46s. However, before the wounded were completely loaded, the enemy mortared Tam Boi and the choppers immediately departed the hot zone. Would we ever get out of this place? After several hours of disgusted wondering and falling morale, the word came down, "Birds inbound, get Alpha on the zone."

Alpha was the first company out, which was easy with the perimeter around the HLZ providing good standoff security. As the perimeter decreased with each departing company, the last company and particularly the last chopper would not have that security belt. Delta drew the lot of being last.

Delta was prepared to make the NVA pay a high price for any delaying action. Smith had shallow trenches dug in the crest of the hill leading to the HLZ to cover and conceal the final squad's movement to the helicopters. Each departing company left its MGs and ammo for Delta's use, and all supporting arms, air and arty, were assigned sectors of adjoining real estate for concentration of fires.

To complicate an already difficult task, the last bird lifting Delta out had to go back in. Riley, while watching Tam Boi get smaller through the hatch of his chopper, happened to spot a gun team running from their position on a ridge to the HLZ. The gun team did not get the word to move; fortunately for them, their leader did not wait for a verbal invitation.

The CH-47s lifting us out were mortared in the HLZ and took MG fire from the ridges while in flight, but the Army kept them moving. The bird flying out my command group made it to VCB, but bullet holes in its hydraulic system kept it on the ground. Our thanks went out to the US Army and LtGen Richard G. Stillwell, CG XXIV Corps. I feel that without Stillwell and his 47s, we would have had to walk out of the A Shau.

All of 1/9 was lifted out on the same day: a piece of luck considering the weather and enemy action. We gathered at Vandegrift, and that base never looked so good. Hot chow, more water than one cared to drink, hot showers, clean clothes, and no enemy looking down our throat changed our daily routine. I had forgotten just how easy life could be. We were not to stay; better things were in store for the Walking Death Battalion.

A truck convoy delivered 1/9 to Cua Viet, a recreation beach on the Gulf of Tonkin. We were there in November and knew to expect steaks, cold beverages, USO shows, and REST! Rest we did, for three days. Some Marines wounded earlier on Dewey Canyon returned for duty; one was Jim Davis, who went back to his platoon.

Light bush duty followed Cua Viet; 1/9 established CPBs west of Dong Ha in the Cam Lo area. My AO was immediately west of Cam Lo with my CP on Hill 37. (Map, page 248) That little hill would be our home for a month, including several short operations that always ended with us returning to Hill 37.

Alpha worked with 2/4 on one of those operations. The battalion conducted a sweep and Alpha was the blocking force. I moved out before daylight on a route that would keep my movement covered in valleys. I hoped to prevent the NVA from learning of my arrival, especially of where I would set up the blocking position. The plan was good; the valleys were deep, with plenty of vegetation to conceal my movement. I did not, however, allow for the weather.

Hayfields and haymows are hot in Virginia's August heat, and Parris Island has its own brand of hot times. Heat has never bothered me, but that morning as I moved under my steel helmet, enclosed within my flak jacket, I felt odd. The sun burned hot, there was no air moving, and I was soaked with sweat. Boots kicked up a low cloud of dust as we moved. I passed my condition off as laziness; all I wanted to do was crawl into a shade and go to sleep. My radio operator brought me out of it.

Heat casualties! Within ten minutes I had three heat cases. The corpsman expected a stroke on one of the cases, if not worse, and rec-ommended an immediate MedEvac. All platoons were out of water. Hell, we were to move clandestinely into a blocking position, not use heli-copters to outline our movement route.

First things first, I had hurting Marines. More Marines would be down if I did not get water. I moved from carrying our heat cases to a full stop, set up security, and positioned as many men as possible out of the sun. A MedEvac with water resupply was called. Two hours later, we were again on the move. As expected, we had no action in our blocking position.

At the time, I did not consider our uniform or even feel that I had the option to do so. Hindsight tells me that a smart commander in this situation would have ordered the removal of helmets and flak jackets, if he had not left them behind in camp. As it happened, I suffered real ca-sualties and these casualties had a negative effect on my mission.

The second day out, Delmar Six was on the radio. "Hammerhand, there is a Change of Command dinner for Bulldozer Six tomorrow night. I would like you to be there; can you? Your Five can handle things; besides, there is no enemy force larger than a squad in your area. Over." (Colonel Smith used his personally chosen call sign for me rather than the official one of Delmar Alpha-Six.)

"Delmar Six, roger, I would like to make that dinner if I were in the area. Can't make it from here. Over."

"Hammerhand, there will be a chopper out for you tomorrow. Turn the reins over to your Five for one day. Be ready. Out."

One chopper to pick up one lieutenant and all for a dinner party; this officer life was taking shape. I returned to VCB in time to clean up and make the reception. Cocktails preceded dinner in the regimental commander's mess. One gin and tonic in my dehydrated pouch really made me feel good, so good that I had the nerve to accept another. Din-ner chimes were all that saved me; I needed food.

The meal was superb, but what followed made my evening. We gathered again in the social room where Barrow spoke. He cut his talk short with a request for his guitar. After a few strums, he started picking and singing "It Don't Rain in Indianapolis." Was there anything that this old warrior could not do?

The gin elevated my already high emotional level: I was flooded with feelings of camaraderie, professionalism, and love for these great leaders before me. Awareness of my pleasure while my Marines were gutting it out somewhere in the bush also haunted me. That evening was full and rewarding, and one I shall never forget.

The team, however, had served its purpose. Barrow turned over the 9th Marines to Col E. F. Danowicz. Later, on 1 April, Smith gave command of 1/9 to LtCol T. J. Culkin. There would be the 9th Marines and 1/9 on the morrow, but there would never again be Barrow's 9th Marines and George Smith's 1/9.

Colonel Smith rated and ranked me at the top on my Change of Reporting Senior Fitness Report as he had on my earlier report. I was the only 1st Lt marked Outstanding in General Value to the Service. Excerpts from his statement:

> . . . is a superb combat officer. Experienced, aggressive, determined, courageous, professionally knowledgeable, and balanced in judgment, his individual performance, and that of his command continuously proved exemplary. . . . No small measure of the success of this operation can be attributed to his daring, aggressiveness, imagination, tactical proficiency, and dedication to mission accomplishment . . .

I had received what I had hoped to gain with my extension. Thoughts of Eakin's death no longer brought raw pain and unanswered questions. His death could never be avenged, but I felt that I had done something in his memory. The little girl of the Christmas shooting a year ago no longer haunted me. She was not my Dixie. It was time for me to go home; I was serving on my last month.

Lessons Learned

1. Some personalities and situations are not necessarily tailored to suit you: zip-up and give 100 percent; you will not be with any one person forever.

2. Another man's war is difficult to conduct, especially in his manner.

3. Positive leadership brings out the best in us.

4. A winning team requires rehearsal and practice of the plays, even while involved in combat.

5. Good ideas come up the chain of command as well as down.

6. Body armor can cause casualties with a negative impact on mission accomplishment.

11
Captain
096702/0302/9953

1 April 1969

My senior commanders visited Alpha on Hill 37, and Col Danowicz promoted me to captain. Donning the T/O rank of company commander was anticlimactic after leading a company for six months in heavy combat. I had met that challenge and had been rated highly satisfactory.

Promotions during the Vietnam War era were temporary. We were selected twice for the same rank, the first known as a temporary-temporary selection and promotion. After the second selection and a period of time, the promotion became permanent. The temporary promotion was of no concern, as I was also a temporary officer. Supply and demand of officer strength had leveled out, and HQMC convened a board to consider temporary officers for retention or reversion. A few were selected for regular status, more as reserve officers, and the largest groups were those appointed to LDO and WO ranks. I was selected as a reserve officer, which was hard to swallow, but at least I would remain a leader.

Meanwhile the war continued with no change at our level although Nixon was determined to scale down US involvement and turn the war over to the Vietnamese. As long as we were in country, we were at war. If we backed off, the NVA picked up operational momentum, gained freedom of action, and selected options favorable to them.

My TAOR was about four square miles, and included the Cam Lo River. Though limited, the NVA were active in the area. In spite of day patrols and night ambushes, we were in effect merely occupying positions. This war had been going on so long, with the same players using the same ambush sites that the enemy knew exactly where and what to expect. Our operational plan needed energizing.

Motivation, new ideas, and freedom of action were needed at the squad level. My SqLdrs were good at their business, they knew the rules, and their followers were efficient and loyal. I unleashed this war machine on the people of the night in the form of Hunter/Killer Teams. My

SqLdrs decided what to do and determined the situational where and when. The who, why, and how were understood. Dividing my area into squad-size TAORs, I assigned them to squads for days at a time. Squads worked their TAORs during darkness, ambushing as desired and for as long as desired before moving to another site. Anyone moving in that TAOR separate from that squad was enemy: it was shoot first and search the bodies later. No air or artillery could fire into the squad spaces without the respective SqLdrs' approval.

Departure was normally during early night, followed by a second night out, and returning at the end of the third night. The squad lay under cover during the day, rested and slept. C-rations were carried, and canteens were filled from streams. The ideal daytime cover site had elevation that allowed observation within the area and where the squad would move that night.

SqLdrs readily took to the plan, and our enemy contact improved 100 percent. This was new to the enemy; they could not figure out our game plan. Most importantly, my Marines used their common sense to find, fix, and destroy the enemy. They used what worked best for the given situation.

Easily identified terrain features outlined the squad's TAOR. A squad owned the path, canal, or feature that served as a boundary, and the area between it and the terrain feature serving as the boundary of the adjacent squad was no-man's-land, or the safety border. Some boundaries located on lightly used trails or paths did not stand out well in the dark, and it was possible for a squad to move beyond its boundary. The safety border and the next boundary would provide a margin of safety. I did not sleep soundly the first few nights, but as time passed with my Marines the clear winners, I relaxed. The work areas and the safety borders did not remain on the same ground, so the enemy was unable to lock on an avenue free for his use. Safety borders this week were killing grounds next week.

A rumor of another operation in the A Shau Valley became a fact; the 9th Marines would determine if the enemy was using the valley. My tour was about over; the idea of becoming hung up in the A Shau again did not interest me. I did not expect to be on hand for the jump-off on Apache Snow, which was scheduled the second week of May.

I was more of a realist with Eakin's death, and the loss of Bill Christman and Lee Herron had hit me hard. The realization of just how close I had come to death upon several occasions on Dewey Canyon made a statement that I could not ignore. I was all right while actively involved in a firefight. The time leading up to the fight was my problem: there was too much time to think. The high probability of leaving my family without a husband and a father worked on me. I was ready to go home.

Culkin visited me requesting that I stay for the operation; he wanted me to take Alpha in on Apache Snow. There had been a large turnover of commanders and he wanted to keep some Dewey Canyon experience aboard. He hinted at my concern for my Marines and said that they needed me. I had not the slightest thought of extending my tour, and his request was a total surprise.

I had already extended my time in this place, and a devoted, loving wife, a daughter, and a new baby needed me at home. I loved the Marines of Alpha and what we as a unit stood for, but I loved my family more. It was now time for me to carry my share of the family load. Dotti Lu had been alone since one month before Amy's birth. Amy was nineteen months old, and knew nothing of her father. My response was a simple, "No, I will not extend again."

That was not the answer sought and my commander allowed his displeasure to show as he departed. I knew where he was coming from, and I would have liked to help. However, when would it end? There would be other operations requiring proven commanders.

My departure Fitness Report was probably influenced by my refusal. Noticeably a major drop from earlier combat reports, it was not the evaluation of an individual asked to serve in expected combat. Most of the marks were in the excellent boxes with the important one, General Value to the Service, marked between Excellent and Outstanding. The report covered the period 1 April to 12 May, but was not signed until 12 June, after the battalion returned from Apache Snow. Section D excerpt:

> . . . Because of the lack of enemy contact during this reporting period, it is felt that the "presence of mind" category cannot be accurately adjudged. . . .

Apache Snow came; my freedom flight to the world did not. The 9th Marines moved out, and we began moving into jump-off positions. As we did earlier on Dewey Canyon, we moved toward the A Shau by bounds, from FSB to FSB. The idea of reentering the A Shau was beginning to brighten; I was losing the dark dread that hung over every thought of the upcoming operation. Maybe I could get Apache Snow out of the way before my flight date. My thoughts became more positive as I accepted the fact that I would be around for the operation. Although Alpha was now manned with about half its ranks full of FNGs (new guys) who had joined since Dewey Canyon ended six weeks earlier, their performance was professional. Squad work in the low-level combat around Cam Lo had woven them into the spirit of Alpha, 1/9.

Darkness of 10 May arrived with Alpha on a hill east of FSB Razor. Word came that my flight date was in; I should board the first chopper into my position the following morning. We were not in enemy contact; the XO could run things until the new Alpha-6 arrived.

It is impossible to put into words the feelings I experienced that night. I was happy; I was sad. Going home to my loved ones was a real high, but leaving these young men, and knowing what was ahead of them, was a load to carry. I was confused, mixed up, and uncertain. My life for six months (when some days had the pain and death experiences of a normal lifetime crowded into each of them) had been these Marines, this collection of grimy, smelly, vulgar, big-hearted, wonderful young men. Planning, executing, and supervising the happenings of their daily lives were important to me, and I needed to share in their accomplishments, their bleeding and their dying.

Everything else was a far-off dream; Dotti Lu, the children, and home all seemed to be in another world. These Marines were real, in this world with me, full of life today with the likelihood of an ugly death tomorrow. Life had become so basic; could I just walk away from it, from all of this? While I felt guilty for leaving when I was needed, as implied by the colonel, I could not deny that I was happy with going.

Early on the 11th, with the 2nd Platoon on patrol, I divided my gear. My Vietnamese pack was bigger than the haversacks carried by Marines. My pack, air mattress, flexible flak jacket (Army type issued to advisors), and everything else desired, were given to my warriors. I gave my good-byes and walked down the hill.

Passing several positions en route to our HLZ, I thought I would lose it. Marines stood and saluted, despite there being no requirement to salute in the bush, and said, "Alpha One/Nine, Sir." I returned the salute with a smile, but words would not come. My emotional level was at a high, and I found it difficult to maintain my composure. Prying loose from the bond of these Marines was not a natural happening. Each step widened the gaping wound that was developing between now and what had been; I was walking from a way of life to which I would never return. Was I doing the right thing? Doubt filled my mind as my emotions were flooded with the awareness of my love for these young men and the purpose for which they stood. At any moment, the weight of a straw would have influenced my decision, and I would have remained. The need for the love, presence, and warmth of my wife kept me walking down the hill.

The CH-46 ride to VCB did not sever the tie with Alpha. Spending the next twenty-four hours in my tent, although the others were empty, was a connection. The day was spent boxing up my meager possessions and collections from the bush and my Hong Kong R&R. My possessions included three 122mm howitzer shells earlier carried out of the A Shau (on a chopper) for me by two homeward-bound Marines.

LtCol Smith was now the G-3 of TF Hotel at Vandegrift; I enjoyed a warm visit with him and departed feeling better about leaving Alpha while faced with Apache Snow. His point was simply that I had done more than my share; it was now someone else's turn. He gave me his wife's phone number, asking me to call Nan when I arrived in the DC area. One day at Danang allowed a departure call and visit with Col Barrow. The legal work required to take my two A Shau rifles home was accomplished, and I was now in the going-home mode.

Arriving on Okinawa the next day, I was greatly disappointed to learn the processing time was four days. Now that I was committed to going home, that amount of time was unacceptable, a pure waste. In true military fashion, we spent four days doing what took four hours of effort. Maybe this was the warrior de-fang period: our time for rehabilitation or adjustment to civilized conduct. Contrary to my feelings on my first night, the time did pass.

Dotti Lu and I had not foreseen a short-notice flight date, meaning that I would be home before a letter could arrive telling her that I was on my way. By the time I landed at Norton AFB in California, I was a six-hour flight from being home. To keep from getting our babies out of bed, I decided to make a surprise arrival and called my sister to meet me at Dulles. Linda met me at 0530 for the thirty-minute ride home.

Dotti Lu opened the front door to my ring and instantly and swiftly slammed the door shut in my face. Just as quickly, the door reopened and we united. The sight of the Marine uniform standing in her doorway was too much for her, thinking I was in Vietnam. Considering what this young lady had been living through, my surprise was inconsiderate, unfair, and crude. Each of her days had contained the dread of a Marine uniform appearing in her doorway with bad news. I have never made any surprise appearances since.

Being home was great, and my thoughts returned to Alpha Marines less frequently. Marine action on Apache Snow was not mentioned on the news media, which meant that there was no enemy contact. The only coverage of that operation went to the Airborne soldiers' problem in taking and holding Hill 937, which they named Hamburger Hill.

Amphibious Warfare School did not start until August, which gave me two months to kill. I hoped to be temporarily assigned to the Recon Section in the Development Center upon checking in on 11 June. A call to the Recon officer, Maj Timothy J. Geraghty, received his affirmative response; he could use some help. The base Adjutant, however, had more business for me than just checking me into the command.

The papers terminating my enlisted and temporary officer status had been following me around since 15 April. Not catching me in Vietnam, it was waiting at Quantico, and I became a reserve officer on 18 June 1969. Both officers immediately up my chain of command, Tim Geraghty and his boss, LtCol Alfred M. Gray, were keen on my getting a regular commission. They helped with the paperwork, as well as getting me a personal interview with BGen Kenny Houghton, Manpower Dept, HQMC. I lost no time in setting up the college-level GED Test, the only thing I needed to qualify for regular officer status. After receiving an acceptable score on the GED, I was sworn in as a regular officer on 29 October 1969, having four and a half months in reserve status.

Recon did not need jump numbers on a particular parachute; time in the water behind Aqua Darts was the push. They were evaluating a motor device that pulled swimmers through the water behind a small, low-silhouetted hull. Throttle and kill switches were on the handles; the swimmer hung on by hand and steered with his trailing legs. I spent many hours in the Potomac River that summer.

Fridays were jumps days, and my 1st Force free-fall (FF) parachuting experience came to good use for training this section in FF parachuting. I ran the FF operation while the section waited for quotas to the Ft Bragg Parachute FF Course. This Recon Section was the only unit in the Marine Corps authorized to FF; Force Recon Companies had been on hold since 1 April 1963 following Captain Johansen's death.[38]

Geraghty suggested that I determine which steerable parachute would best serve the needs of the recon community for my required AWS Staff Study. He could use it to support his evaluation, and he in turn would support my study. I could do the fieldwork by visiting and interviewing current users of steerable parachutes. I went to Forts Bragg and Benning to learn the Army's opinion. Then we went to Orange, Massachusetts, where the father of US sport parachuting was located.

Meeting Jacques Andre Istell at his Orange Parachuting Center after reading and hearing about him was a pleasure. Meeting him was not enough, though; I wanted his D-1 license number in my logbook. Jacques signed my 378th FF.

AWS Class 1–70 started on 18 August 1969; I was pleased to find William C. Fite and John J. Sheehan from the Advisor Unit as classmates. Other personalities from my Vietnam experience were on the AWS staff: MajGen Raymond G. Davis was the Director of the EdCtr, Col Elliott R. Laine was the Assistant Director of AWS, and Maj Joseph B. Knotts was an instructor and conference leader. The student body included other friends and gungy types, among them Richard J. Craig, Roger M. Jaroch, John F. Juul, Edward St Clair, John Telles, and Richard B. Trapp.

The Vietnam War was winding down and Marine forces were withdrawing. Most students had returned from the war within the year; however, our classroom material and computer war games were oriented toward containing the Soviet threat within Europe.

Few of us would return to Vietnam, and the ones who did served as advisors. Capt Douglas O. Ford (infantry) received advisor orders to Vietnam upon graduating and was later KIA. To my knowledge, Doug was the first and last member of AWS 1–70 to pay the supreme price for being a US Marine.

I continued with my steerable parachute study, and jumped with Recon when I could get away from class on Friday mornings. My earlier concerns about holding my own in a classroom environment with college boys proved unfounded. Some might have developed better study habits, but I did not get behind.

Vietnam came back to haunt me at my high level of academia. It started with spells of fever, and over a week's time became worse, with ringing in my ears. Looking through Dotti Lu's medical manual, we began to suspect malaria, but I had taken my malaria pills religiously in Vietnam and for the required period following. The attacks became worse and after a bad evening, I went to Quantico sickbay. The doctor took a blood test and checked me over, but said, "The malaria bug would only show during a fever."

Two days later, 7 October, I awoke very sick with a high fever. Dotti Lu wanted to drive me to Quantico, but I did not want to drag the children along. The doctor had a chance to read the malaria bug this time; I was sicker than I have ever been and was admitted to Quantico Hospital. The saying "you have to get better to die" really fit; dying would have been a relief. Three days later I began to feel and care enough that I might live. My doctor did not doubt that I took my malaria pills as prescribed in and after Vietnam. The pills were only a prophylactic; they did not prevent all strains of malaria but did delay the disease.

My strain of malaria was Vivax, from the highlands of Vietnam, and one for which we had no prevention. By taking the pills, I had simply put off the attack. Instead of getting a break from combat days, I would take time out now in my academic environment, when I could least afford the lost time. On 22 October I returned to duty.

I was two weeks behind in the classroom and further in the running program but managed to catch up in both. An example of Marine lack of enthusiasm for running in 1969 was my placing second in our Run for Your Life program after not running for a month.

AWS 1-70 graduated on 23 January 1970 with Bill Fite as our Honor Graduate. I was happy to complete the course. My mom and dad attended my graduation, which was followed by lunch in Harry Lee Hall, the Officers Club. Our duty stations and job desires had been worked out earlier; I was assigned to the Basic School. Knowing little about TBS, I elected it for my education in officer training. We moved into Quarters 4022 in Lyman Park, and rented out our country home.

I checked in at TBS and was assigned to the Tactics Section. LtCol J. T. Elkins, Tactics Chief, further assigned me to Company Tactics (CoTac), headed up by Maj William I. Ferrier. Capt Kenneth W. Moore was headed for AWS as a student, and I took over his classes. My favorites quickly became the Night Attack and Combat in Built-up Areas. CoTac gave the amphibious warfare instructional package, which I also shared with other instructors. Highly motivated for my classes, I quickly became a subject expert.

Whatever my reason for choosing TBS, it was the right assignment. I loved the work, the professional association with some of the best officers in the Corps, the close, personal, family relationship within the Tactics Section, and the daily association with the future leaders of our Corps. Lifelong friendships were developed during that tour of duty, more so than in any other tour of duty in my experience.

Instructors were responsible for teaching certain classes; the primary taught the classroom portion. The primary would then take the lieutenants to the field for the practical application phase. The company would break down into platoons for our subjects, and the remaining instructors worked as assistant instructors.

We worked long hours, starting early and ending late. Major Ferrier had a brave, commonsense approach to duty, which I greatly appreciated and later used as my model. An example was the Night Attack package that wrapped up with a company night attack on an aggressor position. The attack normally ended about 0200 and all CoTac instructors were involved. After the student critique and gear put-away, the major usually stated, "Enjoy a late breakfast with your wife and come in after lunch."

My first encounter with this approach deeply impressed me. Here was a leader who was genuinely concerned about his Marines and their families; family time was returned for family time taken. My experience up to this point had been roughly along the lines of "You are a Marine twenty-four hours a day. We do the Marine thing all day and all night if necessary; work out your personal time as best you can." From time to time, I saw evidence that Ferrier came in to cover an issue, but he ensured that his Marines had quality family time.

I learned tactics inside and out, and was surprised at how little I did know when it came to the finer points in both the offense and defense. My learning continued as I assisted in providing all the instruction given to a lieutenant. By platoons, we attacked or defended across a piece of terrain. My students, seated on camp stools at one vantage point to another, discussed how we would do it and with what. The walk-through phase was followed with exercises where the lieutenants functioned in all leadership billets of a rifle company, from fire team leader to commander.

Skunk Hats were the trademark of the instructors and student company staff in 1970. Green helmet liners with a three-inch white stripe painted around them readily identified a source of knowledge, wisdom, compassion, and gunginess; instructors stood out under their skunk hats. Student lieutenants wore either their soft covers or the full helmet.

CoTac's amphibious package amounted to classroom presentations, a bus ride to Little Creek Amphibious Base at Norfolk, and a beach assault known as BASCOLEX (Basic School Company Landing Exercise), from land-launched Mike boats. The assault beach was around the coastline on Camp Pendleton, a National Guard Base. We added a couple of days, persuaded the Navy to give us a ship, and moved our assault to Onslow Beach at Camp Lejeune. This way the lieutenants received a feel for the real thing: shipboard life and working with 2nd MarDiv Marines.

Our lieutenants were Vietnam-bound upon graduating from TBS. Lieutenants at any time are motivated to do well in TBS, but those who face the final exam of functioning correctly under fire tend to take school more seriously. We had the cream of the crop, as TBS always has: loyal, intelligent, highly motivated young men who wanted to lead a Marine Rifle Platoon. Infantry was the first duty choice of the majority, and it mattered not that their first command would be in combat. Bill Christman had traveled this route, and his book was not yet closed.

Soon after returning home, I had contacted Bill's parents in Gaithersburg, Maryland, visited with them, and later entertained them in my quarters. Through them, I learned that the Inspector and Instructor Staff in Baltimore would present Bill's wife with his Navy Cross. I informed Colonel Smith, who was then assigned at HQMC, and we drove together to pay our last respects to the memory of one fine young Marine.

The ceremony was proper, but it left me empty and cold. The award was never meant to replace, justify, or correct the loss to this wife and mother of a two-year-old daughter. Nothing and no one but Bill could do that. Trying to sound out my feelings, I received no answers; that day was a reminder of how great a loss this was to a warm, loving family and to our nation.

★ ★ ★

I attended a meeting of the Quantico Sport Parachute Club. With a membership of three, the club was defunct; the air station did not support the club, and the members paid for their jumps at a Stafford County airport. The president recommended that the club be dissolved; there was no interest in the sport. In spite of not being a club member, I asked to speak and left the clubhouse as the new president with the mission of getting the club airborne. A visit with HMX-1 (helicopter squadron at Quantico) leadership solved the aircraft problem with one helicopter every other Saturday, providing I could get a volunteer crew.

Air guys like their Saturdays off, but there are those who love to fly and will do so at every opportunity. We were airborne. A notice in the base newspaper brought new blood into the club; I was soon involved in training new jumpers. The Quantico Skydivers continued to grow from three club members to almost forty during my TBS tour. I trained and jumped both the XO of TBS, Col William Masterpool, and my later CoTac Head, Ed Riley. Neither officer really took to the sport, but they did satisfy their youthful ambition of leaping from an aircraft in flight. Many 2nd lieutenants joined, and stayed with the sport through field grade rank.

During this period of jumping, I started with jump number 379 and ended with number 607. Jump 531 stands out as different from the routine. After a good fall, I pulled, only to have nothing come off my back. Normally, I feel action on my back when the pack opens and the canopy leaves. Feeling no activity, I looked over my shoulder, saw nothing, and immediately pulled my reserve which opened instantly in my face. With the opening shock, my main chute fell below, still in its deployment sleeve. Rather than drop the chute and retrieve if from the woods below, I let it hang. It was a bad decision that I could have corrected at any time but did not, as canopies are hard to get out of trees.

My little reserve required hands-on steering to keep me headed for the DZ. My rate of descent was great enough that I might not clear the woods before touchdown; I did not want a tree landing, so I ignored my hanging chute. Then my sleeve started working off the canopy. There would be bigger problems should that canopy get air and come up into my reserve.

Each time that I released a control toggle to activate a Capewell release, my reserve turned back into the woods. I could not cut away my canopy without increasing my risk of landing in the tall trees. I was low and close to the DZ, so I continued steering. I made it but just barely. As I landed, my Para-Commander canopy cleared the sleeve and began to inflate, driving into my reserve canopy. Never again have I tried to avoid pulling a chute out of a tree.

★ ★ ★

Dotti Lu and I had planned an addition to our family after learning that we would stay at Quantico. Nicole Lyn was born on Saturday evening, 17 October 1970, at the Quantico Hospital. Another beautiful girl with lots of blond hair and big blue eyes, Nicole would be our last attempt for a boy. My parents-in-law had three daughters; Dotti Lu was the third. They had had high expectations for a son with their fourth child on the way; instead, twin girls arrived. We decided that three children were enough, and yes, I could be happy in a house full of girls.

★ ★ ★

CoTac had a complete turnover of personnel; Maj Ed Riley moved over from Platoon Tactics and replaced Bill Ferrier. Now there were two former 1/9 company commanders teaching company tactics, and Jack Sirotniak was the commander of a student company. Other gungy types who joined CoTac included Captains Phil Torrey, Nick Grosz, Fred Bobbitt, Jim Furleigh, and George Hofmann. The CoTac section became tight, socially and professionally.

CoTac's procedure was to pick up a company of lieutenants and introduce all the structors before beginning our instructional package. Ferrier had included the information that I would be awarded the Medal of Honor shortly. These words were meant as attention gainers and to inspire the students with what would come from CoTac. For me, the reference became old. Over a year later, Riley was still using this introduction. Meanwhile, I became more embarrassed about the issue, as it appeared that it would never happen.

George Smith, now a full colonel, was a student at the Army War College. He had tracked the award recommendation through each level of command approval. CinCPac had approved the award with the Sixth Endorsement and SecNav approved it on 13 October 1969. The Secretary of Defense and Congress had acted on the recommendation by January 1970 and authorized its presentation. As he had done upon approval at each level, Smith called me at CoTac in January to say Congress had approved the award. My medal was on the President's desk for presentation, but he was waiting for the "right political climate" to make the award.

Nixon was taking measures to keep the war out of the American home, and the right political climate meant for me a fourteen-month wait after the award was approved for presentation. This also meant a small ceremony in the White House; only immediate family members could attend. I had planned to invite Colonel Smith and all Alpha, 1/9 Marines and corpsmen that I could locate.

Nixon made a production line out of presenting medals to six soldiers and me with room only for immediate family. One war reminder appeared in the news media instead of seven separate accounts. My thought of the whole affair amounted to, "After holding something in such high regard for all of my military life, I get it from Nixon!"

In spite of the ceremony's shortcomings, I was pleased and proud to receive the Medal as recognition for the actions of all the Marines and corpsmen of Alpha 1/9 on 22 February 1969. Collectively and individually, each man had performed above and beyond the call of duty.

Presentation day came on 2 March 1971, and I headed for the White House with my girls. Dotti Lu's parents kept Nicole, less than six months old, at Quantico. My mom, dad, brothers, and sisters (without their spouses and children) attended. Major Donald J. Myers (Corporal Myers of my G 3/5 days in 1954) was now the Operations Officer at Marine Barracks and elected to be my escort. His first duty was to drive to Aldie, Virginia, and deliver my parents to the ceremony.

I wore Dress Blues with the Sam Browne belt. (TBS officers were evaluating the belt for wear by all officers.) My family gathered in Center House at Marine Barracks; government vehicles with police escort delivered us to the White House; and then the usual military "hurry up and wait" followed. Entering the White House was just another of my first-time experiences as a Marine. I guess I had waited too long for this occasion and was not overly impressed. The presence of those who shared the battle with me would have made it a grand affair.

Each recipient's family was staged behind him in the East Room. Nixon entered, traveled around the circle placing the Medal around each neck, shook hands, and departed. A short reception followed where the Secretary of Defense, Melvin Laird, shook my hand so hard that my drink spilled on both of us.

This was my first opportunity to speak with the Commandant of the Marine Corps, and I truly enjoyed my time with General Leonard F. Chapman Jr. I managed to get in a recommendation for his next CO appointment to TBS. Colonel George Smith was the right man for the job, and the Commandant seemed interested in what I had to say about the matter. A tour of the White House followed; then we returned to the Barracks. Marines held another reception in Center House where I met most of the Corps's leaders as well as the officers assigned to the Barracks.

Another enjoyable event took place that night in Leesburg. I arranged a dinner at Johnson's Beef House for my entire family, including in-laws and children. Everyone came, I spoke a few words, and we enjoyed a great meal. The only missing elements for the day's activity were my battalion commander and the Marines and corpsmen of Alpha 1/9.

Majors Joe Knotts and Ed Riley organized a reception for me at Quantico a few days later. Many old friends were there, including Paul Mazerov, my platoon leader of G 3/5 days in 1955. LtGen Richard Stillwell USA attended and read a message from BGen Barrow who was on Okinawa. There were now three MOH holders stationed at Quantico, including Ray Davis and Harvey Barnum.

★ ★ ★

TBS activities and duties as well as teaching parachuting cut into my family time; I would lose more. The University of Virginia gave evening classes at Quantico High School and I enrolled. For most of my time at Quantico, I attended class at least two and sometimes three nights per week, including summers. My resolve weakened at times; thanks to Dotti Lu and her support, I stuck with it.

★ ★ ★

Colonel George W. Smith became the Commanding Officer of the Basic School on 15 July 1971. First Battalion, 9th Marines of the '68–'69 vintage was now well represented at TBS. Smith and his lovely lady,

Nan, brought a genuine professional flavor to the TBS scene. The new Commander shared his time with his lieutenants.

★ ★ ★

HQMC changed the way that we were evaluated on physical fitness. The new test measured three important areas of body fitness: upper body, lower back and abdomen, and cardiovascular. Pull-ups, sit-ups, and the run were scored to a maximum of one hundred points each. Merely passing the PFT, as was the custom on the PRT, was not good enough. Twelve to thirteen pull-ups satisfied me on the PRT; now I had to do twenty for one hundred points. Forty to fifty sit-ups had been my maximum; now, I needed to do eighty in two minutes to max the event. My twenty to twenty-one minutes on the three-mile run must be reduced to eighteen.

My daily workout shifted to focus on these three events. There was progress, but it was slow. Sit-ups were the easiest to improve upon. I left TBS a year later doing eighteen pull-ups, maxing the sit-ups on a good day, and running in just over nineteen.

★ ★ ★

Capt Jack Kelly, from our Walking Death Bn days and now my Monitor at HQMC, called to ask if I wanted to go to Paris, France. The Marine Security Guard (MSG) Detachment position held by Capt Leonard F. Chapman III, another One/Niner, was available. Dotti Lu was in favor of another tour in Paris, and it did not take us long to decide on our next duty station.

My transfer report from LtCol Leemon McHenry was typical of all I received at TBS. I was rated as Outstanding in Overall Value to the Service along with three others. Statement excerpt:

> . . . is truly a superb officer, an extraordinary leader with a
> sincere, absolute dedication to duty, country, and Corps . . .
> superior to his contemporaries in almost every respect. The
> officer students seek him out for his advice and counsel. His
> knowledge of tactics is profound and his good-natured manner
> and willing attitude make him a pleasure to serve with. Capt Fox
> is recommended for promotion ahead of his contemporaries.

On 7 June 1972, I checked out of TBS on leave and en route to Europe. The required briefings at HQMC and State Department were completed and my leave time was free and clear until my port call on 19

June. Each family member received a Diplomatic Passport; we were going to Europe with a little class.

Chapman had been the OIC of the Paris Detachment; it rated an officer because of its size and international importance. The CO of Company A needed help, however, so the billet was closed. Chapman moved to Frankfurt, Germany, and became the XO of Co A, MSG Bn. A MGySgt now headed up the Paris Det, putting it on line with all detachment commanders who were staff NCOs. I was assigned to Frankfurt instead of Paris.

LtCol Hooper[39] met us at the airport and delivered us to our furnished apartment at 13 Ernst Schwendlerstrasse. Located off Platenstrasse, our quarters were on the third floor directly above Hooper's. Our company office and the Marine House of the Frankfurt Consulate were also within this complex. An Army commissary and PX were within a mile and a DOD elementary school was four blocks away.

Lenny and Gail Chapman were on leave and driving around the Scandinavian Peninsula, one of the few times that neither the CO nor the XO was on an inspection trip. Lenny returned and we had a good turnover, including ideas.

Company A had twenty-eight detachments that covered the national capitals from Rome north to Oslo and from Moscow west to Reykjavik. Detachments were inspected twice a year, once by the CO and once by the XO. An inspection trip normally included three detachments, spending from two to five days with each. The number of Marines assigned determined the length of the inspection, with a week at Paris and two days at five-man detachments.

Until 1972, most embassies required Marine guards on duty only during nights and weekends. These embassies were manned by a five-man detachment led by a staff or gunnery sergeant. The bigger detachments, along with Paris, were London, Brussels, Moscow, Rome, and Bonn; all manned one or more twenty-four-hour posts, seven days per week. Terrorist activity was just coming on the horizon, and our embassies were a soft extension of our great country. Due to the threat, a plan was underway to have at least one twenty-four-hour post in all embassies.

The time-consumer on the inspection was a personal, private interview with each Marine. He was appraised on how well he was doing; if he had a weakness, we talked about the problem and what he should do about it. Each was encouraged to present anything that might be on his mind, bothering him or otherwise. Considering the context of these one-on-one sessions, I later found it hard to understand how something like the Longtree incident[40] could have taken place in the Moscow Det. A detachment that large had to have a few Marines who would not be comfortable with what was going on. During these half-hour interviews, any problems became known and were resolved.

Bonn and Hamburg were my first inspections, and on 30 July 1972, I drove up the Rhine and went to work. GySgt Don L. Lohmeier was the Bonn NCOIC and the best for breaking me in on my new routine. He and his Marines were ready and presented themselves well. Lohmeier invited me back that year as Guest of Honor for their Marine Birthday Ball. Prague, Budapest, and Vienna were next on my inspection itinerary.

The inspection included personnel in ranks (in full blues), Marine House, PFT, the NCOIC's administrative procedure, and an audit of the mess and club accounts. A call was made on the Ambassador or Charge of Mission as well as the Embassy Admin or Security Officer. Dets with twenty-four-hour posts required a repeat of the PFT and personnel inspection for those Marines standing watch during the main events. While my travel and most of my inspections were conducted in business suits, I wore blues for the personnel inspection.

My focus was the PFT, and I did the events with my Marines. Upon getting ready for the run, I received the same response from each detachment: "Well, Captain, who will time us if you're running?" This much older (I was forty-two at the time) Marine was not expected to operate in the fast lane.

I answered, "I will keep the time."

"Sir, do you max the run?" After putting forth a good effort, they wanted credit for each second earned.

"No, I have never maxed the run. Anyone who comes in ahead of me gets a hundred points." Laughing and kidding followed with each Marine probably feeling as if he were going to get some easy points. Actually, my time was under nineteen minutes, and with a pacer and competition I did better. I would be close enough to see anyone ahead of me cross the finish line. There would not be many free points given, but it was a motivator. Beat the captain.

Young men start out hard and fast. I had learned that was a miserable way to get through three miles. Fast starts leave you weak with the first mile and you force yourself through the remainder, hurting and trying to regain your breath. On my command "Go," I was usually left behind at the gate. As I warmed into running, my pace quickened and my stride increased. I gave a verbal nudge to each Marine that I passed, "Move over, New Corps, Old Corps coming through." I did not pass up every Marine in each detachment, but those who beat me were running six-minute miles. Later, I learned that most Marines, as they ground out that last mile seeing me get smaller in the distance, made a personal promise that next year would be a different story. The Old Corps would not be coming through them.

I also did the makeup PFT with watch standers in the twenty-four-hour Dets. Running four to eight PFTs per week helped me improve. Most of my runs were gutted out near the eighteen-minute mark. I gave a ten-minute break following the pull-ups and sit-ups and learned to use this time for getting my system up to run speed. My guidance to the NCOIC was to have his Marines on the ready line and ready for the word "go" at a specific time. I timed my warm-up run to arrive at the start point at that minute. Without a pause and with the group yet in front of me, I would yell "GO" while making a show of starting my stopwatch. With my second wind and my body adjusted to running, I easily passed many of the younger Marines. This happened in spite of them being ready for me my second year and intending to blow off my doors. Somehow, the idea of running before the watch starts does not appeal to Marines.

Pull-ups were the last holdup to my maxing the PFT. In 1972–73, Marines were only allowed to do pull-ups with palms facing out. Resting was allowed, including hanging by one hand. I learned to get two more pull-ups by shaking out one arm at a time; after both arms had their rest, I did my twenty. Not long after maxing the pull-ups in this fashion, regulations changed and chin-ups (palms facing in) were allowed. Immediately, I could do twenty no-stop chins for a hundred points.

From 25 July 1972 through 13 May 1974, I took sixty-eight PFTs with scores from 234 to 300. December 1972 through April 1973 saw my lowest scores because of a back problem compounded by the flu. Regardless, I took the test; my back problem surprisingly affected pull-ups and running more than sit-ups. Though I had hit the high 290s several times earlier, it was 12 September 1973 before I maxed the PFT. Seven more max scores were spread out over time, but most scores were around 297 to 299 when I dropped a minute or more on the run.

There were side benefits to my running the PFT. My run-time improved greatly in some detachments, and Brussels was the best example. I was extremely happy at how fast I was completing the required laps of the track. Speedy should have been my name; twelve laps were completed in 15:45.

Nothing would do but to measure the track; I had not gotten that fast. Our run turned out to be three laps short of three miles. Because several Marines had not passed the run by much, I gave the test again. The next day, fifteen laps proved about right as I finished in 18:09. The detachment had three failures. If my run-time was much under eighteen minutes, I measured the course. The word was out, however, and short courses ceased to be a problem.

Many of the detachments could be reached by car. I bought a travel trailer and took my family to those countries that they wanted to visit. Dixie and Amy were doing well in their schoolwork and did miss some school days, but there was an educational value to traveling through Europe. My girls went with me mostly during the summer months and school vacations.

Going through the Iron Curtain checkpoint en route to Prague was an education. We watched while the cars and occupants ahead were thoroughly searched by the border guards. All people were ordered from the car, luggage was opened and personal belongings dumped on the ground, car seats taken out, and the entire car stripped and searched including underneath, in the fender wells, and in the engine compartment. Time was not a consideration; up to four goons spent over a half-hour on each car.

I was thankful that there were only two cars ahead of us. Dotti Lu on the other hand, after seeing how hateful and ugly the guards were, suggested that maybe we should turn around. She did not want to take our children into that country. I assured her that we would be treated differently for the sole reason that we were traveling on diplomatic passports. I hoped I was correct and that these clowns knew the difference.

The car ahead reloaded and left. I moved forward and presented our passports, which were immediately taken. We were directed to move to the side and another car moved forward for the shakedown. We sat for fifteen minutes, grateful that we were not going through what the people behind us were getting. Our guard finally returned, handed over our passports and motioned for me to proceed. While my children had not paid any attention to the word communism before, they were now full of questions. This personal experience motivated them for a lesson on democracy.

Our stay at a Prague campsite was pleasant, and my girls experienced a different atmosphere from the border crossing. The detachment driver showed my family the city while I inspected. The Czech driver became their friend as he chaperoned them to the best shopping places. We left Prague with less space in our trailer, having made room for two beautiful Maria Theresa crystal chandeliers.

Budapest was next with the same entertainment: my family shopped and enjoyed the sights while I worked. A sword chair and other items of small furniture bought on this visit were shipped back to Frankfurt. Our trailer was comfortable for family use but too small to double as a truck. A weekend and the Vienna Detachment finished the trip.

My first visit to Moscow was notable for two reasons: the Marine PFT run conducted while dodging Russian citizens on the streets, and my method of travel from the embassy to my hotel. The embassy drivers were busy taking people home following the Marine House party celebrating the end of another inspection, and I waited my turn. After a while, I decided to run to my hotel. Bidding my escort goodnight, I took off in suit and dress shoes.

I did not intend to run hard enough for my dress to bother me, but I forgot how I might look to others. As I departed the embassy block and headed down the street toward the bridge, a black sedan followed me at a half-block distance. That car kept the same pace while I continued my run. The occupants did not care that I knew they were following but stayed behind me until my hotel door closed.

Besides routine inspections, the CO and XO are on call for all problems occurring at the detachments. For personnel problems a Marine was normally handled by the NCOIC. If required, the CO held Non-Judicial Punishment immediately over the phone. A few Marines traveled to Arlington, Virginia, for a court martial and a transfer. If given a choice, the watchstander always chose NJP. The officer in Frankfurt immediately investigated a major screw up by the NCOIC.

A call for help from Company B, located in Lebanon and covering the Middle East and Africa, gave me an opportunity to get on the continent of Africa: Their CO was away, and the XO, Capt M. F. (Mike) Shisler, was otherwise committed. The Abidjan, Ivory Coast, State Department Security Officer had alleged that his detachment NCOIC was abusing his Marines. On 6 July 1973, I flew in to spend a few days and get the facts. The allegations could not be supported, but there was a personality conflict between the Security Officer and the NCOIC. A transfer solved the problem without the Gunny taking a hit.

Two months later, problems surfaced with our detachment NCOIC in Oslo. As a result of my investigation, the CO relieved him. These special investigation trips added to my problem of continuing toward my educational goal. With only eighteen credit hours from UVA, I was not half way to the sixty hours required to apply for the College Completion Program.

The University of Maryland offered classes in the Frankfurt area. The problem was my work schedule: I was not in the area half of each month. I worked out a plan that gave me nine hours while conducting my inspections on either side of the semester. Hooper approved and for ten weeks, I was a schoolboy. The idea did not work well, however, as it caused too many schedule changes.

A college degree would never have been within my grasp except for the US Armed Forces Institute (USAFI). Learning of USAFI's Subject Standardized Test, I looked through their catalog and applied. First- and second-year course tests were available that dealt with common sense and everyday-life subjects with which one is familiar at age forty, such as health, physical fitness, social problems, speech, and business law. These were End of Course exams (no study, text, or involvement other than taking the final exam) completed, graded, and ranked on a national percentile. The decision to accept and award credit hours based upon percentile placement belonged to the university. I worked hard toward my goal of sixty acceptable credit hours.

★ ★ ★

A tour of MSG duty was two years, and for continuity purposes, the CO and XO were assigned in separate years. Hooper and I started out well, two old Korean War Vets hanging out, in spite of his cigars. That relationship soured, and I never learned why.

Running was not Hooper's style; he was a big man with too much stomach. For whatever reason, he started running and broke his foot while running around the housing area. That did not hold up the colonel; he continued his inspection schedule with a walking cast. Several months later, the cast had been removed and Hooper was on an inspection trip. Mrs. Hooper called: The Colonel was coming into Rhine Mein, would I drive her to the airport? I was in the middle of a detachment problem, the wife did drive, and I was unaware of any limits to her driving. For airport connections, we used the Metro and streetcar system. I answered with, "Why, did the colonel break his foot again?" Anyway, I reported and drove her Mercedes to Rhine Mein.

Hooper's plane was not on schedule so I returned to the terminal to check on changes. Unfortunately, the two were waiting when I returned to the gate. He responded to my greeting with a growl between cigar puffs. The two of them did not say a word on our walk to the car. Still not sure that I was reading the signs correctly, from the backseat I asked about his inspection trip. His curt, smart answer along with a dark scowl convinced me; I was along for the ride.

A situation required our Administrative Officer and my presence in Hooper's office the following morning. Hooper did all the talking and finished with directions for Lt Winter to tell me certain things. Here was a lieutenant colonel putting a lieutenant between himself and a captain. Why not tell me directly, look me in the eye, and tell me where I screwed up or whatever else was bothering him? I made a move to ask Winter to wait outside, intending to close the door and ask Hooper about his problem. Then I realized that Hooper had only two weeks here, and I would be on my inspection the following day. Taking on a boss two pay grades higher was no doubt a factor; I played the same dumb-non-Marine game. I promptly left his office and never entered it again while he was there.

The cause or problem never surfaced. Beyond the crack about another broken foot, I did drive the Mercedes fast, as we had a late start. Fast driving is not a problem with the Germans, and I merely kept up with the traffic. Accelerating while turning at an intersection caused the wheels to spin on the steel streetcar tracks, which brought a glance from Mrs. Hooper. I did not give it a second thought, but the two events together could make a story for the colonel's ears. The Mercedes was their pride, and the telling could have had me abusing it out of spite. We were speaking when he departed, but our relationship never recovered.

My Fitness Report showed a change: General Value to the Service dropped from a mark between Excellent and Outstanding to Excellent, and most of the individual trait and capability ratings dropped from Outstanding to Excellent. One-on-one Fitness Reports (not compared with peers) are not supposed to hurt or help you. While I was the only captain reported upon, the lower evaluation marks in so many areas had to be a consideration by later promotion boards.

Major Thomas V. Draude reported as the new CO. I was the CO of Troops. The Frankfurt MSG Det provided the Marines, and we had a Change of Command ceremony. Our new CO brought a noticeable improvement in morale in Frankfurt, especially within the Fox household.

The Paris Det invited me as their Guest of Honor for their 1973 Marine Ball. In typical Marine fashion, they also figured to save money on the deal. They asked to shift their inspection two weeks so that I would be there officially during their Ball. We did, much to my pleasure.

Dotti Lu and I have attended many Marine Balls, but Paris wins all awards—size, color, grandeur, important people, or any other standard. Much work and money go into that Ball and it shows. Any international figure in Paris who does not get an invitation to the Marine Ball feels slighted. I hope in the future to attend another Paris Marine Ball.

★ ★ ★

During my two years in Frankfurt, I collected twenty-five credit hours with the Standardized Test and twelve hours with USAFI College-Level Continuation Program home study courses. Collectively, with my UVA and Maryland credits, I totaled sixty-four hours; the next requirement was acceptance by a university with a two-year standing. The last step was to apply and be accepted by the Marine Corps College Completion Program Board.

Western State College was my choice based upon the outdoor life available and the opportunity for something other than East or West Coast living. WSC in Gunnison, Colorado, accepted me with a two-year credit standing, and, with a strong endorsement from Draude, I applied for the program. Sometime later, the Board reported out with my name on their list. The only hitch was that I would first do an unaccompanied tour of duty with the 3rd MarDiv. The curse of all family Marines was on me again.

I had been in the States since 1969, and it was my turn for a thirteen-month tour overseas without dependents. As sure as death and taxes, a Marine's unaccompanied tour date is monitored and fulfilled. When due, he goes to the dependent-free 3rd MarDiv: our country's immediate response to a communist threat.[41] My schooling would start in September 1975 if Western State agreed.

In spite of the personality conflict with the Hoopers, our State Department tour was enjoyable. My family and I saw much of the world and its people, and moving among the communists was a valued educational experience. Two years out of the Marines was enough, however, and I was ready to return. We sold our travel trailer and made ready for another military move. On 1 July 1974, I checked out of Co A, MSG Bn, on leave and en route to the 3rd MarDiv.

We bought a townhouse in Pinecrest Heights in Annandale, Virginia, and moved in. Leave time moves on speeding wings when the termination is an overseas assignment without loved ones. My port call was again Travis AFB, a place I was getting to know as well as any Marine base. This time was different.

The Air Force handled me with class; my Medal brought me the VIP treatment. From quarters assignment and waiting in the terminal VIP lounge, to special boarding privileges and seat assignment, the Air Force took care of me. Naturally, I enjoyed the privileges, especially the stares of some colonels who glared at me silently with a look of, "Captain, are you lost?" I did not expect or want special handling in the Marine Corps.

Being a Marine includes competing on an equal basis with one's peers while being evaluated on potential, not history. However, the Air Force made the Medal of Honor mean something. In short, the Air Force extends to the holder of the Medal, regardless of rank, the same privileges enjoyed by pay grades 0–6 and higher. The Medal took me to Okinawa in style, and then it got in my way.

Checking in at division, I sought assignment to the 4th Marines. Al Gray had the 4th, and I had hopes that he would give me a rifle company. Without giving me a chance to talk with Gray, the G-1 gave me the facts. The only battalion in the 4th that needed captains had locked on its company commanders. I could maybe be the S-3A.

I was slated for 3rd Recon Bn. Recon needed captains with reconnaissance experience, so I rode out the tide. My orders were endorsed assigning me to Recon at Onna Point located halfway up the island on the west coast.

Checking in with Major Harper L. Bohr Jr., the CO, I learned why I was assigned. He was at 50 percent officer strength, was losing his S-3 that week, and the few officers he did have had no recon experience. Other than the CO, there was no submarine experience in the battalion, and no officer was SCUBA qualified. The battalion had inherited a Deep Recon Platoon (DRP) when 1st Force had been placed in cadre status. The platoon had parachutes but little jump experience. Bohr was formerly Force Recon but had allowed his SCUBA qualification to lapse. Anyway, he could not run the whole show alone. He assigned me as his S-3 (a major's billet), relieving Captain Robert L. Earl who was homeward bound. The day had been a good one, and I was happy with the turn of events. With the jet lag heavily upon me, I hit the sack.

The following morning at chow, Bohr told me to repack and report to the Chief of Staff. There had been a mix-up; I was to be assigned to the 4th Marines. My seabag did not go with me because I was headed for a fight that I felt reasonable leaders would let me win. Bohr and 3rd Recon needed me, which meant the 3rd MarDiv needed me in Recon. Arriving at Camp Courtney, I reported to the Chief of Staff.

Colonel W. Plaskett Jr. was not much on formalities. Coming directly to the point, he stated, "I'm sending you up to the 4th Marines."

"Sir, if I have a choice, I would prefer to stay with Recon."

"Well, you do not. I have promised my Headquarters Battalion CO a job as the XO of Recon in recognition of the fine job he has done with the battalion. Major Jay Vargas has the Medal of Honor, and it would not do to have you both in one small, under-strength battalion."

Plaskett was aware of Recon's personnel shortage, and I informed him of the total lack of reconnaissance experience. "Vargas has no reconnaissance experience; Bohr needs technical help," I continued. The chief was not swayed; I was 4th Marines bound.

As I did not appear to have a chance at a rifle company, the regiment had lost its lure. Recon was attractive apart from the need for my experience: I would hold a major's billet and be number three in the chain of command. The small isolated camp of Onna Point offered the additional benefit of being a small family compared to the larger camps with their personnel issues.

My problem with accepting Plaskett's assignment was that he was using the Medal against me. It was the stated reason why I would not be assigned to Recon. In a move that was out of character for me, I asked him for an audience with the CG.

MajGen Kenneth Houghton was an old Recon Marine; surely, he would listen to the reasons why I should go to Recon. In addition, I had met him when I worked for Gray and Geraghty in DevCtr Recon. George Smith also had spoken highly of Houghton, so I still had a chance. Plaskett listened quietly to my request, and responded with, "Wait here," then entered the next office, which I assumed to be the general's.

In ten minutes, he returned. "Okay, go back out to Recon. I'll assign you to Harper Bohr."

"Thank you, Sir." I moved out fast and returned to Onna Point. Bob Earl had a few days to turn over his duties, which included the S-2 and the S-3 jobs. As if these two were not enough, my additional duties included Bn Diving Officer, Parachute Officer, Guard Officer, Education Officer, Human Relations, and FORSTAT Officer. Most of these duties did not demand a great amount of time, and some had a staff NCO who was the subject expert. SSgt Johnson was a good example: as my S-2 Chief, he ran our intelligence shop, and I only provided a signature now and then. GySgt Newman was my 3-Chief; he knew the business and provided continuity while I got my feet on the ground.

Other personalities in the battalion were Lt Bob Bittle, the DRP Leader who later served as my S-3A, and Captain B.V. (Vic) Taylor, who arrived a few weeks later and took command of Charlie Company, the battalion's only reconnaissance company. Jay Vargas joined us on 6 September to be the XO.

Company A was assigned and located with the 3rd Marines in Hawaii. Company B was a paper company with no Marines. Company C's mission was to staff, outfit, and train a recon platoon for each deploying battalion. The company usually had three platoons, one deployed, one just returned and losing its personnel, and one building up for the next deployment. The occasional need to deploy two platoons created personnel problems in numbers and training qualifications.

The DRP provided one four-man team with each deploying recon platoon. The one-year assignment to the division dictated that DRP personnel had to arrive as Force Reconnaissance–qualified. Personnel inbound to the division from 2nd Force or the DRP attached to 1st Recon Bn were screened. Second Force was the only Force Recon in existence.

My first assignment was to take our divers to Fuji, Japan. Steel beach matting used to get heavy equipment over the beach sand had been left in place on the Fuji Beach. A recent storm had ravaged the coast and washed the matting seaward. Japanese fishermen were snagging their nets in the matting and our government was responsible; could we help?

We attached lines to the matting pieces as we found them and tractors hauled them up onto the beach. Matting out beyond the surf zone was the easiest. Working easily with SCUBA, we attached lines and surfaced to signal the pull. The surf zone was a different story, as SCUBA gear was more of a problem because of the wave action against our SCUBA tanks. There was no way to keep the tanks from hitting our heads. We finished the job by skin diving for the matting in the surf.

As in Quantico, I found the 3rd MarDiv Sport Parachute Club on the verge of becoming history. The annual turnover of personnel and a shortage of motivated, experienced replacements were the cause. Camp Hansen, located on the opposite side of the island from Onna Point, provided the clubhouse.

I joined the club and took on the leadership responsibilities: getting aircraft support from the Marines at Futenma Air Station and training new jumpers. Jump gear was not a problem, and the old Yomitan Airfield was our DZ. Shortly, with aircraft support and the time of friendly pilots, the club was airborne. Parachuting soaked up much of my free time that year.

In addition to sport jumping, I jumped with our DRP as the Parachute Officer. Most were small team jumps from OV-10s onto Yomitan. We also jumped on small, garden-patch size HLZs in the northern training area for realism and worthwhile training. Recovering from a PLF on an otherwise routine Recon jump onto Yomitan, I was surprised to find myself under the watchful eyes of our CG. General Houghton had driven out to see how reconnaissance training was going. I enjoyed our conversation and his concern for how the battalion was shaping up.

Submarine operations in the Western Pacific were a big step forward from what I had experienced in 2nd Force. We had the *USS Grayback* (LPSS) for four days on 6 October. The *Grayback* was modified and maintained for our kind of work. The greatest improvement was a bubble-like hangar attached to the deck that allowed teams with equipment, including the IBS, to leave the submerged boat together.

Not only could we wear our full equipment, but there were also benches for comfort. Facemasks with air supplied through hoses attached to the bulkhead were provided for each swimmer. We did not worry about losing the bubble after the hatch was opened. The hatch was a big sliding door, wide enough to allow the passage of all men together. Underwater reentry was easy with air stations provided on the way down; ears were equalized while breathing air; and no one delayed you. The entire team could enter the hatch at once. Life in Recon was getting easy.

Onna Point living was also great; our battalion was the only tenant on the small post. Security, mess, club facilities, maintenance, and other housekeeping responsibilities were ours. One mess hall served all ranks, one EM club served the sergeants and below, and one end of our Staff NCO and Officers' Quarters served as our combined club.

Midday was my workout time, and the weather never became too hot. Rice paddies faced our camp on three sides with the South China Sea on the west. Farm service trails wound through the paddies over which I had a good six-mile run course, including a distance down the beach. I ran at least six miles every workday and further on weekends if parachuting was weathered out.

My run time on the PFT remained just under eighteen minutes, allowing me to max the test. Experience also helped; as with my MSG Marines earlier, Reconners preferred to start their run cold. The PFT was S-3 business, and Gunny Newman conducted the test. I supervised and took the test at the same time. During the break before the run, I ran. Newman would have the Marines ready to run and he sounded, "Go" as I approached our start position.

Our PFT run was from our gate, a half-mile out to the main road, a mile down the highway, and return. The last quarter mile before the turnaround rose in a noticeable incline. The highway wound along the coast making for an interesting and scenic run. That hill, however, sucked the wind and strength right out of you. Once you made the turnaround, if you had burned up only nine minutes plus a few seconds, you were home free. I was never first on these runs in Recon, and I always had plenty of pacers.

The North Vietnamese were about to win their war in the south. The 3rd MarDiv was rattling the sword, and commanders were ensuring that they were ready to go into harm's way. Recon Bn with our one-platoon company was for the second time on standby to evacuate Saigon. Houghton wanted Recon to do the job, but with two platoons already deployed, we were not large enough for the task. A rifle company was attached for training in preparation for the mission. This situation had been an on-and-off thing for several months with the call to get ready followed by orders to stand down.

Newly promoted LtCol Bohr sought his staff's recommendations on Recon's options. To a man, we felt that Saigon was not a mission for our under-strength and under-trained battalion. He then took our strength and capability situation to Houghton.

The fact that the attached rifle company was three times the size of our Recon unit caused Bohr to recommend that the parent infantry unit do the evacuation. With Recon in the picture, there were too many strange personalities in the chain of command. Moreover, that chain of command was not clear, especially since Recon could only handle a small corner of the playing field. Recon was relieved of the Saigon evacuation mission; Al Gray's 9th MAB[42] did the operation known as Frequent Wind on 29 and 30 April. (One attached Recon platoon did the in-city evacuation.).

I detached from 3rd Recon on 31 July 1975, and returned home, but we would not stay long at 4516 Maxfield Drive. In the past, house hunting had been done after I checked in for duty. Not knowing anything about Gunnison, Colorado, I decided to fly out in advance and lock on to a rental for my two years at WSC. Getting there was no problem: I caught a hop in an Air Force Lear Jet from Andrews AFB to Colorado Springs and bused to Gunnison.

I went immediately to a realtor's office, but my future steadily darkened over the next two days. There simply were no unfurnished rental homes suitable for my family. There were places available for college students but nothing for a Marine Corps captain with a house full of furniture and children. Dotti Lu and I talked by phone and considered our options: ask for a change of orders or buy.

After all my effort towards getting a degree, to ask HQMC to cancel my orders now and reassign me was tough. We never considered buying a house because we had bought the townhouse the year before; we had no money. Faced with either/or, we had to buy. Dennis Steckel, my realtor, made our situation workable.

A modern, six-room rambler in the Palisades residential area was available for a fair price. The basement in the house at 108 Irwin was partially finished, and when completed would add three rooms and a bath. Dennis worked out a loan with 10 percent down, which I covered with a Dead Horse (an advance on my Marine Corps pay). The coming six months would be lean while I paid it back, but I would at least carry out my orders. Renting our townhouse immediately would be a major factor in our survival; I could not cover that monthly payment also.

Finding renters for our townhouse happened quickly; two young ladies about to attend a local college wanted it. Their fathers, Conway Twitty of country music fame and a friend, signed the lease. We moved to the high country, where I became a full-time student.

My student priorities initially fell behind because of time spent completing our home. We needed to finish the basement, which included adding a chimney for a Franklin fireplace. There was space for a two-car garage that would increase the resale value, and I wanted to take advantage of the garage during my winters there. My life insurance policies financed the building needs; I borrowed money on their cash value.

Elk came into season during my building project. This was my first opportunity at the big elk, so I added hunting to my classroom distractions. I did not get my elk, but gained some hunting tales. My best elk story has a bull elk and me suddenly staring at each other eyeball to eyeball with an expression of "Oh Shit!" in both pairs of eyes.

After still-hunting all morning, I took a break on a flat place on the side of the mountain. Placing my back against a big tree, I started to eat a juicy apple. Several times I ceased chewing, thinking I heard something. Attributing the noise to the squirrels that were active around me, I continued eating. Another sound caused me to rise.

Halfway to my feet, with my rifle across both thighs in my left hand and my right holding the apple halfway to my mouth, I looked around the tree into the startled eyes of a bull elk. Less than twenty yards from me, he stood in full view. We both froze; I am sure confusion showed in my eyes as much as it did in his. I dropped my apple and fumbled to get my rifle up for a shot; he did a midair turn and was instantly gone. I just stood there trying to figure it out, which took some doing. No more apples on hunts! On the other hand, the smell of my apple probably was in his nostrils.

At midterm, I was doing all right in every subject except accounting, where I received a F. Thereafter, Dr. Mattocks and his spreadsheets received my full and undivided attention. By the end of the quarter, I had pulled my accounting grade up to a C, the only C I would get at WSC.

Snow fell for Thanksgiving and stayed for the winter. Cross-country ski gear bought in Oslo received a workout as my neighbor, Jim Pendergraft, and I hit the trail each evening. We skied the Gunnison River

Meadow for a hard hour in the normal twenty-degrees-below-zero temperature. Family ski outings were limited to weekends and my girls, being small, did not really take to the cross-country stuff; there was too much work to it. We did enjoy several picnics on the trail, as well as some overnight camping. My ladies loved downhill skiing, and we skied evenings at the Gunnison Ski Area. Crested Butte and Monarch Pass were easy commutes for day skiing.

Jim Pendergraft introduced me to coyote hunting, at which he was a master. During the fur season, we hunted regularly. Besides the enjoyment of meeting the challenge of the crafty critters, pelts brought up to $75.00 each that year. While coyote hunters can hunt the year around, we slacked off after fur season, electing to save the dogs for prime fur time.

With all the great outdoor distractions, it is a wonder I ever graduated. Jim was a perfect neighbor. In spite of my background, I had much to learn from him, a natural outdoorsman. The spring thaws brought in trout fishing; again, I learned from the master. Jim knew the best brook-trout streams, and my girls loved catching fish in the high mountain waters. My family enjoyed quality outdoor time in the Gunnison County high country. During winter quarter, I figured out accounting, and by the wrap-up of spring quarter my GPA was decent.

The Major Selection Board reported out with my name on their list. The I&I Officer in Denver, the officer and office for my Marine Corps connection, called to inform me of my selection. He beat my copy of *The Navy Times* with the news by one day. My name was not far down the list; summer 1976 was promotion time.

Lessons Learned

1. Captain is the best rank of all in the Marine Corps.
2. Capitalize on the abilities and initiative of squad leaders; give them responsibility.
3. Instructor duty is next best to field command.
4. Evaluations are motivators when the evaluator himself competes in the evaluation.

12
Major
096702/0302/9953
1 July 1976

The Inspector and Instructor in Denver promoted me to Major by phone and mail. Keeping with tradition on the home side, I held a promotion party. Next-door neighbors and the Smiths joined my family in a backyard barbecue. Captain Gene Smith, the Delta Company platoon leader who took Hill 1044 on Operation Dewey Canyon, was attending WSC for his Geology degree. Gene liked the high country; he and his young family had just moved to Gunnison.

Gunnison was great for a workout; initially, a three-mile run in that thin atmosphere fatigued me. Within three months, however, I had adjusted to the thinner air and less oxygen. Running in subzero temperatures in the dead of winter also required an adjustment. I needed a wrap or muffler over my face to prevent lung damage as well as a frozen face. My outer clothing turned white as my body vapor froze and crystallized in the fabric.

Running did not interfere with my academic endeavors. After my first quarter, I functioned in the academic mode. Distractions, however, were plentiful and continuous. I took full advantage of my second and last elk season and enjoyed the hunt. I saw many fresh signs, but the season ended with no elk meat on the table.

Opening morning of my second deer season was promising. Snow had fallen during the night, giving the great outdoors a virgin quality. Walking toward my hunting area before daylight, I enjoyed the feeling of being first into this hours-old wilderness. While yet in the grassland and looking toward the mountain with the breaking light of day, I could just make out dark objects moving on the snow far to my left front.

As light improved, I assumed they were deer as they moved toward my direct front at about 1,000 yards and disappeared into a timbered draw. With excitement building, I moved quickly around to catch them coming out the other side.

A stick beneath the snow snapped loudly under my weight, and the thin morning air carried snorts of alarm with sounds of movement as the animals cleared the covered draw. I watched in amazement as a herd of twelve elk came out of the draw a hundred yards away; elk season was over. A big cow stopped and stared at me. To see how she might react to my movement, I slowly placed my rifle into my shoulder. As I did so, a big bull charged from the herd toward me, stopping fifty paces away, snorting, shaking his head and looking at me.

I could not decide if he was telling me he was "out of season" or trying to identify me. He placed himself in a defensive position between his cows and me; maybe he thought I was another bull. The temptation to shoot was great, but I settled for sighting in on him, raising and lowering my rifle to learn if slow movement bothered him. It did not. I tired of playing with my rifle before they tired of looking at me. Finally, they moved up the mountain.

After still-hunting all day on Flattop Mountain, I started down toward my car. Coming out of timber onto grassland halfway down the mountain, I came across three sets of deer tracks. One pair of tracks belonged to a big animal, and they were going in my direction, so I followed.

The tracks wandered around but always continued in my direction down the mountain, passing over my earlier tracks. The deer tracks were the fresher, and I really took an interest in the pursuit. Out of the timber, these deer had to appear somewhere in the open below. Little knolls and rises in the rough terrain were all that kept them from my view. I tracked on with excitement building; I expected a showdown within minutes.

A rise in the downward slope ahead was all that kept me from seeing the flatland and my car; I readied my rifle in anticipation. A big mule buck exploded from the ground a hundred meters forward; lying down, he had been hidden by the curvature of the ground and the sagebrush. He was running as he came to his feet with a big rack spreading over his back. Instantly my rifle was up, off safe as it went into my shoulder, the buck filled my scope, and I squeezed the trigger, all in the same fluid movement. My 268 Magnum barked and the buck went down. What a sensation for the great white hunter! But, only for a second. The buck rose and disappeared down the hill. Disappointment immediately followed my high, but I suspected that I had hit him.

The snow told me several things: the buck was indeed a big one, and he was hit well, dragging a leg and losing blood. He went straight down the hill. Moving over the military crest, I saw him standing in the meadow far below, looking toward me. One doe was still with him, but she was dancing around, wanting to put some distance between her and this place. The buck just stood there, looking. He was dead by the time I got to him. This was my last high-country big-game hunt. All of my Gunnison County sports were in the home stretch.

I was well into my last year, and it was time to decide what I wanted to do on my next assignment. There are few command billets in the Corps for majors, and I did not want staff duty. My choices were 2nd Force Recon or the Development Center (DevCtr) reconnaissance job. Jim Capers (of my Pathfinder days) had the 2nd Force job locked on, I learned. Capt Robert Earl was the Recon Officer in the DevCtr at Quantico. Bob, whom I replaced as 3rd Recon's S-3, now had the job that Tim Geraghty had held in 1969 when I worked there temporarily before attending AWS. Bob was due to leave and was working his bolt to get me into his job on the Quantico side. I would have to work HQMC for orders to Quantico.

While getting back into the Marine Corps was appealing, I had not had enough of the high country and the wide-open spaces. Gunnison County was to my liking, and I could enjoy a lifetime there. Coyote hunting, fishing, skiing (cross-country and downhill), and academics finished out my year.

Friday, 3 June was graduation; I had achieved the distant objective of those long evening classes back through the years. It was hard to realize that it was over. The preceding two years, however, were real; there was no doubt in my mind that I had been a student. Graduating cum laude was proof that I had accomplished my assigned mission, even if I did have fun along the way.

The high collar of my Dress Whites showed above the neck opening of my black gown. We lined up, moved into the football stadium, received our diplomas, and bid farewell to each other, WSC, and Gunnison.

Physically and mentally, I was prepared to leave Gunnison; financially, I had to sell our home. Keeping the house was not a consideration: we would never again live in Gunnison, and I needed financial relief. My real estate agent, however, had made no progress on the sell. Several major businesses had recently located in the county, and houses were scarce. Selling should not be a problem. No interested buyer came along, and my agent suggested that I was asking too much. Considering what I had paid plus my additions, I did not agree. I held out for my price, and we left Gunnison with the house empty. Fortunately, the house sold within three months.

Assigned to Quantico, I checked in on 23 June, replacing Bob as the Recon Officer. We moved into Quarters 4506, Lyman Park. My family settled in quickly; they liked the base community: swimming pools, teen activities, and the school system.

Adjustment to my new job took longer. The development, acquisition, and procurement system was new to me, starting with the terminology and continuing through the budgeting process. I had a lot to learn. My big problem was that I had to learn it on the job through trial and error. The office rated a captain as the assistant; he would have been helpful with my transition. The billet was empty.

Bob was around for a decent turnover before he headed for his new job with the CIA; but the more he talked, the more I felt snowed under. A few days after Bob's departure, I dreaded the sound of a ringing telephone. There was always someone, somewhere, wanting answers or talking about something of which I had not the slightest clue. We were not talking about means of entry into an objective area, observing and reporting details on the enemy but details in the acquisition process. Bob had kept good files and records of what was going on, but I did not have the benefit of his instant recall or the knowledge of where to look for the source.

Attacking the problem with time, I arrived in my office several hours before the beginning of the normal workday. Digesting the files, I learned the system and our ongoing projects. A prior class on the acquisition process would have been helpful. Recon projects included: inflatable boats, gas-powered air compressors, portable-inflatable recompression chambers, waterproof equipment bags, parachutes, silenced weapons, and burst communications means and systems. To this list, I would add several more needs of the reconnaissance community.

My section was one of several specialty sections within the Intelligence Division of DevCtr of which Colonel Frank M. Manrod was the Chief. Other personalities in the division included Maj Michael R. Lamb, who had been a sergeant in 1st Force with me back in 1960. Maj Jerry Thompson, the Canadian Liaison Officer, was not in our division, but he never missed a ParaOp.

Capt Edward J. Robeson, a recent graduate of AWS with orders to the Royal Marine Exchange Program, was temporarily assigned during my second week on the job. Ed had three months before reporting to the Royal Marines and spent that time as my assistant. MGySgt Hank Henry had become a permanent fixture as the Senior Parachute Rigger. Henry, after eight years in the section, was Okinawa-bound for a year. He left his family in quarters and would return to his old job one year later; I would be glad to get him.

Ed's reporting time in England approached while I sought a replacement. After several conversations with Personnel Assignments at HQMC, S. Joseph Velarde, shortly to be promoted to captain, became my assistant. He was sorely needed, as it was difficult balancing my lab and project visits while also maintaining continuity in the office.

Our biggest ongoing program was the MARS (Marine Amphibious Reconnaissance System). Bob had worked up the Required Operational Capability (ROC); Naval Coastal Systems Center (NCSC) in Panama City, Florida, had the contract and was constructing our boat. A silenced, reliable outboard motor was also part of the project known as SPS (Silenced Propulsion System). To complicate matters, the Army was in on the project; the boat and motor had to satisfy both services. MARS was starting its operational test phase with my arrival on the job.

Bill McCrory was the MARS Project Engineer at NCSC; we would spend much time together over the next four years. We ran tests in the Gulf and up Alabama and Florida rivers as well as off both coasts with the Recon Battalions. All requirements of the ROC were met except weight; just making the boat Marine-proof meant that it would be heavy.

One-hundred-mile open-ocean trips required the boat to be fast and seaworthy. McCrory solved this problem with a wooden transom and a metal beam running from the transom to the bow. The MARS would rear up and go. The SPS was provided by Evinrude; the engine noise was reduced, and the engine could be submerged in water, pulled up days later, purged, and started.

This assignment made clear to me why the government is slow in accomplishing tasks. Between the Army and the Marine requirements, plus the rotation of personnel at the user level (those who are supposed to know what they want), design changes were never-ending. The MARS program was a big circle as we continually reinvented the wheel. Unfortunately, many of the changes added weight as well as cost.

Because of the normal operational loss of IBSs and the supply system's lack of a replacement, commanders of recon units were buying Zodiac boats. Zodiacs had been evaluated under the ROC and found satisfactory in all areas except that they were not Marine-proof. Zodiac boats were light, and Marines loved them. Those that worked the boats were not concerned with the replacement cost or how often replacement was required.

When I left the DevCtr in 1981, the Corps and the Army were in full procurement of the MARS. People changed positions, and that changed the focus of desires and influence; the MARS was dropped.

Millions of dollars went down the tube for nothing: Recon today is using off-the-shelf civilian gear.

Free-fall parachuting was not authorized for any unit except my Recon Section. Fourteen years after Johansen's death, recon teams were still limited to static-line parachute entries into an objective area. This limitation was unsatisfactory because it reduced a commander's options of delivery means in placing his recon teams on the ground. The type of parachute dictates the type of delivery aircraft useable. Static-line deployed chutes usually mean lower flying and slower-moving aircraft. The problem, I learned, was that there was no ROC. I wrote it up and staffed it for action with copies sent directly to commanders in the field for a quicker response.

I included HAHO (High Altitude/High Openings) in the ROC because we were already working with ram-air canopies and the offset delivery idea (high-altitude parachute openings and the parachutists moving great distances over the ground). Within the year, the ROC was approved, and 2nd Force Marines were going through HALO (high-altitude exits with low parachute openings) School.

Every other Saturday there was sport parachuting with the Quantico Skydivers Club. There had been no change or improvement since I set up the schedule back in 1970. Now, all services were represented in our club, so I visited the Army at Camp Davidson to talk about aircraft support.

No one had asked: "What do you want, when and where?" Consequently, we received an Army UH1E from Davidson on the Saturday when we did not have a Marine bird. The National Guard followed shortly with a helicopter on Sundays, any time we wanted it. With official Marine Corps jump operations going every Friday, I was finally getting enough jumping. An exception to the recon-Friday jump was the last week of each month when a night jump was scheduled on Thursday.

Flying the new square parachute was a different parachuting experience. Initially, I found it unnerving: there were just too many little things going wrong on too many jumps that required a decision to cut away from the canopy or ride it down. Incidents of end-cell closures, broken steering lines, and slider (a delayed opening device) hang-ups upon opening were some of the problems. This ram-air canopy, known as a square, was new and had some bugs in it. We worked on the bugs.

A slider hang-up did not allow the lines to separate and the canopy to open. The problem usually worked itself out with a shake of the risers; the slider would move down to where it belonged. Until then, the canopy was slowing his fall, but the jumper was moving rapidly toward ground contact, provoking the question: How long do you wait for it to start the downward movement? Sometimes the slider would hang up on a knot that developed in one or more suspension lines. For the positive hang-ups, the decision was quick and easy: cut away.

A broken or separated steering line was a regular happening in the early days. Several times, I rode a canopy to the ground while being able to turn or correct my flight in only one direction. Pulling the rear riser containing the broken steering line slightly influenced the direction of flight.

Experienced square flyers spoke of end-cell closures (one or both cells on each end of a seven-cell canopy failing to inflate.) End-cell closures caused the canopy to have less lift; the jumper, therefore, would hit the ground harder. The remedy was to pull both turn toggles to the full brake position; that caused the end cells to inflate. That seemed easy enough; now I needed to determine what end-cell closures looked like.

After I had made several jumps on squares, a fellow jumper asked if I had an end-cell closure on my last jump. "No, I don't think so." My canopy looked all right and my landing was soft. His question made me wonder, though, if I would known an end-cell closure if I saw it. I obviously needed more airtime under a square canopy, time to play with it before concerns of where and how I would land it.

Friday, 19 August, during a Marine Corps ParaOp, jump number 655 and my tenth on a ram-air, I decided to pull high and get some flight time. Jumping alone, I pulled my ripcord at 4,000 feet. My opening felt good, and I checked my Strata Cloud canopy. It appeared to be in good shape so I prepared myself for a long ride down.

The DZ was a mile away, with woods under me the entire distance. Deciding to be comfortable, I released my reserve belt and the left snap fastener of my chest-mounted reserve parachute. With the reserve hanging by my side, I checked my canopy again, paying particular attention to the end cells. Now I knew what end-cell closures looked like: I had them.

Pulling full brakes caused both end cells to fully inflate, and I turned loose of my toggles. My sudden release of the brakes caused a violent canopy action that deflated two outboard cells on one side and put me into a hard right spin. Bad news! Pulling full brakes again, my canopy corrected and all cells inflated; I was flying all right. Releasing my toggles again, the two outer cells on the opposite side deflated, putting me in a spin to my left. (I later learned that I had caused the collapsed cells by releasing my steering toggles from the full-brake position rather than a gradual release of the brake pressure.)

Going through the full routine a third time and in a hard downward spiral, I had had enough. Spins were burning up altitude, but I had space if I cut away now. Gripping my Velcro canopy releases, I pulled, freeing myself from the spinning canopy and putting me back in free fall. In a rocking-chair position, back to the ground, I saw the left side of my reserve pack rise in the air above me. I then remembered that I had released one end of my emergency chute.

I reasoned that I would make one attempt to hook that end of my chute and whether it hooked or not, pull my ripcord. The system was made to function with only one side hooked, I reflected. I grabbed my reserve and made a deliberate slide of the hook over the D-ring on my main-lift web, feeling if not hearing it snap shut. With another deliberate act, I grasped my reserve ripcord and pulled.

That canopy exploded off my chest, inflated, and I was again sitting in the saddle, checking a good canopy over me. Because of my higher opening, I had gone deeper into the wind line and well beyond our normal exit point for 2,500-foot openings that would put parachutists on the DZ. Now under a smaller canopy and not a ram-air, and having lost altitude with the spins and cutaway, I would land in the woods. I steered for a less dense area of the woods, finally selecting and landing on a trail through the high brush.

Saturday, the following day, was sport parachuting. Four of us jumped the UH1E at 9,600 feet, two of us going out of each side of the bird at the same instant. We planned to join quickly into a four-man star formation. I was immediately flat and stable outside the aircraft and knew that we would make a quick hookup. Turning left to close on the pin man nearest to me, I received a bump against my left foot.

The next thing I knew, I was in a flat spin. My training had taught me to do a tight-body tuck to get out of a spin. The centrifugal force, however, was so great that it was difficult to pull in my arms, let alone draw up my legs. My attempts at control were not successful; I could not get out of the spin. I thought that I was caught in a whirlwind. In 660 free falls, I had never been in an uncontrollable flat spin. Our exit altitude gave me forty-five seconds of free fall before safe-pull altitude and may be another twenty seconds before ground contact. Initially not overly concerned, I soon lost track of time while trying to get into the airborne tuck. I could not read my instruments and could only see a white blur.

Finally, my tuck effort succeeded, the spinning stopped, the white blur became blue sky, and I was falling on my back. Pulling in an arm, I rolled over, face down. Pushing out into a full spread, I relaxed with the green of earth below me; the trees were yet small, which meant that I was at safe altitude. The needle on my altimeter registered 6,000 feet. Holding the fullspread, I watched the ground and my altimeter and pulled my ripcord at 2,500 feet.

The other jumpers exiting with me saw me fall away in a turn on my back and assumed that I had changed my mind about joining them. I had just gone into a tight body turn when a jumper hit my foot, adding unexpected force to my turn. I was not aware of going over onto my back. In that spin, I was only aware of the centrifugal pull and black and white.

One other major jump incident occurred during my first year in the Recon job. On 2 June 1978 and my 797th jump, I experienced a double malfunction (when both the main and reserve parachutes malfunction). Making my third jump of the day on a Recon ParaOp, I did relative work with two other parachutists during our fall from 10,000 feet.

We pulled at 2,500 feet, and my chute opened in a gob, spinning me madly. Without hesitation, I pulled my canopy releases, cutting away the mess. Again in free fall, I pulled my reserve ripcord without thinking of my body position. Tandem rigs, which I was using, mount the reserve on your back above the main parachute. Ideally, back mounts should be opened while in a face-down fall so that the canopy has free flow into the air stream. My cut-away left me facing skyward; I should have rolled over before my pull. I did not for two reasons: I was concerned about my low altitude, and all of my experience had been with chest mounted reserves, which favors falling on your back.

I received opening shock, but my head was held forward and down by my twisted risers. Checking my canopy was impossible because I could not get my head back through my risers. Turning my head sideways, I could see that my canopy lines were twisted together tightly, up to my canopy skirt. This twist caused reduced lift area in my canopy, and I was dropping fast. Finally working the twist up to free my head, I saw that I also had a Mae West in my canopy: two or more of my suspension lines were over the canopy, making two smaller canopies.

I was losing altitude faster than originally thought, well beyond safe ground-contact speed. My biggest concern was the Mae West, but nothing could be done about that until I untwisted the suspension lines. At the rate I was turning (a parachutist twists himself under the canopy to unwind the lines), I would be on the ground before the lines straightened out. Kicking helped increase my spin rate, but the trees in Training Area 8 below were getting bigger, fast. I had doubts that I would solve both problems before I hit the ground.

Dizziness was building up from my spin, but I kept it going. The lines finally unwrapped, but my spin momentum began wrapping up again in the opposite direction, in spite of my outstretched arms. When my spinning stopped, the Mae West had worked itself out, probably when my lines swung free from the twist.

There was just time to realize that I was landing in a forest of young trees. I hit the ground, hard, feet and ass, no PLF. Conscious and hurting all over, I lay there, fully enjoying the pain; it was proof that I was alive. No bones were broken; this was another jump from which I would walk away.

Almost immediately, three 2nd lieutenants (part of a concurrent TBS training exercise) were standing in front of me with their rifles at port arms, asking if they could be of any help. They had watched my descent, and knowing nothing about parachuting, knew that I was in trouble. "Yes! No! I'm okay, thanks!" I was alive!

Parachuting was not the only excitement provided by my new job. Several DevCtr Officers took advantage of Major Thompson's offer of cold weather training experience with a Canadian regiment. On 2 February 1978, I went along with three other majors to Valacitier, near Quebec, Canada. We were hosted by the French-Canadian 33rd Regiment on Winter Exercise Nes Rouge. While much of what I encountered reminded me of my Korean War experience, the Canadians do have the cold weather figured out. Shelters and stoves were the big differences between my two experiences. A shelter and a heat source make the cold bearable; they keep one within the realm of reality and aware of the desire to live. Two weeks later we returned to Quantico.

I was selected to attend the 1978/79 Command and Staff College (C&SC) at Quantico. Col Joseph Scoppa, an Operation Dewey Canyon veteran (artillery), was the Director of C&SC. Another one-niner and fellow student, Lenny Chapman, and I were sharing the same command now for the third time. From my 3rd Recon Bn days were Baynard (Vic) Taylor and Jay Vargas. Probably no other class of C&SC has had two Marine MOH holders seated simultaneously. Our class had talent, and we applied it conservatively while preparing ourselves for bigger roles within our Corps.

Colonel Manrod's plan and my desire were for me to return to the Recon desk after C&SC. He kept the job open with only Velarde running the section, and I stayed abreast of the projects and jumped with the section when there was no class conflict. Completing school, I returned and Velarde resigned as planned. Capt David Weber inbound with Recon experience replaced Joe. MGySgt Henry returned from his

Okinawa tour, so my section was in good shape with personnel. Experienced parachutists, and especially Top Henry, were needed to wrap up our parachute program.

Ram-air parachutes with a four-to-one glide-to-descent ratio offer the commander another option for inserting his teams into an objective area. Known as offset delivery, this method of parachuting was supported by my earlier ROC. While the Recon Section jumped these parachutes weekly, jump operations were routinely conducted with canopy activation at 2,500 feet, the same as with other parachutes.

Upon my return to the Section, I started deploying our parachutes at a high altitude, miles from the ground objective. Factors influencing the offset from exit to landing point are altitude, glide ratio of parachute, wind, and navigation. Other problems were identified and solved as we worked the program (i.e., keeping team members together during descent on a dark night).

The offset concept includes jet aircraft, exit altitude over 20,000 feet, and the use of oxygen. However, our primary jump aircraft was the CH-46 with a regulation altitude limit of 10,000 feet; sometimes we had a pilot willing to take us to 15,000 feet. Starting nearer the DZ, we worked further away with our offset until we were leaving the aircraft over Camp Upshur. This exit gave us nine air miles to fly before we touched down on our DZ in Training Area 8.

The prevailing wind line was from Camp Upshur to TBS, and with a strong wind, we would have to burn off air to get down on our DZ. Sometimes the wind line was different, and we would fly over strange countryside. As all of Quantico west of I-95 is woods and parachutists do not like tree landings, we worked outward gradually. A miscalculation or sudden wind change sometimes forced us to pick alternate DZs. In addition to small clearings in the woods, my alternate landings included the Rifle Range, the Tank Park, the EOD Range, and the Ammunition Dump.

Wind direction at altitude on the day of my Ammo Dump landing was ninety degrees off from my brief by the weather desk. Ground winds we read on the DZ; wind speed and direction every thousand feet above ground were provided by the weather forecaster.

Out and open under a good canopy at 10,000 feet and well south of TBS (distance from exit to the DZ was about six miles with TBS between the two points), my team was on the wind line to our DZ, down to 8,000 feet. Then, the wind shifted, coming against my left side. I turned into the wind to compensate for the wind speed with my canopy's forward speed. The wind was so strong, however, that I continued to back up, about fifteen miles per hour.

Though not an immediate threat, I-95 was now behind me, not on my right flank. My canopy received lift while facing into this wind, causing me to dump air so as to get down and not back up to I-95. The west wind continued until 4,000 feet, where it shifted back to the south. Now I was far off my earlier wind line with the DZ on my left front.

After crabbing (angling the parachute to one side of the wind line) for a while, I realized that I could not make the DZ. Moving smartly with the wind at 2,000 feet and the DZ passing far to my left, I looked forward for an alternate landing spot. The Ammo Dump was ahead, but I doubted that I could make it. I decided to try for a roadside landing on my side of the Ammo Dump.

Initially concerned about whether I could fly so far, I arrived over the road too high. Not wanting to chance the wind backing me into the fence, I turned around and flew into the secured Ammo Bunker area. I assumed the sentry saw me as I passed over the fence at two hundred feet, near his guard shack. After gathering up my gear, I approached the sentry from his rear; the shock on his face expressed his complete surprise. "Where in the hell did you come from?" he stuttered.

"I just dropped in," I responded. He did not give me any hassle, or call out the guard, but opened the gate as though he was eager to be rid of me. Such experiences were common as we continued to learn more about the offset delivery business.

My last cutaway and reserve activation, while doing the testing and evaluation thing, happened on jump number 930, on 7 March 1980. Pulling my ripcord, I swung slowly in the saddle under something reducing my fall rate, but no opening shock told me immediately that something was wrong. Looking up, I saw that the slider was hung up just below the canopy skirt and attempted one riser shake to brake the slider loose.

Without losing more altitude, I cut away, went stable face down, and pulled my reserve. A good canopy opened over me but it was smaller and round; I would not make the DZ. I picked the open ground of the EOD Range on my wind line and made a good landing with nothing exploding under me. My walk out of the range area was happily uneventful.

Modern methods of inserting a recon team require the team to navigate long distances to reach its objective after launch from the delivery craft. A MARS team might leave a submarine one hundred miles off the targeted coast, and an air entry team might cover twenty to forty miles over the land. These teams need a navigation means from point of exit to their objective. In the early eighties, the old handheld magnetic compass was all we had; it might land the boat team on the right coast or the flyers within several miles of where they wanted to be. We had to do better.

The Navstar Global Positioning System was under development, but it was too big and too heavy for our needs. Weight and size are not so much a problem for the boat teams, but a smaller system would be beneficial to them too, once they were ashore. Airborne teams needed something smaller and more responsive.

Thinking the requirement through, I worked up the ROC. Ideally, the system would be small and light so that it could be mounted on the chest of the parachutist, no more than four by six by two inches in size and one pound in weight. The user must be able to enter his insertion and destination grid locations and receive a constant illuminated arrow pointing toward the destination. Also required was a readout of current grid location and distance to destination, when queried. The unit must be passive so as not to give away the presence of the team.

While writing up the ROC late one evening, I came around to the name. I wanted one that identified the system with a catchy acronym. A four-man recon team would be the user of this navigational system. My first try was a success: Small Unit Navigation System came out immediately as SUNS. If the right acronym is the secret to acceptance of a new idea, my ROC was a sure thing. I turned off the lights and went home. There have been modifications along the way to my original idea of the SUNS, but today small units move long distances to point targets, the flyers unhampered by weighty navigational equipment.

Monday, 4 August 1980, was the start of my 31st year as a US Marine. For some time, I had planned to mark the occasion with my 1,000th FF parachute jump, followed by running the PFT with a perfect score. We had some great jump days in June and July causing me to jump static line, saving the big FF number for the special day. Hank Henry was also on the rag line, saving his free falls so that he could make his 2,000th on the same jump.

LtGen John H. Miller, the CG of MCDEC, agreed to my jump on the parade deck in front of Lejeune Hall. Two jumpers would exit the aircraft at 10,000 feet, free-fall for fifty seconds, open their chutes at 2,500 feet, and drive their ram-air parachutes onto the parade deck. Miller would present my USPA Gold Wings and Hank's Gold Wings with Diamond upon our landing.

Late Friday, 1 August, the Director EdCtr, MajGen Bernard E. Trainor, called; he wanted to jump on the parade deck with me the following Monday. Well, putting out static-line jumpers was not what I had in mind, and I explained that I was making one pass at 10,000. The general countered with the suggestion that I could put him out while I climbed to altitude. True enough, and he had told General Miller that he would jump with me.

Monday morning I attempted to reconstruct my special jump that had grown from me to two and now three. We met at our Paraloft on the bank of the Potomac behind Larsen Gym and I conducted the training and the jump briefing for the day's ParaOp. Other jumpers were on hand for the following regular ParaOps. It had been years since the general's last jump, and he had no experience on a steerable canopy. I explained the difference in the canopies, what to expect, and how to steer, emphasizing the importance of not turning below two hundred feet. He went through his reserve activation procedures while hanging in our practice harness and did some PLFs.

Thinking over the situation, I did not want the general jumping alone so I assigned an experienced jumper as guide. Following the sergeant off the ramp, Trainor would always face the same direction as the guide. Then Murphy's Law took over.

Reaching the exit point on jump run with my head extended out the side door, I dropped my arm signaling "GO!" With my head back in the aircraft, I saw the master sergeant leave the ramp and looked out the side door again to watch the general's body position. The master sergeant fell away below me but no general.

Looking inside, there I saw my general standing on the ramp, held by a major. Both were looking at me for the obvious command to jump. Meanwhile, the chopper was moving away from the DZ at the rate of sixty feet per second. I yelled and signaled the general to jump. He was to be with the experienced jumper who was now on his way down.

We were well over the creek. The exit was long, but if the wind held and the general faced the parade deck the entire time, he should make the DZ. As we circled while climbing up to ten, I watched the general turn his back to the parade deck. He did that twice before we flew too high and too far to see detail; I had little hope that he would make it. The Top's chute landed on the parade deck, which made me feel better, but I could not see the second chute. Lady Luck was off duty. DZ Control radioed up to me that the general had broken his leg. What a way to celebrate thirty years!

Hank and I made our leap, drove our chutes with combat equipment hanging below us up to the crowd on the parade deck. Trainor watched our jump, then was on his way to the hospital. General Miller presented us with our wings and seemed to find the entire show amusing.

What happened? This dippy major who jumped with us now and then as a straphanger (term for a jumper under permissive orders) took the opportunity to score some brownie points. While I was lining up the aircraft and watching the exit point come under us, this major stood up and for no earthly reason, grabbed the general's parachute's main-lift web. He hung on to the general when the Top jumped, waiting for a second jump command. There is only one jump command given for an entire stick of parachutists that wants to land together. If the Top was to be of any benefit as a guide, the two parachutists needed to be close together. Murphy's Law was not yet finished.

After both chutes were in the air, the Top decided that he needed to get the general closer to him. He turned around to face the general with his back to the parade deck. The general did exactly what he was told to do: face the same way as the Top. While they did not hold long in this direction, turns cost altitude and Trainor had none to spare. The Top did this turn act once more, which ensured that the last chute would run out of air before reaching the parade deck.

General Trainor's story picks up at the traffic circle beside the parade deck when he realized that he would not make the DZ. His glide path would land him on the main road, and a beer truck was bearing down on the same spot. He remembered my caution about low turns but realized that he had two options: the beer truck or a hard impact. He turned his chute, spiraling into the uneven roadside, taking most of the impact on one leg. We finished our ParaOp, and I lost interest in running the PFT.

The following day, Henry and I flew to Petawawa, Canada, for their Military Jump Bivouac. Jerry Thompson had worked an invitation for us to attend the Canadian Airborne Regiment's annual jump session. The purpose of this jump week was to bring together all Canadian parachutists serving in other-than-jump billets for refresher training and requalification.

Going through the airborne training routine did not interest me, especially the PLFs and swing-landing trainer, but we needed to do things the Canadian way. Other than the foot stomp while leaping from the door, I noted no difference. The experience and the Canadian Jump Wings were my objectives. Five jumps on 7 and 8 August made us Canadian jumpers, and we were presented with the red-maple-leaf jump wings.

One week later we did our annual thing at the Naval Academy. My recon section conducted a ParaOp, both FF and static-line, including water jumps into the Severn River. We also rappelled from our helicopter and jumped from a very low, slow-moving chopper into the river with a technique known as Helo-Cast. Then we were lifted from the river on the SPIE (Special Patrol Insertion/Extraction) rig. While the show was for the benefit of the entire class, Marine option midshipmen were collected and lifted out on the SPIE rig for a fly-over of the academy grounds.

Other annual occurrences that required recon expertise were the Armed Forces Day show at Andrews AFB and the Marine Air show held at the Air Facility, Quantico, for the summer officer candidates. Depending upon our time slot in the show and what was desired, we did pretty much the same as our USNA shows minus the water work. Timing at Andrews was always a problem; as we were only a small part of the show, we had to get in, do our thing, and get out.

Quantico's air show was not as rushed, and we had a bigger piece of the action. We did an offset delivery from 10,000 feet and from several miles down the Potomac. Rappelling and SPIE lifts entertained the crowd while we rode the ram-air chutes the ten minutes needed to touch down. Most of these shows, and especially the USNA, required more personnel than the four in my section. Straphangers filled in for numbers; some, like Jerry Thompson, were regulars and could be counted upon to muster when needed.

Powered hang gliders and ultralight aircraft caught my attention during my school year when Palestinians made a deep unobserved or ignored penetration into the heavily defended and electronically controlled Israeli airspace. In another incident, Canada was unaware of the airborne entry of an American who intended to fly across the Atlantic from her coast. Lapses in border control between Canada and the US might be explained, but the Israeli penetration was noteworthy. The possibility of use by our reconnaissance units deserved further study.

I wrote up and staffed a ROC for Powered Hang Gliders and Ultralight Aircraft that identified the need for multiple options for delivering recon teams into an objective area. The four members of a team on their separate gliders would take off well behind the front lines in the middle of the night. Climbing to an altitude of 6 to 10,000 feet, they would cut their engines, enter enemy airspace, and glide miles toward their objective. A great advantage to this method compared to Offset Delivery is that the team uses the same craft and technique to return upon mission completion.

The radar signature of a man under a fabric wing or sail is small to nothing, depending upon the sophistication of the radar system, and the alertness of the operator. At 0400 in the morning, sleepy, red eyes miss a lot, even with good equipment. The idea offered good potential; the Marine Corps bought it.

Exploratory money for the project was approved the following year. I ordered a hang glider and enrolled my section in a hang glider beginners' class with Kitty Hawks Kites at Kill Devil Hills, North Carolina. With the project money, I bought two powered hang gliders and contracted with the Navy Laboratory at China Lake, California, to evaluate these gliders in accordance with the requirements of my ROC. Glider training for my team took place from 8 through 11 September 1980.

We returned to Quantico, qualified for flight and eager to get our hang glider in the air. Enthusiasts in the area use a hill known as Taylor Ridge located on a farm east of Fredricksburg. On 16 October, we tied our new Phoenix 6D Sr on top of my old pickup and headed for the farm and some flight time. Taylor Ridge is 250 feet above sea level, but the hill was only 110 feet high for our purpose. The open pasture allowed the run to be limited only by the wind. Hang gliders took their place along with ram-air parachutes and inflatable boats in the recon section's weekly routine.

Meanwhile, the program was not doing well at China Lake. A Navy test pilot flying our glider was killed only twenty feet off the runway. The glider turned upside down and crashed; the pilot died of a broken neck. The Navy put the program on hold during the investigation; I continued to fly off Taylor Ridge. My section flew our Phoenix throughout the fall and winter of 1980/81. Strong winds gave us good lift and longer flights, but we learned the hard way not to fly in gusty winds when a sudden gust overturned my glider during launch. I managed to break my ring finger in the pileup, which secured my flying. Later, when I left the DevCtr, the program was still on hold; it was canned before another year was out.

Powered hang gliders offered another entry/exit option. Unfortunately, the way we (the military) do business requires that someone push through any idea that is not already proven and accepted by the status quo. This someone has to be a believer, a doer, a mover, and a shaker to accomplish the difficult, uphill push. Because of the death in the program and the end of my tour of duty, the Marine Corps dropped the program.

Colonel James E. Mrazek USA (Ret) wrote positively on "Ultralights—New Generation of Military Aircraft" in the October 1981 issue of *Armed Forces Journal International* and stated, " . . . only the Marine

Corps seems interested." Sorry Jim, by the time your article appeared, the Corps was no longer involved or interested in powered hang gliders and ultralights.

Completing my fourth year at Quantico, I began thinking of duty choices. I was in the Selection Zone and if selected my next duty would be that of lieutenant colonel, regardless of promotion date. I asked my monitor for a slot in the 2nd MarDiv and orders followed with a reporting date during June 1981.

MajGen Al Gray, Director of the DevCtr, was also going to the Division. In the passageway one day, he confronted me with, "I guess you want 2nd Recon Battalion?"

"No, Sir," I replied, "I want your worst infantry battalion."

He smiled and moved down the passageway trailing the words, "We'll see."

Monday, 1 June 1981, I checked out of the DevCtr and the development and acquisition business. Our children's school was still in session, and there was a waiting period for base housing at Lejeune. Quantico gave me a one-month extension on vacating quarters, and I reported to Lejeune alone.

Assigned to 2nd Recon Bn, I headed for Onslow Beach, the home of my new command. Greetings from members of Recon were followed immediately by the words, "Return to the Division CP; you are not assigned to Recon." While I was satisfied to command Recon, I really wanted an infantry battalion. Unit activity was the key: Recon did not do anything as a battalion; they trained and deployed as teams, platoons, sometimes as companies. The CO was responsible for the training and efficiency of his Marines; his fun and involvement ended there. Infantry battalions trained and deployed together as a battalion, all over the world. The problem was my misconception that I would get only one command; Recon Bn was a command.

Major Sean Leach, from my advisor days, had checked into the division ahead of me. Sean, while waiting for a command assignment, worked the officer's slate for General Gray. Both Marines knew I preferred an infantry Bn to Recon. Instead of Recon, I was assigned to G-3 as the Training Officer; my battalion would come later. Sean took over Recon for a year and followed that with command of an infantry Bn. It WAS possible to get two commands, and back-to-back at that.

Major Carlton Fulford, a C&S College classmate, was the outgoing G-3 Training Officer. He and Mary Ann would also be our next-door neighbors in base housing. While Carl took command of the next deploying battalion in the 8th Marines, I settled in for desk work. Two gungy captains, Michael L. Rapp and James E. Snell, kept my head above the waterline throughout the following year. Tim Geraghty became the G-3 before the summer was over.

Our time ran out at Quantico with no house available at Lejeune. On 22 July we packed up, moved, and let our household goods sit in storage. Meanwhile, my girls got enough beach living to last them a while as we lived in our travel trailer on Onslow Beach. My name came up for a house, and on 5 August, we moved into MOQ 2608.

My primary duty was not training the division, as the title implies, but mastering the division's dog and pony shows. All visiting dignitaries saw the division in action. Casper Weinberger's visit as Secretary of Defense caught me first, which made all following visits easy. Weinberger's was the biggest show of the year as we lined Mile Hammock Bay Road with the entire Division's stock of tanks, amphibious tractors, and artillery pieces. These big warrior items lined up side by side were impressive, even to Marines. An amphibious landing and an air assault took place at the right time to further entertain our guest.

Command guidance talked down shows; I was encouraged to show regularly scheduled training. That sounded good, but it seldom worked because of event times, locations, and types of training. Marine field training was at least 50 percent at night and VIPs usually have other things to do after dark. Dog and pony shows were out in name only. While field training could be shown for all events, if the VIPs had not bothered us, the units involved would not have done that training (entertaining) event. Units would also not have wasted training time rehearsing those special events.

My job also included designing and installing training plans for the division to meet the combat requirements of World War III. Our smaller Marine force would take on and hold the Soviet Bloc forces until our nation mobilized. In meeting this challenge, certain people who felt that Marines needed to fight differently became involved. William S. Lind had determined from his readings that Marines could do a better job of fighting wars. Lind spent several days trying to impress us with what he and others termed Maneuver Warfare. It mattered not that Lind had never worn a uniform nor had any practical experience with what he preached; he had done his book study and gave a good pitch.

We sat for his lectures and modified what we did and how we did it to fit the model. One of the buzz phrases at the time was "free play." The idea was that a commander did or reacted with what he thought was needed to handle a particular situation based upon his commander's mission and the latest information on the enemy. Commanders were not tied to a specific course of action, they were not to be concerned with real estate but oriented on the enemy force.

Complying with this manner of conducting warfare is easy when one mind controls the play for both sides. However, the opaque cloud of warfare, battlefield confusion, and breakdown in communications could cause free play to be a disjointed effort going nowhere.

My problem with the whole issue of Lind-and-party's Maneuver Warfare was that Marines have always fought that way when possible. Offense is what Marines are all about, but the situation or a higher commander was not always in support of an aggressive offense. A case in point is the WW II Okinawa battle in which Marine generals wanted to make additional amphibious landings while clearing the southern part of the island.[43] They hoped to avoid the meat grinder of a frontal attack, but the overall commander, General Buckner, never approved the plan. Both Army and Marine forces conducted the less complicated maneuver of attacking directly forward as expected into the enemy's defense and suffered high casualties.

General George Smith, during his presentation of Operation Dewey Canyon to students of C&S College, answered the question, "Did we use Maneuver Warfare in that operation?" He stated it best with his interpretation: "Maneuver warfare is nothing more than fighting smart. With that definition," he said, "Yes, we used Manuever Warfare in the A Shau Valley." Marines have not won all of their battles by fighting less than smart. When it comes to winning wars, others are involved. They, the politicians, are the ones who lose the wars. Case in point: Vietnam.

The T/O rank for the Training Officer billet was lieutenant colonel; I was only a major. That lasted four months: my name appeared on the October promotion list.

Lessons Learned

1. Developing new ideas and a better means to accomplish an old task is interesting and exciting.
2. Repetitive training causes near instinctive reaction during life-threatening situations.

13

Lieutenant Colonel
096702/0302/9953

1 October 1981

General Gray promoted four lieutenant colonels on 7 October 1981 in the division conference room among family and friends. He asked, "Do you swear that you will . . . , " and quoted the Officer's Oath from memory. We responded with, "I do." Our wives assisted with pinning on our rank insignia, and our General left-handedly socked each of us in the shoulder as he shook hands.

All battalion command slots had been filled the past summer so I had eight more months as the Training Officer. Meanwhile, Dog and Pony shows, Division Schools, and shooting with the Division Pistol Team kept me busy. I had time to become involved in our children's activities: Dixie Lee's cheerleading along with her graduation from high school, Amy's swim-team competitions, and Niki's horse shows. My family enjoyed a close relationship with our many neighbors and we participated in the base-sanctioned activities. Dotti Lu's love for tennis and long-distance running kept her involved; she did not miss many 10-K races and placed well in all.

Getting a battalion was a hassle. All lieutenant colonels wanted one, and there were not enough to go around. The routine was a last-minute decision on an individual basis. The rumor mill kept us informed and, not long after the rumor, we received an invitation to attend a change of command that was only days away. The months passed, battalions started turning over, and I was not one of the commanders-to-be.

Earlier, I had met General Gray in the passageway on his way to my office. He asked, "Do you want to go to the Army War College next year?"

"No, Sir, I want a battalion."

"Well, you'll get your battalion, and you can also make that class. That is the best Top Level School available. That's where I went, and it will be good for you."

I assumed that he had been talking with someone at HQMC. The average command time was only a year so I could work it, although I really wanted more time with the division. "Yes Sir, I'll take the War College."

Because of my request a year earlier, Gray may have been saving me for his less-than-ready battalion. In typical fashion, I learned late Friday, 4 June 1982, that I would get 1st Battalion, 6th Marines. Geraghty informed me of the plan, and I followed immediately with a call to LtCol Eugene T. Nervo, the CO of 1/6. Gene was geared for a change of command on 11 June, as he was on a short fuse to his next command in 2nd Force Service Support Group. We had four days to put it together starting with my visit to the battalion first thing on Monday, the 7th. There was no comfortable time to work out a guest list, mail out invitations, and receive responses, but we tried.

En route to 1/6, I paid a call on Col Randy Austin, the regimental CO. He responded to my thanks for the opportunity to command 1/6 with the remark that he had no say in who commanded his battalions. Initially, I took that comment to mean that he had someone else in mind, but later realized he simply made a statement. The assignment of infantry battalions in his regiment was done above his pay grade.

Nervo spoke highly of his battalion while also informing me of its shortcomings. It was a catch all for short-timers and others who could not deploy with their battalions in the deployment cycle. In addition, because 1/6 was not in the deployment cycle, they received what was left of incoming personnel.

With something of a home guard mission, 1/6 did not go anywhere or do anything interesting. The AWOL, drug involvement, and general misfit list was high, but Gene was in the process of cleaning the ranks. CMC's hassle-free discharge of misfits made the process easy. There was no battalion XO, but most other essential billets were filled. Gray had given me what I asked for; this battalion was far from his best in operational readiness.

On the plus side, the 6th Marines were now in the deployment cycle to the 3rd MarDiv. We would shortly receive quality personnel and training because we would relieve 2nd Bn, 4th Marines in January 1983. We had a lot to do and six months in which to do it.

Squad-Leader Course seats within Division Schools had not been filled for the summer class because of the heavy activity schedule; commanders could not free up their young leaders. I had considered dropping the summer course because of lack of students. My last act as the Training Officer was to assign all seats in that course to 1/6. A phone call to Capt Michael G. Whitten, the S-3 of 1/6, ensured that all squad leaders would be graduates of the course. That was one of the best things I did in preparing the battalion for what lay ahead. As personnel would be on maximum leave following the change of command and before we started our train-up, the young leaders would not be missed.

Eleven June came, 1/6 formed up on AP Hill Field, and Gene passed the colors to me. I had attended many of these ceremonies over the past year, each time thinking that mine was coming. The time had arrived, and I searched in vain for some sense of attachment to this grouping of young men in Marine green. I knew from experience that these feelings toward a unit develop over time, but still I felt a void. Something was missing. I reasoned that my problem reflected the quick turnover: there was no time for an emotional buildup, no time to get to know a little about my new command. What you see is what you get; this was my battalion, and I gave them my first order: "March the Command in Review, Sir!"

I was promised the next inbound major as my XO. The PIO at HQMC had asked me to represent the Commandant at the World's Fair in Knoxville over the first weekend in July. While I would have liked to do so, I would not go without an XO to run things in my absence.

Major Earnest A. Van Huss reported aboard during the last week of June. I returned from watching a drill competition to find Ernie waiting outside my office. We talked a while about 1/6 and followed with a rundown on Ernie. I was impressed; I liked his way of thinking and his manner of communicating his thoughts. Ernie and I had the same outlook on life and Marine business; together, we made a strong team.

Captains Thomas F. Western and Jerry W. Honea were recently assigned as Charlie and H&S Company Commanders, respectively. Lieutenants commanded my other companies until current graduates from AWS reported aboard. Inbound within the month were Captains Timothy R. Larsen, Carl J. Ericson, and John Demarco. If schools were a benefit to a command, 1/6 was shaping up.

Hiking (known as humping) was not popular in the mechanized 2nd MarDiv. Recent studies by think tanks had determined (once again[44]) that the foot soldier was obsolete. Foot mobility was deemed to have no place in a war with the Soviet Union. However, if that war should come, Marines would defend and later attack through the mountains of Norway. This action would be on foot, but troop carriers were now getting all the attention. Few units did much hiking at Lejeune in 1982. Unit commitments, available time, and priorities were all reasons not to hike; commanders had more to do than time allowed.

My experience had been that Marine infantry moves by foot, so I put 1/6 on the trail. The main gate was our march objective for our first hump during my second week, with half the battalion on leave. Weekly hikes with increasing mileage and weight became our routine. If we could not do a hike because of higher commitments, I tried to do a run of several miles. My first attempt with the run did not go well.

When all had returned from leave, I moved out at double time with the battalion behind me. Shortly, stragglers lined our path down the Main Service Road and back on River Road. In spite of my extremely slow pace, there were many who were not going to break a sweat. My rear company commander set his own pace and kept his company far to the rear, shuffling along at walking speed. This poor performance by a sizable number of my Marines was my first challenge.

I had talked earlier with each group—officers, SNCOs, NCOs, and Marines and covered what I expected of them, what they could expect of me, and where we were going with our battalion. That talk appeared not to be enough; I needed to use stronger language. There was a lack of spirit, or maybe pride, in their unit and themselves. A quarter of these people would be leaving because they did not have the time to deploy. Some, who had recently joined in preparation for our deployment, had developed no attachment to this battalion or its commander. It was time to get my Marines' attention.

Returning to our battalion area, I held all personnel in formation, waiting for the stragglers. When all had taken their position in ranks, I began, "Before we left on this run, I told you that we were going to do a two-mile run at a slow pace. Any Marine is expected to do as much in boots and utes, especially infantry units. We ran two miles at a ten-minute-mile pace, and some of you could not keep up—you dropped out, you simply quit. Why?

"Only one person, one mind, can make the decisions for this battalion, and I have that responsibility. This means I call the shots; I determine the what, when, where, why, and the how. Marines do not select those things that they want to do. If that were the case, we would never win any battles. This battalion will always win at anything we attempt.

"I will never expect or ask you to do anything that I cannot or do not want to do. As with this run, I will be out there with you, sweating and bleeding if necessary. We are 1/6 and therefore 1/6 will be only as good as you and I. If this is not the best infantry battalion in our Corps today, it will be by the time we deploy in six months. That is my promise to you.

In return, you have to produce, get good at our business of kicking butt, and the way to do that is to do what you are told.

"Now, if any of you don't like what I am saying and the way I run this battalion, you need to come and see me. We will find somewhere else for you to wear the uniform. Any comments or questions up to this point?"

The stony faces did not reveal any progress toward my purpose. I was doing all the talking; I needed a verbal response. That thought brought forth an idea. The word ATTACK was painted on three consecutive steps going into the Bn CP. ATTACK, ATTACK, ATTACK was placed in several other places, causing me to ask why. Somewhere along the way, the words had been presented as the battalion's motto. Initially, I did not care for the manner presented; it was too elementary. At this moment, however, the idea fit; I liked the words. I continued with: "I understand that the motto of this battalion is ATTACK, ATTACK, AT-TACK. I like that, because that is what Marine infantry battalions are all about. We take the fight to the enemy.

"Well, with what I saw this morning I might be short of help if I had to quickly move 1/6 to meet the enemy. You can do it. Our problem is a lack of team spirit and individual motivation. I want to use our motto, to keep it in front of us so that we never forget who we are and what we do.

"From this moment at formations, when I turn the companies over to the commanders, I want to hear you shout, 'ATTACK, ATTACK, AT-TACK.' You will sound off upon the termination of my return salute. Is that clear?"

It was now test time. "BATTALION, TEN-HUTT! COMMAN-DERS TAKE CHARGE OF YOUR COMPANIES AND CARRY OUT THE TRAINING SCHEDULE." I followed with my return salute.

"Attack, Attack, Attack," came the response from something like half of my battalion and not very loud. Some of my Marines were with me, but clearly, the majority was not sold on my intentions.

"That was more like what I would expect from a squad of boy scouts. I want to hear you sound off as though you mean it, that you can attack." The turnover was repeated.

This time was better, at least louder, even if it was from the same number of Marines. Two more times I gave the cue for the response with the last one being acceptable. Probably to get me to go away, the majority was now sounding off. Satisfied that my Marines had a better understanding of what I expected of them, I left the companies with their commanders.

My slow company commander was the next to develop an understanding. He was one of the recent AWS graduates and received a one-on-one with me. His reasoning had been that he wanted to keep his company intact; he had too many Marines falling out. "Good point, Captain, except that you are part of my formation, and I set the pace, not you. You may not always know the mission of your higher commander, who might just have to get somewhere with whatever number that can make it. The pace of this battalion will not be geared to the slower or weaker quarter in anything that we do. Marines in 1/6 will move out or get out."

I would later learn that this otherwise hard-charging captain did not like to run. He was never a run problem after that and became one of my essential officers as well as a strong force behind much of our success.

One/Six Marines became good at moving by foot under a load; we were coming together and none too soon. The Marine Corps Combat Readiness Evaluation System (MCCRES, which all battalions must pass before deploying) was staring us in the face. Block Training was underway by the last of July with mechanized/counter-mechanized warfare and mine demolitions.

Division tasked me with the aggressor mission for the MCCRES of 2/2, which helped me work out the manner in which I would later fight my battalion. Known as OpFor for opposing force, 1/6 moved into the field for three days, 18 to 20 August 1982. Information on 2/2's plans, requirements, and mission was not available; I would first have to find my enemy. My reconnaissance background came into use; I wanted eyes and ears forward.

Captain Kenneth S. Harbin, my S-2, followed through with a plan to organize our Surveillance/Target Acquisition (STA) Platoon into four-man recon teams. These motivated, capable Recon wannabes had a good idea of what Recon types do. Ken and I merely gave them their head, and they ran with it. Ken provided on-the-spot training and deployed the teams. Shortly I knew where my enemy was and what he was doing. I retained that recon capability for my time in command, and those teams proved essential later during our MCCRES and CAX (Combined Arms Exercise).

For the time being, the officials and evaluators of 2/2's exercise hamstrung me. I could not always react to a situation as I might choose. My action had to fit the overall scheme of the evaluated battalion's posture. The MCCRES for the most part was free play for the unit being evaluated. OpFor, however, was held within certain limits and boundaries to ensure that all areas scheduled were fairly evaluated. We played the game and 2/2 passed.

Time was moving too fast: the big events in our near future were the MCCRES, CAX at Twenty-nine Palms, California, and our deployment to Okinawa. Deployment was several months away, but our MCCRES was next. Two weeks after playing OpFor, 1/6 was evaluated. I would have liked more preparation time, but early Monday, 6 September, I moved the battalion into the field at LZ Bluebird.

Monday night found my assault companies in amphibious tractors moving up the New River with a raid mission on a fixed enemy position west of the river and south of Camp Geiger. My command tractor lost power in the river; it could not move fast enough to hold against the current. The amtrac that took us under tow developed engine problems and stopped dead in the water. Great! This was some way to start a war. We would be evaluated on our flexibility, if nothing else.

My company commanders were in the game, however, and carried on. By the time I arrived ashore, they were in their assault positions. With the arrival of first light, my assault hit the enemy, finding most in their sleeping bags. Other than the amtrac breakdown and no sleep for thirty-six hours, we were looking good.

Next was an uneventful movement back to Bluebird. As our return route was obvious to anyone concerned (amtrac movement was restricted by the base environmental policy to certain approved trails), I expected ambushes. Each choke point was covered well with arty and air preparation that should have pleased the umpires. I would like to think that we moved too fast for OpFor to react. Several satisfactory company-size evaluations followed over the next two days while my CP remained at Bluebird.

With one exception, I lucked out with great company commanders. Fresh out of AWS for the most part, they thoroughly knew the infantry business. With checklist regularity, they ensured that all points were covered before each evaluation started. The two non-AWS commanders had been in the battalion as lieutenants and knew what was expected of them. The coming CAX would focus on my weak commander, who managed to lose his national security communications codes during this MCCRES exercise.

The last MCCRES evaluation was a full-force assault on an enemy position of considerable strength. The enemy force was positioned in the northeastern section of Lejeune requiring me to move some distance.

Again, the limited number of trails did not give me many options in the Movement to Contact phase. The OpFor commander no doubt knew my location. If he deployed his force correctly, he could raise havoc with me strung out on the restricted vehicle-maneuver trails. It was time for Ronnie Recon to go to work.

While the smaller unit actions were being evaluated, I deployed my recon teams. Harbin began placing the enemy on our situation map. There were contacts on all trails except the northern loop. My recon teams were compromised in only two instances, meaning that the majority observed the enemy from cover. The two exceptions were both motor patrols taken under fire while moving on trails. OpFor seemed to expect us to take the southern, more direct trails. We would go north. We did and had no OpFor contact en route. Our dawn assault came off in textbook style and the evaluation ended. One/Six did well on the MCCRES, and we were certified ready to deploy.

One month following our MCCRES, we were en route to Twenty-nine Palms. The purpose of the CAX is to ensure that commanders employ supporting arms effectively, use airpower and artillery together without degrading the effectiveness of either. Pilots do not like to fly through air filled with artillery rounds. The enemy gets a break if artillery shuts off while the air is coming on target. Proper coordination and control allow artillery to fire until the aircraft are actually going down for their strike. Artillery then closes the door immediately behind the pullout of the last aircraft, allowing no break for the enemy. While every Marine in the battalion had a role, the people essential to our success were our supporting-arms types. Captains Tim Larsen, my Weapons Company Commander/Fire-Support Coordinator, and Steve Carlson, the Air Officer, put it together and made it work.

Flying out on 12 October, we set up in the desert at Camp Wilson, and continued training. Live-fire assaults supported by live-air and artillery ordnance added realism to our training, and we became deeply involved. Living out in the desert might have had some influence on our involvement; there was nothing else to do. For ten days, we attended periods of instruction on all aspects of fire support, followed with practical application. All of this was preparation for the big evaluation, which was a four-day live-fire exercise with 1/6 in a mechanized infantry attack utilizing all supporting arms to the fullest extent.

Before dawn on Friday, the 22nd, we moved into our assault position behind the high ground of Dime Dingo. At daybreak, and under a rolling artillery barrage, we jumped off in our attack up the Delta Corridor toward Noble Pass. With a company of tanks attached and leading my assault, Charlie covered my right front in AAVs, and truck-mounted Bravo covered the left. Alpha was my air assault element and would go in at H + 8. My command was in two AAV command tractors close behind Charlie.

One/Six's attack was by the book; we did nothing fancy. Aggressors opposed us and kept us honest. For safety reasons, the areas that we worked over with live fire were make-believe enemy positions. Time had to be allowed for the aggressors to vacate their positions before we called in air and arty. My assault stalled at midmorning with my command tractor stopped at the foot of a hill.

Taking a radio and operator, I moved to the top of the hill to observe the battle. Shortly after I arrived at the top, Bravo dismounted and assaulted the enemy position on our left flank that had caused the holdup. I was impressed with the scene below me. My entire front was visible as I watched the tiny figures move about their business.

Carl Ericson's Bravo Marines dismounted quickly and, in the same fluid movement, were in the assault. They were not moving because someone told them to; Carl's Marines moved as though they each had a special purpose, as if this were the real thing. The action below made me proud of my new command.

Ken's recon teams worked the ridges of Bullion Mountain and both sides of the corridor to prevent any surprises. We moved ahead of our attack schedule with events occurring as planned, and it was time for me to exert my influence on events. I wanted my XO to have some of the fun: so I planned to declare myself a casualty on the last day.

The chopper I ordered the evening before arrived as scheduled at daylight on the last day. I flew over to Alpha's position to get a feel for their situation. Umpires had been briefed earlier on the plan that I put into effect upon deplaning with Alpha. The chopper took off without me while the umps informed Ernie that the plane went down, and all personnel were assumed lost. That was all Ernie needed. My plan had two purposes: to give Ernie a chance to fight the battalion, and to determine the source of my Alpha commander's problem.

Alpha's mission was to make an air assault on Noble Pass and hold it until we moved through it. Their umpire had hit the company with heavy casualties from artillery fire because they did not disperse following their air assault. Hours later, they were still on and around the zone, so the umps hit them again. I was concerned about the tactical knowledge and efficiency of this commander. He had just graduated from AWS, so I expected better of him. He was already on my concern list for losing his copy of the national radio code and frequency book during our MCCRES. I saw him as strong on show but short on competency; my talks with him had not gotten results.

Morale in Alpha was not up to that of my other companies, and receiving the air assault mission in this major mechanized exercise did not help, because we did air assaults at Lejeune all the time. After observing the captain's actions, or lack thereof, I stopped talking and decided to do what I could to replace him.

Alpha held the high ground until Ernie moved through. That ended the exercise and Alpha heli-lifted back to base camp. One/Six had done well. Maybe all commanders get the same lines, but many CAX instructors and evaluators told me that 1/6's operation was flawless. They said that we had a better CAX than any before us. We flew home, ready for deployment. No other major event was scheduled between CAX and our flight date.

I talked with Col Austin at 29 Palms about my commander problem, telling him what I had learned. In fairness to the individual, more time was needed for closer observation. My deployment date did not allow that luxury, as I must deploy with competent commanders. My solution was to swap captains with Lieutenant Colonel Andy Beeler of 3/6 upon my return to Lejeune; I wanted Chuck Deisher.

Austin was at Twenty-nine Palms for 2/6's CAX when I approached Andy Beeler, my old C&S College classmate, with my proposal. Capt Charles Deisher had moved from the G-3 Training Office to 3/6. His duty performance in the training office had been superior, and we had served together in 3rd Recon. Chuck had just taken a pass-over for selection to major and was otherwise an unknown to Andy. I felt that I could help Chuck on his next promotion board, and Andy had time to work with my problem captain.

We swapped captains like a couple of horse traders. HQMC assigned all personnel below the commander to deploying battalions, and local commanders had no influence in the matter. I did something for which I had no authority, did not talk loud enough about my intentions at Twenty-nine Palms, and was in trouble for conducting the trade. True, my colonel did not say, "Do it," but he did not say "no" either. Austin, however, made it work; Chuck deployed with Company A.

Smaller tasks filled our remaining days. Some could not qualify as tasks: our Jane Wayne Day was enjoyable, while others, such as the dental check requirement, were a pain. Jane Wayne Day was an opportunity for our wives to learn firsthand what we did and how we did it with as many of our infantry activities as we could conduct in one day. Starting in the garrison area, sergeants formed up the ladies into platoons, taught them drill movements, and marched them in Close Order Drill. Other presentations followed, including chow in our regimental mess.

From garrison, we moved to the field and wrapped up the day with a mech/counter-mech presentation, followed by the girls getting a chance to drive the armored vehicles. Dotti Lu fell in love with the M-60 Tank and handled it as easily as she did our Olds. C-Rations in the field closed out our efforts, which were rated a high success by all the ladies. They each had a better understanding of our jobs.

Six months had made a noticeable difference in the battalion. Those individuals wearing the uniform but not measuring up to the mark of a Marine were dismissed. These undesirables did not go to another unit for further action but home without their uniforms. My ranks were now filled with gungy Marines who would take the fight to the enemy. While my squads were filled mostly with young Marines fresh out of the Infantry Training Regiment, they were ready and led by quality corporals and sergeants. My heavy-handed use of Division Schools was paying dividends.

Maximum deployment leave was authorized over the Christmas holidays. One/Six Marines scattered to the fifty states for their last family visit for six months. Deployment was sweet and sour for me: the thought of leaving my family again was hard, but I would be doing Marine things twenty-four hours a day.

In the past, deploying battalions had dropped from the Lejeune scene on their departure date with little acknowledgement. Their return was also without much fanfare. Low-key movements are needed in wartime, but otherwise, Marines and their families deserved more attention. Why not community recognition upon our deployment to the front lines of the world?

My solution was a parade en route to our division commander's send-off talk. With the battalion in a column of companies on a four-man front, we would march down River Road, pass in front of Division Headquarters, and end up at the Base Theater. The word went out to family and friends, and 1/6 Marines prepared their uniforms.

We formed up at 1300 on 7 January. After a close look, ensuring that our best-turned-out Marines were on the flank files, we marched down the road. There was little cadence call, as everyone was pumped up for the occasion. Six hundred pairs of heavy boots made the cadence; this was our time to shine and everyone had the spirit.

Loved ones, friends, and fellow Marines stood along our route with the heaviest concentration lining the street by the Division CP. General Gray and staff members were on hand for my "Eyes Right" and our pass in review. When the heart is involved, a rehearsal is not needed. I was greatly impressed with my battalion's performance and heard nothing but the same from all who saw us.

Our march ended at the Base Theater where we moved inside for our send-off talk. General Gray gave us his pump-up, building upon what he had observed of the battalion for the past six months. He finished; I called the battalion to attention and asked, "WHAT DO YOU DO BEST, ONE SIX?" Gray was about to step from the stage when the "ATTACK! ATTACK! ATTACK!" hit with a near-deafening response. Though startled, he was clearly pleased with his 1/6 battalion as we shook hands upon his departure. We kissed our loved ones good-bye outside the theater, boarded buses, and headed for Cherry Point for our 2030 flight.

No time is a good time to leave those whom we love, but evenings have to be the worst. The future is dark enough without the blackness of night facing you, and Marines do not have the heaviest load in this unit deployment business. We are doing new and different things in a different place while enjoying an adventurous feeling. Our family members, on the other hand, are left with the same daily routine and an essential member missing. There are daily reminders of this void within the family leadership structure and a constant feeling of disruption, if not loss.

Ernie Van Huss and our Advance Party of sixty Marines had arrived on Okinawa a month earlier and paved the way. Ernie and I had talked weekly about the happenings within the 3rd MarDiv. We were informed of the CG's policy of no facial hair, green skivvy shirts, and doggie-style sleeve-roll-up on the utility jacket.[45]

Some Marines shaved off their mustaches before our flight. Others were taking the hard-line approach: Marine Corps grooming regulations allowed mustaches, and they would not shave. Some Marines, depending upon their lovers' likes and dislikes, had an image to uphold at home. Overseas, away from home, they should not be overly concerned.

Colonel James P. McWilliams was the CO of the 4th Marines and Camp Schwab, the northernmost Marine Base on Okinawa. (He became the S-3 of 1/9 after Major Kennon was killed on Operation Dewey Canyon.) McWilliams met me at Kadena AFB, and I rode with him to Camp Schwab and my new home. Second Battalion 4th Marines was at Kadena ready to board our plane for the return trip to Lejeune; we assumed each other's roles, including the sign-over and acceptance of all organizational gear from weapons to barracks.

MajGen Robert E. Haebel, the 3rd MarDiv CG, fit the gungy mold. He took care of his Marines and expected certain things in return. Of the Old Corps school, he discouraged the growth of mustaches in his division. Wearing green skivvy shirts with the camouflage uniforms made good sense, why have a white flag showing over your chest for a point of aim? As for rolling up the sleeves of the utility jacket, one way or the other did not matter to most of us. Therefore, my immediate problem was the mustache. I chose a frontal attack to solve the problem.

After a triple-ATTACK response from my battalion seated in the Base Theater at Schwab, I warmed up to my purpose. I spoke of all the good training and deployment opportunities ahead for us. "The best battalion on this Rock will get the better assignments, and we know which is the best. We merely have to ensure that our CG knows which is his best. That opportunity is coming up in two days; the general will be here to welcome us aboard.

"We all know the regulations on grooming standards. It is obvious that some of you feel strongly about your rights regarding mustaches. I am on your side when it concerns your presence with your wife or girlfriend. We have left those lovely ladies in the States, so now the issue is simply you liking what you see in your mirror. If it is something else, like a local business girl charging you double fare for her attention because you don't have hair on your lip, I'll cover your additional cost. Otherwise, you had a mustache upon leaving your loved one, and you will have one when she sees you again. Between these times, I ask each of you to shave off your mustaches and do so in time for the general's visit. As a battalion, we stand to gain; we will capitalize on doing the things we want to do instead of sitting on this Rock for six months."

After a pause to allow what I said to sink in, I continued with, "Give me an attitude check, ONE/SIX."

"ATTACK! ATTACK! ATTACK!"

The next day's results confirmed my earlier assessment of the theater talk. All mustaches were gone; my Marines and corpsmen were with me. By nature, Marines do not like things shoved down their throat, but they always come through when asked to do something. In this case, providing the justification also helped.

At 0830 Monday, 17 January, General Haebel was seated on stage in the Camp Schwab theater for his welcome aboard address. I started my introduction of the general with, "The situation is hopeless! You are out of ammo and the enemy is overrunning your position! WHAT DO YOU DO, ONE/SIX?"

"ATTACK! ATTACK! ATTACK!" shouted my Marines enthusiastically rising to their feet. Habel was clearly impressed and welcomed us with promises of interesting events in our future. We would not be stuck on the island. The smooth, clean faces added to his pleasure, and he clearly liked the attack spirit. (He would prove that point on our departure inspection in six months.) He later asked that the attack response be provided upon the occasion of several demonstrations that we conducted for important persons visiting the division.

Company C conducted an amphibious assault demonstration for General Inamuri and Japanese politicians the following Thursday. A week later we did it again for General Murai, Chief of Staff of the Japanese Defense Force. Rehearsals naturally preceded the demo, all of which soaked up good training time. These first two weeks turned out to be typical of our time on the Rock. Serious battalion training was impossible to conduct because of all the requirements placed on us by higher commanders.

Battalion strength, counting the advance party, upon leaving Camp Lejeune was 704. That number included 38 officers, which remained satisfactory, but the enlisted numbers fell far under the mount-out requirement of 85 percent of our T/O. Leaving the States 15 percent under my T/O, I quickly dropped to twice that number missing from my ranks due to housekeeping and support requirements.

The 3rd MarDiv Fleet Assistance Program (FAP, a means of housekeeping at less expense to the taxpayer) drew off thirty quality Marines. These men were lost to me for the entire deployment while they performed division-level duties from rifle range coaches to school instructors. Another thirty Marines were pulled for Camp Schwab base support, such as guard, mess duty, and other requirements, but they were returned to me when we deployed off the island. My problem was that these Marines did not train with us and missed our daily involvement with the issues as they surfaced.

Other draw-downs of my personnel strength while on the island were a rifle platoon assigned to Naha Port for security and rifle company training opportunities assigned by division. In the later category were Incremental Training in Korea for three weeks, the Combat Skills Course in the Okinawa Northern Training Area (NTA) for one week at separate times, and other tasks placed by higher commanders. Planning for these individual company training times, I requested all available leadership and weapon seats in Division Schools.

Personal conduct was a big issue at this time throughout the Marine Corps. Generals Wilson and Barrow had rid our ranks of the problem people, but units were still having a run on unauthorized absences and drug and alcohol incidences. All leaders within 1/6 were in the attack to ensure that we had no disciplinary problems during our deployment. I reached this goal by holding squad members responsible for each other. After all, that is what Marines are all about: taking care of your buddy, not only in a firefight, but whenever he needs you.

If the buddy idea did not work, my procedure was that all alcohol incidents be referred to me. My plan worked. There was firsthand evidence of Marines saving their buddies, usually from alcohol trouble while on liberty.

Our ATTACK response was working well and the battalion possessed and showed great esprit and élan. I went another step with the attack word. I suggested that Marines salute all officers, not just those of 1/6, with the greeting of "One/Six, Sir." Let it be known that 1/6 was in the area, and that the Marine or sailor was proud of his battalion. Battalion officers would return the salute with the greeting of ATTACK, ATTACK, ATTACK. My Marines responded enthusiastically, bringing favorable comments from officers on Camp Schwab.

I continued my humping program with two purposes in mind: no disciplinary problems and keeping all hands in top physical shape. Every Saturday was hump day with a progressive distance to exhaust my young people physically. Tired Marines are not as likely to go out and get themselves into trouble.

We hiked down Highway 2 and into the Central Training Area (CTA). The first march distance was twelve miles, and a mile was added each week after that. Though we were combat loaded with weapons and packs, I ran the battalion periodically for short distances to keep our muscles limber. The run was more of a shuffle, but it rejuvenates lungs and muscles when they stiffen into the walking pace.

Part of the time I carried something from the 81 Mortar Platoon to keep me in touch with the more heavily loaded Marines. On the first hump, I just happened to have an 81mm baseplate on my back at the turn-around point. Individuals continued forward to the turn-around point so I was marching back through the formation while turning the battalion around. The positive response, the "ATTACK, ATTACK, ATTACK" I received while moving back through my entire battalion ensured that I would have an extra load at all future turnarounds. It is good to set the example when and where it can be seen and is especially motivating when Marines are sweating, hurting, or bleeding.

Although we were on Okinawa for only about half our deployed time, we did some humping. We finished our time on the Rock with thirty-mile humps. All were at forced-march speed, four miles per hour, which returned us to Schwab in the middle of the afternoon. Our departure time moved up into dark hours as the temperature rose with summer heat and our distance increased.

My younger Marines enjoyed a quicker recovery time than I; however, most did not leave camp for the rest of the weekend. We all nursed blisters and sore muscles. My real payback was that I had no doubt that my battalion could get to wherever it needed to be, by whatever means, and be able to do whatever had to be done.

One/Six boarded ships on 4 March 1983 as BLT Bravo en route to Korea and Operation Team Spirit. My command group, H&S, and one rifle company went aboard the USS Denver (LPD-9). On 10 March, we arrived off Pohang, Korea, where my staff joined Korean Marines and Navy staff to work out details of the rehearsal. The plan called for two battalions to land in surface assault and two by vertical assault inland. One/Six and a Korean battalion would do the beach assault. The final landing plan was worked out and we hit the practice beach on the 12th.

All went well during the practice landing until the Koreans broached one of their LSTs on the beach and could not retrieve it. In what was obviously a loss-of-face situation, all Korean officers, Navy and Marine, became tight-lipped and less responsive to the requirements of command and staff action. The Korean commander did make a decision: there would be no Korean battalion landing over the beach. One/Six would be the only surface-landed unit. I back-loaded my battalion, and we moved to sea for the approach to the real assault. Now the forces committed at H-hour were one by sea and two by air.

Tok Sok Ri was our assault beach, and we hit it shortly after daylight on the 14th. A collection of important people, including the media, was on the beach. Most were Koreans, and I wondered if there was not a hope among them that the American Marines would screw up. Everything came off as planned, however.

Big white "Fs" appeared on the hulls of the amphibious tractors as they cleared the water coming ashore. The letter preceded the serial numbers painted on each tractor hull, and I wondered about the coincidence of the letter and my last name. Johnny Johnson, my S-4, later confirmed that he had taken the letter from my name while working up the landing tables.

Assault companies continued inland to their initial objectives before dismounting the tracks. Little time was spent in the beach area against the small aggressor force, and the rapid displacement ashore over-ran them. Ground action continued for three days against a constantly retreating aggressor force. The exercise ran its course without any signif-icant actions or events beyond the routine occupation of key terrain va-cated by a retiring defense.

Team Spirit ended but not our time in Korea, and Sunday, 20 March, we began a two-week war on mud. We moved into Muchuk, a Korean Forces base near Pohang that soon became known as Mudchuk. The entire camp compound was covered with six inches of mud churned up by thousands of boots. During our time there the mud nei-ther dried nor increased in spite of rain or no rain.

We lived in tents, had a mess hall, a small PX, and several civilian concessions to accommodate us. However, the second you stepped into the compound or walked out a door, you were in the soft slushy mud. Of course mud stayed on boots and was tracked into the buildings, so we never were away from it.

One way of getting out of the mud was training. We were there for Incremental Training and made good use of the opportunity. Companies moved through the different training cycles set up for the Korean Marines. Rappelling, cliff climbing, rope bridges, rifle/pistol ranges, live fire exercises, and mine/booby trap warfare were some of the training opportunities. I was out of the mud while observing training.

Another out-of-the-mud opportunity was liberty call. Pohang was close and it was a good liberty town, meaning women and booze. A lib-eral liberty policy was in effect, and my one requirement was that all hands conduct themselves as Marines with zero disciplinary problems. If anyone felt the need to get drunk, he was to do so in camp where his buddies could look after him. There were small infractions of Korean law, but we had no problems.

On 6 April we left the good liberty and life in the mud and boarded ships for our return to Okinawa. Three days later we debarked but re-tained the mission of BLT Bravo. This requirement placed the battalion on an eighteen-hour standby for move-out with a six-hour standby for one rifle company.

Marines and corpsmen of 1/6 savored the feeling of an elite within an elite and looked the part. Admittedly, mine was a biased opinion, but I could identify a 1/6 Marine from a distance just by the sharpness of his utility uniform and his carriage or posture. Pride in person and the unit were evident; disciplinary problems remained nonexistent. The hard Sat-urday humps helped, but the overall reason was the concern exercised by individual Marines, policing themselves. We did have a thief in the barrack, however, and Charlie Company seemed to be his area of operations. Money, wallets, and paychecks disappeared; we could not catch him.

Marines in Kansas City later caught our thief. Many months after our return to the States, Marine Finance Center in Kansas City inquired about the validity of a certain gunnery sergeant's endorsement on so many Marine paychecks. These checks had been deposited into his bank account. BANG! The thief was caught, court-martialed, and put away for a long time in Leavenworth.

Our WestPac Deployment was everything I had hoped it would be, with deployments off the island; one was successfully behind us and one was on the horizon. Haebel gave the nod for 1/6 to be the air-landed ground force for the Joint Airborne/Air Transportability Training Exercise (JA/ATT 83-2) scheduled in May.

Assigned as the 35th MAU, the battalion was airborne aboard four C-141s en route to Tinian on 11 May. A Recon team from 3rd Recon Bn's DRP was to jump on Tinian as we flew over en route to the Rota airfield.[46] The big troop carriers could not land on Tinian. At Rota, the battalion would reload on C-130s for their air assault on Tinian.

The Recon team was on my plane for a purpose: I had approval to jump with them. Following the team out the door gave me my first jump from that big plane. This was one of the few times, if not the first, that the commander was on the ground hours before his assault forces. With no enemy to face, the act was easy enough. While Recon did their thing on the island, I waited by the little airstrip for my battalion to arrive.

After landing on Tinian, my rifle companies pushed out in Movement to Contact formations from the airfield perimeter. There were no aggressors facing us so the operation ended early with Marines swarming over the island. We may not have been the first unit to secure the island after the Marine action in WW II, but I would wager that this was the first time that 1/6 maneuvered on the island since fighting the Japanese there during the war. The few inhabitants surely were excited by our presence.

By nightfall, the battalion bivouacked along the airfield on the northeastern coast, looking across the water at Saipan. Living in shelter-halves, we ate C-rations and roasted in the hot sun. There were no shade trees within our camp, and therefore no relief from the intense midday sun except while training: When we could, we conducted our training in the wooded portions of the island that offered some break from the heat.

Rifle platoons were evaluated by MCCRES standards with time for practice and rehearsals. The evaluations ran the breadth of events from patrolling to combat assaults including live-fire. Safety was the watchword, but no holds were barred because we were isolated and someone could get hurt. It was great being on our own little island, but the routine became old fast. We were ready to leave after five days of isolation.

On the 17ᵗʰ, D-day, we assaulted the island of Guam. Bravo conducted a helicopter air assault on Northwest Field, Anderson AFB, and secured the airstrip. The rest of the battalion arrived in C-130s. From there, we attacked down the coast to the Naval Station against aggressors supplied by Marine Barracks. The daily routine of the populace took some edge off our attack, but the aggressors kept us honest. One/Six received good local media coverage, and our attack wrapped up on the second day.

We pitched shelterhalves on the air base and settled in for more training. One difference now was liberty; Marines in camouflage utilities were all over the island. Guam's five-day experience was a much better deal for my Marines, but more quality training was accomplished on Tinian.

Mount Fuji, Japan, was next and still part of the JA/ATT, with the Air Force moving us on the 24ᵗʰ by C-141s. With me tagging along, the Recon team jumped onto the Fuji Training Area. All the thrills of the jump vanished with a hard landing in the thinner air. One/Six landed at Yokota AFB and moved by bus to the Fuji transit-training camp. With the camp as our base, we continued training with major emphasis on firing all weapons on all ranges.

Ernie Van Huss had earlier suggested that 1/6 climb Mt. Fuji while we were there. I liked the idea and its time had come. The mountain was not open to the public, but most of the snow was gone from the top. Rising out of the ground for 12,385 feet, Fuji could not be missed, but it also did not look to be a real climbing challenge. My plan was straight up from our tent camp, which was on the backside of the mountain from the tourist trail.

During the afternoon of 1 June, I hiked the battalion to the base of the cone. That night I conducted a class on mountain climbing, passing on what I had learned in the Korean War. I stressed the importance of the knee lock with each climbing step, which allows muscles to rest while bone supports bone. On 2 June, we went up that mountain.

Leaving our sleeping bags and extra gear on trucks, we started climbing at 0400. Individual march gear included a belt with canteens and a field jacket. Unfortunately, the warm weather at the base caused many to leave their jackets behind for a lighter load in the climb.

Initially, the incline was moderate, and footing was solid; we would be at the top in less than four hours at the rate we were moving. About halfway up, the situation changed dramatically: the incline became steep and the footing was soft, rolling volcanic ash. A twenty-inch step upward moved you less than ten inches because of the slide back. I changed our climbing routine from a ten-minute break every fifty minutes to frequent halts of several minutes; we stood in place and caught our breath. Every half-hour we sat for ten minutes.

Completing three-quarters of the climbing distance, I gave a chow break although it was midmorning. We needed fuel. Climbing became tougher, and while most of my Marines and sailors hung in with me, some could not or would not commit to the effort. SgtMaj Hunt enjoyed the challenge as well as the climb, but much to our disappointment, several staff NCOs quit. Noting the absence of several company gunnies and 1st Sgts on one of my movements back along the line during a halt, I was informed of their early dropout. Company C's sticky-fingered gunny was one of the early dropouts.

Climbing was more difficult, and the incline seemed to be more than 45 degrees. A stride forward did not always move the climber up but ended in a negative gain or loss in the loose, sliding ash. Physical exhaustion along with less oxygen in the thinner air was affecting most of us; I was nearing my limits.

Base Camp radioed HQMC's authorization to promote three of my 2nd lieutenants. At the next break, Ernie and I talked about the promotion, and I decided to do it on top of Fuji. Mentally working up the ceremony helped take my mind off my pain.

Climbing became even harder as we neared the top and the temperature continued to drop. It appeared that we would never make it; each objective we thought was the top while looking upward turned out to be a bump in the slope. Studying the mountain from a distance had caused me to think that a climber could always see the top while climbing. Not so, I learned, as one disappointment after another revealed more mountain yet to climb.

Finally, we circled a few big boulders, and there was our objective. Before me, with a fence around it, was the volcano crater: one big hole in that mountain. We were on top of Fuji by 1100, which gave us a climb time of seven hours. I did not hold a muster, but 80 percent of those who started the climb were there with me. Company commanders had a list of those who dropped out and for what reason with the majority due to exhaustion.

Right off, I was struck by the extreme drop in temperature. Wind on that mountaintop was so strong that a person had difficulty standing, let alone moving. The wind and low temperature made the windchill well below zero, too much for our light field jackets, never mind those who did not bring them. We could not stay; there would be no on-site enjoyment of our accomplishment.

Realizing the urgency of the moment, I collected my officers and singled out the three lieutenants to be promoted. Meanwhile, Marines checked out Fuji, looked down into the volcano crater, and sought shelter from the wind behind boulders. My ceremony included a statement of the Commandant's message and a repeat of the Officer's Oath. The ceremony did not take five minutes, and I followed with the word to move out. One/Six moved off Fuji's summit but not soon enough; I had three hypothermia litter cases. Three Marines were down hard from exhaustion plus the cold and were carried from the summit. Their buddies would have carried them all the way down, but I felt that walking would help restore their body heat. They walked, and the problem went away.

Leg muscles received a full workout that day, between the earlier climbing and now a difficult restraining effort. Holding back developed into a major task: it was tiring and difficult to keep from running. To let loose and run or roll was the natural and easier thing to do. An advantage to going down was that all movement was positive. The ashes slid us in our direction of movement so that a two-foot step moved us four feet. With the steep decline behind us at the halfway point, I let off the brakes, and we did the last half of the mountain in a fast shuffle.

Again, 1/6 had achieved a difficult objective. Major Van Huss ensured that all who made it to the top had the following Service Record Book entry: "He entered the realm of Buddha, faced the Rising Sun and conquered Mount Fuji."

Two days of liberty call followed, with most Marines going to Tokyo where they spent all of their money. Some of us older guys spent that time recuperating. For both reasons, there was very little movement in and around our camp.

Ernie and I decided to hold an officer's Mess Night in the nearby town. We wore utilities, sat on the deck oriental style, and enjoyed to a great degree the pleasures of a unit mess night. The highlight of the evening was a challenge by the battalion XO to wrestle anyone—sumo-style—on the spot. Lt Robert G. Burge quickly accepted, they stripped to bare chest, and got with it. With his closely shaved head, Ernie looked the part of a sumo warrior, and his flair for theatrics ensured our entertainment. Bob held his own in the stage play and the two settled the match as a draw.

Camp Fuji was a fun change of pace from the daily life of infantry Marines on Okinawa. Here we had live-fire exercises and quality liberty nearby when the training day ended. However, those benefits had limitations: we shot up our ammo allowance, and each Marine spent his paychecks and more. It was time to leave.

On 9 June, we flew in C-130s back to Okinawa. Our time on the Rock was running out, as we had one day less than a month to do. Ernie and his Advance Party headed for Lejeune. Other than some humps into the CTA, our training slowed to a mark-time. Inspections of ordnance, equipment, and Marines filled the days.

General Haebel's departure inspection of us was scheduled at 1400 on 1 July. I had the battalion standing tall in a column with companies on line. The general arrived, dismounted his sedan, and approached me as I stood front and center on the parade deck. About twenty paces from me he stopped and asked loudly, "What do you do best, One/Six?"

"ATTACK! ATTACK! ATTACK!" came the instant, thunderous response while I stood dumbfounded. I was about to report but wondered why he was stopping so far away from me. My mind was still working out this change from the expected when the battalion response erupted.

This one was clearly on me. Haebel approached with a chuckle and a favorable comment on the Marines standing before him. We had already passed the CG's inspection. He trooped the lines asking a few personal questions. Liking what he saw, he had no comment on the obvious beginnings of a few mustaches. The facial hair was started in accordance with my earlier position on that issue: grow them back before we go home.

Excerpts from John P. Kalish's (an insurance salesman for American Fidelity Life) letter to General Haebel are provided to give an outsider's view of 1/6:

> In my 21 years as a General Agent on Okinawa, I have never written a letter about a commissioned officer, but I feel compelled to do so now lest my impressions go unnoticed.
>
> . . . In the course of talking to hundreds of his Marines, I heard many stories about Lt/Col Fox. Mainly, they were about this great American war hero and the pride every last man felt about being a member of 1/6. I never saw anything like it in 21 years in the business. I had the feeling that every last Marine would have followed Lt/Col Fox to the very gates of hell if he led the way. . . .

Maintenance Stand-down and rifle, pistol, and swim requalifications filled our last days. Then it was flight time. On Friday, 8 July 1983, we were replaced by 3/6, and we flew east to where our wives and children had been working on our welcome home in the 1/6 spirit.

Excerpts from General Haebel's personal message to General Gray dated 19 July 1983:

> I believe Wes and his guys had about as good a deployment as any I have observed. 1/6 truly hit the island with both feet moving and they never stopped until they departed. From the very outset, everyone here was generous with their compliments concerning 1/6 and the comments remained positive throughout its deployment. . . . One of the techniques that Wes routinely employed was the use of SNCOs, wherein he turned the battalion over to the SNCOs while he and his officers accomplished officer training. It did much to enhance the prestige of the SNCOs and increased even further the mutual respect between both groupings. 1/6 and its commander enriched our division and its readiness posture during their deployment. When you think of leadership by example, you think of Wes Fox. He leads as combat ready an outfit as I have observed during my tour. It was a privilege having them serve with us.

The day following my return, my family and I drove up to the War College at Carlisle for the weekend to check out the housing situation. We also worked in a family trip to Auburn University where Dixie Lee had decided to attend. All the while I had a Change of Command staring me in the face with Marines who deserved to be on leave. The battalion was not a problem, however; my Marines and corpsmen answered the call as they had all year, with spirit, professionalism, and can-do. A couple of rehearsals were enough.

The big day was the 26th, and at 1000, 1/6 marched on WP Hill Field in a way that swelled my heart with pride. They stood for the routine ceremony and heard the old and the new commanders say their unimpressive pieces. One major difference was, when the CO of Troops, Ernie Van Huss, directed, "Deliver the Colors to the Commanding Officer," the battalion sounded off with its most thunderous "ATTACK! ATTACK! ATTACK!" My chest swelled with emotion, and it was good that I did not have to speak, as it would have been futile. Colonel Randy Austin's Change of Command message was read; an excerpt follows:

. . . Under your command, the 1st Battalion has distinguished itself in every activity. In the demanding months that preceded the deployment to WESTPAC, and while in WESTPAC, you led the battalion in a variety of difficult evolutions that included a nearly flawless Combined Arms Exercise, a large-scale Amphibious Exercise in Korea and an ambitious JA/ATT Exercise in the Marianas.

Throughout, you and the Marines and sailors of 1/6 have been a credit to this regiment. You can be justly proud of the success that the battalion enjoyed, and the esprit of every man in it must be linked directly to your efforts—specifically to the example and strong personal leadership that you exerted. . . . I know that you will continue to attack.

LtCol Thomas D. Stouffer took command of my battalion. Not only was I out of a job, but I felt as if I had lost a big part of myself. One/Six passed in review for their new commander and walked out of my life, forever. Thirteen months was all I had, and I would have given much to double that time. If I had it to do over, I would have given up the War College for one more year with 1/6. I feel General Gray would have been agreeable. That idea surely plagued me throughout the coming year.

I had some great duty in the Corps, and I have warm memories of great Marines and mission accomplishments. However, short of my combat units and Force Recon, 1/6 was the best in Marines, activities, attitude, morale, esprit de corps, and you name it. Gungy 1/6 had it all. In thirteen months we covered much ground and did it all the Marine Corps way. When the young American is motivated to do something, it is done and the doing does not take long. In less than six months, privates and lieutenants joined 1/6 and were ready and eager to take on all comers. They proved it to the 3rd MarDiv for six months. I found it very difficult to turn loose of that magnificent warhorse, more so because I had a major play in the building of it.

A Meritorious Service Medal for my tour with 1/6 would catch up to me months later at the War College. That MSM would be my first peacetime award. End-of-Tour Awards were part of the New Corps: Marines now expected to receive medals for doing their job.

The War College was waiting, and I moved into the next chapter of my Marine experience, again a student. My household relocated in base quarters at 588 Sumner Road, Carlisle Barracks, Pennsylvania. This was our one assignment close to Dotti Lu's home, but the pleasure had been taken away by the death of her mother the summer before. Being close to her family members during that time helped her adjust to her loss.

I had a major adjustment problem also. Student life was like dead stop in the water after the fast pace of 1/6 in both divisions. Classroom time was mornings only, leaving the afternoons for individual study, reading, research, and thinking. Well, that just was not enough activity, and I found that I had not mentally detached from the 2nd MarDiv.

After the frustration of not being able to talk by telephone with anyone in 1/6 because they were in the field, I called General Gray. I was that desperate: I have never called a general officer just to pass the time of day and to find out what was happening. There was no relief from his office either, as he was also in the field. After several weeks I adjusted somewhat to the slower pace of the classroom, only to have the Beirut barracks bombing and the Grenada invasion take place. Grenada was particularly hard to sit through, as that was just the operation for my 1/6.

The school year started with a load of material to read for background. Other students had received their reading packages four months earlier, while mine had not caught up with me by the first week of school. There was no way I could catch up, but I skimmed the surface.

I found that I could think about military matters just as well while lying in ambush for groundhogs. A nearby farmer gave me standing permission to diminish his abundant groundhog population, and I spent many afternoons doing so. Deer and bear hunting seasons also provided relief from the boredom of study. It was great to hunt with my in-laws on a resident hunting license. Pennsylvania is a sportsman's paradise, especially if the game protector is your brother-in-law. I did not get a bear, but I did bag a deer during muzzle-loading season.

The short school days came and went; we had some good speakers, and we worked some worthwhile seminars on worldly issues. We fought the Soviet Bloc Forces in WW III, and the computer declared us the winner. I wrote the required papers, did some community speeches as is usually requested of a local Medal-of-Honor holder, and was the guest speaker for the Camp David Detachment's Marine Ball. The year went by fast enough, and then it was time to be concerned about my next duty station.

This was one of the few times when I had not identified a preferred assignment. Joint duty was getting a buildup, and the word was that it was needed for promotion. I went to HQMC to find out what was available. My monitor, LtCol Joe Dwyer, shot down joint assignments because I did not have a tour at HQMC. In other words, I could not speak the party line. He wanted to assign me to Headquarters, saying that the experience would be good for my career.

"Probably true, but what are my options?"

"Well, as you just had a FMF tour, I have to assign you to an identified Top Level School (TLS) billet, and there are not that many available after taking away Joint Duty."

"Do you have anything at Quantico?" That base was far from my first choice because of the jobs available to lieutenant colonels, plus the fact that I already had two tours at Quantico. Joe really had my attention; I had spent thirty-four years as a Marine without duty in the Head-shed, and I did not want it now. I would take most anything, anywhere.

"Yes, let me check. I believe there is a TLS billet in the C&S College open yet." Joe made a phone call; the job had not been filled; and I could have it. The day would come that I would regret that choice.

We graduated on a pleasant and comfortable summer day. We wore uniforms for the occasion after wearing civilian clothes in the classroom all year. Seven other Marines graduated with me. Only one of the eight, lawyer Gerald L. Miller, was later selected to brigadier general rank. We moved into Quarters 334 at Quantico.

My billet requiring a TLS graduate was Head, Battle Studies and Strategy. I should have predicted the consequences; the job would not have been filled if I had not asked for it. Proof of this statement is the fact that the job was not filled one year later: it was deleted from the school's T/O. Reason: There was nothing to do.

LtCol Don Bittner had a doctorate in military history, and as the college's historian, taught Battle Studies. Fully capable LtCol Burt Quist covered the strategy studies, which amounted to several classroom presentations. Students did not get much out of either course, and both instructors were locked on to their subjects. Neither they nor their courses needed a "Head" to coordinate, negotiate, or hold their efforts together.

That C&S College tour was not good for my career as a future promotable Marine officer. As my job was not demanding, I did not sit around before and after regular duty hours in my office reading newspapers and smoking cigars, as did certain other individuals. I did not fill space for the sake of show. When my den members went home, I went home, and we came in at the same time. I learned later that the Director, my Reporting Senior, was taking note of who were his space fillers.

Meanwhile, I felt that I was contributing to the college mission within the bounds of my job description. We instructors were in the bullpen together, to share and help each other. I volunteered to give presentations in support of the operations sections. Other than one class on reconnaissance, I never received an offer. The gunfighters were slow to accept help from the history and strategy guys; there appeared to be a bit of turf protection in play. I failed to read the signals that sharing and working together was out; the in thing was making oneself look good.

The only good thing about my year at the C&S College was the student body. Young, motivated majors, the pick of the Corps, kept me in tow. They, the students, were organized into conference groups, known as dens. I had a great group, and as the den daddy, I found my job both motivating and interesting. Some of the young stallions in my den were Majors William A. Whitlow, Jan C. Huly, Lee F. Lange, Jan M. Durham, William M. Charles, Zackery Forrester, Michael W. Sullivan, and James N. Strock. The benefits of my assignment ended there, however.

Counseling sessions for our semiannual Fitness Reports came up in November, which in my case covered a four-month period. The Director, an aviator, started mine off with, "You will get your regiment; you are a quality Marine and deserve that position." He followed that statement by expressing his desire to help those officers who had been hurt on their Fitness Reports by his predecessor. He did not dwell on that issue but went on to read to me what he had written in my Section C. His reading was flattering enough, and I never returned him to the obvious: to help some on their Fitness Reports has to be at the expense of others. Excerpts from his long, detailed Section C:

> . . . extremely dedicated, totally honest officer. His professional
> demeanor and obvious dedication to the Corps establishes
> immediately the ultimate in rapport with juniors, peers, and
> seniors alike. A team player, orientated to the accomplishment of
> the mission in every respect, he excels in building high morale
> and enthusiasm. . . .

What this director did not address with me was his ranking of lieutenant colonels. His words meant nothing considering his spread in 15a, Estimate of this Marine's General Value to the Service. I was marked with three others in the box between Excellent and Outstanding; there was one mark of Excellent; and eight were marked above me as Outstanding. Those eight, I suppose, were the ones that needed the help; they were also the office space fillers, for the most part. I learned these facts several years later.

A highlight of the year was my winning the Marine Corps Association's Major General Edward A. Wilcox Award for professional writing.

My final paper at the War College was on command and leadership and I titled it "On Leadership." Feeling good about my work, I sent it on to the Editor of the *Marine Corps Gazette*. Colonel John F. Greenwood USMC (Ret) printed it after working with my grammar and changing the title to "Herringbones, Boondockers, and Leggings."

The article was printed in the July 1984 *Gazette* which later judged it the best article published that year by the professional magazine for United States Marines. I needed that plug for my writing ability. I wrote several more articles for the *Gazette* over the next three years. John can make anyone's writing look good, and he also impressed on me the thought that maybe I had something about which to write.

Still unaware that my situation with the C&SC was career negative, I was surprised when the Director told me that General Hudson (MGen John I. Hudson was the Director of the EdCtr) wanted me to take over the Staff NCO Academy. My response was negative; I liked my conference group of young majors in spite of the Battle Study and Strategy job. Several days later I was informed that General Hudson wanted to see me; I would have to tell him that I did not want to head up his SNCO Academy. I reported; if the general wanted me as the Director of the Staff NCO Academy, I wanted the job. June would be the changeover, so my den members and I would depart at the same time.

The months passed and it was time for the required counseling session with my send-off Fitness Report. As with the first report, the director read to me what he had written in Section C, full of flowery words but death where it counts. Considering this report, it is a wonder that I was selected for colonel. The spread now was one marked Excellent, two of us marked between Excellent and Outstanding, and ten marked as Outstanding. Except from Section C:

> . . . Despite a continual flow of new problems, instructional packages and additional Division Head responsibilities associated with the second half of LtCol Fox's first year he has provided sound direction and guidance to his more experienced subordinates. In addition, he has concentrated his efforts in organizing, coordinating and developing a completely new day-long presentation titled "Battlefield of the Future. . . .

Our school year closed, and on 7 June 1985, I relieved LtCol James Williams as the Director of the Staff NCO Academy. I had earlier accompanied Jim on his inspections/visits to the other two Staff NCO Academies located at Camp Lejeune, North Carolina and El Toro, California. The Directors of those two academies received guidance from the Quantico Director. We would be the last officers to hold these positions.

All major command NCO Schools were also under the academic supervision of the Quantico Academy. We provided the Program of Instruction to ensure a Marine Corps–wide knowledge standard. Quantico was responsible for keeping all seats filled within the seventeen NCO schools.

Thirteen officers helped me run the Academy; three of them were majors. Major Gary C. Allord was my Deputy and helped me get into the saddle. Two sergeants major, two master gunnery sergeants, 1st first sergeant, one master sergeant, seventeen gunnies, and four staff sergeants rounded out the instructor assignment. SgtMaj Bernard P. Ross, another gungy Marine, was my favorite academy sergeant major.

My physical fitness scores dipped at this time. No longer was I mastering a perfect score, although I took the test each time students or permanent personnel were tested. Pull-ups and sit-ups were no problem for max points but the run cost me. I could not do the three miles in less than twenty minutes. Even at that run time, few finished ahead of me. My goal was to get my time down to six-minute miles, but I did not work at it hard enough. There were plenty of distractions.

Family activities kept me involved, especially with the high-school scene. I suppose the father of three beautiful daughters ought to expect as much. Amy was on the Queens Court for Homecoming at Quantico High. I was getting good at this duty, as Dixie Lee had been the Queen at the same school. Amy graduated in 1986 and enrolled in Southern Seminary College in Buena Vista, Virginia.

The academy work and atmosphere were enjoyable, and I put my heart into my job. Initially of the opinion that the Staff NCO Academies were nice to have, I came around to feeling that staff NCOs should attend. The Marine Corps was still recovering from robbing the staff NCO ranks of their best 5,000 for the temporary officer program in 1966. The most capable individuals, who performed the daily leadership tasks at the action level, had been lost. Probably most important was the loss of positive role models for the young NCOs coming up the ranks. Many less effective individuals who moved into these important leadership slots gave the impression to young NCOs that all one had to do to be a senior sergeant was to show up and collect a paycheck.

My opinion is that the Corps would have fared better with SNCOs leading and fighting their platoons and companies in Vietnam than with making them lieutenants. Leadership would have been where it was needed, and equally important, young NCOs would have had positive role models.

Along with weaker SNCOs was McNamara's Project One-Hundred-Thousand.[47] Because of Corps-wide disciplinary problems (to which I feel the lower category Group Fours were a major contributor), officers were directed to perform what had been SNCO responsibilities. Higher commanders, including CMC, issued directives requiring officer presence in the barracks after working hours and in all places where Marines collected, including the nearby towns. These actions reduced the SNCO authority and command presence. Over time, this requirement became the norm as junior officers advanced in rank and continued the policy. They expected and required their subordinate officers to be in the barracks and to look over the sergeant's shoulder, if not do his job. Sergeants came to expect the lieutenants to be always on hand for order, discipline, and decisions. Middle-level leadership by sergeants took a back seat.

This leadership problem of the 1980s was not caused entirely by the temporary commissioning and McNamara's project, however. The Corps had changed from my staff NCO days when I learned the NCO role and duties. No longer was the staff NCO a twenty-four-hour Marine; he did not live in his unit's barracks or even in the Staff NCO Quarters. Lost to the Marine was the staff NCO's constant touch and the benefit of an hourly role model. His seniors were not on hand to show him how or to suggest solutions to the ever-occurring middle-level-leadership problems.

My Marine Corps had become a commuter force. Not only were the staff NCOs married but most of the NCOs and too many rank and file Marines maintained a home and family. The Corps had become on the order of an eight-to-four job, maybe six-to-six in many situations, but my point is that now another life shares most Marines' twenty-four-hour day. Marines now have families and homes to share their time, interest, and responsibilities. At some point in his day, a Marine sheds his uniform and picks up his other life. He is no longer in a daily continuous learning cycle within the Marine environment. The things I learned on the job (including in the barracks after working hours and on weekends) about performing staff NCO duties now needed to be taught in the classroom. Thanks to the many good schools brought on board for the SNCO (unheard of before the Vietnam era) and awareness on each commander's part, our Corps has recovered and developed a strong SNCO corps.

I traveled to all major commands and talked of the importance of our training, visited with our Mobile Training Teams teaching at distant commands, and kept HQMC moving toward requiring completion of course work for promotion. Staff sergeants had to complete the Career Course for promotion to Gunny, who in turn had to complete the Advance Course before selection to 1st or Master Sergeant.

During his turnover, Jim Williams had presented the idea of staff NCOs running their Academy and their professional education. The idea grew on me, and I began to work it. BGen Gene A. Deegan, Director of the EdCtr, was all for the idea, as were these involved at HQMC. I began placing staff NCOs in positions to support that idea. An example was the officer assignment at the Quantico Academy for my second year, which had dropped to three field- and three company-grade officers. The senior staff NCO numbers increased to five E-9s and six E-8s. Then I began a search for three sergeants major to fill the three director billets.

Three factors determined the field of sergeants major for the Director positions: command potential, availability to move, and personal desire. The final selection board was convened at Quantico where David W. Sommers was selected for the Quantico Academy, Ronnie A. Chamberlain to receive the helm at Camp Lejeune, and Carl O. Stucker at El Toro.

After all that fuss and bother, Sommers only lasted a month, as he was selected as the Sergeant Major of the Marine Corps. I was never sure if that was a step up or down. He was great as the Corps' Sergeant Major, but as the Director, he would have done great things for staff NCO education.

On the home front, my family enjoyed living on the hill, but it was that time again; we were due for a move. I visited my monitor at HQMC, hoping to influence his decision on my next assignment. As I had been selected for promotion to colonel, the colonel's monitor would move me. I was surprised to learn that I was due again for an unaccompanied overseas assignment, meaning Okinawa.

The six-month deployment with 1/6 did not give me a new tour date but only added a year to my old one. I never had a chance to get another six-month tour with the 2nd MarDiv. Now I was looking at twelve months added to the six still fresh in my family's memory. "What are my options, Matt?"

LtCol Matthew E. Broderick, the Colonel's Ground Monitor (also selected for colonel) responded with, "The Fleet Marine Officer job with 2nd Fleet will be open. Skip Sweetser has his two years in this summer and will move. Fleet Headquarters is aboard the USS Mount Whitney and based out of Norfolk. I understand that the ship seldom goes to sea but it is still sea duty. Two years of sea duty will cover your unaccompanied overseas requirement. Do you want to talk with Skip?"

"No, I know Skip; if he is doing it, the duty is right for me. I'll take it."

Getting credit for an unaccompanied tour while walking to my office aboard ship sounded too good to be true. I did not want another year away from my family, and I did not need any more time on Okinawa.

Several house-hunting trips to Norfolk determined one fact: we would have to buy. Navy housing had close to a two-year wait for 0-6s, and we could not find any decent rentals in good school districts. As in the past, Dotti Lu had done her school search well, and we focused on the top three high schools. We bought a house on Timberwood Lane in Virginia Beach, and Niki would go to Cox.

The change of directorship was conducted in the Breckinridge Auditorium, and SgtMaj Sommers took the helm of the Academy. Staff NCOs were now completely in charge of their professional military education. General Deegan frocked me to colonel in the same ceremony.

A point of humor to some and a shock to me came during the receiving line, which we quickly set up outside the auditorium entrance. My friends came through the line with congratulations and handshakes. One good friend decided to give it a little Al Gray touch. MajGen Robert F. Milligan shook my hand and at the same time with his left hand firmly slapped one of my collar eagles.

Deegan and Dotti Lu, after inserting my eagle pins into my shirt collar, had not placed the clips on the pins. My pain must have been telegraphed as June Milligan immediately reprimanded her husband. I pulled the insignia from my flesh wondering why he did that. Then I realized that he was as surprised as I was.

Lessons Learned

1. A battalion of Marines is not too large a unit for the commander to enjoy personal involvement in unit activities.
2. When a commander communicates with his Marines, they will respond, give up, and do without in spite of the sacrifices to themselves—because he asked.
3. If your billet or job can be dissolved upon your departure, maybe you ought to speed up the process.

14
Colonel of Marines
096702/9906/0302/9953

1 May 1988

I reported to the Commander, US 2ⁿᵈ Fleet, at the Norfolk Naval Base
on 12 June 1987. Vice Admiral Charles R. Larson also wore the NATO
hat of Commander, Strike Fleet Atlantic, and was located with his staff
aboard the Amphibious Command Ship, *USS Mount Whitney* (LCC-20).
The *Mt Whitney* was referred to as the USS Never-Sail, but during my
time, that name did not fit. A fast-paced schedule started with my arrival and before I had my family settled. This was my sole career experience of leaving before unpacking our household goods and settling
the home front.

Skip Sweetser encouraged me to attend a planning session at
NATO Headquarters in Brussels, Belgium. Job continuity required that I
attend although Skip would be the key player. That pace did not slacken
for the next two years. If the ship was not involved in an exercise, then I
was off to Europe on a planning phase for the next exercise or observing
a Marine Expeditionary Unit Special Operation Capable (MEUSOC)
exercise at Camp Lejeune.

My job identifier was N-342, Plans, and I was responsible for setting
up and planning all Fleet exercises. My shop was within the Plans and Exercise Section, or N-34, which was under the N-3, Operations. Two Navy
commanders and one Army lieutenant colonel worked with me. All of
the N-34 officers, usually numbering about ten, shared office space.

In port, the *Mt Whitney* tied up at Pier 25, which gave me a commute time of half an hour at 0500 going in and an hour or longer returning home in the evenings. Usually the staff would depart around
1500, which gave us a head start on the rush and shaved thirty minutes
off the homeward travel. Aboard ship, I enjoyed a single room with head
and shower on the 01 level. I was a member of the Flag Mess; breakfast
and lunch were served on workdays in port, and you paid whether you
ate or not.

Teamwork-88 (a major NATO biennial exercise in defense of Norway against a Soviet threat) was the big focus in the near future; everything was geared to and paced by that exercise. Also, we were involved in five other annual and semiannual exercises. As if these exercises were not enough, we also fought with computers in war games at Newport, Rhode Island. Our enemy was always the Soviet bear. Other national exercises were FLEETEXs (Fleet Exercises) and MEUSOCs.

Exercise Teamwork planning usually took place at NATO's AFNORTH (Armed Forces North) Headquarters located in a security bunker deep under a mountain in Norway. I logged many miles on PanAm Airlines working out the planning details.

Returning from Brussels with Skip, I had a week to settle my household before going to Newport for my first war game. Dotti Lu had not waited for me to place our home in order; our household goods were unpacked and our home functioning. The Soviets did not win the war game, and I returned home for a couple weeks. Next was a Caribbean tour, compliments of the Marine Corps, for colonels recently assigned to FMFLANT. We flew in a C-9 to Cuba, Puerto Rico, Panama, and Key West and spent several days in each place receiving briefings on the local US strength and weakness in light of the Soviet threat.

One week later we sailed on Exercise Ocean Safari, catching Halifax and the Grand Banks on our way to the Vestifjord in Norway. Arriving in the fjord, I flew by chopper to the Forrestal where I was catapulted in a COD for the flight to Bodo, Norway. I got my feet on the ground, looked around, and met with the planners and exercise officers involved. The return trip rewarded me with my first arrested landing. While routine for Navy people, carrier flights are special events for most Marines.

Typical of our exercises, we capped this one off with port visits to Plymouth, England, followed with three days in Lisbon, Portugal. Luck was with me, as I had to attend a Teamwork meeting in Oslo immediately following Lisbon. That caused me to miss the boat ride home and have to ride PanAm again. Tough but somebody had to do it!

The first three weeks of October were spent in port with time at home. Then the *Whitney* got underway for the Virginia Capes for a couple of days while I attended a Teamwork-88 conference in Little Creek, Virginia. October went out with me returning from London, having attended an FMF Europe conference involving Marines with whom I would work in that quarter of the world.

January 1988 started at the normal pace with most 2nd Fleet headquarters heavies (principle officers from the admiral downward) in Newport for war games. We had not much more than started when Haiti hiccuped with a leadership change. Second Fleet went on Stand-By, and we left the games with the attitude and fanfare of going to war, while our game contemporaries were stuck with the computers. Larson directed the *Mt Whitney* to get underway for the Caribbean via the Florida coast where we joined the ship sixty miles off Mayport.

Other service planning groups arrived aboard to include the 2nd MarDiv guys that included Ernie Van Huss. Ernie's abilities and efforts made the planning task easier for all of us as we got down to the business of planning for the "What ifs" on Haiti. The issues were: how would the fleet evacuate the US citizens, and what might we do to preserve or restore civil order? The collected talent worked around the clock and came up with several acceptable plans that gave the commander options to suit the situation as it developed.

All of those candle- and diesel-fuel-burning hours were for naught, as the Haitian government handled its affairs. American lives were not threatened. After several days, we steamed for Norfolk with a port visit in Nassau. I missed the port visit because I had to observe the MEU-SOC Exercise taking place at Lejeune.

Spring and summer of '88 went by with the normal planning conferences and exercises. Dixie Lee's graduation from Auburn helped to break up my work routine. Another break from the norm was the 2nd Fleet Change of Command.

Vice Admiral Jerome L. Johnson relieved Larson on 11 August. This was my only time standing in Navy ranks, and I had something to learn. All personnel were formed up on deck in three formations: enlisted, officer, and one made up of O-5s and O-6s of the fleet staff. The N-3 was front and center of this third formation. All three formations were given Parade Rest in preparation for the talks with no following commands.

I stood at Parade Rest (Marine style) while everyone else shifted weight, scratched butt, and wiped noses at will. Even working with the Navy, I was surprised at their lack of knowledge of or respect for commands. We were not given At Ease, which the command should have been. My muscles were stiff when I did move an hour later, but Marines know the position of Parade Rest as a modified position of Attention; one does not move.

Teamwork-88 had been on the horizon and my focus for so long that it did not seem right when its time came. On 26 August 1988 the *Mt Whitney* churned out of Norfolk Bay, formed up the carrier group, and headed for the North Sea and the Norwegian coast. Commanders played games listed as Free Play in the waters between Iceland and England while our force took on the NATO flavor. Ships from other nations joined the combatants, one side or the other. Continuing north, we rehearsed the amphibious landing in the Trundheim area, then moved into the Vestifjord.

Operating in the Arctic Circle, BGen Jack Sheehan's 4th MEB hit the beach doing the Marine thing, while I was stuck on board the *Whitney*. I did get ashore to visit with Marines, but that did not fulfill my need. Clearly, I was a staff pogue no longer involved with action at the front. I had to suffer with white sheets and tasty, hot meals.

The land, sea, and air exercise came off with no problems. All NATO operational objectives were achieved, and the exercise ended as scheduled on 21 September. Debriefs and critiques known as Hot Wash Ups follow NATO exercises. However, the Wash Up was not scheduled until after several port visits. Different ships sailed to different ports: the *Mt Whitney* (with the influence of COMSTKFLTLANT) drew Keil, Germany and Copenhagen, Denmark, but my time in Copenhagen was soaked up attending the Post Exercise Debrief taking place in that city. Our third port visit was Portsmouth, England, where I left the ship to attend the Teamwork Hot Wash Up in Oslo. A planning conference on the coming Exercise Bold Guard 89 was scheduled in Oslo following the Wash Up. These two meetings caused me to miss the *Whitney*'s return again.

A FLEETEX in the Caribbean, a SOCEX at Lejeune, and another planning conference in Oslo finished out the year. Planners were already working on Teamwork '90 while we had a full schedule of operations and exercises scheduled for the spring of 1989.

President George Bush's inauguration was the first major event of the new year, and Dotti Lu and I attended with the members of the Congressional Medal of Honor Society. While inaugurations unfold for the Society with a more or less normal routine, Bush's was different in several ways. First, he was a warrior; he had been there and related easily to members of the Society. In addition, attendance of our membership was noticeably higher, and I believe all attended who were physically able.

My time with 2nd Fleet would end that summer so I took advantage of being in the Washington area and visited my monitor at HQMC. Ross Brown, ground colonel's monitor, quickly closed the door to my first choice of duty. Second Fleet time counted as FMF time, and I was now due for post and station duty, making an infantry regiment at Lejeune not an option. My FMF time was over, forever; it would be several years before I realized that fact.

TBS was my next choice of duty, but I allowed that I would be happy with OCS. Ross thought that I had a good chance at either, and I left with the impression that he would focus on TBS as my first choice. Somehow, my choices were turned around. (Several months later Ross would call me aboard ship with the news that I would get OCS and seemed surprised when I asked why not TBS. He inferred that CMC wanted me at OCS, and I never learned what shaped the results at the commander bargaining table.)

The big naval exercise of the spring was North Star; it would take the fleet back into the North Sea. Preceding the big exercise was FLEE-TEX 2-89, conducted in the Caribbean; it moved the *Mt Whitney* out of Norfolk on 9 February. A port visit at St. Martin followed the Fleet Exercise, and the *Mt Whitney* continued northeast for the North Star Exercise on 24 February.

While underway to North Star we played the computer and radio war game of WINTEXCIMEX, killing two birds with one stone. The computer game took the boredom out of the sea travel in that it kept us busy, and we met the requirements of the war game at no cost to family time. The computer war game ended in time for us to move into the play of North Star. For me, North Star amounted to keeping the admiral abreast of what the Marines were doing ashore. Staff work inside a ship does not give one much of a feel for action; one day is no different from the next, and in that manner, North Star ran its course. The exercise ended on 17 March, followed by a three-day port visit to Antwerp.

While at sea, my physical fitness routine amounted to working out in the gym with the universal weights and running on the *Whitney*'s weather deck. Running on steel decks probably was a negative gain when bone-joint damage is considered, but there were no fresh-air alternatives. Running in circles was not motivating; the ship was big enough, however, that twenty laps gave a good run, especially at a fast pace.

On the family side, 1989 was a benchmark year. Dotti Lu worked with a Virginia Beach surgeon, Dixie Lee was a Flight Attendant with Delta Airlines, Amy became Mrs. Andrew Hill and the dependent of a Naval Flight Officer, and Nicole graduated from Cox High School and was accepted at the University of Virginia. The Fox household would again relocate.

Colonel Raymond P. Ayres Jr., the CO, Marine Barracks, Guam, received orders to replace me. Ray rented our house, which made my departure easier by not having to dispose of it. The summer of '89 was busy enough with a PCS, settling into another home, and learning a new job. Ray's 30 June arrival time in Norfolk influenced my departure date, as my job required a contact relief. Compounding that problem, my new billet also required a contact relief and Colonel Claude W. Reinke, whom I would replace, had a report date of 10 July in the 3rd MarDiv, sooner than I could get away from 2nd Fleet. Summer is a heavy work period for OCS, and Claude and I needed time together for the turnover. I made it work by driving back and forth between Norfolk and Quantico.

Three days at Quantico during the latter part of June gave me a feel for Claude's duties and responsibilities. Then it was back to the ship for Ray's arrival and turnover, which took several days. Change of Command at OCS took place on 7 July so that Claude could meet his schedule, only I was still in Norfolk. I drove to Quantico to assume command, followed by a return to Norfolk to pack up and move my household.

Our new home was Quarters 351, which had been scheduled for renovation and sat vacant for several years. No work had been done on the house due to lack of funds; it was cleaned, a fresh coat of paint applied, and we moved in. As might be expected, we had everything that goes with an old, vacant house, from a broken steam pipe to a backed-up sewer. I did not need the home front hassle along with the OCS summer schedule. Dotti Lu tried to manage the home affairs, but the house problems were ongoing.

A top priority was to settle my family in quarters so that I could give full attention to my mission of screening and selecting the future officers of the Corps. LtCol Norm Wiggans, the OCS XO, made my task easy as he ran the command superbly during the commander transition. Norm is one of those country boys who, like Ernie Van Huss, has the facility for keeping a finger on the pulse of a unit and taking instant corrective action before most of us have a hint of a problem. Norm was good for OCS and me.

One hiccup did occur early on the job when I went home to move packing boxes and lay carpet so that Dotti Lu could finish unpacking and get the house functional. My day had started with reveille in the candidate barracks at 0500, followed with candidate PT and a good run over the Hill Trail. About 1000, my assistance was required at home. As the day's schedule was light with academic activities, I told Norm that he was in charge and I would be at my quarters until mid-afternoon.

About 1100, I received a call from a headquarters captain; a brigadier general was in the CP. The general wanted to have lunch in my mess hall with his nephew, a candidate undergoing evaluation. Another captain had told the general that he could not do so, following which the general wanted to talk with someone in charge. Of all of the times to be away from my post! I told the captain to pass the phone to the general. This Marine knew his way around OCS; I told him to enjoy his meal.

After my departure that morning, Norm had attended the base's monthly staff meeting concerning housekeeping affairs. Had I known of that meeting, I would have waited until Norm returned before doing my home work. Anyway, there was no commander's reception for the general's surprise visit. After lunching with his nephew, this general (a personal friend) stopped by my quarters to greet Dotti Lu and caution me on my lackadaisical approach to command. He was not around, however, when I tucked my young candidates into bed at 2200 that night. Eighteen-hour workdays do not leave much time for the other things requiring a Marine's attention, and short of combat assignments, my family's needs are not far down in my pecking order.

LtGen William R. Etnyre was the CG of Marine Corps Combat Development Command (MCCDC)[48] and liked to drive through my area. OCS was high on his show list for VIPs, active duty Marines, those no longer in uniform, and non–Marines who liked to see us in action. Two good entertainers were the Tarzan and the Combat Course. The Tarzan consists of a series of ropes up in trees over which candidates move and ends with a cable Slide-for-Life over a pond of water to the ground. The Combat Course is a series of obstacles and rope bridges to include a muddy creek that candidates must negotiate, mostly submerged underwater, within a specific time. No one obstacle by itself is difficult for most candidates, but to complete them all properly within a decent time is a workout. With freezing temperatures thrown in, most found the Combat Course a challenge.

Major Mike Winter[49] was my S-3 and Operations Officer. All SNCOs and officers assigned to OCS were top quality, which made a tough job easy. Each summer I was augmented with more quality hand-picked Marines to do our task of screening and evaluating.

BGen Gary E. Brown was the Director of Personnel Procurement Division, HQMC, and I paid him a visit for my marching orders. He spoke my language and made it plain and simple: "Keep those candidates whom you feel will make good officers and send the others home. The more you send home, the harder my people must work, but if they do their job correctly in the first place, we all gain."

While TBS had been my first choice of duties, OCS quickly convinced me that I had the better duty of the two. TBS may be more prestigious because of size and popularity; it has the important mission of educating and training our lieutenants. OCS, however, decides who those future leaders will be and sets the mold for their thoughts on the requirements of a leader of Marines. I eagerly responded to the task with leadership by example.

Shipboard life had not allowed me to prepare for my new task, a fact that hit me hard during the first PFT after my arrival. Our Change of Command ceremony had doubled with the graduation ceremony of the first six-week increment of the summer. The second and last six-week increment of the PLC and Bulldog[50] candidates was aboard and ready for the Inventory PFT. I elected to run the test with a Bulldog Company and maxed the pull-ups and sit-ups along with more than half of the candidates. Then we moved to the grinder (parade field) for the run where I did my usual by starting behind the group. The three-mile run course was four laps around the parade field and the headquarters area.

Last was my start position and there I stayed. The body of runners quickly narrowed as the faster candidates moved ahead. By the time the lead runners made their second 90-degree turn at the south end of the grinder, I was only halfway down the field. I was bothered by the distance between the slowest candidate and me; he was leaving me farther behind, the first time ever in my experience. One lap, two laps, and I wished that I could just disappear quietly between the buildings. Physically, I was hurting; there was no more speed in me and the gap grew. Worse, the lead runners began lapping me. Finally, I ended the pain with a twenty-four-minute run-time, two minutes behind the last runner. Changes were in the wind; I would not embarrass myself like that again, and I would be involved in all PFTs.

I hit the OCS running trails with a purpose; my time improved but six-minute miles were beyond my reach. I continued my warm-up runs before the time started, but they no longer gave me the desired edge.

Many PFTs are conducted at OCS during the summer schedule. Each company does an inventory and a final PFT for the record. While my aim was to do the PFT with each company; one per day was enough. I ran with one company for the inventory and caught the sister company for their final PFT. In addition, OCS conducted two OCCs and five NCO School classes during the other nine months of the year. I enjoyed running the PFT with the NCOs, as there were fewer antelopes in the group, and I moved nearer the lead.

OCS running trails have to be the most enjoyable in the world. They wind through the shade of the OCS forest and along the Chopawamsic Bay water. Trails are graded and packed with stone dust that provides a malleable impact surface. Deer, turkey, geese, and other birds and animals constantly add interest to the run. Then there is the infamous Hill Trail with no grading or stone dust. The Hill Trail lies in its natural state with only the boot wear of many thousands of officer candidates marking its trace. Interest in animals encountered on the Hill Trail is reduced by the hurt of the pull on the four major hills encountered. After hearing about the OCS Hill Trail for forty years, I finally met it. I loved it.

The toughest job for me at OCS was telling a young man who wanted very much to be a Marine that he did not fit the officer role. It happens in the next-to-last week at OCS, known as the Commanding Officer's Board. This is the last step for a candidate on his way out of OCS without the coveted commission. The route to the commanding officer is through the sergeants, the captain of his platoon, then to the company board headed by the commander, a major. By the time a candidate reaches the CO, the commanders have a long list of reasons why he/she should not be commissioned. Very few came before me as physical-fitness or academic failures; failure to show leadership potential was by far the most common candidate weakness.

A candidate's leadership potential is evaluated to identify those without, or short in, a take-charge personality that causes others to comply. Platoon staff, consisting of two staff sergeant drill instructors, a platoon sergeant who is usually a gunny, and a platoon leader with the rank of captain, live with their candidates from reveille to taps. They note who does what, when, and how. Candidates are evaluated while filling all leader positions within a company, from fire team leader to company commander. Who has the respect of his peers, who gets response from them, who accomplishes the mission?

Results are documented and filed. Another evaluation that I considered closely is that of his peers; how do they see this candidate? Ratings like 16 of 16 and a justifying statement that ends with something like, "I would not follow this candidate to get a drink of water," make a point, especially when all fifteen members of that squad make the same point. Yes, he is or will be a college graduate, but does the Marine Corps need him as an officer for three years? Of equal importance, I feel, is concern for that individual. Which is the better plan for the future of this young man or woman: To change now to something that he can handle, or play Marine for three years and then start his life forward with something at which he can succeed?

OCS has many courses and exercises that challenge young men

and women to come forward and move others when they have no en-
ergy or motivation left to continue. These evaluation tools include the
Combat Course, the Battle Fitness Test, Endurance Course, Leadership
Reaction Course, and Small Unit Leadership Evaluation I and II (SULE
I & II).

SULE-II is an excellent identifier of those who do not have that
which we seek. Candidates are awakened at midnight and moved out on
an eight-mile forced march followed by two days of constant movement
with little sleep and time to eat. They function as members of squads and
fire teams in the attack on different objectives all over the OCS wooded
hills. Each candidate is evaluated on his performance as a leader within
those unit actions. Each fire team hikes from the boonies to the Reaction Course at Brown Field (two miles each way by the trails) for a leader
evaluation. Only one member is evaluated at a time, meaning that they
make that fast hump four times in addition to the ongoing field evaluations. The fourth trip in on the last day really taxes the leader of the spent
team, as he must work hard at receiving an acceptable response from his
team members in accomplishing his mission on the Reaction Course.
The other three have been evaluated, they are exhausted, and they have
lost interest in what is taking place.

SULE-II easily separates the leaders from the followers, and ends
with all candidates knowing that they have handled a tough assignment.
Marines in my time did not need a pocket card to remind them of what
they had endured or of their future obligations and responsibilities to
their fellow Marines and their Corps.

Drop on Request (DOR) is the term for those who decide at OCS
that the Marine life is not for them, and this category usually equals the
leadership failures. DORs come along at all times, as do those candidates
who do something to raise questions about their integrity. If a candidate
wants to DOR, he normally comes to the CO during his fourth week
of a six-week or the seventh week of a ten-week program, states his reason, and is gone when the paperwork is completed, usually in about two
days. A few refuse to stay the minimum required time, and I see no benefit to the Corps in requiring them to do so. A good example is two candidates who on their arrival day refused to get a haircut; they were going
home and would not need a haircut. (More on these two birds later.)

An integrity case is completed quickly. Because of the need for
leaders with unquestionable character, any question concerning someone's integrity brings the subject candidate before the CO. A few (about
one in five hundred) do something like allow their eyes to rest on

another candidate's test paper. The biggest temptation appears during the PFT when a candidate might inflate his number of event repetitions. OCS sergeants are always observing, looking, counting, checking, and verifying. Doing fifty sit-ups and reporting sixty to the scorekeeper is a sure ticket home.

Some candidates touched me with their statements about their integrity, how they just did not think, they forgot, it was an accident, it would never happen again, and how badly they wanted to be Marines. We all have weak moments; however, six or ten weeks do not allow much time for observation of the true person inside the candidate uniform. Claude Reinke impressed on me the importance of allowing no second chance for an integrity violation during the candidate's time with us. While the OCS acts when a candidate's integrity is merely called into question (proof is not a requirement), administration is quick and simple. All integrity cases go through the full board sequence with the subject facing his accuser and speaking in his defense.

As all cases in my experience involved lying and cheating, there was not much room for a defense. He did or he did not! All candidates were fairly warned: they received the word during my welcome aboard talk as well as each company commander's and platoon leader's talk: "Don't do anything to raise a question about your integrity. To do so is an automatic drop at the time, no excuse accepted." I also felt that several candidates used the integrity issue as a quicker exit than the DOR.

A command visit to Parris Island gave me some ideas for additions to the OCS way of doing business. I brought the concept of team pugil stick fighting to the OCS woods. Selecting a small hill with a trail on each side, we built a bunker on the hill for focus. Candidates in numbers of one to three were sent from both sides simultaneously to engage at the bunker. The meeting engagement was full flurry with pugil sticks.

One side might send up three fighters to find only one from the other side. (Because of the hill and woods between them, neither side could see the other's commitment until they met face-to-face at the bunker.) Numbers alone did not always determine the winner. Many times a single fighter won against three by maneuvering to keep one between him and the group, taking them on one at a time. Candidates loved the mix-up on the hill.

Parris Island, with Gen Etnyer's encouragement, also influenced me to do something for candidate parents. Most parents arrived Thursday for the Friday morning graduation parade so I set up Family Day for Thursday afternoon and presented my Command Brief and the

OCS movie in the base theater. Candidates were then released to their parents with guidance to visit the Marine Corps Association bookstore, the Museum, and the Marine Exchange. After dinner with their parents, the candidates returned to their barracks. I received many favorable comments, written and verbal, from family members, especially those who had attended an earlier OCS graduation. Family Day added a family touch that serves our Corps and country well, and I give my thanks to the leaders of boot camp for showing me how.

The mission of OCS was to determine who might make it as a Marine Corps officer, but I felt that there was something missing in the process. We did the determination part well enough, and along the way provided the candidates with some education on Marine basics. The problem was that one day the candidate was handled worse than a private and the next day he was a lieutenant, an officer and leader of Marines. Other than what he might gain from professional chats presented by his Staff Platoon Leader on one end of his barracks (and these chats were limited to the motivation of his platoon leader), he bridged the gap alone through trial and error. Something was needed before he checked in at TBS.

I developed and presented a lecture on the Marine Corps Officer that quickly grew from one to two-plus hours. Following are some of my main points:

Leadership is one thing and rank is another; do they automatically go together, or can a person have one without the other? Bill Christman's story followed as a motivator and attention gainer. Bill had both rank and leadership, and I gave examples of how he led his Marines. Bill was blessed with natural leadership, but I believe good leadership can be learned, practiced, and exercised. Learning leadership includes knowing what others expect and like to see in their leader. For Marines, a leader is someone who cares about them, communicates with them, and sets a good example, one who sweats and bleeds with them.

My main theme was the importance of good individual character, including principles, integrity, and ethical standards. Personal interest conflicts hound many high-powered politicians, judges, and other highly placed leaders; the Marine Corps Officer is and must remain above that. A man's word is his bond. A Marine officer does not lie under any circumstances. There is no middle ground or gray area in the meaning of integrity. You do or you do not; you will or you will not. The same idea fits the rating of loyalty: you are or you are not loyal to your Marines, your Corps, and your country.

My talk included the conduct and appearance expected of officers; he or she is always a gentleman or a lady. On duty or off, an officer is always presentable. In the Marine Exchange on Saturdays or anywhere and anytime you encounter a Marine officer, you see a clean-shaven, well-dressed leader, not a bearded someone in shower shoes and shorts. Our society is in dress decay but not our Marine Corps community. The Marine officer wears the uniform or a businessman's attire, not jeans and a sweatshirt while traveling on a commercial carrier and under official orders. Regarding tattoos: back in the fifties I understood that you could not be commissioned in the Marines if you had a tattoo. Do officers need ink stamped into their body today? Have we lowered our standards? A Marine's tattoo is his war wound.

My approach to duty places the officer's care and concern for his Marines as his top priority; he is their leader, teacher, provider, and disciplinarian. He must ensure that he and his Marines are always prepared to go into harm's way at a moment's notice in our national interest, to accomplish the assigned mission. I talked about the Pusan Perimeter situation when other forces ran before the North Korean T-34 tanks because the 2.6 Bazooka could not stop them. That same Bazooka in the hands of Marines stopped those tanks. They simply waited in their fighting holes until the T-34s rolled over them, then fired into the tank's thinner sides and rear.

I spoke of the Marine captain in Beirut, Lebanon, who stopped an Israeli tank platoon from going through his checkpoint with a caliber .45 pistol. That captain placed his pistol against the defiant tank platoon commander's head and impressed him with the fact that he was a dead man if he tried to move his tanks through that checkpoint.

The Marine Officer is an optimistic, sentimental fighter who makes the tough decisions and moves out. He is a winner, a member of the First Team, and "part way" or "almost" does not suit his style. He joins the ranks of a tight band of brothers who live by a well-defined code. He is an accomplisher, as expressed by the phrases, "The Marines Have Landed and the Situation is Well in Hand" and "Tell it to the Marines." He never leaves a fellow Marine on the field of battle, and he takes care of his own. He will find his job difficult and demanding, but then he would not be a Marine if he found it otherwise. Roosevelt's statement of raising the Marine Corps strength to 600,000 for the war against the Japanese brought this response from his Secretary of the Navy: "Are there that many men in these United States good enough to be Marines?"

We are always proper and correct. Vulgarities are not used and their use by Marines is discouraged. The naval language is ours—use it. Notice that I use the word Marines instead of troops. Why? Does not the word Marines better identify those to whom we are referring? (This resulted in the word Marines being placed over the word Troops on all base-installed traffic warning signs in the OCS area: "Marines on the Road".)

★ ★ ★

From 1988 through 1991, OCS alone determined who would be a Marine officer. Thanks to Colonel John Ripley, the Senior Marine at the Naval Academy, and James Webb, the Secretary of the Navy, the last loophole missing in OCS determination of qualification for a Marine commission was closed. USNA midshipmen who chose the Marine Corps had to complete the six-week Bulldog program with NROTC midshipmen. Justification included the fact that academy midshipmen were behind the power curve at TBS compared with other lieutenants. In short, they were not Marine Corps oriented in everything from uniform wear to tactics. Ripley and Webb should know; they went the academy route.

On the negative side were the Canoe U alumni, including Marines, who felt that two screening courses were unfair to the individual. Their real objection, I feel, was allowing another institution to select over the academy's product, and the Navy having to commission Marine rejects. By 1992, USNA midshipmen choosing the Marine Corps were required only to attend a familiarization course at OCS. Academy Marines would recommend those midshipmen who should be commissioned to CMC.

We can make anything work. Most midshipmen who became Marines before the OCS requirement did well, as did those commissioned during this OCS era, and so will those who follow, whatever the screening process. Some go the distance and some do not. The issue as I see it is the individual: what is in his or her best interest? Would a study show that a greater percentage of midshipmen who were screened by OCS continue with a full Marine Corps career, if desired?

Over the years, I had served with academy officers, and they did not stand out in either direction. Now at OCS, I had midshipmen who wanted to DOR and others presented to me as unsuitable for a Marine commission during final boards. NROTC units and the academy provided the officers and staff NCOs who screened and evaluated the candidates of Bulldog Companies; OCS staff did not do this evaluation. These companies held their boards, the platoon staff presented their findings, and the company commander made the decision: give him a change or send him up to the colonel.

When candidates came before me, I knew the staff had given up on them and wanted them gone. The captains presented strong cases, backed up by their major, which was usually good enough for me. (This held for all OCS Boards.) Each candidate was given a chance to speak, and at this stage, he or she knew how they stacked up with their peers. Midshipmen before me, I felt, had the greatest reason for leaving OCS. They were intelligent, capable, and willing; they just fell short on the personality side. We did not see the leadership potential they needed to be successful in the Corps, and we did not need technical officers. These young people could have a successful technical field in the Navy where their talents were needed.

OCS, at the time, provided real-life examples. Three USNA graduates were on my staff and in professional trouble, two captains and a 1st lieutenant. All three were considered twice by their promotion boards, not selected, and released from the Marine Corps. Two of these I rated highly, and I received top-quality work from them. One captain was my Adjutant and the lieutenant was Head of Academics in S-3 and directly responsible for bringing OCS into the computer age. Both officers would have had a long and successful technical career in the Navy. A fair screening and evaluation system benefits both our Corps and the individual. Of course, the counter to my position is that all cannot be promoted up the leadership pyramid anyway. Yes, but when talking with a young man, I am interested in him and his future. What is in it for him?

A few candidates, some with tears in their eyes, stated how much and for how long they had dreamed of being Marines. Those were tough decisions: concur with my officers who knew the capabilities of this person or consider his or her feelings of what being a Marine meant? Seldom did I go against the commander's recommendation on the final board. I focused on convincing the wannabes that their best interest was served by taking their education and strengths into something in which they could do well. If I had a fault at OCS, it was that I did not always listen to my captains. Sometimes the candidate's statement of wanting to be a Marine worked on me and I allowed him or her to be commissioned. I have often wondered what percentage of those given the chance made a worthwhile contribution to the Corps.

Candidate Kurt pointed up my captains' competency during final Boards of a Junior PLC. I agreed with the company recommendation and sent Kurt home in spite of his emotional statement of losing his childhood dream. Kurt's father, a former Marine, later wrote a motivating, informative letter regarding his son's continued work toward preparing himself for the Marines. I remembered Kurt's plea during my Board action and responded with a strong recommendation for Kurt to return to OCS during the following summer's PLC Junior Class. He did. In five weeks, Kurt was again before me with the recommendation from a different company staff that he lacked the required leadership potential. Kurt was a great follower, he would do anything that anyone hinted needed doing, but he could not tell anyone else what to do. He handled the stress of OCS poorly, and his peers saw him as a man with no force or command presence.

General Brown at HQMC had not been concerned with my attrition, which continued with its historical average of 36 percent. Brown's replacement focused on the high black-candidate attrition rate of 55 percent. The facts on this rate dealt directly with whom OCS received as candidates.

Officer Selection Officers (OSO) were pressured to enroll African-Americans, who were also heavily recruited by industry, business, and politics. Graduates with the best potential and capabilities were siphoned off by big-money offers while the Marine Corps came along offering a uniform and a hard time. Except for those who truly wanted to be Marines, OCS received what was left after industry was satisfied with its numbers. In addition, some of those sent to Quantico did not want what OCS offered.

I mentioned earlier two candidates who reported and refused to get a haircut because they were not staying. They were two black men who bought the OSO's line about Marine officer's life, did not see it that way at Quantico, and wanted out. Other than suggesting that they live up to their commitment, I did not keep them.

That high black attrition rate caused some to look at OCS with an eye toward racial prejudice. If anything, it was in the other direction. Sixty-four percent of my drill instructors were black. First off, I feel that my DIs were fair and cut only those who did not show leadership potential. The prejudice might come from black DIs not wanting some future black officer embarrassing their race with incompetence. From my position, those whom I sent home did not stand a chance of making it at TBS, let alone as an officer. TBS is a good barometer of the success of OCS.

Up through my time at OCS the Basic School lost a student lieutenant now and then because of involvement with alcohol or some other conduct reason. Seldom was a lieutenant's commission revoked because he could not handle the TBS load or because he wanted to quit.

Someone later decided that OCS was wasting assets; attrition was far too high and should be reduced. OCS's focus, if not its stated mission, changed from screening and evaluating leadership potential to training entry level officers. Attrition moved to TBS.

It appears to be in everyone's best interest to have the quitters out sooner, reducing the expense to the individual and the taxpayer. In addition to the higher attrition rate, TBS recycled lieutenants through the course. If they failed, they repeated it until they got it right. Can these recycled lieutenants possibly provide future leadership by example? How many chances will they get to lead their units out of something like the Chosin Reservoir?

My problem with all of this concern for attrition has to do with thoughts on "A Few Good Men." Are we at the point that we should keep all who come to try the Corps on for size? Have the words "A few good men" come to mean "anyone who wants a paycheck"? A bachelor's degree alone is not proof that one is qualified to lead, motivate, and inspire others, particularly Marines. He graduated from high school, so he has what it takes to be a Marine? Will training at Parris Island give him the intestinal fortitude to do those things Marines before him have done? When crossing the beach on Iwo, walking out of the Chosin, or humping the A Shau Valley, it is too late to identify those who cannot function under extreme stress. Even normal OCS screening does not catch all who should not be commissioned: example, Rutland in Company A on Operation Dewey Canyon in 1969.

The following comments from the CG's letter to a father typify the average candidate dropped from OCS during my time. This father, a prior Marine and a big guy in the FBI Academy, could not accept the fact that his son did not pack the gear as a Marine Officer. After exhausting several political strings with me,[51] the father wrote to General Cook[52] who responded with these facts:

> The record of the board proceeding includes the following:
> —He failed the night compass course, Combat Course, Reaction Course, Small Unit Leadership Course #1 and failed to complete the obstacle course (twice) due to rope climb failure.
> —He had been a run straggler (three times), performed below average on the weapons and the tactics exams, received 15 unsatisfactory interview sheets ranging from lackluster performance to failure to follow simple instructions, and failure of the Platoon Sergeant's personnel inspection.

—His performance as a squad leader resulted in an unfavorable evaluation noting a lackluster, timid, and confused candidate.

—His appearance before Col Fox was confused, slow, and timid with a notable lack of self-confidence and bearing.

—He was ranked 18 out of 18 by the members of his squad.

—He was ranked 57 out of 57 by his Platoon Commander on his command evaluation.

This candidate's comment to the board was that he came to OCS unprepared and that fact had caused him to lose confidence in himself.

Should this young man be included as a leader of "The Few"? Not on my watch; I owe him a chance to look for something in which he can or at least might do well. He will never make it as a Marine leader, and if we keep him around, how many others might he take down with him?

Leaders must be able to reason and make rapid-fire decisions under extremely high-stress situations. OCS is not the final evaluator, but it is a good start. If a person cannot handle the OCS load, he will not be a leader of Marines. Two years at TBS is not going to change that.

I will close the attrition situation with this letter from Waukegan, Illinois:

Dear Colonel Fox:

I would like to thank you for all the consideration given to me during my brief five-week stay at Officer Candidate School. As you may or may not know, it was entirely my idea to join the United States Marine Corps, a decision I do not regret even though I passed up many better paying positions to do so. I will always respect you and your efforts in following the United States Marine Corps tradition of wanting just a few good men.

I consider your program at Quantico especially good for people like myself who when exposed to what the United States Marine Corps is really about can bow out gracefully by being dropped out of the program.

If I am ever in a position to help a Marine or the United States Marine Corps, I will do so. I will always consider my experience at Officer Candidate School as a positive experience. It increases my appreciation for people who choose to serve our country in the United States Marine Corps.

Sincerely,
JML

★ ★ ★

Graduation days are big events at OCS, not just for the candidates but also for parents and friends. A parade starts the day at 0900 and is followed with a commissioning ceremony in Little Hall auditorium at 1300 for the OCCs. Of course, the PLC and Bulldog candidates depart OCS following the morning parade; they have school yet to complete. I learned quickly the value placed on OCS events by the families of candidates.

My first summer wrapped up with companies graduating in late August, and the day broke with rain having fallen throughout the night. As the rain continued intermittently, I held off canceling the parade. At 0815, I walked outside to get a feel for the rain situation, cancel or go? The bleachers in the reviewing area were already filling with people in spite of the mist blowing over Brown Field. If the parents did not mind the rain, a Marine was not going to say it was too wet. Do it!

Although the mist and light rain saturated our clothing, those parade attendees exhibited great enthusiasm for our purpose. Candidate performance was an order of perfection: rifle carriage was exact, all movement smart and distinctive, and all commands given with the voice of authority. As the lead company completed its last left turn to approach and pass in review, spectators in the stands rose and came forward onto the drill field. The spectator surge forward was so strong that I feared they would be in the path of the oncoming companies. The march route was crowded, but no spectator was trampled.

Three changes were implemented after that parade: First, ropes were placed forward of the bleachers to prevent spectators from crowding the marching companies. Second, I devised a scheme to introduce the staff of each candidate company. Up to this point, the Marines responsible for these future Marine officers were lost in the crowd, usually standing around to the rear of the bleachers. I directed the staff, one company at a time, to march on line across the drill field to our direct front and halt at fifty yards. Our narrator introduced each Marine as he stepped off to the rear of the VIP stand. There was a formal thank-you with applause to each name and position called, from the company commander to the last sergeant. Third, a tent cover was placed over the VIP stand. While the tent over me might appear contrary to my idea that the leader should share life's rough spots with his Marines, that rainy parade convinced me that the CO's guests did not have to suffer. I shared the elements, as I was forward on the parade deck anyway, awarding outstanding candidates, trooping the line with the Reviewing Officer's inspection, and standing for the Pass in Review.

Our commissioning ceremony included our Reviewing Officer from the parade speaking as our guest in Little Hall. He followed his words with the presentation of awards and graduation certificates. The CO of OCS wrapped up the ceremony by giving the oath of office to the group, less those who were to be sworn in individually by a family member or friend.

Before giving the oath, I quoted it one line at a time, giving my interpretation of the words as I understood them and discussed their meaning as follows:

"I DO SOLEMNLY SWEAR. If the use of the word swear bothers you, you may use the word affirm. Your sincerity and dedication are sought and the meaning is as important as life. You should expect that life, your Marines' and yours, to possibly one day be at risk by accepting the responsibilities of this oath.

"THAT I WILL SUPPORT AND DEFEND THE CONSTITUTION OF THE UNITED STATES. Note that your oath is to support and defend our constitution, not some individual, group of people, or any other idea. You will defend our constitution, that was given to us by our forefathers and preserved with their blood, that document that gives us our way of life and our freedom.

"AGAINST ALL ENEMIES, FOREIGN AND DOMESTIC. Your oath focuses on enemies of our constitution, foreign enemies that you may confront on foreign soil, as has been our national good fortune for over a hundred years. The enemy is easily identified with manner, purpose, and dress. Our Corps's history is full of such campaigns and meeting our enemy has never been a problem for Marines. Note, however, that your oath acknowledges the possibility of a domestic enemy, one who may do us more harm as he works from within. Drug dealers are an example; you may well be involved in combating this enemy.

"THAT I WILL BEAR TRUE FAITH AND ALLEGIANCE TO THE SAME. Not only will you fight when fighting is called for, but your every word and deed shall support our constitution and its ideals. You shall live by our constitution with your every action and thought. Your Marines will better understand our constitution through you.

"THAT I TAKE THIS OBLIGATION FREELY, WITHOUT ANY MENTAL RESERVATION. It is your desire and your decision to be a leader of Marines, to support and defend our constitution. You have no doubts about that fact. There has been no push by someone who wants you to be a Marine more than you do.

"OR PURPOSE OF EVASION. Accepting your commission is not the lesser of your options; you are not accepting this commission in order to avoid another obligation or responsibility.

"THAT I WILL WELL AND FAITHFULLY DISCHARGE THE DUTIES OF THE OFFICE ON WHICH I AM ABOUT TO ENTER. Your office will be those young Marines placed in your charge. Always have their best interest foremost in your mind and heart. Take care of them, provide for, teach, train, and guide them. Never forget that when you do right by your Marines as their leader, they will charge right up the enemy's gun barrel for you with a moment's notice and never ask why.

"SO HELP ME GOD. These words need no explanation, but for me, I equate them with my vows to my wife—until death do we part. As United States Marines however, death does not always part us immediately. Despite the difficulty, the pain, and further death, through the snow fields, from the depth of jungles, and across burning sand, Marines bring their dead from the field of battle."

I followed with asking if there were any questions regarding the oath or if anyone was not ready to give their oath at this time. "Candidates, please stand. Those who are to be given the oath by someone else following this ceremony do not raise your hand or repeat after me; all others raise your right hand. Will our guests please rise for the oath." In unison and with looks of deep sincerity, my candidates repeated after me one phrase at a time. The guests' applause and response to the oath was so long and loud that I began to wonder how to turn them off. My new lieutenants loved it.

The following is taken from a Northbrook, Illinois, father's notes and states the situation best:

> . . . Arlene and I went to the commissioning ceremony on December 8, 1989, at Quantico. It was a terrible day with snow and cold, but the weather did not make any difference. What I want to try to do is to convey to you the best I can the sense of pride and emotion that I saw that day. Visualize with me an

auditorium filled with families and young men in winter green uniforms. There were 160, more or less, of more than 200 who had started over two months earlier. You could feel the motivation and dedication that existed in that room. You could literally feel the pride coming through when they swore their oath to serve and protect our country from all enemies, foreign and domestic. It was one of the most moving experiences I have ever known. The pride that showed in all their faces at being Marine Officers had to be seen to be understood. You also have to have been through it to know the pride in Mike that Arlene and I felt when we pinned his lieutenant's bars on for the first time.

★ ★ ★

Saturdays are full workdays during the OCS summers, and 4 August 1990, a Saturday, rolled around with me not giving much thought to it being my fortieth anniversary as an active duty Marine. I would be in the field most of the day, so I wore an old set of jungle-camouflaged utilities rather than the later Woodland style; I would not be on stage. BGen P. K. Van Riper, Dpty Cmdr, Trng/EducCtr, had called the evening before asking that I come over at 0800 to discuss the academy midshipman issue. The discussion led to my reading a report on the issue that he had prepared for CMC. Did I have a problem with any part of it? About 0850 the aide entered to say that LtGen Cook wanted to see Van Riper immediately.

Our discussion terminated, I headed for Brown Field with the intention of joining my candidate companies in the field. On the way, I thought it odd that an earlier neighbor, BGen Butch Neal, now stationed at HQMC, passed me with his wife, Cathy, going toward Brown Field. I knew something was up when I crossed the railroad tracks to see a Marine directing traffic at the intersection as though we were having a parade. My driver made an unexpected left turn instead of driving straight ahead to my CP, and I was surprised to see candidates in formation and people in our reviewing stands. My driver continued with a purpose right up to the reviewing area where Butch and Cathy were dismounting. BGen Sheehan was seated in the rear row of the VIP stand; he answered my question of what was going on with: "Your Commanding General is up front waiting on you."

Still without a clue, I noted the stand was full of friends as I headed for Cook. Dotti Lu and my daughters were seated in their normal parade seats. "Sir, you are supposed to be in your CP. General Van Riper is on his way to you," I reported.

"Hey, Wes, we are having a parade in your honor and you are holding it up. Have a seat so that we can get on with it."

Five candidate companies were lined up on the drill field to our front. The formalities began with Van Riper speaking; he then passed the mike to me. Starting with, "If this affair was for my benefit, why should I work by having to speak?" I gave my thanks for everyone's time and interest, reviewed some highlights in my life since riding that milk truck to the recruiting office forty years earlier, that morning, and remarked about how quickly forty years passed. Then there was "March the Command in Review." Dotti Lu was escorted to my side for the Pass in Review. I must admit that I loved it, even if it did mess up a day of screening and evaluating. A reception followed under tents erected behind the VIP stand.

★ ★ ★

Our Command and Staff College faculty presented a battle study on the Dewey Canyon Operation in the Vietnam War. A commander at each level was invited. They included: Gen Richard G. Stillwell USA, CG 24th Corps; Gen Raymond G. Davis, 3rd Division Cmdr; Gen Robert H. Barrow, 9th Marine Rgt Cmdr; MGen George W. Smith, 1st Bn Cmdr; and me as a CoCmdr. The students spent several days studying the battle. During the morning of 1 June 1990, we commanders each gave a talk about our experience, and the afternoon was given to questions and group discussions. Our presentation and the battle study were rated so highly by the students that we were invited back for the next five years. Our last presentation on 2 June 1995 was taped for future use. Guess we old commanders were getting too costly for the college, and the death of General Stillwell two years earlier had broken up our team.

★ ★ ★

OCS is great duty unless war clouds are on the horizon. Because of the possible need for a personnel increase, the personnel acquisition and training pipeline is frozen initially. Saddam Hussein did his thing and there I sat while all Marines everywhere headed for the Middle East. I did not get excited about missing any action because I felt that it would not happen. The war cloud did kindle community interest in the warrior and brought about many parades and speeches when it was over.

Front Royal and Harrisonburg, Virginia, both asked me to be their Parade Grand Marshall and give a talk. I accepted and took along my OCS Drill Team as an element of their parades. We provided a Marine Rifle Squad moving in the Approach March formation with fire teams shifting through their combat formations. In combat dress, Marines carried squad T/O weapons at the ready, and the crowd loved them. Dotti Lu and I also participated with the Medal of Honor Society in the big victory parades in Washington, DC, and New York City that summer.

My time at OCS saw the heaviest national-guest-speaker demands of my career. Many of these engagements were with NROTC units in universities all over the nation, and Mess Nights and Marine Corps Birthday Balls usually were the occasions. Other organizations such as Don Williams' Texas Association of Former Marines in Houston, Texas, invited me for several visits.

★ ★ ★

Outstanding officers and SNCOs serve at OCS (My Sergeant Major Alford L. McMichael, later SgtMaj of the Marine Corps is a prime example), but they need help to do 85 percent of their annual work during three months of summer. Twenty-five captains from AWS and six majors from C&SC augment OCS each summer. NROTC units throughout the country send in the staff, both officer and enlisted, to cover the Bulldog Companies. SNCO and Sgt DIs come on temporary duty from units aboard Quantico where they are assigned with the expressed purpose of spending their summers at OCS. The system works because of quality personnel, but does it have to be this way?

I developed a level-loading plan where OCS could do its business with its own permanent staff. Summer candidates would be only PLC Juniors and ROTC Bulldogs. PLC seniors would be ordered to OCS after they graduated from college. Ten-week PLC classes would also report sometime during the year following their college graduation, which would make them no different from an OCC that would be scheduled only during the nine months after summer. As it is now, all PLCs, ROTCs, ten-week PLCs, and usually an OCC go through the three months of summer. Normally, there is one OCC in the fall and one in the spring, but the spring OCC dropped out on me one year. OCS is the sleeping giant nine months of the year.

Why was my level-load plan not accepted? HQMC, meaning the budget people, like to commission most of our officers just as the fiscal year ends to save Y-months of Z-number of lieutenants' salaries. No one has figured up the cost of running OCS the way we do, but I doubt that we save any money. Level loading would create less personnel turbulence and hardships, but hey! "We are the Marines. It is not supposed to be easy."

My three years at OCS saw four Reporting Seniors. BGen Van Riper held the job the longest in spite of joining the war that never happened. (Reserve B/Gen G. R. Omrod came on active duty during Van Riper's absence.) Van Riper's Fitness Report on me for the period of 1 July 1990 to 6 January 1991 is typical for the period; he marked me down the page as Outstanding. An excerpt of Section C:

> ... Had General Lejeune known Colonel Fox, he could have well served as a model for the General's essays on leadership. When the Corps wants to put its best foot forward, it could find no better representative. . . .

My first look by a BGen Selection Board took place that spring. The Board members were more influenced by my ranking as third of six colonels reported upon, rather than the flowery words of Section C. Van Riper's following report included:

> ... came time to consider a replacement as he neared two years in command, I couldn't think of an equal. Recommendation that he remain as the CO of OCS concurred with by entire chain of command, including CMC. . . . and possessed with a *natural command* presence, all to the nth degree! Looks and performs as an officer 20 or more years younger. He displays a special ability to motivate Marines; a superb mentor to junior officers. . . .

On this report, he ranked me sixth of ten colonels in the truth-teller box. These are not reports that will get one promoted to the top positions in the Marine Corps. Not being selected was a major disappointment, but I suppose I should have expected as much: I was sixty years old.

On the personal side, two big events occurred during my time at OCS: Dixie Lee married and the end of my life as a Marine approached. Dixie Lee met James D. (Mick) Davis at the Officer Pool while he was a student at TBS, and she was on leave from her Delta Flight Attendant job. Romance burst into full bloom, and the following summer the two married in the Quantico Chapel. Dixie Lee continued to fly with Delta out of Los Angeles, while Mick went off to the Middle East to help wipe Saddam's bothersome nose.

Terminating my Marine life was never a serious consideration. There were always far-off thoughts of retirement in Montana; however, leaving the Corps was never seriously considered. While I did not expect to serve into old age, I did not see attaining the age of sixty as a negative factor. Maybe doing better than the average young candidate on the field humps, runs, and PFT confused the issue, but age did not concern me. It had slowed me down a little in some areas but, in all ways, I was a better Marine than I was in 1950. I knew the Marine Corps Manual stated that one could not serve beyond age sixty-two without a presidential waiver. I expected to ask for a waiver, as I thought that I had a good chance of being selected to brigadier in 1990. (I was not aware of my peer rankings in my later reports.) After promotion, I would have two years of service before hitting age sixty-two.

My failure to be selected for promotion brought the issue front and center: turn out to pasture or fight the battle to serve beyond age sixty-two. Maybe at another time I would have pursued the issue, but with the Corps downsizing and having to let great, young Marines go, why keep me on board? One thought is that the taxpayer would keep a Marine in the ranks at one-quarter pay (I would receive three-quarters pay in retirement). From a personal viewpoint, why work for one-quarter pay? But then, I had been drawing one-quarter pay for thirteen years, so money was not the issue. I realized that I would be retired from active duty and started the job hunt.

LtCol Richard Alvarez, a C&SC instructor with me in 1985, had retired and now worked at Virginia Tech. He had several years earlier called me aboard the *Mt Whitney* to inform me of a search to fill the Commandant position with the Corps of Cadets; he felt that I was the man for the job. I was not interested then, but now I gave him a call. Networking with Richard, I visited the cadet corps and gave a presentation on leadership. There was no immediate opening in the cadet corps, but I liked what I saw.

At age sixty-one, my third year completed at OCS, no retirement job in line, and Niki in college all added up to serving another year. Naturally, I wanted to do that at OCS and pursued the issue, but there was a roadblock. A concerned individual was in position to directly influence the attrition rate at OCS. "No, Fox will not have another year at OCS. Get him out of there."

I was going to remain on active duty; what would I do? Checking with my monitor for one-year opportunities at HQMC was no help. His boss, the same person who influenced the OCS option, said that I could have the Marine Colonel position on the upcoming Presidential Inauguration Committee and that was it. The job and I would both go away together in a year. That offer put HQMC out of consideration; I checked out other possibilities at Quantico.

My good friend and fellow Vietnamese Marine Advisor, Colonel Tom Taylor was the CO MCB, Quantico. I asked Tom for the Base Inspector Job only to find that someone else had been slotted for it. Tom replied that he would look into it, and later called me back with the job. I moved into Lejeune Hall, becoming the Inspector, after turning OCS over to Colonel Pete Osman. Our OCS Change of Command doubled with the graduation parade of the first summer increment of candidates on 10 July 1992.

Routine was the word for my year as the Inspector; nothing happened to draw national attention to Quantico. The job was more interesting than I had expected, which helped the year to move. I worked the resume circuit hoping to land a job, attended all of the required departure lectures, and made myself ready for my new life.

In June 1993, I was invited down for a job interview with MajGen Stan Musser USAF (Ret), the Commandant of Cadets at Virginia Tech and was offered the job as Deputy Commandant to start on 15 August. On 26 July I went on terminal leave and left the active duty ranks of Marines. General Mundy, as CMC, gave me a letter authorizing me to wear the Marine uniform with the Corps of Cadets. Not many Marines have had to be concerned with haircuts, shined shoes, and squared-away uniforms for so long.

Terminal leave allowed me to work at Tech, though I would not retire from the Marines until 1 September 1993. I returned to Quantico for my retirement ceremony on 13 August. Pete Osman and BGen Pete Pace, President, MC University, agreed to my retirement ceremony being included in the ten-week OCS graduation parade.

General Mundy retired me. All of my family and friends were there for support on my last big Marine Corps day. MajGen George Smith traveled from Los Angeles for the occasion as did Bill Donahoo from Brownwood, Texas, Cousin Nelson Fox from Florida, Ernie Van Huss from Tennessee, and Frank DeAngelis[53] from New Jersey. Frank surprised me with a shadow box display of my decorations in both ribbons and medals, including a genuine Medal of Honor.

Contrary to my earlier expectations of a difficult adjustment period upon leaving the ranks of Marines, I have found the experience easy. There are times that I have had to pause and remind myself that I am retired and no longer a real, live, kicking Marine. Of course, the Corps of Cadets is the answer: I continue to wear the Marine uniform, work with young people, and leadership is the name of the game. My duty with the cadets is not that different from my three years at OCS. My daily work centers on encouraging young people to make the most of their lives and to do so soonest in order to reap a longer benefit. There are the 10 percent problem cadets, just like Marines, that soak up most of my time trying to get them squared away or out the door.

The major similarity of the two duties is helping those who want to lead others learn what is required. Correctness of self and integrity of the individual are the starting blocks, then knowledge, capability, and dependability add to the value of the leader. Courage overshadows all traits; without it, one falls short in the others. Cadets, like Marines, who desire to be leaders must study the art of leadership and learn what it takes during trying situations to cause others to reach deep down inside themselves and pull up that quality that they did not know they possessed.

My retirement in August 2001 from the Corps of Cadets gives me fifty-one years of proudly wearing the Marine uniform. There is life for a gungy Marine after the Corps.

Lessons Learned

1. Young people must select and shape their goals in accordance with their capabilities. In this instance, desire is rated less than 50 percent.

2. The art of leading others is so important to our society, why are there so few institutions of higher learning that offer a degree in something so important to the people?

3. The ability to handle stress is key to combat leadership. Those who cannot function under life-threatening situations are not suited for the Marines.

Glossary

03	Marine Infantry
1–MC	Shipboard intercom
1st Lt	1st Lieutenant
1st Sgt	1st Sergeant
2nd Lt	2nd Lieutenant
31–MC	Submarine intercom
AAV	Amphibious Assault Vehicle
AFB	Air Force Base
AK	AK–47, Communist assault rifle
ALC	Anchor Line Cable
ALMAR	CMC Message to All Commands
Amtrac	Amphibious Tractor
AO	Area of Operation
ASPD	Armed Services Police Department
AT	AntiTank
AWOL	Absent Without Leave
AWS	Amphibious Warfare School
BAR	Browning Automatic Rifle
BAS	Battalion Aid Station
BASCOLEX	Basic School Company Landing Exercise
BGen	Brigadier General
BLT	Battalion Landing Team
Bn	Battalion
BOQ	Bachelor Officer Quarters
Buoyant Ascent	Air assisted rise from water depth
Blow & Go	Buoyant Ascent
Brown Bagger	Married Marine
C–1A	Later designation for TF–1
Capt	Captain
CAX	Combined Arms Exercise
CG	Commanding General
CinC	Commander in Chief

CMC	Commandant of the Marine Corps
CMD	Command Military District
Cmdr	Commander
CO	Commanding Officer
Co	Company
COD	Close Order Drill
COD	Carrier Onboard Delivery
COG	Corporal of the Guard
Col	Colonel
CoTac	Company Tactics
Co-van	Vietnamese word for Advisor
CP	Command Post
CPB	Company Patrol Base
Cpl	Corporal
CTZ	Corps Tactical Zone
CWO	Chief Warrant Officer
Dead Horse	Advance pay
Det	Detachment
DevCtr	Development Center
DI	Drill Instructor
Dir	Director
Div	Division
Diwe	Vietnamese for Captain
DMZ	Demilitarized Zone
DRP	Deep Reconnaissance Platoon
DZ	Drop Zone
E & E	Escape and Evasion
EdCtr	Education Center
EOD	Explosive Ordnance Disposal
FEBA	Forward Edge of the Battle Area
FM	Field Master
FMF	Fleet Marine Force
FMFLANT	Fleet Marine Force Atlantic
FMFM	Fleet Marine Force Manual
FMFPAC	Fleet Marine Force Pacific
FO	Forward Observer
FSB	Fire Support Base
FSSG	Force Service Support Group
FT	Fire Team
GED	General Education Development

Group Tightner	Slang for increasing discipline
Guns	Machine Guns
GV-1	Earlier naval designator for C-130
GySgt	Gunnery Sergeant
H & I	Harrassment and Interdiction
H & S	Headquarters and Service
HAHO	High Altitude Exit High Opening
HALO	High Altitude Exit Low Opening
Hashmark	Slang for Service Stripe
H-Hour	Time a unit crosses the LOD
HLZ	Helicopter Landing Zone
HMX-1	Quantico Helicopter Squadron
HQMC	Headquarters Marine Corps
Hqrs	Headquarters
HST	Helicopter Support Team
IBS	Inflatable Boat, Small
IP	Initial Point
JA/ATT	Joint Airborne/Air Transportability Training
JM	Jump Master
KIA	Killed in Action
KMC	Korean Marine Corps
LAW	Light Antitank Weapon
LCpl	Lance Corporal
LDO	Limited Duty Officer
Ldr	Leader
L-Hour	Landing Hour
LOD	Line of Departure
LP	Listening Post
LPM	Landing Party Manual
LSNCO	Landing Site NCO
LST	Landing Ship, Tank
LtCol	Lieutenant Colonel
LtGen	Lieutenant General
LZ	Landing Zone
MAB	Marine Amphibious Brigade
MAC	Military Airlift Command
MACV	Military Assistance Command, Vietnam
MAF	Marine Amphibious Force
MAG	Marine Air Group
Maj	Major

MajGen	Major General
MarDiv	Marine Division
MARS	Marine Amphibious Reconnaissance System
MATA	Military Assistance Training Advisor
MAU	Marine Amphibious Unit
MB	Marine Barracks
MCCDC	Marine Corps Combat Development Command
MCCRES	Marine Corps Combat Readiness Evaluation System
MCI	Marine Corps Institute
MCRD	Marine Corps Recruit Depot
MEB	Marine Expeditionary Brigade
MedEvac	Medical Evacuation
MEF	Marine Expeditionary Force
MEU	Marine Expeditionary Unit
MG	Machine Gun
MGen	Major General
MGySgt	Master Gunnery Sergeant
MLR	Main Line of Resistance, later replaced with FEBA.
MOH	Medal of Honor
MOS	Military Occupational Specialty
MSG	Marine Security Guard
MSgt	Master Sergeant
NAS	Naval Air Station
NCO	NonCommissioned Officer
NCOIC	NonCommissioned Officer in Charge
NCSC	Naval Coastal Systems Center
NGF	Naval Gun Fire
NRA	National Rifle Association
Obj	Objective
OCC	Officer Candidate Class
OCS	Officer Candidate School
OD	Officer of the Day
OIC	Officer in Charge
OpFor	Opposing Force
ParaOp	Parachute Operation
PCS	Permanent Change of Station
PFC	Private First Class
PFT	Physical Fitness Test

PIO	Public Information Officer
PLC	Platoon Leadership Class
PLF	Parachute Landing Fall
Plt	Platoon
PltLdr	Platoon Leader
PltSgt	Platoon Sergeant
PMI	Primary Marksmanship Instructor
PMO	Provost Marshal Officer
PPB	Platoon Patrol Base
PRT	Physical Readiness Test
PT	Physical Training
Pvt	Private
R-4D	Earlier Naval designation of C-47
R-5D	Earlier Naval designation of C-54
ReconEx	Reconnaissance Exercise
Rgt	Regiment
RLT	Regimental Landing Team
ROC	Required Operational Capability
Rocker	Stripe at bottom of chevron
ROK	Republic of Korea
RPG	Rocket Propelled Grenade
RS	Recruiting Station
RTB	Recruit Training Battalion
RTC	Recruit Training Command
S-1	Administration
S-2	Intelligence
S-3	Operations and Training
S-4	Logistics
SAR	Sea Air Rescue
SCUBA	Self-Contained Underwater Breathing Apparatus
SecNav	Secretary of the Navy
SF	Special Forces
SFC	Sergeant First Class
Sgt	Sergeant
SgtMaj	Sergeant Major
SHAPE	Supreme Headquarters Allied Powers Europe
SitRpt	Situation Report
Six-by	Military truck with six-wheel drive
Slick Arm	No service stripe
Snake and Nape	Rockets and Napalm

Snapping In	Practice in rifle firing positions
SNCO	Staff NonCommissioned Officer
SOG	Sergeant of the Guard
SOP	Standard Operating Procedure
SPIE	Special Patrol Insertion/Extraction
SPS	Silenced Propulsion System
Sq	Squad
SqLdr	Squad Leader
SSgt	Staff Sergeant
STA	Surveillance/Target Acquisition
Stick	Group of parachutists jumping together
SubOps	Submarine Operations
T/O	Table of Organization
T/OE	Table of Organization and Equipment
TAD	Temporary Additional Duty
TAOR	Tactical Area of Responsibility
TF	Task Force
Thungwe	Vietnamese for 1st Lieutenant
TLA	Temporary Lodging Allowance
TSgt	Technical Sergeant
TBS	The Basic School
Tubes	Mortars
USNS	US Naval Station
Utes	Utility Uniform
Utilities	Marine Field Uniform
VC	Viet Cong
VCB	Vandegrift Combat Base
WestPac	Western Pacific
WIA	Wounded in Action
WIA(E)	WIA Evacuated
WM	Woman Marine
WO	Warrant Officer
XO	Executive Officer

Notes

1. Naval time is shown on the twenty-four-hour clock as 1825 for the equivalent of 6:25 p.m. (1825 − 1200 = 6:25)
2. Lynn Montross, Hubard D. Kuokka, and Norman W. Hicks, "The CCF January Offensive," *US Marine Operations in Korea* Vol IV, *The East Central Front* (Washington, DC: Historical Branch G-3 Headquarters, U.S. Marine Corps, 1962), 31. Reprinted 1987 by Brandy Able 1, Austin, Texas (hereafter Montross et al., *Marine Operations in Korea*).
3. CMC waived promotion exams (never to be reinstated during my time).
4. Montross et al., "The CCF Spring Offensive," *Marine Operations in Korea* states on page 126 that the 5th Marines relieved the 38th Infantry. Third Bn, 5th Marines Historical Diary, May 1951 dated 18 July 1951 (hereafter 3/5 Historical Diary) states the Bn set up in defensive positions and the 3rd Bn, 38th Inf moved rearward through the lines.
5. At the time, I assumed that Company I was on the hill with us and at this writing was surprised to learn from the 3/5 Historical Diary that the three platoons were in separate locations.
6. 3/5 Historical Diary states for the night of 20 May: "I Company reported that a small group of enemy had made a slight penetration of the lines at DS 0518K [sic, typo for 0581] but were being contained." (The "small" enemy force was 167 soldiers smaller.)
7. Montross et al., *Marine Operations in Korea*, 126. Also, the 3/5 Historical Diary states elements of the 580 Rgt, 33rd Div, 51 Corps, CCF launched an attack across the entire Bn front. And Billy C. Mossman states in "The Counteroffensive" on page 466 of *Ebb and Flow Nov50-Jul51* (Center of Military History, US Army, 1990), (hereafter Mossman, *Ebb and Flow*) that the only attack across the front on the 20th was conducted by the 34th Div, CCF against Co C, 9th Inf.
8. Ibid., 126.
9. Ibid., 126.
10. Not his actual name.
11. Mossman states in "Battle Below the Soyang" on page 474 of *Ebb and Flow* that the 5th Marines recovered eleven soldiers of the 2nd Div near Hill 1051 on 23 May.
12. Ibid., 16. Mossman mentions the "scene of a very disastrous attack by the enemy upon units of the 38th Infantry."

13. Ibid., 456. Mossman co-locates the 1st and 2nd Bns, 38th Inf at Hills 910 and 975.
14. Montross et al., "Advance to the Punchbowl," *Marine Operations in Korea*, 146.
15. Ibid., 148.
16. Women Marines (WMs) were organized into their own company for billeting and administrative matters while they performed administrative tasks aboard the Base.
17. For more on this event see Allen R. Millett, *Semper Fidelis: The History of the United States Marine Corps* (New York: MacMillan, 1980). Hereafter Millett, *Semper Fidelis.*
18. The Corps had a double rank system as a result of adding the two pay grades E-8 and 9. Sergeant Major became a pay grade and Lance Corporal was the E-3. For several years, the pay grade was shown following the rank to show which corporal, E-3 or 4, through which master sergeant, E-7 or 8. Technical Sergeant was renamed Acting Gunnery Sergeant.
19. Not his actual name.
20. The PCA was the forerunner of today's United States Parachute Association.
21. For more information on this program, see Millett, *Semper Fidelis,* 578.
22. John's first tour in Vietnam was with an infantry battalion. On his second tour in 1972 as an advisor to the Vietnamese Marines, he alone destroyed the Dong Ha Bridge in the face of a North Vietnamese Army assault. John G. Miller tells this story in *The Bridge,* published by the US Naval Institute in 1989. John received the Navy Cross; my opinion is that his actions were deserving of the Medal of Honor.
23. This is a later designator for the TF-1.
24. The phrase "Lost the bubble" probably means different things to different people. A Recon's bubble contains his life supporting air and if he loses it, he has two options: exit and rise to the surface or open the blow and try to make another. The bubble is lost by the sub rolling over, causing the open hatch to rise into the bubble area.
25. Not his actual name.
26. Not his actual name.
27. Combat Arms positions were always filled. During R&R and hospital, a combat support advisor moved into the field position.
28. The SKS is a Soviet-developed semiautomatic rifle also made in China and provided to communist forces.
29. Dewey Canyon started with a ground sweep from established FSBs with new FSBs opened as rifle companies moved forward, always under cover of an artillery fan.
30. M. R. Conroy, in *Don't Tell America* (Red Bluff: Eagle Publishing, 1992), page 302, relates personal accounts of members of this water detail firing at

snipers inside my perimeter. This did not happen. The only enemy soldiers near us were the dead from the earlier bunker encounter. Regardless of this water-detail sergeant's negative action with me, statements of this sort from him and his friends worked him an award of the Silver Star Medal many years afterwards. He has also written a book of fiction concerning that day.

31. HM2 Charles M. Hudson USN was my senior corpsman and moved with my command group. He was swamped with work. I salute the Navy corpsmen who serve with the FMF; they are as gungy as Marines.

32. One hundred mercenary soldiers (Nungs) led by SF SNCOs as PltLdrs and Meadows as the CO.

33. Joe Garner, *Code Name Copperhead* (NY: Pocket Books, 1995), 334. Garner quotes Meadows as saying he offered to carry my casualties, and then to take the lead. There are many inaccuracies in Garner's story, e.g., his rescue mission of a half-dead, bottled-up Marine rifle company (page 310). If it were not for that SF company, 1/9 would have been out of the A Shau a week sooner. Garner writes on pages 332 and 333 of an enemy attack against the SF position Hill 1044 on and provides a quote from me regarding such. These things happened only in Garner's imagination.

34. Ibid., 335.

35. Ibid., 336. Garner writes that Col Smith asked SF to "Close the back door" on Tam Boi and states that they did so. He follows with the SF company being tasked to protect our battalion extraction from Tam Boi. Again, all pure fantasy; neither of these events happened.

36. Ibid., 338. Garner states that he and Meadows were to be decorated for the Marine rescue mission by General Stillwell, but that it did not happen. I am not surprised: General Stillwell knew what took place, what was going on, and who did what. He visited us several times in the A Shau; Stillwell was a soldier.

37. This is my field count and does not include Marines who may have later died of wounds.

38. Captain Peter Johansen was killed during a 2nd Force Recon FF ParaOp. The resultant investigation determined that the procedure and equipment used were not approved by HQMC.

39. The T/O rank of the billet was Major; Hooper (not his actual name) had been recently promoted.

40. Longtree was a Moscow MSG found guilty of providing information to the Soviets through his Russian girlfriend. MSG Marines during my time were forbidden to have any relationship with any person of the Soviet States.

41. Unit Deployment has since replaced most of the unaccompanied manning requirements.

42. Marine units of combat arms, combat support, and combat service support form together under one commander for independent operations.

Smallest to largest, these are the Unit with an infantry battalion, Brigade with an infantry regiment, and Force with a Marine Division. The name was Expedition, such as MEU, MEB, and MEF. The word Expedition changed to Amphibious during the Vietnam War to satisfy politicians and avoid any inference that the US had an expeditionary interest in Vietnam. Long after the war, the name returned to Expedition.

43. Millett, *Semper Fidelis,* 435.

44. The infantry was considered obsolete following WW II. The next conflict, if any, would be a push-button war and easily handled by our new air force.

45. Only white skivvie shirts were issued and authorized for wear with all uniforms. Army personnel roll their sleeves with the outside sleeve material showing. Marines roll theirs with the inside material showing over the roll, country style.

46. Part of the JA/ATT is paradrop qualification for pilots, thus the non-realistic ParaOps on this and the later Fuji exercise.

47. SecDef McNamara wanted to help society by requiring the military services to accept 100,000 lower-mental-category Group-IVs who otherwise did not meet entry prerequisites. See Millett, *Semper Fidelis*, 579.

48. The base was known earlier as Marine Corps Development, Education Command.

49. Mike was the sniper in the A Shau Valley on 22 February 1969 who was wounded while helping with one of my radios after that mortar round hit my CP.

50. The OCS programs include the Platoon Leader Course (PLC) that is two separate six-week or one ten-week course; Officer Candidate Course (OCC) that runs for ten weeks; and Bulldog, a six-week evaluation of Marine Option, Naval Reserve Officer Training Corps (NROTC) midshipmen.

51. Oliver North phoned me to say he had known this lad since birth and knew him to be Marine officer material. Ollie asked me to give the guy another chance. Another friend, Jim Kalstrom, visited me from the FBI Academy to ask for a second chance. Then the father tried the CG of MCCDC.

52. My three years at OCS saw three CGs of MCCDC. LtGen Walt Boomer replaced Etnyre and Ernie Cook followed Boomer.

53. Frank is a friend of all Marines. He has done much in the line of scholarships and support for the MC University Foundation. Frank's love for his Marines dates back to WW II when he served aboard one of the ships debarking Marines on the hot, fire-swept beaches in the Pacific. He has been in awe of Marines ever since.

About the Author

Colonel Wesley L. Fox, USMC (Ret.), retired from the Marine Corps in 1993 after forty-three years of distinguished service. In addition to the Medal of Honor, he received two awards of the Legion of Merit, a Bronze Star with Combat V, four awards of the Purple Heart, and numerous commendations. From 1993 until his full retirement in 2001, Fox served as Deputy Commandant of Cadets at Virginia Tech. He lives in Blacksburg, Virginia.

INDEX

1st Bn 6th Marines, 317–40, 346
1st Bn 9th Marines, 231–71, 279
1st Force Recon, 93, 114, 122, 124–67, 231, 289
1st Marine Brigade, 32, 46, 48
1st MarDiv, 8, 33, 35, 46, 48, 83, 86, 92–93, 149
1st Marines, 41, 45, 62
2nd Brigade, 9th Inf, 227
2nd Fleet, 346, 348–53
2nd Force Recon, 184, 187–200, 229, 291, 298
2nd MarDiv, 22, 275, 313, 318, 340, 346
2nd Recon Bn, 313
3rd Force Recon, 231
3rd Bn 5th Marines, 28–79, 93–100
3rd MarDiv, 126, 140, 157, 228–30, 288–89, 292, 317, 339, 353
3rd Recon Bn, 163, 289–93, 333
4th Replacement Draft, 25, 56
5th Marines, 27–28, 35, 40–41, 45, 48, 50, 62, 66, 72, 75, 77, 93, 97, 131
7th Infantry, 45
7th Marines, 45, 48–49, 139
9th Marines, 177, 243, 258, 266, 268–69, 279
9th MEB, 351
29 Palms, 323–25
35th MAU, 333
36th Replacement Draft, 87–88
38th Infantry, 64–65
38th Parallel, 3, 46, 66, 96
187th Airborne, 35

Adams, Maj Rayford K., 115, 117–18
Allord, Maj Gary C., 334

Alvarez, LtCol Richard, 373
A Shau Valley, 244–45, 258, 261, 264, 268–69, 271
Armed Service Police, 84
ASPD, 84–86, 88–89
Asplund, A1/C Daniel, 175–77
Atsugi, 88
Austin, Col Randy, 317, 325, 338
Ayres, Col Raymond P., Jr., 352

Baird, L/Cpl J. R., Jr., 256
Baker Block, 94–95
Baker Co., 1/2, 22, 24
Baker, PFC Gridley, XIV, 55–56, 68, 70–71
Bales, CWO Pappy, 84, 86
Barnum Capt Harvey C., 243, 279
Barrow, Col/Gen Robert H., 236, 265–66, 271, 279, 329, 370
Beeler, LtCol Andy, 325
Bell, GySgt John A., 114, 126–27, 148
Benewah, USS, 227
Beyerlein, Sgt David A., 254
Biggers, Lt Archie, 250
Bittle, Lt Robert, 290
Bittner, Maj Donald, 341
Blanco, GySgt David, 118
BLT Bravo, 331
Bobbitt, Capt Fred, 277
Boehm, PFC L. J., 256
Bohr, Maj/LtCol Harper L., Jr., 289–90, 293
Boland, Cpl Robert F., 131, 138, 154
Bonora, Capt Steve, 88–89
Boyd, PFC Hilton E., 93
Boyle, LCpl Dennis, 161–62
Branch, Cpl Billy T., 131, 133–34

Breckinridge, LtCol James, 225
Brimmer, Lt Donald R., 29, 42–43, 46, 55, 63–64, 68–71, 73
Broderick, Col Matthew E., 346
Brown, Cmdr John C., 174–76
Brown, BGen Gary E., 354, 363
Brown, Col Ross, 351
Budd, Maj Talman C., 203
Buffalo Line, 45
Burge, Lt Robert G., 336
Burhans, Capt, 125
Burke, Pvt Joe W., 106–07
Burroughs, Lt Aaron C., 257, 262
Bush, President George, 351
Butler, PFC F., III, 256

Camp Blanning, 172
Camp Courtney, 289
Camp David, 340
Camp Davidson, 301
Camp Delmar, 124, 138, 140
Camp Fuji, 291, 334–35
Camp Geiger, 322
Camp Hansen, 291
Camp Lejeune, 177, 185, 189, 313–14, 318, 326, 329, 337, 344, 348
Camp Matthews, 106–7
Camp Pendleton, 98, 100, 110, 124, 127–28
Camp San Margarita, 98, 100
Camp Schwab, 162, 327–28, 330
Camp Sukiran, 157, 163
Camp Upshur, 306
Camp Wilson, 323
Capers, Cpl/Maj James, 154, 161, 167, 298
Carlson, Capt Steve, 323
Carr, PFC, 88
Chacon, L/Cpl D. A., 256
Chamberlain, SgtMaj Ronnie, 346
Chambers, PFC W. J., 56
Chapman, Gen Leonard F., Jr., 279
Chapman, Capt/Maj Leonard F., III, 280–81, 305
Charles, Maj W. M., 342
Cheatham, Lt Earnest C., Jr., 101
Chittester, PFC N. P., 256

Christen, PFC/Cpl John, 93, 106, 108–10
Christman, Lt William J., III, 241, 247, 251–54, 256, 263, 268, 276, 359
Chung, Maj, 204, 206–8, 210, 212–13, 221, 223
Chungju, 35
Clancy, Capt John J., III, 200
Colburn, Pvt, 109–10
Coleman, Cpl, 106
Coleman, Cpl J. T., 244
Congressional Medal of Honor Society, 351, 371
Cook, LtGen Ernie, 369–70
Corbett, Col L. V., 228
Corps of Cadets, 373–75
Corsairs, F4U, 42, 67, 69, 70, 82
Crowe, Col Henry P., 110
Culkin, LtCol T. J., 266, 269
Culver, Lt Richard, 126–27

Da Krong River, 244–45
Danowicz, Col E. F., 266–67
Darby, USNS (T-AP-127), 27
Daves, PFC, 7, 9, 14, 18
Davis, Lt James D., 372
Davis, Lt James H., 241, 252, 254, 256, 264
Davis, Cpl Myron J., 31–33, 38, 41, 44, 46, 48–49, 51, 53, 76
Davis, Gen Raymond G., 273, 279, 370
Day, Capt James L., 113
DeAngelis, Frank, 374
Dedek, PFC J. E., 256
Deegan, MGen Gene, 346–47
Deisher, Capt Charles, 325
Demarco, Capt John, 318
Denver USS, (LPD-9), 331
Dime Dingo, 323
Disciplinary Platoon, 113
D License, PCA, 175, 177
Donahoo, Sgt William B., 90–92, 95, 115, 124, 374
Dong Ha, 237, 264
Dozer, SSgt, 167

Draude, Maj Thomas V., 287–88
Duerr, GySgt Ronald G.,242–43, 259–60
Duffy, Capt Patrick E., 126, 135, 139–40, 142, 154–60, 162–64
Durham, Maj J. M., 342
Dwyer, LtCol Joe, 340

Eakin, Sgt/Lt Shelton L., 93, 95–96, 98–100, 106–8, 110, 122, 125, 128, 155–56, 179, 182, 185–187, 210, 213, 266, 268
Earl, Capt Robert L., 289–90, 298–300
Eckert, Sgt Charles W., 28, 31
Elkins, LtCol J. T., 274
El Toro, 86–87, 154, 344, 346
Ericson, Capt Carl J., 318, 324
Etnyre, LtGen William R., 354, 358
Exercises: Bold Guard, 351; Nes Rouge, 305, North Star, 352; Ocean Safari, 349; Team Work 88, 349–50; WINTEX-CIMEX, 352
Ewing, MSgt William H., 115, 117

Farlee, GySgt, Richard E., 184
Ferrier, Maj William I., 274, 277
Fite, Lt/Capt William C., 225, 273–74
FleetEx, 351–52
Florence, MSgt Joe, 118–19, 121
Flynn, Linda, 1, 271
Foran, PFC Robert L., xiv, 55
Foreman, Maj C. D., 241
Forrester, Maj Zachery, 342
Fox, LtCol George, 258
Fox, Nelson, 2–4, 374
Fox Ray, 1, 4, 5, 22, 200
Fox, Stephen, 2
Franzone, PFC Amedeo U., xiv, 55–56
Front Royal,Va., 1, 371
Fryman, Sgt Roy, 155
Fulford, Maj Carlton, 313
Furleigh, Capt James, 277

George Co 3/5, 93–100
Geraghty, Maj/Col Timothy, 187, 272, 290, 298, 314, 317
Giles, SSgt James, 113
Giles, SSgt Jess, 189
Goggin, Capt William F., 83–84
Goulaillier, PFC/LCpl Frank M., 131, 138–39, 154, 163–64
Gould, Lt, 167
Gray, LtCol/Gen Alfred, 272, 289–90, 293, 313, 316–17, 327, 338–40
Grayback, USS (LPSS), 292
Greenwood, Col John, 343
Gresehammer, Pvt, 109–10
Grossiano, PFC, 137–38
Grosz, Capt Nick, 227
Grover, Lt Arden R., 76
Guam, 334
Gunderson, Pvt Eugene G., 15
Gung Ho, 31, 124
Gungy, 31, 58, 90, 92–93, 95, 179, 225, 237, 241, 273, 275, 277, 314, 326, 328, 339, 344, 375
Guy, Sgt Ottus, 97

Haebel, MGen Robert E., 328, 333, 337–38
Hagen, Lt, 168
Hainsworth, Capt John, 225
Hall, PFC John B., xiii, xiv, 54, 58–59
Hall, PFC Patrick G., 154
Hancock, USS (CVA-19), 158
Happy, Sgt Robert E., 126, 129, 148, 154–55
Harbin, Capt Kenneth S., 321, 323–24
Harris, Capt John B., 114
Hayes Line, 77
Hein, Capt, 203–15, 223, 225
Henry, MGySgt Hank, 299, 305–310
Herron, Lt Lee Roy, 242, 254, 268
Hill Trail, 353, 356
Hill 37, 264, 267
Hill 686, 246–47

Hill 710, 62, 64
Hill 719, 62, 64
Hill 729, 66
Hill 821, 67
Hill 975, 64
Hill 1038, 67
Hill 1044, 257–60, 296
Hill 1051, 64–65
Hill 1316, 67
Hinkle, Sgt Carl D., 154, 167
Hinson, Cpl John, 93
Ho Chi Minh Trail, 251, 257, 259
Hodges, Cpl R. P., 256
Hodgson, Sgt Donald, 168
Hoengsong, 35, 40
Hofmann, Capt George, 277
Holden, BM1/C Red, 175–77
Holiday, Maj, 54
Holland, PFC C. J., 23
Honea, Capt Jerry W., 118
Hongchon, 40, 50
Holzbauer, LtCol J. F., 181
Houghton, MGen Kenneth, 272,
  290–91, 293
Huly, Maj Jan C., 342
Hudson, HM-2 Charles M., 255–56
Hudson, MGen John I., 343
Hunt, Maj Robert G., 125
Hunt, SgtMaj Homer S., 335
Hwachon, 48
Hygienic Unit, 7

Inje, 75–76
Istell, Capt Jacques Andre, 150, 172
Item Co., 3/5, 28–96

JA/ATT, 333–34, 339
Jenson, SSgt Robert, 254
Johansen, Capt Peter, 272
Johnson, Adm Jerome L., 350
Johnson, Capt Johnny, 331
Johnson MSgt Caribou, 88
Johnson, SSgt, 290
Johnson, PFC A. L., 256
Junior Jump, 128, 163
Junkins, Capt K. S., 260
Justus, Cpl Robert N., 129

Kalish, John P., 337
Kammeier, Capt Cyril, 225
Kansas Line, 66, 72, 77
Kelly, Capt John, 241, 250, 280
Kennon, Maj D. N., 238, 240–41,
  246
Khe Sanh, 231, 237, 243
Kirchoff, L/Cpl Wilber G., 155
KMC, 46, 48, 77
Knotts, Maj/BGen Joseph, 243, 273,
  279
Koontz, Capt G. C., 109–10
Kothe, Capt Frank R., 100

Lackey, John Washington, 2
Laine, LtCol Elliott R. (Sonny), 258,
  273
Lamb, Maj Michael R., 299
Lane, SSgt Michael, 254
Lange, Maj Lee F., 342
Lansing, Joi, 110
Laos, 245, 250–51, 260
Laotian Border, 245, 251, 258
Larsen, Capt Timothy R., 318, 323
Larson, Adm Charles, 348, 350
Leach, Capt/Col Sean, 313
Leek, BGen F. E., 149
Lenawee, USS (APA-195), 157
Levangie, Cpl Robert H., 69–70, 72,
  74
Lind, W. S., 214
Lloyd, Capt W. F., 5
Lloyd, Lt, 97
lockout and in, submarine, 189–96
Lohmeier, GySgt Don L., 282
Love, TSgt, 114
Lyke, PFC H. G., 56
Lyons, MSgt, 100

MAG-11, 88–89, 93, 114
Malone, Lt George, 239, 254, 256,
  263
Manrod, Col Frank M., 299, 305
Martin, Cpl/Lt William E., 154
Massaro, GySgt John R., 128
Masterpool, Col William, 276
Mazarov, Lt/LtCol Paul, 101, 279

McAlister, Maj James S., 149
McBride, Sgt James, 97, 99
McCarthy, Capt Pete, 225
McCartney, GySgt Joseph P., 179
McCrory, Bill, 300
MCCRES, 321–23, 325, 333
McFarlane, LCpl, 258
McGowan, Capt Mike, 225
McGowan, BM-1 Robert, 120
McHenry, LtCol Leland, 280
McKeon, SSgt Matthew C., 111
McKinstry, Lt/Maj William E., 93, 203
McMichael, SgtMaj Alford L., 371
McMonagle, Lt James J., 93
McNulty, L/Cpl Thomas, 128
McVey, Cpl Lavoy D., 155
McWilliams, Col James P., 327
Mead, PFC Ralph E., 75
Meadows, Cpt USA, Richard (Dick), 261
Meerdink, Capt George, Jr., 241, 257
Merrill, PFC Lowell H., 155
MEUSOC, 348–50
Michael, Col Richard L., Jr., 203, 225, 228
Miller, SSgt Duke, 115
Miller, Cpl/LtCol Edward, 154
Miller, Col Gerald L., 341
Miller, LtGen John H., 308–10
Miller, Cpl Orville L., 51, 56, 60, 69
Milligan, MajGen Robert F., 347
Minyard, PFC Robert L., 43
Monroe, Betty L., 1, 134
Mountrail, USS (APA-213), 88
Moore, Cleo, 110
Moore, Capt K. W., 274
Mount Whitney USS (LCC-20), 346, 348–49, 352, 373
Mrazek, Col USA, James E., 312
Mt Fuji, 334–36
Muchuk, 332
Mundy, Gen Carl, 374
Murphy, PFC K. R., 14–16, 18
Musser, MGen USAF, Stanton, 374
Myers Cpl/Maj Donald J., 93, 97, 100, 278

Nash, MSgt James, 89
Neal, BGen Butch, 369
Nervo, Col Eugene T., 317–18
Newman, GySgt, 290, 292
Nixon, President Richard, 278–79
No Name Line, 50, 64
Norris, Maj Donald, 200
Northington, LCpl William, 258
Norton, Capt Robert J., 118, 121

Oceanside, 110, 124, 134, 138–39, 142, 148
O'Neill, Sgt Peter J., 114
Onna Point, 165, 289–92
Operation Apache Snow, 268–69, 271
Operation Dawson River/Afton, 238
Operation Dawson River/West, 243
Operation Dewey Canyon, 243–70, 315, 370
Operation Habu, 162
Operation Killer, 35, 41
Operation Pershing, 213
Operation Ripper, 41
Operation ScotlandII/Afton, 236
Operation Silver Sword, 155
Operation Son Ha-3, 213
Operation Song Than, 38–68, 203, 213, 227, 704–68
Operation Team Spirit, 331–32
Operation Thuong-Xa, 236
Operation Tulungan, 158
Osman, Col Pete, 374

Pace, BGen Peter, 374
Parnell, Cpl Randall B., 252–53
Parris Island, 6–20, 115–17, 358
Parrish, Lt, 93
Parrish, GySgt Jullian, 135, 149
Parrish, PFC S. J., 244
Pasker, Dr. Ray, 249
Patterson, GySgt Bobby Joe, 128, 150
Pendergraft, James, 294–95
Phillips, LCpl J. R., 244
Phillips, Capt John W., 131, 148, 162

Pirman, Lt Frank R., 102
Plank, Chaplain David W., 148
Plaskett, Col W., Jr., 289–90
Platoon 107, 109
Platoon 181, 102–14
Platoon 88, 6–20, 24
Pohang, 27, 331–32
Pollard, PFC R., 256
Porter, Sgt Horace H., Jr., 72
Potter, PFC Channing J., 74–75, 77
Pratte, Lt Joe, 225
Prichett, SSgt, 118
Puhkan River, 49–50

Quantico Line, 48
Quinn, PFC James E., 68
Quist, LtCol Burt, 341

Rapp, Capt Michael L., 314
Rayburn, SSgt, 118
Recruiter School, 114–15
Reczek, Capt Gerald F., 131, 148
Reed, Capt R. M., 185
Reinke, Col Claude W., 353, 358
Reiser, Cpl D. W., 6–16, 102
Renville, USS, 97
Ridolfi, Lt USA, A. J., 181, 184
Riggs, Lt R. J., 157
Riley Capt/Maj Edward, 241, 255–
    57, 263, 276–79, 361
Ripley, Lt/Capt John W., 187, 229
Riverine Force, 227
Roberts, SSgt Thomas G., 116, 124
Robeson, Capt Edward J., 299
Rodney, LtCol G. W., 225
Roop, Cpl James B., 58, 69
Rosas, Cpl J. A., 155
Ross, SgtMaj Bernard P., 344
Round Hill, Va., 5, 22, 79
Ryan, PFC Francis J., 43, 55

Saint Croix, 189
Saint Thomas, 189, 196
Saipan, 333
Schober crystal, 182
Scoppa, Col Joseph, 305
Sea Lion, USS (APSS-315), 188–89

Shapley, BGen Allen, 112
Shaw, Sgt Jack B., 90–92
Sheehan, Capt/BGen John, 225,
    273, 351, 369
Sheppard, Lt Albert V., 233, 257
Simpson, Clifton N., Jr., 119
Sirotniak, Capt John S., 232, 234,
    238, 277
Sledge, LCpl D. R., 258
Smith, PFC C. L., 258
Smith, Lt/Capt Gilbert E., 257, 296
Smith, LtCol/Col George W., 232,
    240–43, 246–47, 249–51, 255–56,
    261, 263, 265–66, 271, 276,
    278–79, 290, 315, 370, 374
Smith, Capt John Elm, 115
Snell, Capt James E., 314
Sommers, SgtMaj David W., 346–47
Soyang-gang, 46, 75
Spainhour, Lt Walter J., 155
Stacy, GySgt Kurt, 157
Stillwell, LTG USA, Richard G.,
    264, 279, 370
Stone County, USS (LST-1141), 155
Stouffer, LtCol Thomas D., 339
Strock, Maj James N., 342
Stubblebine, PFC Thomas, 37
Stucker, SgtMaj Carl O., 346
Sugama-oska, 89, 91
Sullivan, Maj Michael W., 342
Sweetzer, Capt/Col Skip, 225, 346,
    348–49

Talbert, MSgt 116
Talley, SSgt 241, 262
Tam Boi, 258, 260–63
Taylor, Capt B. V. (Vic), 290, 305
Taylor, Capt/Col Tom, 225, 305
TET, 214–22
Thomas, PFC A., 256
Thompson, Maj Jerry, 299, 305,
    310–11
Thompson, Pvt J. S., 9
Thurston, PFC John W., 56, 58
Tinian, 333–34
Tok Sok Ri, 331
Torrey, Capt/Col Philip, 277

Trainor, MGen Bernard E., 308–9
Trinidad, 188
Tuggle, PFC Estel, 39, 41, 56–58
Twitty, Conway, 294

Vallario, PFC/GySgt Thomas J., 154, 164–66
Van Huss, Maj/LtCol Earnest A., 318, 324–25, 327, 334–38, 350, 353, 374
Van Ness, Sgt J. H., 104
Van Riper, BGen P. K., 369–70, 372
Vandegrift Combat Base (VCB), 236, 241, 264–65, 271
Vapor Trails, 173–74
Vargas, Maj Jay, 289–90, 305
Velarde, Lt/Capt Joseph S., 300, 305
Vestifjord, 349, 351
Virginia Tech, 373–74

Ward, Maj Doug, 218, 221–22
Warner Springs, 139–43
Webb, Jack, 113–14
Webb, Secretary of the Navy James, 361
Weber, Capt David, 305
Weinberger, Secretary of Defense Casper, 314

Western, Capt Thomas F., 318
Whitlow, Maj William H., 342
Whitten, Capt Michael G., 318
Wiggans, LtCol Norman, 353–54
Wilcox Award, 342
Williams, Don, 371
William, LtCol James, 343, 346
Williams, Capt John, 218
Wilson, Gen Louis, 329
Winter, PFC/ Maj Mike, 255, 354
Winter, Lt Warren, 287
Wisengarber, LCpl, 258
Wisner, LtCol Ralph, 105
Wonju, 35

Yamassee, 6
Yomato, 89
Yanggu, 66
Yokosuka, 58, 78
Yomitan, 57, 291
Yongchon, 28
Young, PFC/GySgt Edsel Ford, 154, 161

Zeihmn, Lt Michael V., 257
Zeorb, Sgt/Capt Dennis R., 145, 154, 167
Zwiener, Lt Robert, 199